DRAWINGS AND WATERCOLOURS IN THE CALOUSTE GULBENKIAN COLLECTION

Manuela Fidalgo

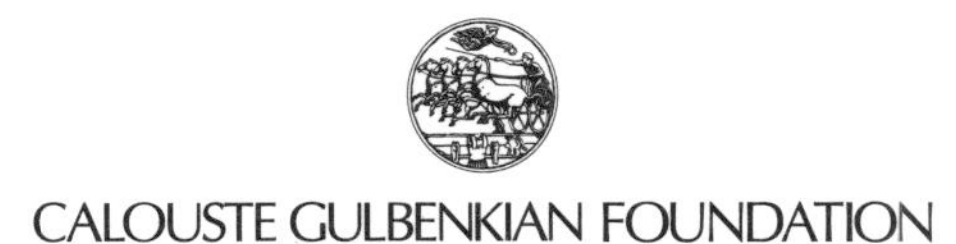
CALOUSTE GULBENKIAN FOUNDATION

DRAWINGS AND WATERCOLOURS IN THE CALOUSTE GULBENKIAN COLLECTION

Le Dessin est tout, c'est l'art tout entier.
Jean-Auguste Dominique Ingres

Le charme particulier de l'aquarelle...
tient à cette transparence continuelle du papier
Eugène Delacroix

In line with the aim of making all of the collections brought together by Calouste Gulbenkian available to the public, a book devoted to the drawing and watercolour collection is now being published. ¶ Many similar works have been published on a wide range of subjects, including Greek coins, Egyptian art, jewels, Mameluk glasse, painting, European sculpture, medals and plaquettes, Iznik tiles and pottery, Chinese porcelain, eighteenth-century French furniture, and the jewellery and glassware of René Lalique. Further studies are awaiting publication on other subjects including French ivories, illuminated books, French jewellery, Japanese lacquerware, oriental carpets, and Islamic and European textiles. ¶ Thus, a broad and systematic view of the collections is given that would be impossible to provide in the permanent exhibition since works are subject to a natural hierarchy of heritage values and because, as is broadly understood, it is not the number of pieces on display that demonstrates the richness of the collections but the rigour behind the selections made. In this respect, Calouste Gulbenkian's principle of always wanting 'only the best' is respected. A large number of works, many of international importance, have been made available to visitors in the museum's permanent exhibition. ¶ The collection of drawings and watercolours has always been treated differently since it can only be exhibited partially and briefly due to the conservation rules that apply to works rendered on paper. Such works are rarely put on display, being kept away from the public eye, and are therefore less well-known. ¶ Although purchasing works in these genres was not a priority for the collector, it is possible to identify some of the great examples of European drawings and watercolours produced between the sixteenth and twentieth centuries. With a logic that is natural and almost organic, these works reflect Calouste Gulbenkian's idiosyncrasies as a collector, which include a predilection for the perfection of human genius and for the tactile quality of images. Noteworthy examples of this tendency include Albrecht Dürer's watercolour of a dead duck; the remarkable page of studies of a woman's head, drawn by Watteau; the disquieting atmosphere of Turner's watercolour; and the calligraphy of Millet's desolate branches. ¶ Since the 1980's, the curator Manuela Fidalgo has been responsible for keeping, studying and making the collections of graphic documents widely available, which include printed and illuminated European books, prints, watercolours and drawings. The year in which she retires, 2014, sees the publication of a book 'Drawings and Watercolours in the Calouste Gulbenkian Collection'. This publication is sure to be a worthy complement to the exhibition devoted to these works that is being held in the same year. ¶ It marks the culmination of a career that has been governed by great technical and scientific rigour, sustained by high personal and professional standards, and coupled with outstanding human qualities that include commitment, loyalty to the institution, an extraordinary capacity for work, both individually and in a team, and a natural liking for others. ¶ As a publication that plays an essential role in increasing the public's knowledge of one of the Calouste Gulbenkian Museum's least well-known collections, this book is also an expression of the gratitude that is rightly owed to its author.

JOÃO CASTEL-BRANCO PEREIRA
Director of the Calouste Gulbenkian Museum

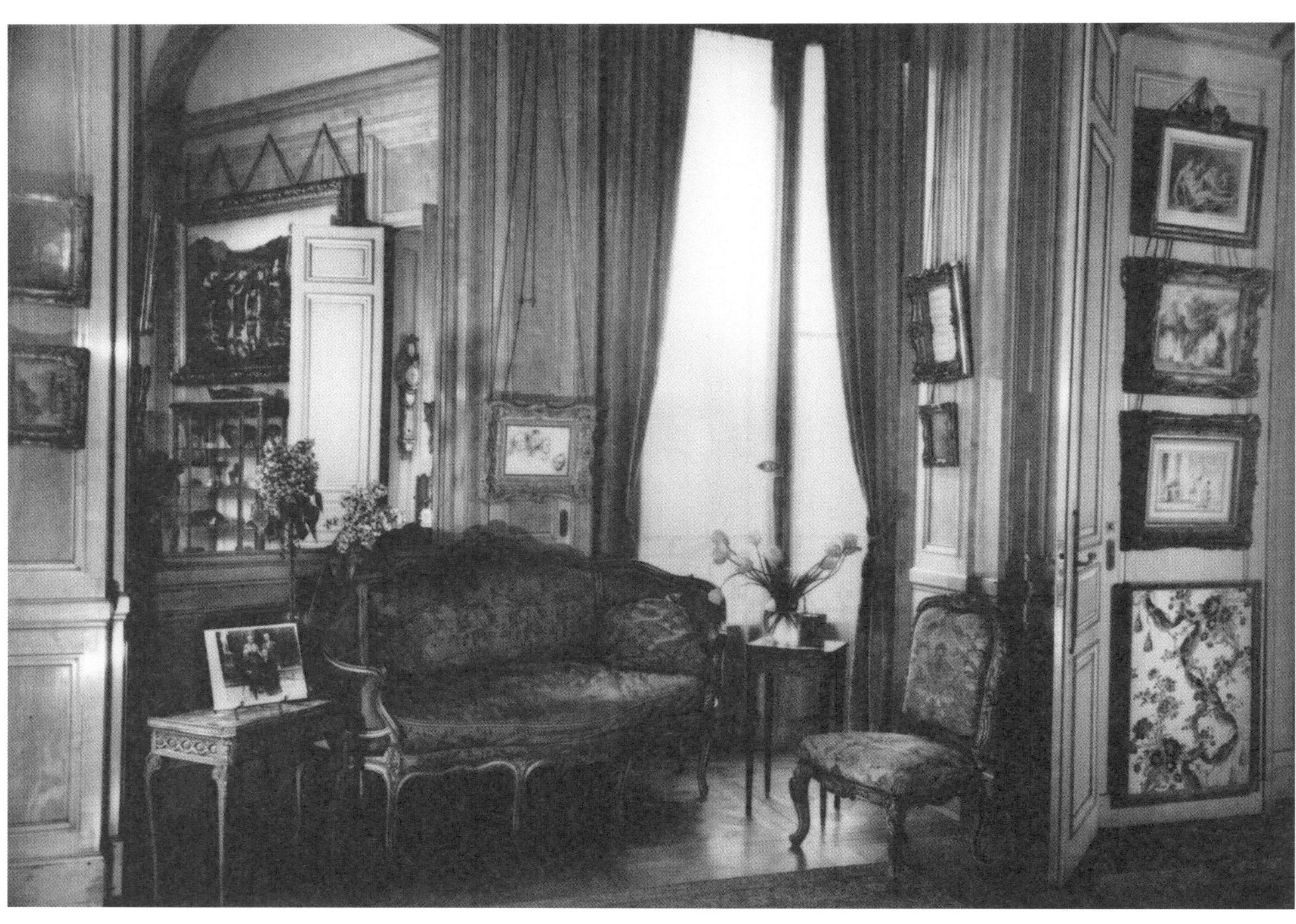

– fig. 1 –

Salon Sycomore, partial view.

Calouste Gulbenkian's house at avenue d'Iéna, Paris.

Photo: Mário de Oliveira

CONTENTS

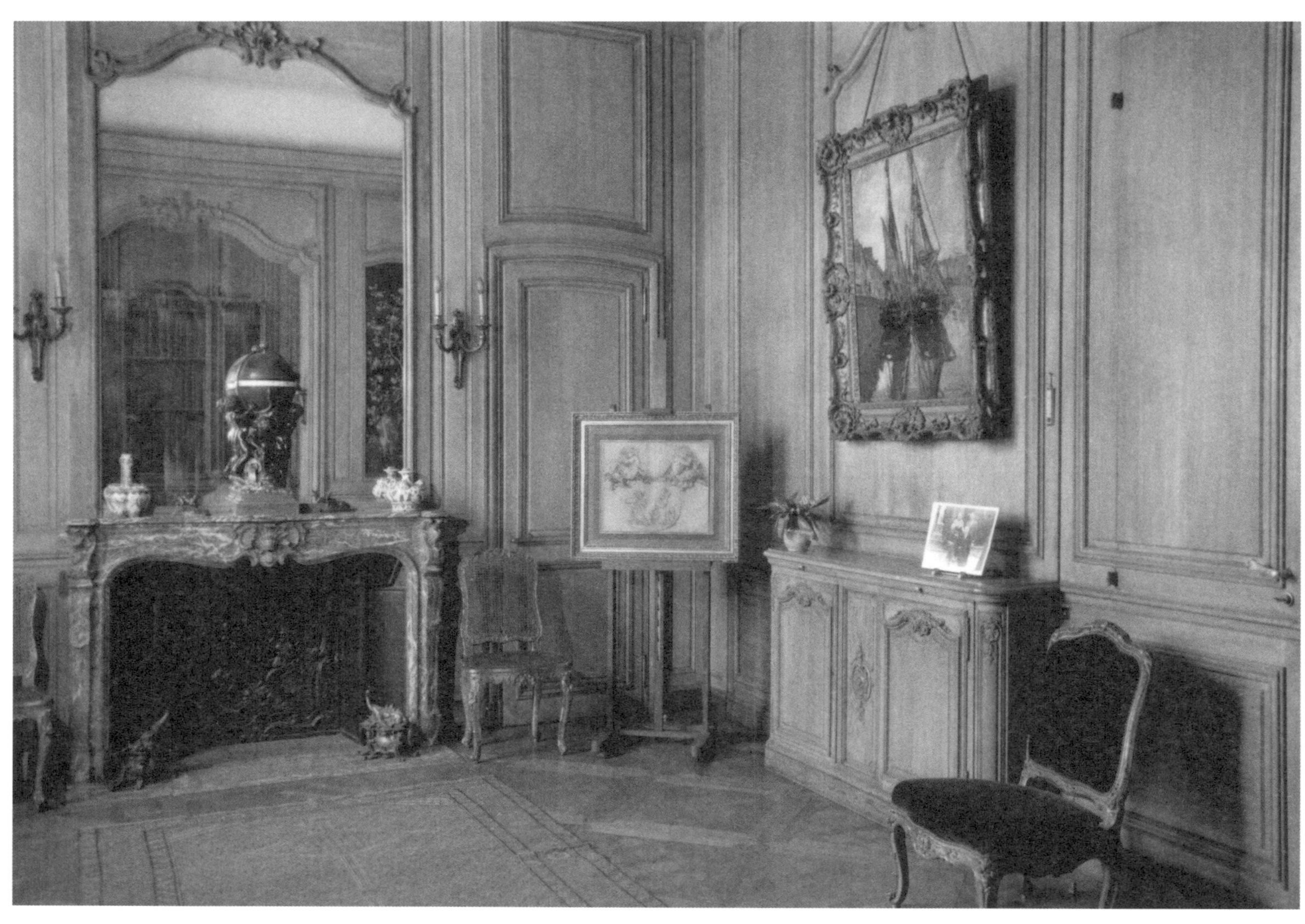

– fig. 2 –
Cabinet de Travail, partial view.
Calouste Gulbenkian's house at avenue d'Iéna, Paris.

Photo: Mário de Oliveira

CALOUSTE GULBENKIAN AND THE ART OF DRAWING

IN 1922, CALOUSTE GULBENKIAN (1869–1955) purchased a Parisian mansion that had previously belonged to the art collector Rodolphe Kann. Once he had made the necessary improvements and adaptations, he moved into the property with his family in December 1927, bringing with him the works of art that he had already acquired, a remarkable series of pieces which made him one of the most renowned collectors of his time. ¶ Photographs of the house as it was then reveal that the living spaces were filled with magnificent paintings, furniture, silverware, ceramics, textiles and books, creating a perfect symbiosis between European and Oriental art. The walls of the various rooms were hung with drawings of the highest quality. Protected by glass (in line with the most basic conservation standards, which Gulbenkian knew and practiced so well), these pieces helped, along with other works, to embellish the spaces in which they were displayed (figs. 1–2). In fact, Calouste Gulbenkian brought together a small number of drawings which, despite not ranking among the most outstanding sets in his collection, contained major pieces by renowned masters such as Dürer, Watteau, Boucher, and Millet, among others, to which Gulbenkian's artistic knowledge and sensibility were not indifferent. ¶ However, it cannot be said that Gulbenkian was a collector of drawings in the full sense of the word. Indeed, only forty or so drawings (associated, for reasons of management, with a similarly small number of watercolours) can be found among the approximately 6000 pieces that comprise the collection, which is currently housed in his museum in Lisbon. But if the collection contains few drawings, this is not because Gulbenkian lacked the opportunity to find works of quality on the market that could rival the other pieces that had interested him. ¶ The correspondence kept in his archives reveals that, from the early 1930s until shortly before his death, Gulbenkian constantly received offers to buy drawings belonging to well-known collections that had been put on sale, including works by such renowned artists as Van der Weyden, Rubens, Watteau, Gravelot, Fragonard, Gainsborough, Constable, Guardi, Rodin and Toulouse-Lautrec, among others. For various reasons, these drawings failed to attract his attention. ¶ When discussing other areas of the collection, such as painting, manuscripts or textiles, Gulbenkian's correspondence constantly refers to the nature of the works that most interested him and the periods, artists and genres that he preferred or rejected. In this regard, it is worth noting that mentions of drawing are virtually absent, although some sporadic references can be found in a few letters that give us a better understanding of his views on the subject. ¶ In response to an offer of some preparatory studies and sketches for paintings, Gulbenkian rejects the proposal by saying: "I do not think that preparatory studies, however well rendered, could interest me. I definitely prefer finished paintings"[1]. For this reason, when the chance arose to buy the preparatory drawing for Fragonard's exceptional painting *The Isle of Love* (inv. 436), Gulbenkian reiterated: "I must confess that having the picture, I am not much attracted by the drawing, however if it is of exceptional quality and beauty, I might make up my mind differently"[2]. ¶ The antique merchants and art dealers with whom he dealt most frequently were well aware of his preferences. Hence, before showing him a new drawing that he might wish to purchase, the manager of Sotheby's in London began by saying: "Although I do not think it is in your line, I feel that I should let you know that we have coming up shortly an absolutely genuine Roger van der Weyden drawing"[3]. ¶ Gulbenkian himself restated his desire to buy a Gainsborough drawing. "I am informed that there is at Mr. Léger's gallery a very beautiful Gainsborough drawing of which I have a photograph [...]. The composition is charming and, although I do not usually buy drawings, I would like you [...] send me your report about it"[4]. ¶ When Gulbenkian was given the opportunity to purchase some drawings by Greuze, his secretary replied: "He regrets he does not collect drawings by Greuze. In fact, only very seldom does he acquire drawings, the exception being in favour of transcendent works by great masters"[5]. ¶ Finally, after agreeing to examine a drawing that was offered to him to purchase, Gulbenkian succinctly summarised his feelings about buying drawings: "Now and then, I acquire drawings when they are of exceptional interest and in perfect condition"[6]. ¶ It can therefore be concluded that the drawings that make up Calouste Gulbenkian's small collection were purchased because he considered them to be works of exceptional quality and beauty in a perfect state of conservation and not because they were examples of artistic expression attained through the specific language and techniques of drawing.

PROVENANCES AND ACQUISITIONS

The drawings belonging to the Gulbenkian Collection were bought between 1905 and 1937 at auctions of renowned collections or sales held at artists' studios through his trusted intermediaries (Agnew & Sons, Colnaghi, Graat et Madoulé, Wildenstein, and Hans Steibel, among others), all of whom were well acquainted with the Collector's requirements. He also bought them from well-known galleries (Sotheby's, the Georges Petit Gallery, the Boerner Gallery, Colnaghi's),
particularly in London and Paris, or directly from the artists who created them, [31]
as in the case of *Black Panther and Serpent (Python)* by Paul Jouve. ¶ In March
1905, Calouste Gulbenkian bought the first two drawings that would consti- [13]
tute the starting point of his collection: *Birth of Louis XV* by Cochin, and *Study of Hands*, Attributed to Van Loo, which he bought at the auction of the Alfred Beurdeley Collection in Paris (fig. 3). ¶ By the early 1920s, he had bought around
ten drawings. At the sale of the Marquis de Biron collections in Paris in June 1914, [11–12]
Gulbenkian bought three pieces, including *Pair of Cupids with Basket of Flowers* by

1. "Je ne pense pas que des esquisses, même poussés, puissent convenir. Il me faut plutôt les tableaux tout à fait finis." Letter from Gulbenkian to Rosenberg, dated 9 November 1936.

2. Letter from Gulbenkian to Mr. Pilkington of Sotheby & Co., 6 April 1946.

3. Letter from Mr Pilkington of Sotheby & Co., dated 20 April 1948.

4. Letter from Calouste Gulbenkian to George H. Davey of Knoedler & Co. of London, 2 July 1946.

5. Letter to William H. Sehab of New York, dated 15 October 1950.

6. Letter from Gulbenkian to Mr. Pilkington of Sotheby & Co. in London, dated 27 April 1948.

François Boucher. ¶ In the 1920s, one of the golden periods in Gulbenkian's life
as a collector, he oversaw the purchasing of drawings from important collections.
[10] [23] From the collection of the Marquess of Lansdowne, which went on sale in London
[3] in March 1920, he selected *Reclining Female Nude* by Boucher, *Portrait of Two*
[5] *Young Ladies* by Henry Edridge, *Female Figure with Children*, by an artist in the
[15] circle of Leonardo da Vinci, and finally, *Ford in a Wooded Landscape* by Ruisdael.
Back in Paris in December of the following year, he bought *Portrait of the Marquis*
de Marigny by Cochin at the Le Breton sale. From the collection brought together
[1] by Max Bonn, two works passed to the Gulbenkian collection when the former
[4] went on sale in London in February 1922: Dürer's watercolour *Dead Duck*, and
Study of Armour, attributed to Van Dyck. Some months later, in May, at the sale
[28] held by the Marseillais collector Alfred Baillehache in Paris, Gulbenkian bought
a series of fifty-seven watercolours illustrating *La Fontaine's Fables* and produced
[29] in France around the turn of the century. In June of the same year, in London, he
bought the watercolour *The Church of Santa Maria della Salute, Venice* at the sale
of William Newall's collection. When the collection brought together by Max and
[8] Maurice Rosenheim was broken up and made available to the public in London
in May 1923, Gulbenkian bought *Pastoral Scene*, the last drawing by Boucher
[25] that enriched the group of works by this artist now in the Gulbenkian Museum[7].
Lastly, in December 1926, he bought Félix Ziem's drawing *The Entrance of the Old*
Port of Marseille at the sale of the Le Roy collection. ¶ The 1930s were equally
fertile years for Gulbenkian's purchasing activities: he oversaw the acquisition
[30] of five drawings, most of which came from reputed collections, including Paul
Jouve's drawing *Royal Eagle* which had belonged to Madame J. Danthon's collection, the sale of which took place in Paris in May 1933. Gulbenkian added the
last drawings to his set in 1937 with four works purchased, two at the sale of D.
[19] [16] David-Weill Collection, and the other two from Count Greffulhe's. At the former he bought *Satyrs*, a piece inspired by the work of Clodion, and also *Qu'en*
[17] [7] *dit l'Abbé?* by Fragonard, while at the latter he bought two pieces of equal importance: *Inside a Roman Park*, also by Fragonard, and *Three Studies of a Young*
Woman's Head by Watteau (fig. 4). ¶ It should also be mentioned that, in order
to carry out one of its original functions – that of studying the works in its care –
the Calouste Gulbenkian Museum decided to buy two drawings related to pieces
[20] already found in the Collection, both of which give us a better understanding of
the artists' creative processes. The first, Francesco Guardi's *Capriccio with Roman*
Ruined Arch and Circular Temple, was bought in New York in January 2002 and
[14] is a preparatory study for a painting by the same artist which also belongs to the
Collection (inv. 531). The second, Cochin's *Female Figure*, which was bought in
[13] Paris in June–July 2003, is a preparatory study for one of the key drawings in the
Gulbenkian Collection: *Birth of Louis XV*.

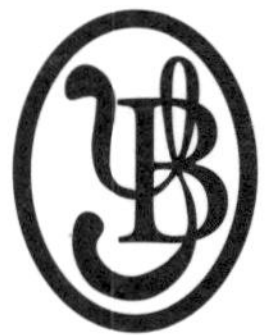

– fig. 3 –
Collection mark of Alfred Beurdeley [13, 18]

7. Gulbenkian bought a total of six works by Boucher: a painting entitled *Cupid and the Three Graces* (inv. 433); a six-volume edition of *L'Œuvre de Molière* (inv. LA247), with illustrations by the artist and an original sanguine drawing introducing each volume; and four drawings [8, 10, 11–12] with which a fifth [9], a copy of a painting by Boucher, is associated.

– fig. 4 –
Jean Antoine Watteau
(1684–1721),
Three Studies of a Young Woman's Head,
ca. 1716–17.
Detail of [7].

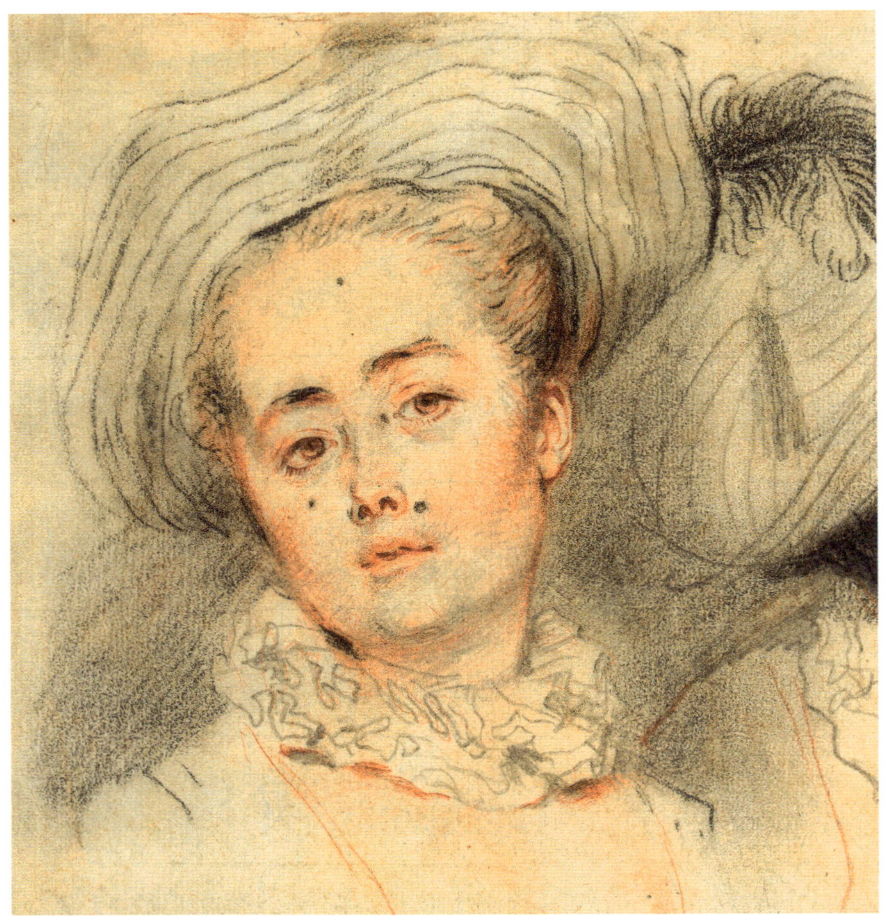

THE DRAWING AND WATERCOLOUR COLLECTION

The Gulbenkian Collection's set of drawings contains around forty items produced in the main centres of European art (France, the Netherlands, Flanders, England and Italy) between the sixteenth century and the early twentieth century. The themes on which it focuses are common to those depicted in other parts of the Collection, that is, landscapes, portraits, genre or religious scenes, still lifes, and representations of animals. As is true of the other groups of works acquired by Gulbenkian, the Collector's proximity to French culture explains the large number of pieces of French origin that he bought, most of which were created in the eighteenth century. ¶ Although Gulbenkian bought an even smaller number of watercolours, the works that he owned in this genre include several notable [21, 22] pieces, those by Turner, *Ruins of Tintern Abbey*, and *Plymouth with a Rainbow* [29] and Sargent *The Church of Santa Maria della Salute, Venice*. The importance of this group of works was increased by the acquisition of a series of fifty-seven [28] watercolours created to illustrate the fables of Jean de La Fontaine. In order to conserve them better, they were brought together in an album commissioned by Gulbenkian from Jean Dunand (1877–1942). The artists responsible for these works were encouraged by commissions placed by collectors who, under the influence of English painters such as Turner and Bonington, greatly appreciated the spontaneity, immediacy and transparency of the watercolour. Many of the art-

ists involved in this project were linked to the founding of the French Society of Watercolourists. ¶ An excellent medium by which to capture reality, drawing performs several functions in the creative process and most of the various types of drawing that exist can be found in the Gulbenkian Collection. The genre can
[24] be used either to register the spontaneous expression of a 'first thought', as in the example found on the back of a drawing by Millet, in which the artist uses only a few summary but expressive lines to capture the outline of a female figure who would later appear in a painting now kept at the Metropolitan Museum Of Art in
[4] New York (fig. 24.1); or it can represent phased studies of all or part of a motif, as in the unfinished work *Study of Armour*, attributed to Anton van Dyck. It can also
[1] highlight an artist's hesitation or reveal a correction introduced into the composition, as in the case of Dürer's watercolour; note the sketched pencil lines on the tail of the duck, which point to other possible paths that the artist abandoned. It
[6] can also serve to present detailed studies intended to serve as a preparation for
[20] [5] paintings. Examples of this use include the drawings by Willem van Mieris and Francesco Guardi. Finally, as in the case of Ruisdael's landscape, it can appear as a finished, independent work with its own artistic qualities.

8. Letter from Gulbenkian to George Davey of M. Knoedler & Co., dated 12 April 1943.

THE COLLECTION'S ARTISTIC JOURNEY

As he stated himself, Calouste Gulbenkian lacked the temperament of a scientific collector of periods or series[8] and, as was noted above, he brought together only a small but significant number of drawings. Even so, they include works that establish a link between the most influential trends in the history of art from the time of the Renaissance to the art that first appeared in the first quarter of the twentieth century, that is, the modernity of the innovative artistic language of Art Deco that Gulbenkian found so appealing. ¶ The first three works mentioned reflect the main artistic movements that dominated the early sixteenth century; on the one hand, the legacy of northern gothic art and, on the other, the blossoming of
[1] Renaissance ideas in the south of Europe. They are translated by Dürer in his drawing *Dead Duck*, which was created from objective observations of nature and inspired by the motifs of classical culture, and also in the artistic expression of
[2] [3] Holbein's late German gothic, which served to inspire the artist who produced *Annunciation*. Another related work is *Female Figure with Children*, which was initially attributed to Bernardino Luini but is now considered to be the work of a sixteenth-century Milanese artist who absorbed the influences of Leonardo da Vinci's aesthetic. ¶ The collection contains only two works from the seventeenth
[4] century, both of which originate from the so-called northern schools. One of these works is *Study of Armour*, which is attributed to the Flemish artist Anton van Dyck, whose work reflects not only the assimilation of the baroque aesthetic of Rubens, of whom he was a disciple and collaborator, but also the main themes of
[5] the Venetian pictorial tradition, especially that established by Titian, whom he greatly admired. The second drawing, *Ford in a Wooded Landscape*, by the Dutch artist Jacob van Ruisdael, is an excellent example of a finished autonomous work which highlights its creator's excellence as a landscapist. ¶ The eighteenth century is represented by a greater number of works by renowned masters from England,
[6] the Netherlands, France and Italy. At the beginning of the century, Willem van Mieris produced the work *Tarquin and Lucretia*, which represents an episode in the

legendary history of ancient Rome. Created in a highly detailed descriptive language, it is a preparatory study for a painting on the same theme. Watteau, one of
the greatest geniuses of French painting, who so skilfully conveyed the aesthetic
ideal of the rococo in conceiving a new pictorial genre known as *fête galante*, is the [7]
creator of *Three Studies of a Young Woman's Head*, one of the most remarkable [8, 10, 11–12]
drawings in the Gulbenkian collection. A group of four drawings and a related [9]
copy were conceived by François Boucher, one of the greatest interpreters of the
joie de vivre of an elite, carefree and sensual social group. The Gulbenkian drawings by this artist unequivocally represent the way that, in a rocaille style, he
recreated a timeless and illusory world of mythological, pastoral and country
scenes. Three drawings in the collection were produced by Charles-Nicolas
Cochin the Younger, the academic and theoretician who inspired neoclassicism in
his country and a renowned name in the world of French graphic arts (drawing,
printmaking, illustration). Two of these drawings, created in a miniaturist lan- [13]
guage, depict episodes related to the history of France: *Birth of Louis XV*, the [15]
future king of France who succeeded the Sun King, and *Portrait of the Marquis de
Marigny*, who was a prominent statesman under Louis XV, the brother of Madame
de Pompadour, and the Director General of the King's Buildings, Gardens, Arts,
Academies and Manufactories. Tackling an enormous range of themes in an array
of techniques, Fragonard, an artist who worked in the Rococo tradition, was especially successful in achieving spontaneity in his drawn work, which is [16]
represented here by two examples: in *Qu'en dit l'Abbé?*, he depicts another of the [17]
elegant scenes that so appealed to society at the time and in *Interior of a Roman
Park*, he conveys his interest in the Italian landscape, which was revitalised on a
second trip to Italy in the company of his patron Bergeret de Grancourt. The best
represented painter in the Gulbenkian Collection, with twenty works, is Francesco
Guardi. This group of works was enriched by a drawing by the Venetian artist, [20]
Capriccio with Roman Ruined Arch and Circular Temple, a preparatory study for the
painting *Capriccio* (inv. 531), which is also owned by the Gulbenkian Museum.
This imagined view, created at the height of the artist's maturity, emerges in the
drawing through short, broken lines that are frenziedly interrupted and restarted
in a way that brilliantly conveys the quiet decline of the city of Venice in the late
eighteenth century. A commitment to the aesthetics of classical antiquity and the
language of neoclassicism is evident in the work of Clodion, one of the most versatile French sculptors of the second half of the eighteenth century. His aesthetic [19]
language and themes are reflected in the drawing *Satyrs*, which was initially attributed to the French master but is now considered to be the work of a disciple or
follower inspired by him. William Turner's skill as a watercolourist is evident in
the technique that he always employed to masterful effect in works ranging from [21]
the landscape scenes that he painted as a young man, such as *Ruins of Tintern
Abbey*, to rigorously rendered series such as *The Ports of England*, which includes [22]
Plymouth with a Rainbow, a piece that already shows glimpses of the visionary
imagination that would be intensified in the more poetic conceptions of his mature
years. ¶ The work of the portraitist Henry Edridge, the British artist with whom [23]
the group of nineteenth-century drawings begins, can be seen in *Portrait of Two
Young Ladies*, a piece whose neoclassical characteristics make it typical of his output. Jean-François Millet, one of the founders of the Barbizon School, was a realist
painter of rural scenes, in which he depicted the peasantry's modest yet epic life
and humanity as well as the nature surrounding them. The artist was the creator [24]
of one of the most beautiful drawings in the Gulbenkian collection: *Landscape at
Dusk*, a view of the Barbizon countryside that he knew and loved so well. A paint-

[25] er of acknowledged merit and a talented watercolourist and drawer, Félix Ziem
was the creator of the drawing *The Entrance of the Old Port of Marseille*. The south
[26] of France, particularly Martigues and Marseille, appears with obsessive regularity
in his drawings and paintings, as do Venice and Istanbul. *Faneuse au repos* is a
study by Jules Breton of one of the characters featured in his painting *Juin* (Arnot
Art Museum, Elmira, New York). In the work of this artist, which was dominated
by rural themes, the harshness of the daily lives of the peasants was overlooked in
favour of depictions of the harmony that characterised the traditional agricultural
[27] community. In chronological terms, this group of nineteenth-century drawings
ends with the work of another British artist Muirhead Bone: *Shipbreaking Talmouth*.
Bone, who came to be seen as the greatest British etcher of his time, was a prolific
drawer and watercolourist who became interested in themes concerned with daily
urban life, the architectural aspects of changing cities, shipbuilding, portraits, and
landscape. ¶ Finally, the twentieth century finds its expression in drawings by
John Singer Sargent, Paul Jouve, and Léonard Tsugouharu Foujita. Of American
descent and a Florentine by birth, Sargent always harboured an intense passion for
[29] the city of Venice, which, in the Gulbenkian's watercolour, he represents through
one of the city's most emblematic monuments, the Church of Santa Maria della
Salute, a work in which he employed an impressionist grammar and paid particular attention to the use of colour and the treatment of light (fig. 5). The animal
world, which greatly interested Paul Jouve and would become the predominant
[30] [31] theme in his work, is depicted in two drawings found in the Gulbenkian Collection:
Royal Eagle and *Black Panther and Serpent (Python)*. In both cases, the artist seeks
not only to convey artistically the anatomical veracity of the beasts but also to
express their secret life and the subtlety of each animal's behaviour. In chrono-
[32–35] logical terms, the Gulbenkian Museum's collection of drawings ends with four
works by Foujita, an artist of Japanese origin who subsequently became a French
national. These drawings were intended to illustrate the literary work *Les huits
renommées* by Foujita's compatriot Kikou Yamata, which was published in 1927.
The Gulbenkian Collection owns the no. 1 of the first edition of this work as well
as the other original drawings chosen for the illustration of the book and assembled in a second volume (inv. LM441 A/B).

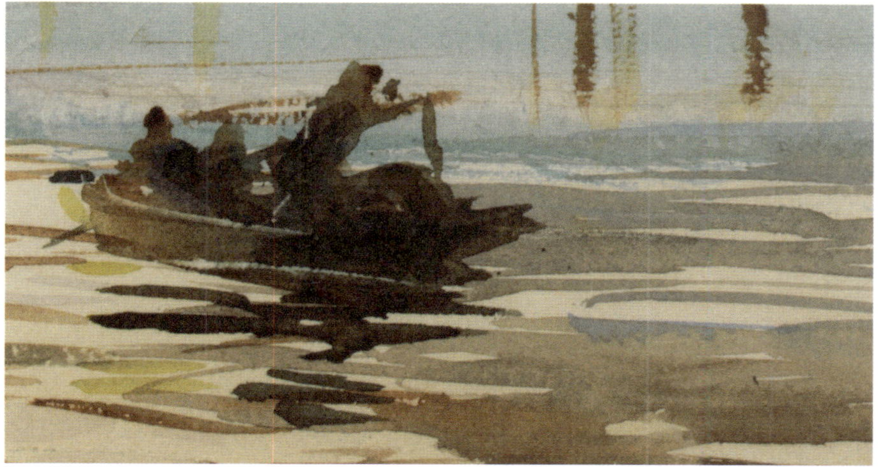

– fig. 5 –
John Singer Sargent
(1856–1925),
*The Church of
Santa Maria della Salute,
Venice*, ca. 1904–9.
Detail of [29].

9. PERDIGÃO, 1969, pp. 12–13.

10. Letter dated 10 February 1953.

11. Opened on 2 October 1969 in the Parque de Santa Gertrudes, (today Parque Calouste Gulbenkian), in Lisbon.

12. The Prime Minister under King José I and the man responsible for rebuilding Lisbon after the 1755 earthquake.

As mentioned above, Calouste Gulbenkian lived among his collections in the house that he bought in Paris on the Avenue d'léna. He valued these pieces so greatly that he rarely allowed anyone the privilege of seeing them[9]. As he neared the end of this life (Gulbenkian died in Lisbon in 1955), he became concerned about the uncertain future of these works and in 1953 he wrote to his friend and adviser John Walker, who was then Chief Curator of the National Gallery of Art in Washington:

> «I fully realise that it is high time that I should come to a decision with regards to the future of my collections. It is without the slightest exaggeration that I consider them as 'my children' and their welfare is one of my dominant anxieties. They represent fifty or sixty years of my life and I have collected them, at times with immense difficulties, and always and exclusively guided by my taste and judgment. Of course, as all collectors do, I have sought advice, but I do feel they are mine, after my own heart and soul»[10].

It was in Portugal, where he arrived from wartime Europe in 1942, that this important financier of Armenian origin, an influential specialist in the oil sector and the owner of a collection of works of art of unrivalled quality, found the solution that he had sought in vain for years. When negotiations to bring his artistic heritage to other cities (London, Washington, New York) broke down, Calouste Gulbenkian chose Portugal as the country where he would set up a foundation with educational, artistic, scientific and charitable aims. Having been attracted by the country's mild climate and by the warm welcome that he received there, he bequeathed the nation the magnificent collection that he had amassed over the course of a lifetime, thereby realizing his long-held dream of bringing all his works together under one roof. ¶ In the capital, plans were made for the construction of the building[11] that would definitively house the Gulbenkian legacy. Meanwhile, in 1958, two years after it was established, the foundation bearing his name acquired an eighteenth-century palace located on the outskirts of the city, in Oeiras. The palace was designed by the architect Carlos Mardel and had belonged to Sebastião José de Carvalho e Melo (1699–1782), the Count of Oeiras and subsequently the Marquis of Pombal[12]. There, it was provisionally stored the works of art that had recently arrived in Portugal from France, England and the United States of America. To ensure the safe preservation of the important artistic heritage entrusted to this magnificent building, despite it being a temporary resource, the foundation carried out the museological adaptations that were deemed to be necessary. ¶ Between July 1958 and July 1960, the collection was transferred from Paris to Oeiras in Portugal. Taking advantage of this hiatus, and with the aim of granting the public access to the extraordinary artistic heritage that was now in the care of the Calouste Gulbenkian Foundation, several exhibitions were organized, the first taking place in France and the others being held in Portuguese cultural institutions. Reference can be made to the most noteworthy exhibition held in Porto at the Museu Nacional de Soares dos Reis in 1964, entitled "Artes

Plásticas Francesas de Watteau a Renoir" ("French Visual Arts from Watteau to Renoir"). Several watercolours and ten of the best drawings in the Collection were shown there for the first time[13]. ¶ In July 1965, on the tenth anniversary of Gulbenkian's death, the rooms of Pombal Palace were opened to the public. Due to the lack of available space, the works were initially shown on a rotating basis. Around three hundred pieces were presented, distributed on the ground floor and the *piano nobile* of the building. On the latter floor, room no. 12 was used to display ten drawings as well as several pieces of furniture[14]. These works were subsequently kept in the palace's storerooms, where they were located in November 1967.

13. PORTO, 1964, nos. 56 to 65 (repr.).

14. OEIRAS, 1965.

15. For a more detailed account of these events, see: "Calouste Gulbenkian Foundation. 4th Chairman's Report. Jan. 1966–Dec. 1968." Lisbon: FCG 1970 (1st part, chapter 7, pp. 55–66).

THE FLOODS OF 1967

The night of 25 November 1967 might have been no different to countless others on which, after the public had left, the lights had been switched off and the doors had been closed, the works of art were returned to the tranquillity of the surrounding silence. On this occasion, however, this tranquillity would be disrupted[15]. ¶ As night began to fall, exactly one year after the city of Florence was flooded by the River Arno, heavy rain poured down on Lisbon and the surrounding areas. In a few hours the intense rainfall, together with the rising tide, caused floods that killed hundreds of people, spreading chaos across riverside regions and causing a massive amount of material damage, some of which was irreparable. ¶ The Palace of the Marquess of Pombal, being situated close to the Ribeira da Lage (a water stream), did not escape the fury of its waters, which were swollen with mud, tree trunks and detritus dragged along by the current. Eventually, the torrent broke through the strong wall protecting the property and invaded the surrounding gardens, destroying everything in its path. The water level quickly rose around six metres up the sides of the palace walls, destroying the air conditioners installed near the ceiling of the two vaults where a substantial number of works of art were kept (fig. 6).

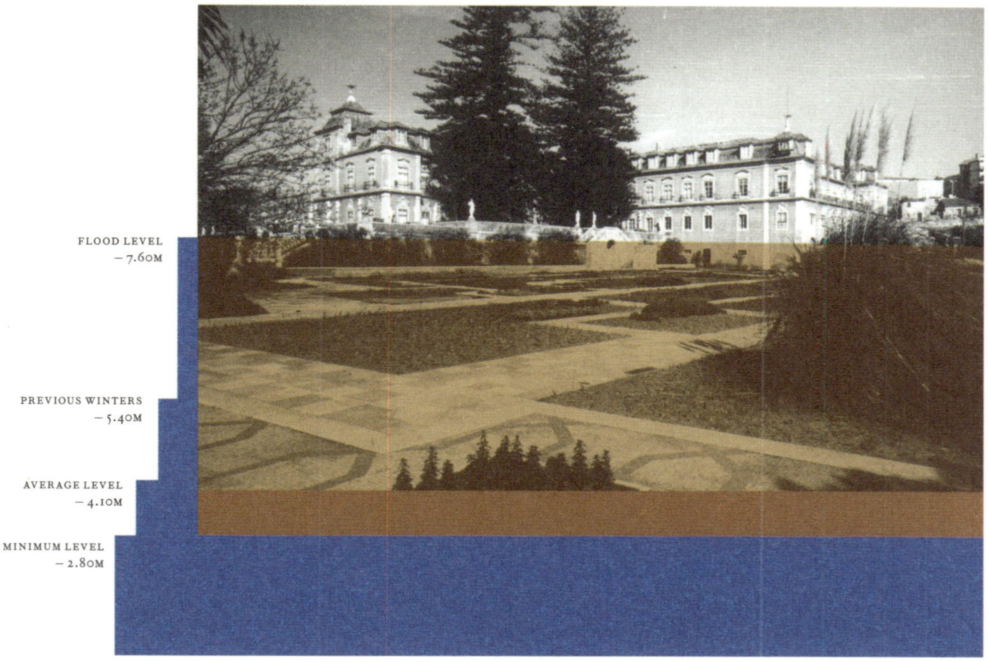

FLOOD LEVEL – 7.60M

PREVIOUS WINTERS – 5.40M

AVERAGE LEVEL – 4.10M

MINIMUM LEVEL – 2.80M

– fig. 6 –
Palace of the Marquess of Pombal, Oeiras.
The 1967 floods: water level measurements.
© Calouste Gulbenkian Foundation / Calouste Gulbenkian Museum
Photo: Carlos Azevedo

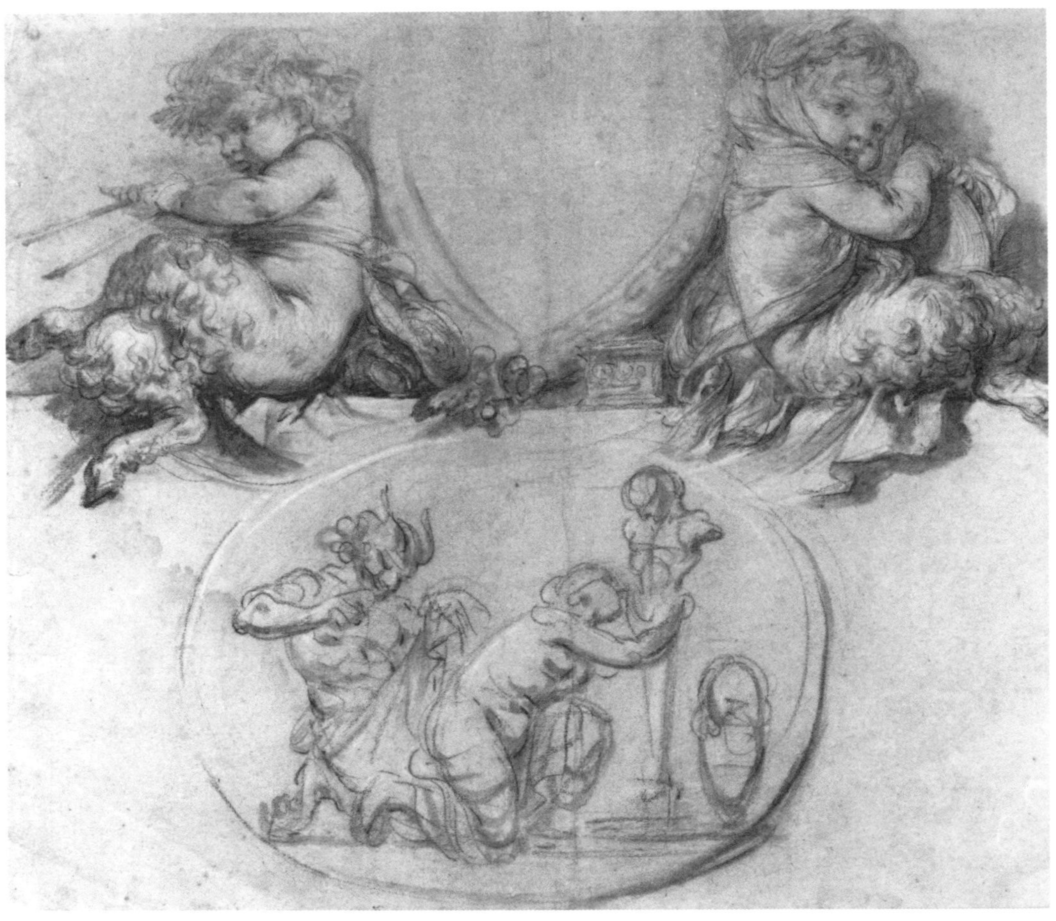

– fig. 7 –
Satyrs drawing after Clodion, before the 1967 floods [19].

Photo: Mário de Oliveira

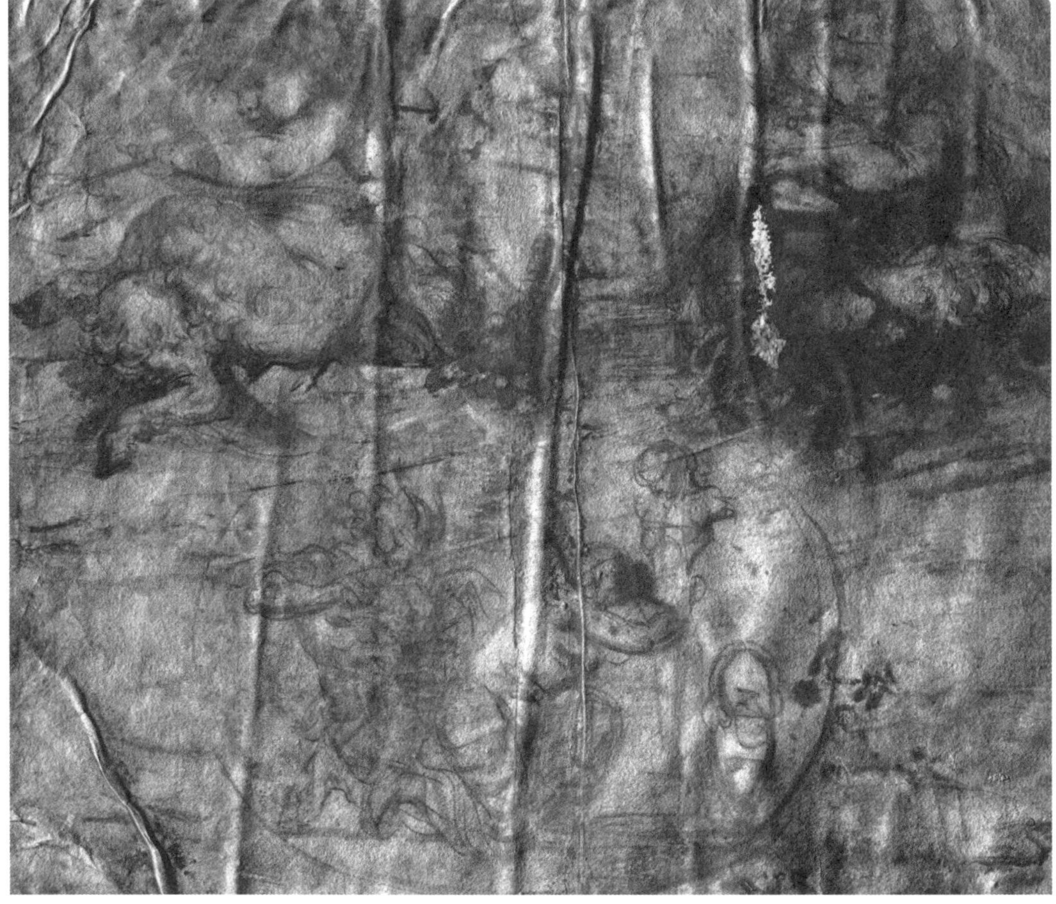

– fig. 8 –
Satyrs drawing after Clodion, following the 1967 floods, and before restoration [19].

Photo: Reinaldo Viegas

The torrent entered through the openings, completely covering everything. This dramatic event left its mark (to a greater or lesser extent) on paintings, drawings, prints, Japanese prints and lacquerware, ceramics, European illuminated manuscript books and Oriental books and bindings belonging to the Gulbenkian collection. ¶ Once the first rescue operations commenced in an improvised workshop at the Palace, the affected works began to be restored with the aid of Portuguese and foreign experts who quickly responded to the Foundation's appeals for help. These experts were joined by several institutions, located in Lisbon, Conímbriga, Paris, London, Amsterdam and Istanbul, to which groups of works were entrusted for treatment. Restoring the affected works thus became a priority in the life of the Foundation, which spared no efforts to provide continuous training to its own experts in the form of courses, visits and internships at prestigious institutions where restoration work was more developed. ¶ The collection of drawings was affected in its entirety, with damage being caused by immersion in water and, after the water had receded, by the brownish layer of mud that covered the surfaces of the works, penetrating the fibres of the supporting paper. The Management and the Restoration Workshop of the Prints Department of the Rijksmuseum in Amsterdam generously offered to help restore the affected pieces at their facilities in the Netherlands, where they were sent in mid-1968. Once the works had been carefully examined and the first restoration attempts had been made in conjunction with senior staff at the Gulbenkian Foundation, the Dutch experts proceeded to treat and restore them, taking into account the fragility of the materials used in creating the drawings and aiming to restore the legibility that had been partially or totally destroyed while also ensuring that their intrinsic qualities would not be irreversibly lost. Initially, the efforts of the restoration team were focused mainly on the group of French drawings, since the possibility of including them in the programme of the Calouste Gulbenkian Museum was being considered (although this did not in fact take place). ¶ Once careful restoration work had been carried out on the drawings (which retained some traces, still visible today, of the harmful effects of the flood), they were sent back to the Calouste Gulbenkian Museum, which was now open to the public in Lisbon. However, four drawings and one gouache[16] were returned in the state that they had been received since the Dutch restoration experts, not being able to guarantee the required results due to the serious damage that the works had suffered, preferred not to subject them to any treatment. Years later, thanks to scientific advances in the field of art restoration and the skill and bold initiative of the experts at the
[11–12, 19] Calouste Gulbenkian Museum's restoration workshop, these pieces were treated and restored (figs. 7–8). Three of them have been selected for this book. ¶ The Gulbenkian Collection is generally noted for the excellent state of conservation of its heritage and, to better understand the current state of the drawings, it is essential to take into account the unexpected circumstances of this natural catastrophe that left indelible marks on some of the Gulbenkian Collection's greatest treasures. ¶ When, on 2 October 1969, the Calouste Gulbenkian Museum finally opened to the public in Santa Gertrudes Park in Lisbon, some groups of works belonging to the collection were not put on display. One such group was the drawings. Created from organic materials subject to natural changes, these items are highly vulnerable to variations in temperature and humidity and to environments that might be polluted. Thus, although the possibility of including an area devoted to drawing in the galleries was initially considered, the circumstances mentioned above and the acknowledged physical fragility of the works confined them definitively to the

16. *Satyrs* after Clodion [19]; *Pair of Cupids with a Basket of Flowers* by Boucher [11–12]; *Female Figure* attributed to P.P. Prud'hon (inv. 171); and *Concert in the Garden* by Lavreince (inv. 237).

17. "Comme vous le savez, je m'intéresse aux livres français du XVIIIe siècle lors qu'il sont vraiment hors-pair tant au point de vue reliure qu'illustrations, et si vous en connaissez vous pouvez me les envoyer pour examen." Letter dated 2 December 1932.

museum's storerooms, their characteristics preventing them from being shown to the public except as part of certain short-term initiatives.

DRAWINGS AND WATERCOLOURS IN THE ART OF THE BOOK

Calouste Gulbenkian's interest in drawing and watercolours, within the parameters outlined above, was not limited to the purchasing of autonomous works such as those that have been described. This interest is equally reflected in many of the printed books that make up his magnificent library, the contents of which are mainly distinguished by the bindings that cover them and the illustrations that elevate the written texts within them to levels of great visual beauty and artistic quality. As Gulbenkian himself told the art dealer Josef Baer: "As you know, I am greatly interested in French books [...], provided that they are exceptional both in terms of the binding and the illustration. If you have any works with these characteristics, please send them to me so that I may examine them"[17]. ¶ Of the illustrations found in the eighteenth-century editions, it is the interpretive line of the intaglio prints that particularly stand out. By contrast, the original drawings related to them can rarely be found in the collection. In this respect, outstanding items in the Gulbenkian library include the 1734 edition of the plays of Molière,

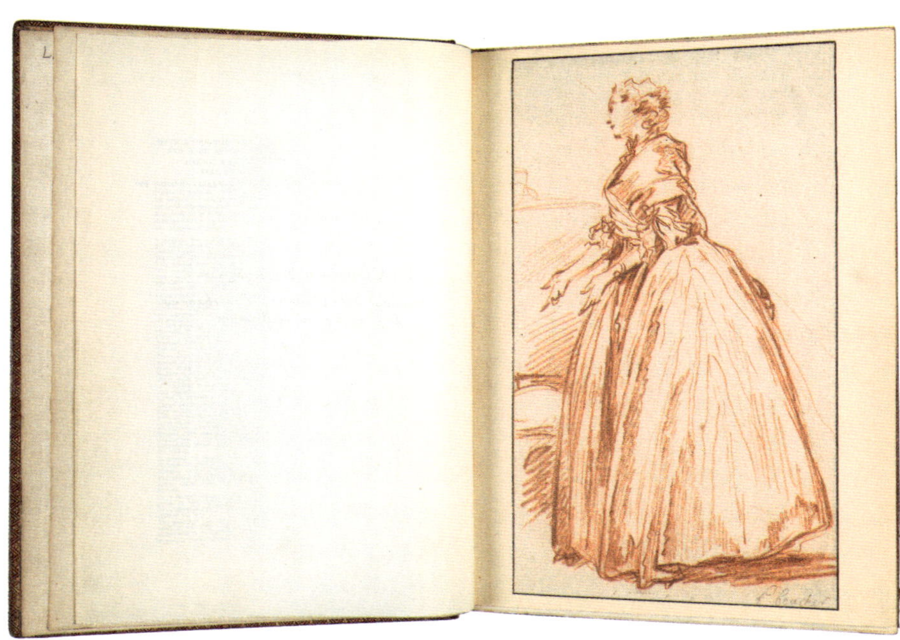

– fig. 9 –
Red-chalk drawing by François Boucher (1703–1770) for the character "Comtesse d'Escarbagnas" in the play with same name, at the opening of vol. I of *Œuvres de Molière*. A Paris : [Prault], 1734, Lisbon, Calouste Gulbenkian Museum, inv. LA247.
© Calouste Gulbenkian Foundation / Calouste Gulbenkian Museum
Photo: Catarina Gomes Ferreira

which is illustrated by François Boucher (1703–1770) and engraved by Laurent Cars (1699–1771). This work is made special by the fact that each volume begins with an original red-chalk study by Boucher of the characters that feature in the pieces inside (fig. 9). ¶ The majority of later books in the collection, being products of the nineteenth and early twentieth centuries, contain etchings or wood engravings as well as drawings and watercolours by renowned masters which embellish and interpret the contents inside and were doubtless one of the reasons why the collector became interested in them. Noteworthy examples include the watercolours by Auguste Renoir (1841–1919) (fig. 10) and Gustave Moreau (1826–1898) that appear at the beginning of two copies of the 1869 edition of Hesiod's odes; Steinlen's drawings, which were hugely influential in illustrating not only Victor Hugo's *Cinq Poèmes*, published in 1902 to commemorate the centenary of the poet's birth, but also the 1910 edition of Jean Richepin's *La Chanson des Gueux*; the excellent drawing by Robert Engels (1866–1926) that introduces the work *Le Roman de Tristan et Iseut* by Joseph Bédier, published in 1900 (fig. 11); or the 250 watercolour drawings by Henriot (1857–1933) that appear throughout the handwritten pages of Guy de Maupassant's *La Maison Tellier.* These are just a few of the many examples that could be mentioned.

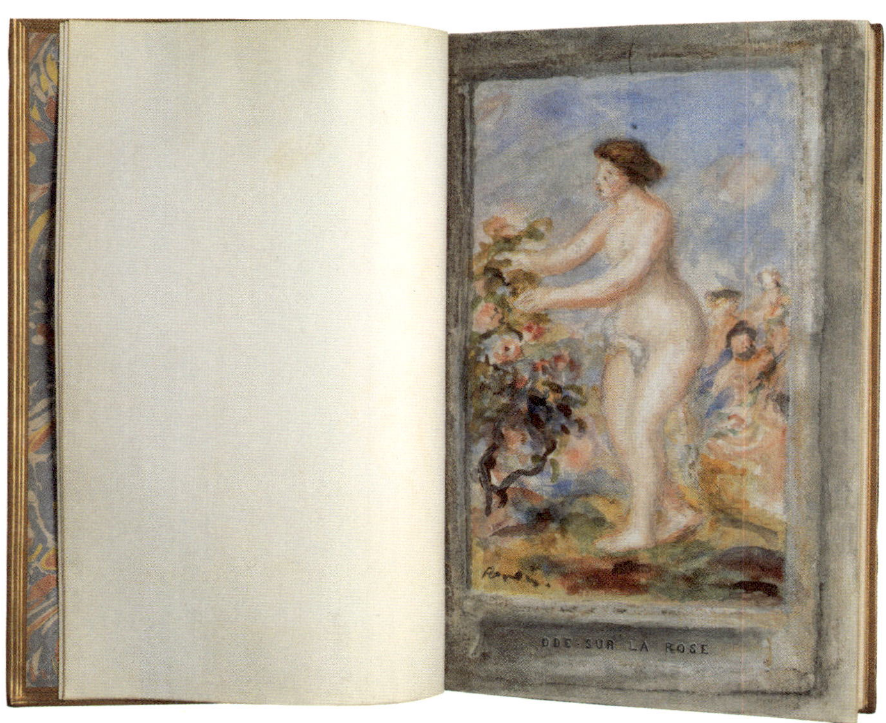

– fig. 10 –
Watercolour by Pierre-Auguste Renoir (1841–1919), *Ode sur la rose*. Illustration for *Odes Anacréontiques*. Paris: A. Lemerre, 1869. Lisbon, Calouste Gulbenkian Museum, inv. LM117.
© Calouste Gulbenkian Foundation / Calouste Gulbenkian Museum
Photo: Inês Oliveira e Silva

The Calouste Gulbenkian Collection is a mirror not just of the personality of the man who amassed it but also of his artistic sensibility and of the scientific knowledge that he acquired during his life as a collector. Naturally, the small group of drawings and watercolours that belong to the collection also reflects his preferences. Thus, the book now being presented initially sought to give the public some insight into the relationship that clearly exists between this area of the collection and the collector's taste. Secondly, it aimed to shine a light, in a general way, on the greatest works in this group from the artistic point of view. It is true that the damage caused to the items shown here by the aforementioned floods, the fragility of the respective supports, and the fear that their condition would be worsened by frequent handling that they might suffer all helped to keep the works in a state of 'in-limbo' maintenance that would allow them to be preserved for future generations. With the exception of widely known masterpieces (by Dürer or Watteau), these circumstances prevented the scientific community from giving their full attention to such pieces in their work. Thus, little by little, information was gathered about the items now being presented. This information was sometimes inconclusive and in some cases doubts remain about origins, creators and dates, questions which, as everyone knows, cannot easily be resolved in the genre of drawing. In spite of this, and leaving aside the desire to search ceaselessly for new data and to hunt down other instructive links, it was felt that the time had come to convey in a systematic manner not only the conclusions obtained but also, and especially, the many doubts that remain when such a diverse collection is examined. Thus it might be possible, sometime in the near future, for this small but important group of works in the Calouste Gulbenkian Collection to become the subject of a better informed and more thoroug study.

—

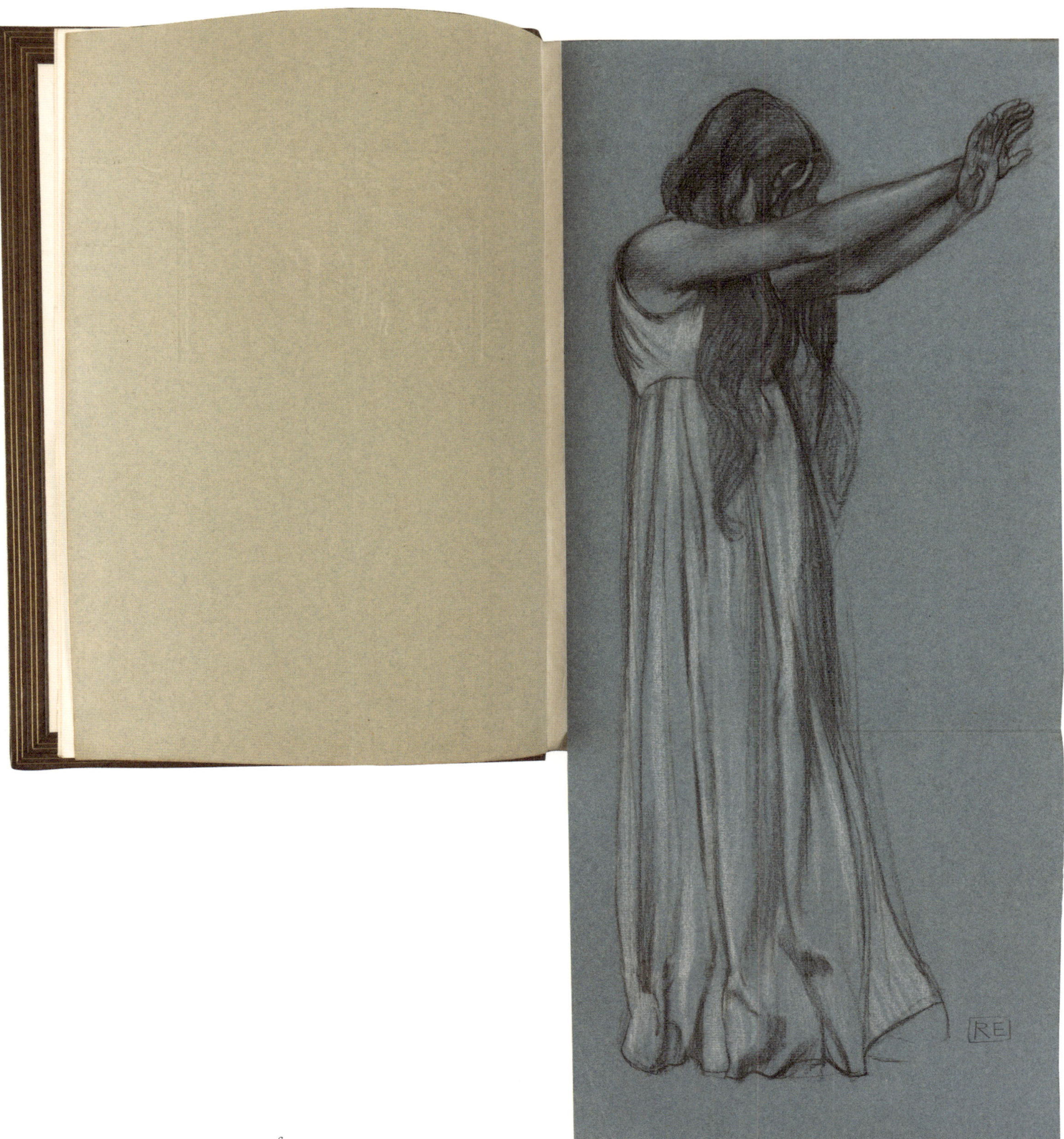

– fig. 11 –
Drawing in black chalk and white highlights, by Robert Engels (1866–1926). Illustration for *Le Roman de Tristan et Iseut*, by Joseph Bédier. Paris: H. Piazza & Cie., 1900. Lisbon, Calouste Gulbenkian Museum, inv. LM29.
© Calouste Gulbenkian Foundation / Calouste Gulbenkian Museum
Photo: Inês Oliveira e Silva

SELECTED WORKS

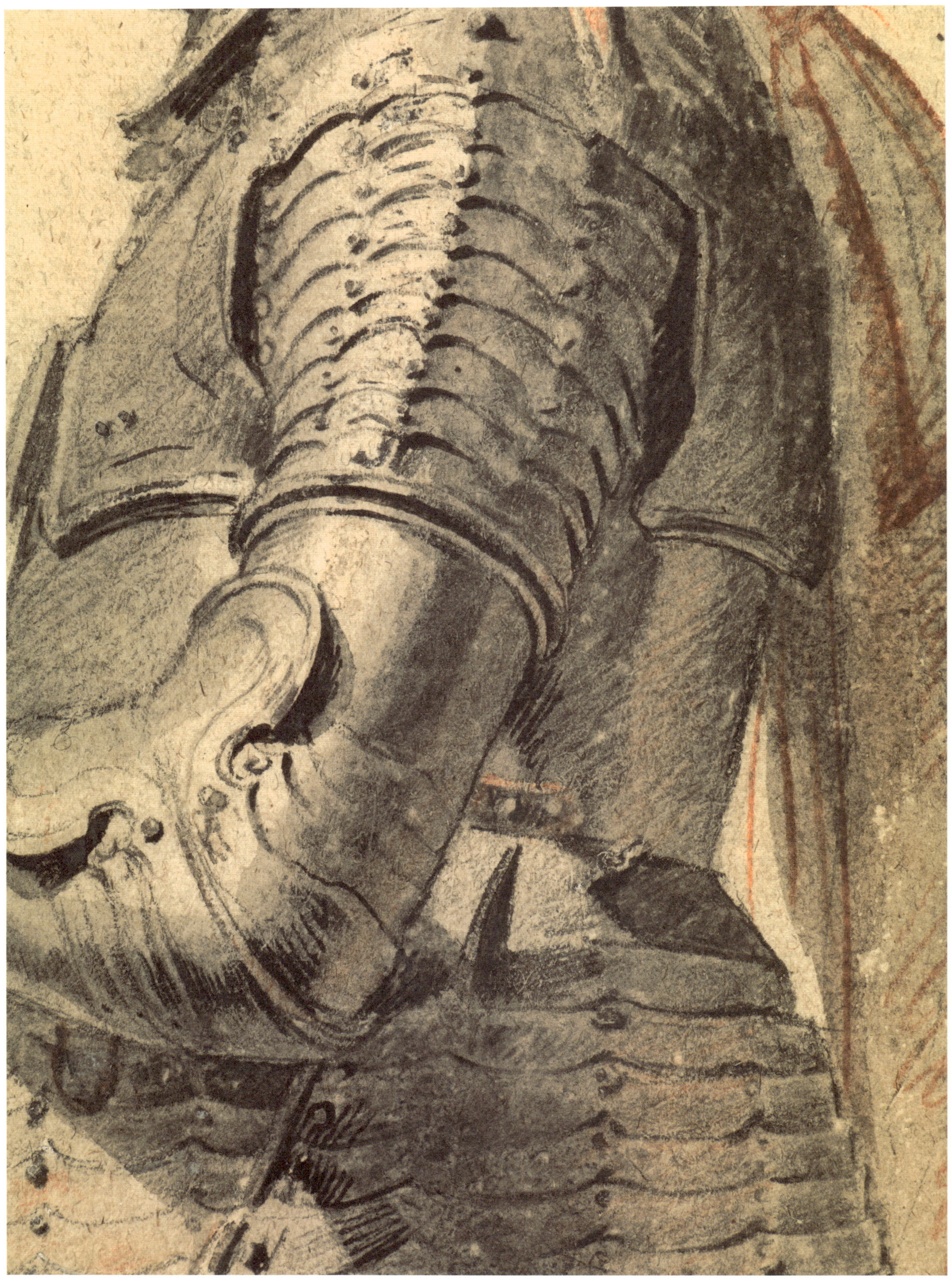

SIXTEENTH CENTURY
—
SEVENTEENTH CENTURY

[1]

ALBRECHT DÜRER

Nuremberg, 1471–1528

DEAD DUCK

Germany, ca. 1502 (?) or ca. 1512 (?)

Pen and brush, watercolour, gouache, black ink,
graphite tracing with gilded heightening on parchment.
22.6(4) × 12.4 cm.
Date and monogram near
the bird's head: "1515 AD" (false).
Inv. 140

Dürer's vast body of work is located on the turning point between two eras in the transition between the Middle Ages and the Renaissance. Born in Nuremberg at a time of intense social, religious, cultural, and political change, Dürer's art melded the legacy of the German late-Gothic[1] with the humanist ideals that were flourishing in Italy at the time, and which he assimilated especially over the course of his two stays there in 1494–95 and 1505–7[2]. ¶ He was a precociously talented artist, and in his quest to go beyond the limitations of his formative years Dürer was naturally drawn to Renaissance ideas. This was conveyed in his work through a rationalist world view and through his search for classical references, some of which he was already familiar with through Italian art and aesthetics[3]. ¶ Talented in all forms of artistic expression, particularly printmaking, Dürer was unsurpassed in his drawing, which was the key to his entire body of work and his preferred medium for all his artistic reflections. This can be seen in the vast array of preparatory studies for his engraved and painted subjects and in his autonomous studies of landscapes, plants or animals that were then frequently expressed in watercolours. ¶ In his search for universal values, Dürer, like Leonardo da Vinci, took nature as his continual source of inspiration. He was a patient and objective observer and he successfully communicated the individual characteristics of every element through drawings that were so full of life and technical virtuosity that they seemed almost real, as exemplified in the studies *Young Hare* and *The Great Piece of Turf*[4]. ¶ The drawing *Dead Duck*, which belongs to the Gulbenkian Collection, is one of Dürer's finest nature studies. In this composition the German master shows a diving duck (*Athya ferina*), a common breed in Northern and Central Europe that is easy to identify by its hazel coloured neck and blue-grey plumage. The bird is depicted as a hunting trophy, hung from a nail in the wall on a string strung through its nostrils. It is shown in sharp profile from its beak down to the start of its body, with its lower half turned only slightly to the left. The way that the heavy body is hung has distended the neck muscles,

1. His artistic roots in the Gothic tradition and his interest in exquisitely detailed decorative elements came from his training as a goldsmith in his father's workshop between 1485 and 1486 and from his apprenticeship in the studio of the painter/printmaker Michael Wolgemut (1433/1434–1519) until 1489. In the former he discovered the world of drawing and metal engraving, and in the latter he entered the world of painting and printmaking for book illustration.

2. Even before these trips, Dürer had already been won over by the humanist culture that had come to his attention through his compatriot and long-standing friend, Willibald Pirckheimer (1470–1530), and through his contact with the intellectual circles that surrounded him.

3. The concept of perspective and the canons of proportions for the human body that had always interested him encouraged him to continue his studies and to research the writings of Vitruvius on the subject. In the final years of his life he published several treatises on these theories: *Unterweisung der Messung* [*Teaching of Measurement*] (1525); *Treatise on Fortification* (1527); and *Vier Bücher von menschlicher Proportion* [*Four Books on Human Proportion*] (1528, the last two of which were published posthumously).

4. Vienna, Graphische Sammlung Albertina, inv. 3073 and 3075.

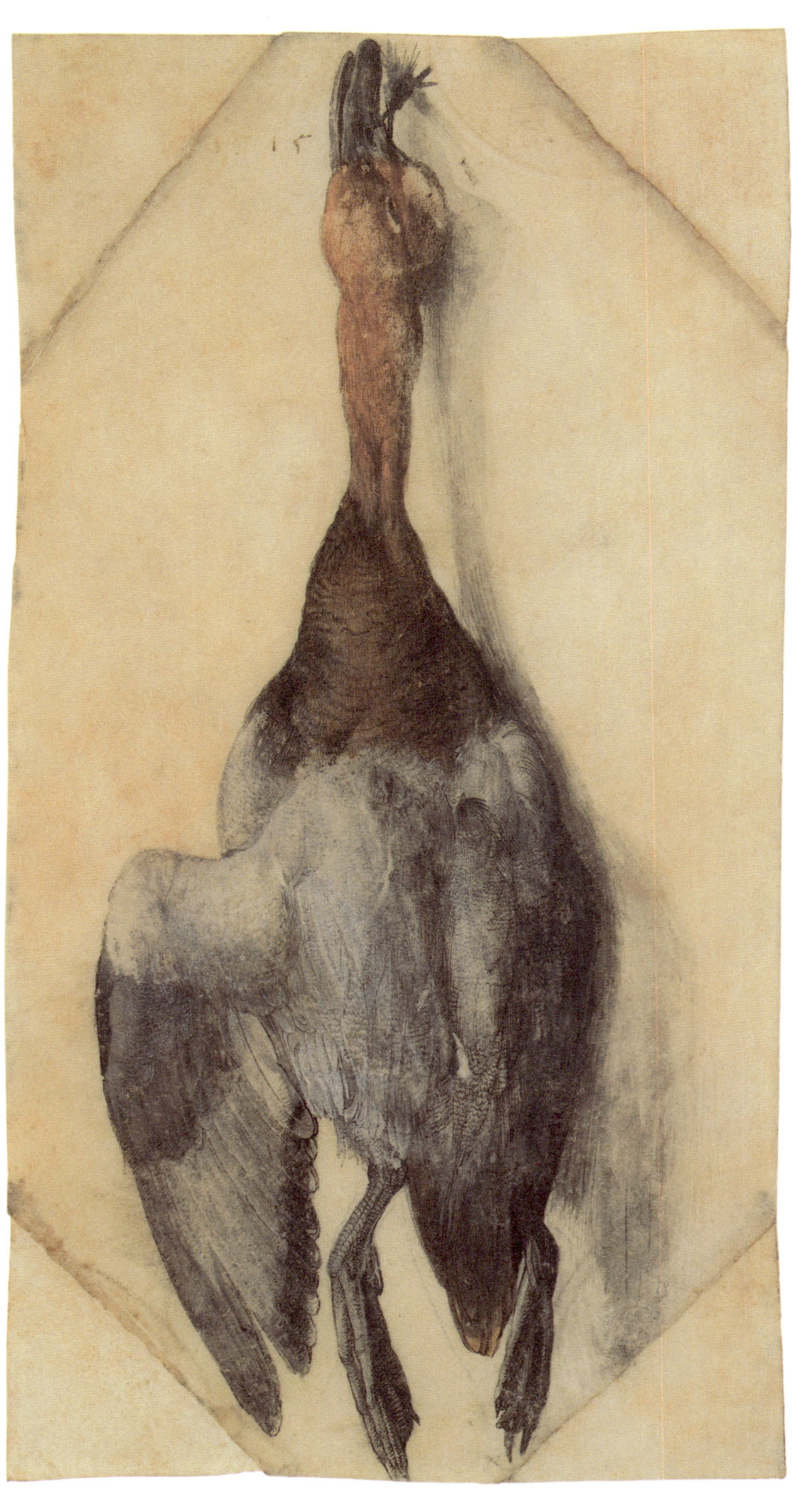

which, being stretched and long, contrast with the bulk of the trunk. The shadow of the inert bird projected on the wall from which it is hung emphasises the relationship between the bird and the space that it occupies, granting the work a sense of veracity. ¶ The work is drawn on a sheet of parchment whose four corners are cut off, making it more difficult to interpret the original composition. Dürer uses a miniaturist's detail and a limited, almost monochromatic, palette of opaque and washed colours that include browns, yellowish-browns, greys, blues and white, with faint touches of gold at the tips of the tail feathers. He employs a brush for the larger areas and a pen for the fine lines used for the contours of the plumage. Short wavy lines delineate the volume of the body, in which darker areas contrast with brighter ones in the lower half of the composition. The numerous feathers over the bird's body are treated differently, both in their form and in the highly convincing use of colour. Near the tail and feet there are pencil lines which are still visible and show alterations to the drawing in relation to the final version. The fact that the parchment was soaked in the aforementioned floods of 1967 unfortunately and inevitably meant that it lost much of its depth of colour. ¶ The originality of this work in the Gulbenkian Collection, that is, its attribution to the Master of Nuremberg, has never been called into question by the sheer number

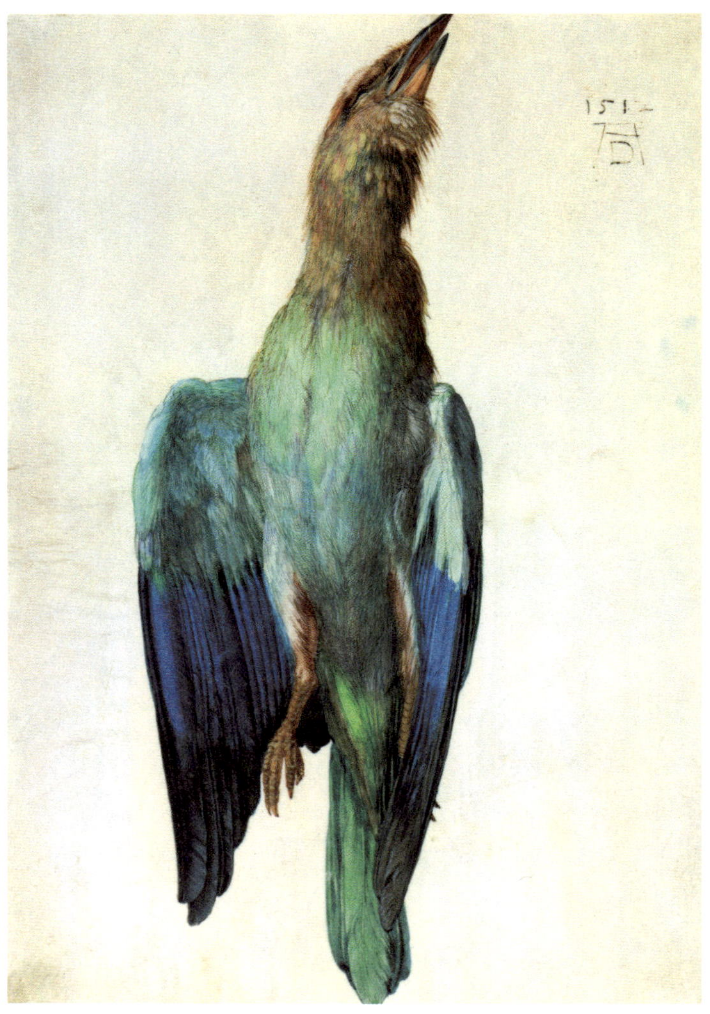

– fig. 1.1 –
Albrecht Dürer (1471–1528), *Dead Blue Roller*, 1512. Watercoulor and gouache on parchment, 27.4 × 19.8 cm. Vienna, Graphische Sammlung Albertina, inv. 3133.

of experts who have devoted themselves to its study. Its date has been the subject of widespread speculation within academic circles as neither the monogram nor the date (1515) next to the bird's head are original[5]. ¶ Musper[6] has suggested that it was executed before 1500, probably around 1498; Eisler[7] believed it was made in about 1500, at a time when Dürer was greatly influenced by Jacopo de 'Barbari (1440/1450–ca. 1516); Flechsig[8] has placed it prior to 1502, as it does not have the date or the original monogram which Dürer began to use that year to identify his drawings as his own; Panofsky[9] suggests circa 1502, which is analogous with the date of the famous *Young Hare* in the Albertina; Winkler[10] proposes a date around 1512 as it is close to that of the *Dead Blue Roller*[11] (fig. 1.1), which is also held by the Vienna Museum; Tietze[12] dates it around 1515; and, due to the technique that the artist used, Koreny[13] associates it with the previously mentioned works *Dead Blue Roler* and *Wing of a Blue Roller*[14], both from 1512. However, he points out that most recent studies tend to favour a date closer to 1502. ¶ The study of the origins of Dürer's subject matter in the Gulbenkian drawing is necessarily associated with the work of Jacopo de 'Barbari and in the relationship between the two artists, as a result of which the two men came to exert a mutual influence on each other. ¶ Dürer met Jacopo in Venice in 1495 on his first trip to Italy, where

5. According to Flechsig, they can be attributed to Hans von Kulmbach, an assistant and collaborator who worked in Dürer's studio. See FLECHSIG, II Bd. 1936, p. 100, cit. *in* VIENNA, 1985, p. 48, no. 7 (note 1).

6. MUSPER, 1953, pp. 126–28, (repr. 59) and p. 344.

7. EISLER, 1991, pp. 63–64 and pp. 75–76 (repr.).

8. See note 5.

9. PANOFSKY, 1948, vol. II, p. 129, no. 1317.

10. WINKLER, 1938, pp. 60–61, no. 616, (repr.).

11. Vienna, Graphische Sammlung Albertina, inv. 3133.

12. TIETZE, TIETZE-CONRAT, 1937, p. 108 and p. 261 (repr.); TIETZE, 1951, pp. 35–36 and p. 60, no. 52.

13. KORENY, Fritz, *in* VIENNA, 1985, pp. 48–49, no. 7 (repr.).

14. Vienna, Graphische Sammlung Albertina, inv. 4840.

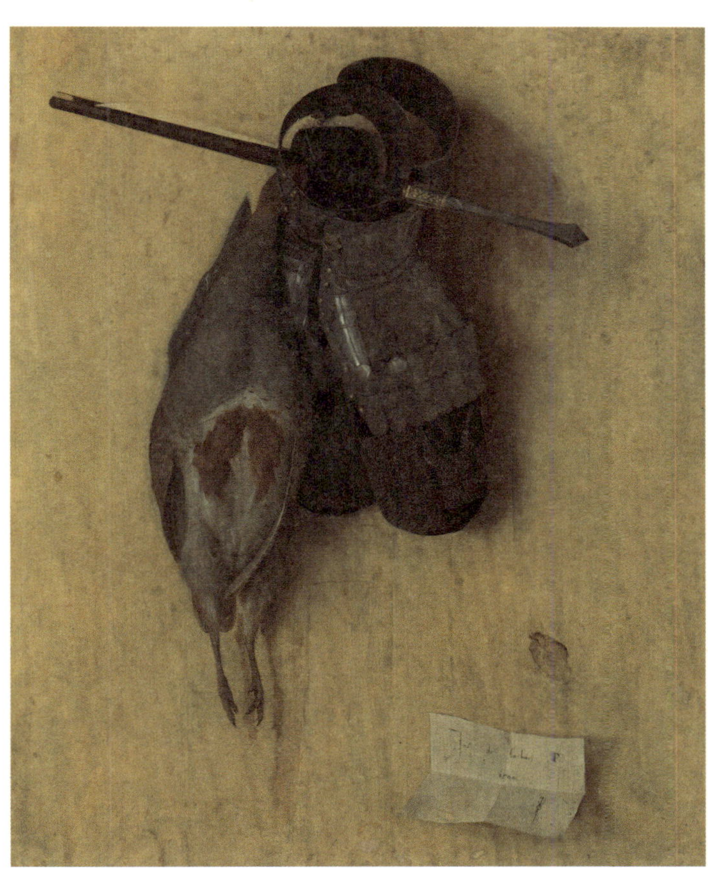

– fig. 1.2 –
Jacopo de' Barbari (ca. 1440/1450–ca. 1516), *Still-Life with Partridge and Armour*, 1504. Oil on panel, 49 × 42 cm. Munich, Alte Pinakothek, Bayerische Staatsgemäldesammlungen, inv. 5066. ©2012 Photo Scala, Florence / BPK, Bildagentur für Kunst, Kultur und Geschichte, Berlin

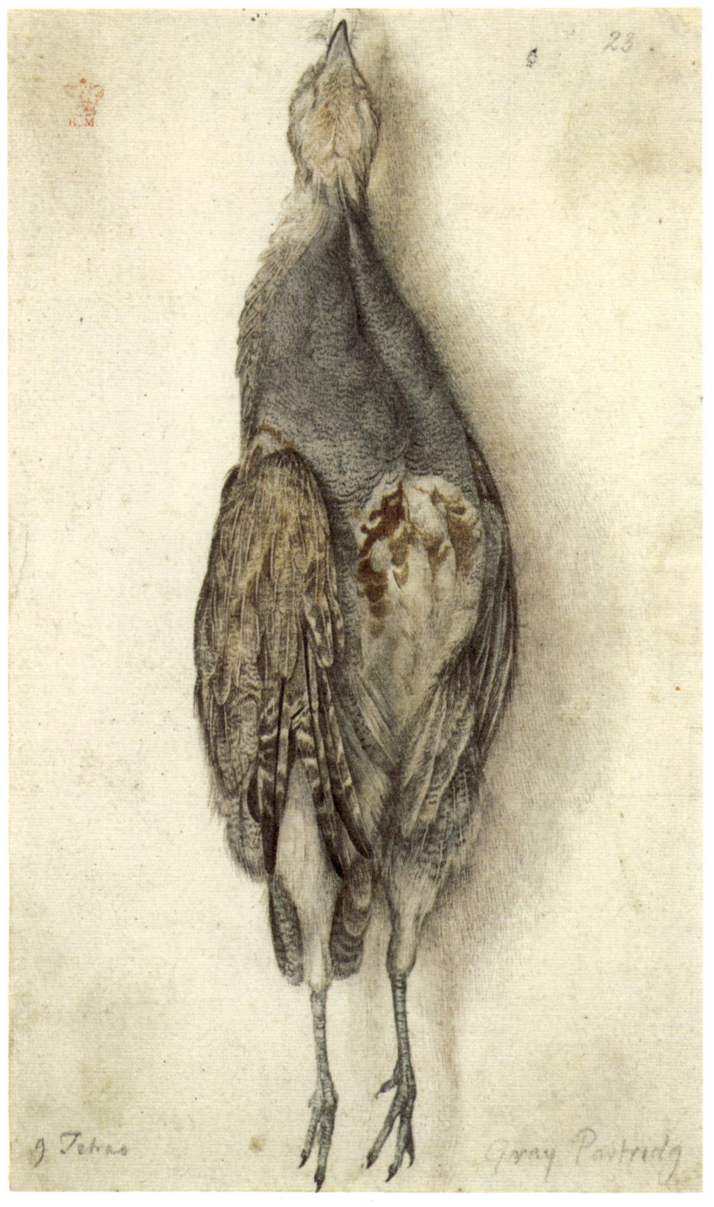

– fig. 1.3 –
Jacopo de' Barbari (ca. 1440/1450–ca. 1516), *Study of a Dead Grey Partridge*. Watercolour, 25,8 × 15,3 cm. Department of Manuscripts, British Library (Add 5263–6). PD SL 5264.23.

15. This is the first still-life painting of its kind in Europe.

he became fascinated by his theories on perspective and the proportions of the human body. They met again in Nuremberg, where, at the invitation of Maximilian I, the Venetian artist took up a position as a court painter. Later, between 1503 and 1505, he worked for Frederick III of Saxony, the Wise, and, after a brief return to Italy, he moved to Holland, where he ended his days in the service of Margaret of Austria, from 1509 onwards. ¶ During his stay in Nuremberg between 1500 and 1503, 'Barbari was able to visit Dürer's studio and study the German master's watercolours, including *Young Hare* (1502). Dürer's influence on his use of the watercolour technique, which was still used only rarely by Italian artists in the fifteenth and sixteenth centuries, is clear. For his part, 'Barbari also brought to the attention of the German master the subject matter of dead birds presented as hunting trophies, which had been decorative elements used in frescos since Antiquity. The Saxon court's enthusiasm for hunting would have encouraged the Italian artist to show the subject in *Still-life with Partridge and Armour*[15] (fig. 1.2), which is signed and dated 1504, and in a watercolour from the same year, *Study of a Dead Grey Partridge*[16] (fig. 1.3), both of which works would subsequently influence other painters, particularly Lucas Cranach[17]. ¶ With regard to its subject matter and date, the relationship between Dürer's study in the Gulbenkian Collection and 'Barbari's aforementioned works is still far from clear, although several possible hypotheses exist: on the one hand, Dürer could have 'invented' the subject, created the Gulbenkian work around 1502, and then influenced 'Barbari, who later, in 1504, painted the two works already mentioned; on the other, Dürer's watercolour may have only been made after the appearance of the Venetian artist's painting and drawing, which would place it at a later date, possibly around 1512.

16. VIENNA, 1985, pp. 44–47, no. 6 (repr.).

17. *Ibidem*, pp. 50- 51, no. 8 (repr.).

PROVENANCE

Pierre-Jean Mariette Collection, sold in Paris in 1775, no. 895. At the time of the sale, the artist Gabriel de Saint-Aubin (1724–1780) made a sketch of Dürer's "Duck" in the margin of his copy of the catalogue (this volume is in the Museum of Fine Arts, Boston); General-Count Antoine--François Andréossy Collection; Sir Thomas Lawrence Collection; Sir Horace Walpole Collection (provenance unconfirmed); Max J. Bonn Collection. Acquired by Calouste Gulbenkian at the sale of the last collection, through Colnaghi at Sotheby's in London on 15th February 1922, lot no. 6.

•

EXHIBITIONS

PARIS, 1775, no. 895, p. 138; LONDON, 1836, no. 22, p. 12; LONDON, 1917, no. 11, p. 13; PARIS, 1967, no. 166, p. 112; LISBON, 1976, no. 72; PARIS, 1978, no. 150 (repr.); LISBON, 1985, no. 3, p. 20, p. 128 (repr.); VIENNA, 1985, pp. 48–49, no. 7 (repr.); NEW YORK, 1999, pp. 48–49, no. 20, p. 48 (repr.); CAMBRIDGE, 2000, no. 75, pp. 170–71, p. 171 (repr.); LISBON, PORTO, 2000–2002, no. 75, pp. 170–71, p. 171 (repr.); MADRID, 2002, no. 48, pp. 118–19, p. 119 (repr.); KARLSRUHE, 2011, pp. 146–47, no. 1, p. 147 (repr.).

•

LITERATURE

DODGSON, 1915, no. 19, p. 8, n. 3; LIPPMANN, 1929, p. 14, no. 807; FLECHSIG, II Bd. 1936, p. 100; TIETZE, TIETZE-CONRAT, 1937, p. 108, p. 261, no. 632, repr.; WINKLER, 1938, III, no. 616, pp. 60–61 (repr.); PANOFSKY, 1948, II, p. 125, no. 1317; TIETZE, 1951, pp. 35–36 and p. 60, no. 52; MUSPER [ca. 1952], no. 59 (repr.), pp. 126–28, p. 344; WINKLER, 1957, no. 127, p. 251 and p. 364; ZAMPA, 1968, pp. 98–99, no. 79 (repr.); STRAUSS, 1974, vol. 2, p. 596, no. 1502/3, Appendix 2, p. 1102; STRIEDER, 1981, p. 204, no. 239 (repr.); PIEL, (1983), p. 143, no. 62; EISLER, 1991, pp. 63–64 and pp. 75–76 (repr.).

[2]

Copy after

HANS HOLBEIN, THE ELDER

Augsburg, ca. 1460/65 – Issenheim, 1524

ANNUNCIATION

Germany, after 1502

Pen and brown ink, grey washes and metal point tracing, on paper.
30 × 18.5 cm.
Inscription on the base of the stand: "1419" (false)
Mark of William Mitchel Collection
on the lower left of the verso – WM (Lugt 2638):
Mark of Edward Habich Collection
on the lower left of the recto (difficult to read).
Inv. 457

Studies of the provenance of this drawing point to its inclusion in the major collections of Andrew Fountaine, William Mitchell and Edward Habich, whose public sales took place in the second half of the nineteenth century (1884, 1890 and 1899). In the respective catalogues it appears, in the first instance, without a title or author, and in the second as a piece by "an anonymous Master from southern Germany in the second half of the fifteenth century"[1]. By the start of the twentieth century it was considered to be a work by Hans Holbein, the Elder, and when this hypothesis was later rejected, it has been seen as a copy of a piece by the Master, thought to be a drawing that has since been lost. The attribution of authorship to the study, acquired by Calouste Gulbenkian in 1925, thus involves complex analysis, and was made even more difficult by the damage suffered in the flooding of 1967 (see Introduction). ¶ Hans Holbein, the Elder was one of the foremost artists of the late German Gothic style. He carried on the German pictorial tradition only slightly influenced by the Renaissance, which brought with it novel ideas that only feature in his very latest works. ¶ There is little in the way of precise biographical information about the place[2] and date[3] of the painter's birth, and exact details about his artistic training are also lacking. It is, however, worth noting that his earliest pieces bear traces that reflect the works of Martin Schongauer (ca. 1450–1491), in the outline of the figures, the idealised structure of the faces, and the arrangement of the drapery[4]. These early works also reveal the influence of Flemish artists such as Jan van Eyck (ca. 1390–1441), Rogier van der Weyden (1399/1400–1464), Hans Memling (ca. 1430/1440–1494) and Hugo van der Goes (ca. 1440–1482), especially in the realistic way in which the themes are presented, the elegant treatment of the figures and the bright, intense colour palette. In the *Annunciation* drawing owned by the Gulbenkian Collection, the composition, spatial distribution and the appearance of the figures are reminiscent of the work of Van der Weyden in his *Annunciation*, from his *St Columba Altarpiece*, an oil painting created by the artist in around 1455, and found today

1. "Anonymer Meister der niederdeutschen Schule aus der zweiten Hälfte des XV Jahrhunderts". See LISBON, PORTO, 2000–2002, p. 168, no. 74.

2. He is thought to have been born in Augsburg, where his father, a tanner, had moved from Basel in 1448.

3. Around 1460–65. This date was established on the basis of the first dated paintings by the artist, as well as the portrait of the Master produced by his son, Hans Holbein the Younger, in 1515. For more information on issues relating to the origins of Holbein the Elder, see AUGSBURG, 1965, pp. 15–21.

4. For more information on the connection between Holbein the Elder and Schongauer, see WOLTMANN, 1872, pp. 43–44.

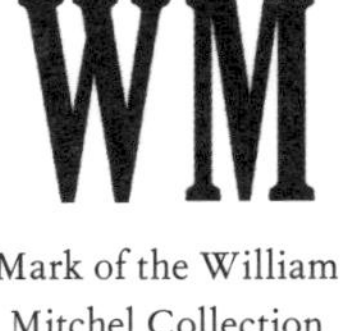

Mark of the William Mitchel Collection

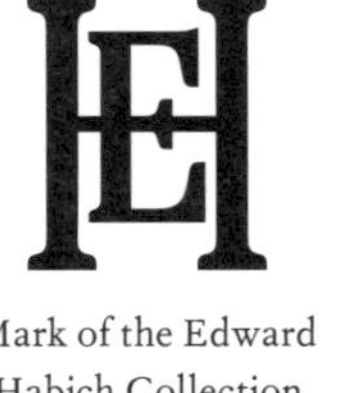

Mark of the Edward Habich Collection

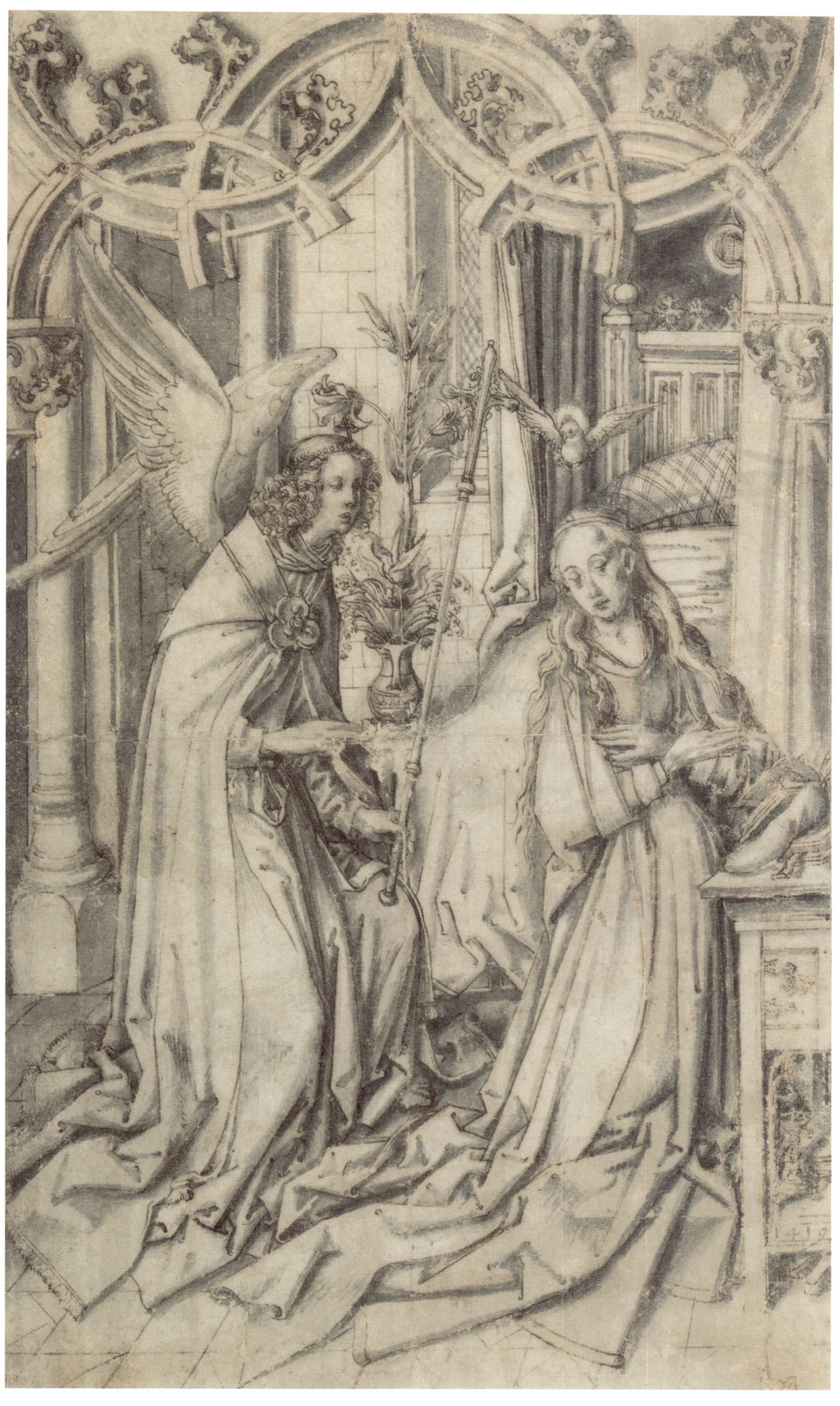

in the Alte Pinakothek in Munich. In the early sixteenth century Holbein gradually distanced himself from Flemish influence by imbuing his pieces with a more personal character and imagination. ¶ Although there are references to Holbein the Elder as a citizen of Ulm in 1493, from the following year he based most of his activity in Augsburg, where he lived, albeit with some interruptions, until he left the city for good in 1515 or 1516. With the help of his studio, where he was assisted by collaborators such as his youngest brother Sigmund (ca. 1470–1540) and his two sons, Ambrosius (1494–ca. 1519) and Hans the Younger (1497/98–1543), he not only carried out countless commissions for religious institutions in the city but also those from a broader geographical area, including Frankfurt and the Alsace region. ¶ A prolific artist, he left behind many paintings with a religious theme (scenes from Christ's Passion, the life of the Virgin Mary and the lives of the saints) and an important body of drawings in which portraits drawn from direct observation of the model and then given a strong naturalistic interpretation are particularly notable. ¶ Drawing was an inextricable part of Holbein's creative process, and he used it to prepare every detail of the composition that he was about to tackle. He would work exclusively with a silverpoint, particularly on portraits, or use it to sketch out his preliminary ideas and then add lines in ink, and the outer edges in pen, with straight lines predominating. Finally, he would highlight certain values and the modelling by applying washes with subtle brushstrokes, sometimes in monochrome and sometimes in shades of colour. ¶ Joseph Meder was one of the first scholars to establish a link between the drawing in the Gulbenkian Collection and the work of Hans Holbein the Elder, and to suggest that it was a preparatory study for one of the panels (*Annunciation*) of the wings of the altarpiece at Kaisheim Abbey, near Donauwörth[5]. ¶ Holbein worked on this altarpiece, which is signed and dated 1502[6], as a commission by the abbot Georg Kastner, who, between 1490 and 1509, was in charge of this Cistercian monastery, renowned as a place of devotion and famous for the splendour of its interior decoration. The sculptor Gregor Erhart and panel maker Adolf Daucher also worked on the altarpiece. On the outside of the wings of the alterpiece are scenes from Christ's Passion[7], where a more mechanical style shows the work by assistants from the Master's studio. On the inner side are scenes from the life of the Virgin Mary[8], the quality of which reveal them to be Holbein's own creations[9] (fig.2.1). ¶ The present work is a finished drawing that features minute detail[10], a common practice in the artist's work. ¶ In this drawing the scene of the Annunciation occurs indoors, in a very intimate atmosphere, under a tri-lobed Gothic portico. Mary kneels in front of a prayer stand, upon which rests an open book of hours[11]. She turns away from her prayers with a devout gesture as the angel appears to her. The spiritual nature of the divine message, announcing the birth of the Son of God, is accentuated by artistic and iconographical elements that have stood the test of time: a dove – the symbol of the Holy Spirit – hovers above Mary's head, while in the foreground the vase of lilies represents the Virgin's purity. The angel

5. SCHÖNBRUNNER, MEDER, 1896–1908, pl. 1180.

6. The sixteen plaintings that comprised the wings of the altarpiece currently form part of the collections of the Alte Pinakothek, Munich.

7. *Christ on the Mount of Olives*, *Christ's Arrest*, *The Crowning with Thorns*, *Ecce Homo*, *Christ before Pilate*, *The Scourging at the Pillar*, *The Way to Calvary* and *The Resurrection*.

8. *The Presentation of Mary at the Temple*, *The Annunciation*, *Circumcision*, *The Adoration of the Magi*, *The Visitation*, *The Nativity*, *The Presentation of the Child Jesus at the Temple* and *The Death of the Virgin*.

9. For the altar at Kaisheim, see WOLTMANN, 1872, pp. 48–51; *Alte Pinakothek München*, 1963, pp. 96–102.

10. Some of these preliminary sketches were known as *Visierungen*. These were intended to give the person who had commissioned the painting an idea of how the finished work would look.

11. On the base of the stand is a date (1419) which was added later and is certainly false.

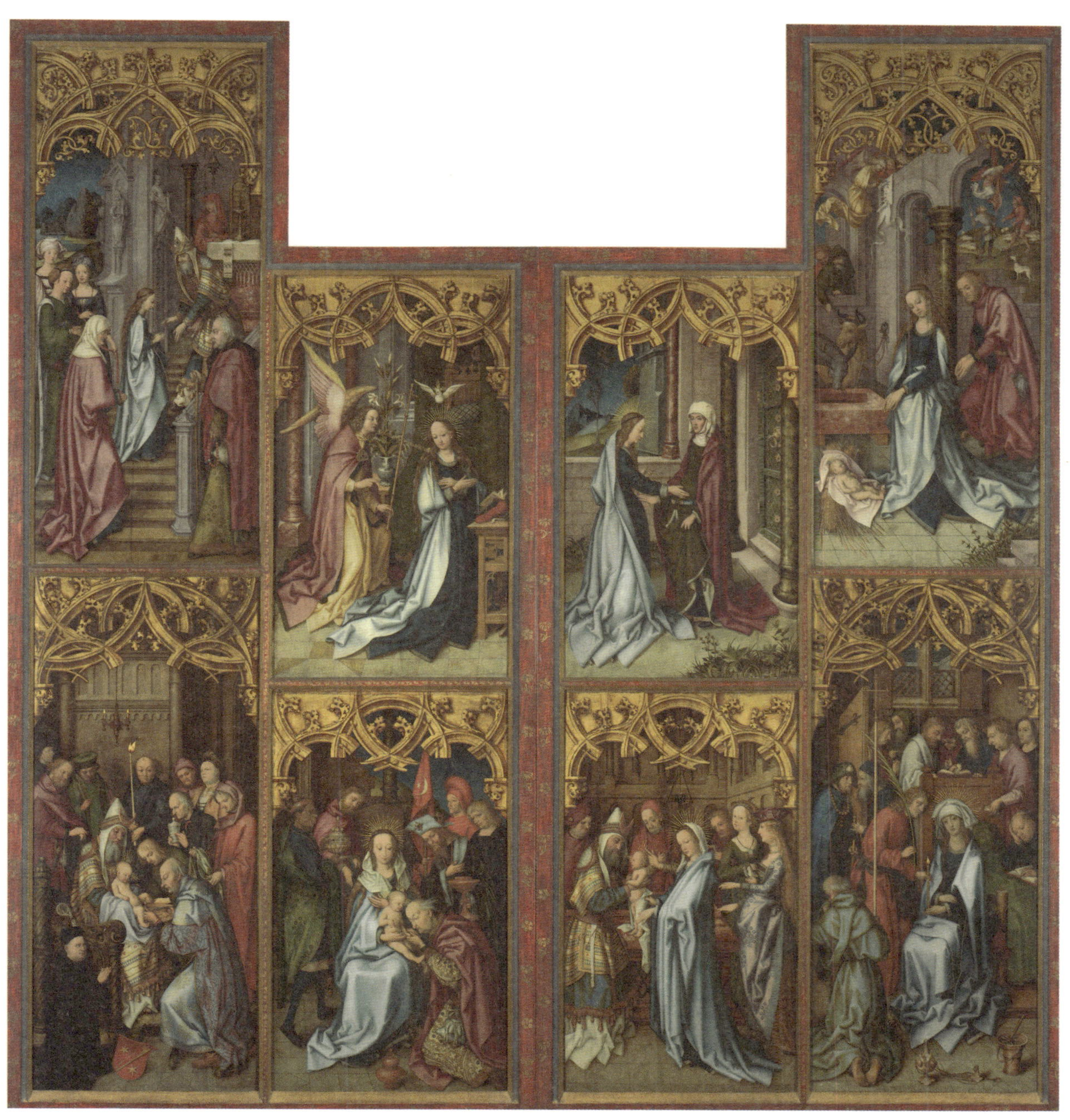

– fig. 2.1 –
Hans Holbein, the Elder (1460/65–1524),
Wings of the *Kaisheimer Altar* (inner side), 1502.
Painting on panel. Munich, Alte Pinakothek,
Bayerische Staatsgemäldesammlungen

12. LIEB, STANGE, 1960, p. 83, cat. no. 91.

gives his words greater impact by pointing to Mary and holds a cross-shaped staff, prefiguring the Passion of Christ. ¶ The parallels that can be drawn between the drawing of the *Annunciation* in the Gulbenkian Collection and the painting in the Kaisheim panel (fig. 2.2) are particularly evident in the general composition and the treatment of the very finest details. However, clear distinctions can be established between them due to the more sacred features look that Holbein gives to the faces of his figures. ¶ Studies carried out in the 1960s, in particular by Norbert Lieb and Alfred Stange[12], classify the piece as a copy of a work by Holbein the Elder that was created by one of the assistants from his studio. It is clear that it

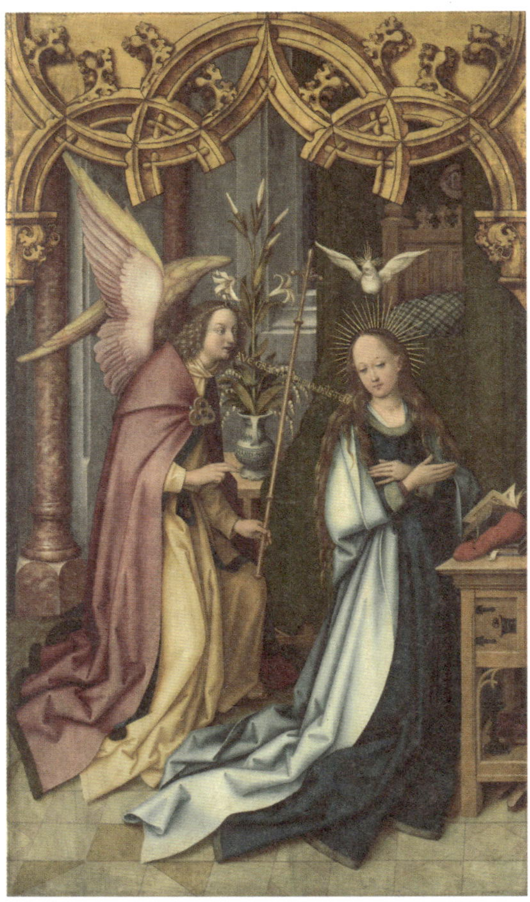

– fig. 2.2 –
Hans Holbein, the Elder (1460/65–1524), *The Annunciation*, detail from the wings of the *Kaisheimer Altar* (interior), 1502. Painting on panel. Munich, Alte Pinakothek, Bayerische Staatsgemäldesammlungen, inv. 7271.

closely imitates the stylistic features developed by the Master in the late fifteenth century. This means that it is a copy based not on the Kaisheim painting but on a related drawing, which has since been lost. Research carried out on Holbein the Elder's works, and in particular his drawings, has allowed scholars to distinguish his pieces from those of his assistants or followers such as Jörg Schweiger (act. 1507–1533/34) or the artist's youngest brother, Sigmund Holbein (ca. 1470–1540). Such knowledge cannot fail to contribute to a more rigorous approach to the issue of authorship of this study in the future[13].

13. I would like to thank Fritz Koreny for sharing his opinions on this matter (1989). Thanks are also due to Christian Müller for the views that he shared on this matter (2010).

PROVENANCE

Andrew Fountaine Collection, Narford Hall, Norfolk, sold at Christie's, London, 7–10 July 1884; William Mitchell Collection, sold in Frankfurt, 7 May 1890, lot no. 3; Edward Habich Collection, sold in Stuttgart, 27–29 April 1899, lot no. 358; Archduke Frederick of Habsburg-Lothringen Collection; Graphische Sammlung Albertina, Vienna, inv. 18085. The drawing ceased to be part of the Albertina Collections after 1920. Acquired by Calouste Gulbenkian at Colnaghi's, London, on 12 October 1925.

•

EXHIBITIONS

LISBON, 1976, no. 73 (repr.); LISBON, 1985, no. 4, p. 20, p. 129 (repr.); CAMBRIDGE, 2000, no. 74, pp. 168–69, p. 169 (repr.); LISBON, PORTO, 2000–2002, no. 74, pp. 168–69, p. 169 (repr.); MADRID, 2002, no. 47, pp. 116–17, p. 117 (repr.).

•

LITERATURE

ALTDEUTSCHE MALEREI, 1963, (pp. 96–102), p. 100; EISENMAN, 1890, II, no. 8; LIEB, STANGE, 1960, p.83, cat. 91, repr. 172; SCHILLING, 1993, Bd. XII, pp. 315–22, p. 317 (repr.); SCHÖNBRUNNER, MEDER, 1896–1908, il.1180.

[3]

ARTIST FROM THE CIRCLE OF LEONARDO DA VINCI

FEMALE FIGURE WITH CHILDREN

Italy, ca. 1520 (?)

Red chalk on paper.
27 × 19 cm.
Signature: *Bernardinus. Lovinus. Mediol.s f.*
Inv. 426

This red-chalk drawing has been attributed to Bernardino Luini (ca. 1481/82–1532)[1], in part due to the artist's signature on the lower left-hand side of the composition. However, as with many drawings by Renaissance artists, the question of its authorship is controversial and studies of the work have led to several different hypotheses. ¶ The attribution of the drawing to Bernardino Luini is supported by Angela Ottino Della Chiesa, who refers to it in her 1956 monograph[2] and suggests that it may be related to the fresco on the façade of the Ospizio della Carità in the Piazza della Scala in Milan, which has since disappeared[3]. In 1989, Monseigneur Enrico Galbiati from the Ambrosiana Library took up Chiesa's theory and agreed that, as well as being the work of Luini, it is also likely to be related to the lost fresco[4]. ¶ Under the title *Woman Carrying a Child*, the drawing was acquired by Calouste Gulbenkian in 1920 and has been related to the representation of the theme "Charity", a classical allegory of one of the three theological virtues, which are a recurrent theme in painting, sculpture and drawing. The work, like many others that depict this theme in varied ways, shows a young woman with children around her. In the case of the Gulbenkian drawing, the female figure, who is wearing a draped tunic that leaves one of her breasts bare, is carrying a child and using her free hand to lead a second little boy. The three figures are united by their shared gaze. In the fresco depicting the theme of the *Crucifixion,* which was created by Luini between 1529 and 1532 in the Church of Santa Maria degli Angeli in Lugano[5], there is a group on the left consisting of a woman and two children, which, despite certain differences (the young woman is fully dressed, and the relative position of the three figures is reversed) could well have been adapted from our drawing[6]. ¶ Evidence supporting the attribution of the drawing to Luini includes the fact that, despite the damage suffered by the work in the aforementioned floods, its fine lines are compatible with those in other studies by the artist. In addition, the genre and the physical presentation of the woman and the two children are common features of the painter's other

1. Very little is known about Luini's life and Giorgio Vasari barely mentions him. See VASARI, Giorgio – *Les Vies des Meilleurs Peintres, Sculpteurs et Architectes* (édition commentée sous la direction d'André Chastel). Paris: Berger-Levrault, cop. 1981–89 (12 vol.), vol. 6, p. 20; vol. 8, p. 301.

2. DELLA CHIESA, 1956, p. 147, no. 34.

3. *Ibidem*, p. 150; TORRE, 1714, p. 279, the academic describes the "Luogo Pio della Carità" and one of the frescos that adorned it with Charity and other figures handing out food.

4. I would like to thank this scholar for sharing his opinions with me on the subject (1989).

5. See Piero Chiara *et al. in* LUINO, 1975, p. 103, fig. 103.

6. I would like to thank Catherine Whistler of the Ashmolean Museum, Cambridge, for sharing her opinions on the subject with me (1989).

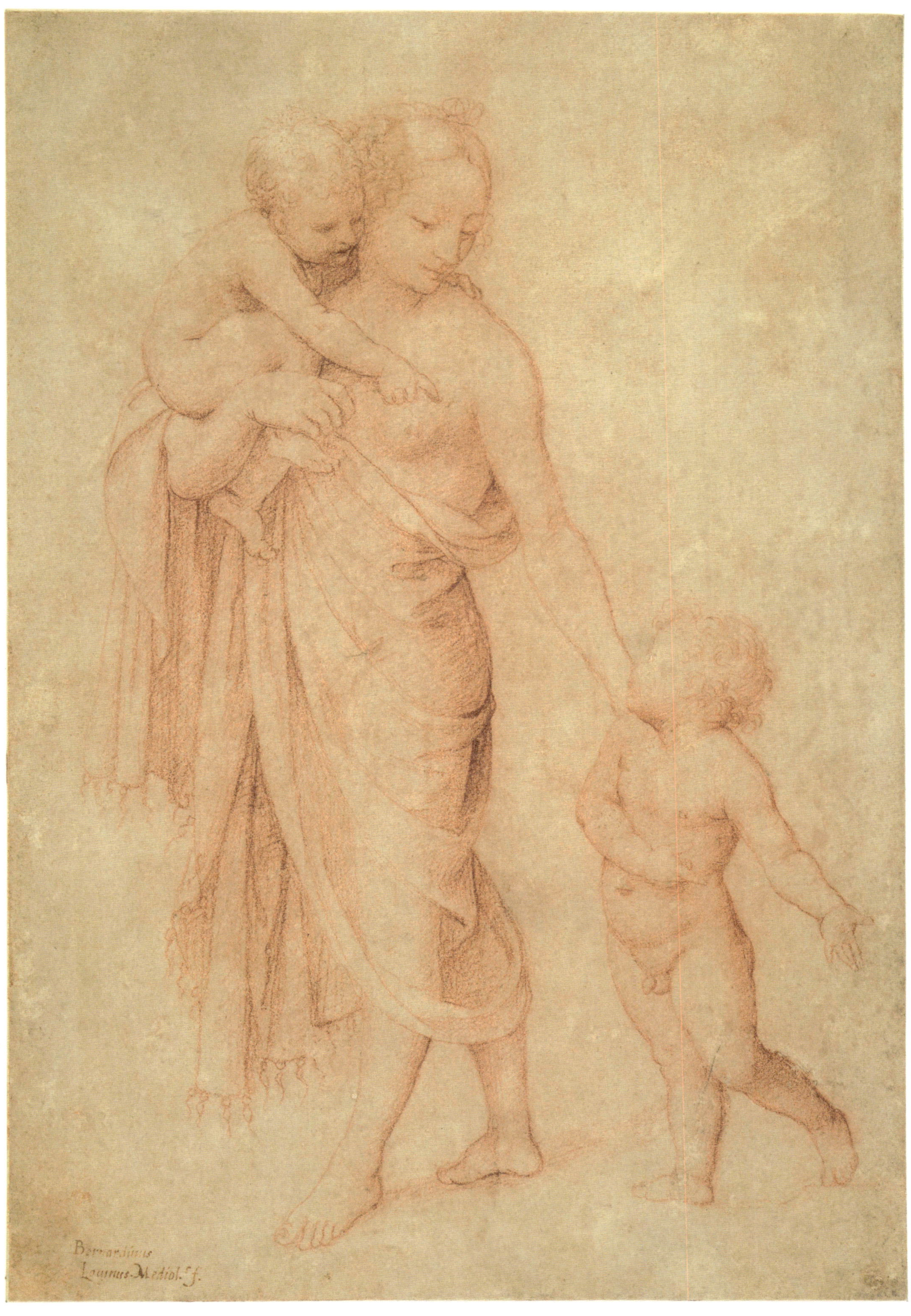
Bernardinus
Louinus Mediol. f.

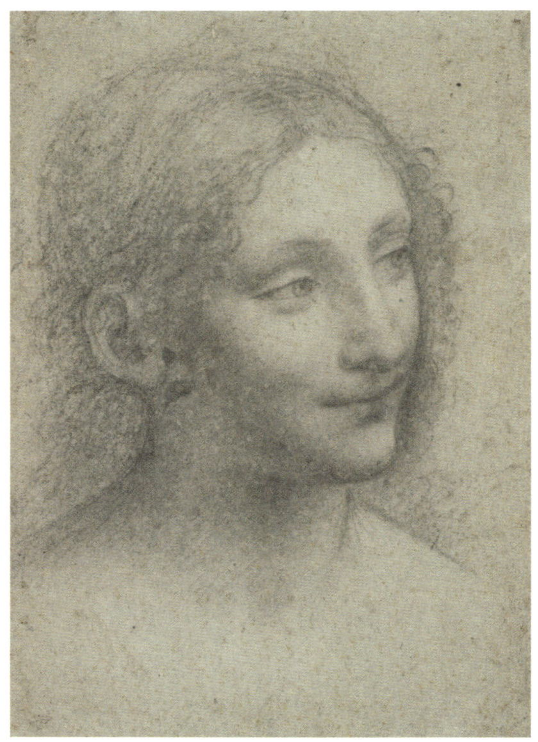

– fig. 3.1 –
Bernardino Luini (ca. 1481/1482–1532), *Head of a Girl*, 15th century. Black chalk or charcoal on blue paper, 29.4 × 20.9 cm. Harvard Art Museums / Fogg Museum. Gift of Meta and Paul J. Sachs, inv. 1959.161. Photo: Imaging Department © President and Fellows of Harvard College

works. Anna Forlani Tempesti refers to another later fresco, *The Animals Enter Noah's Ark* in the Monastero Maggiore di San Maurizio in Milan, which has been attributed to Aurelio Luini (1530–1592), the artist's eldest son[7]. This work shows a group of figures that is extremely similar to the one in the Lugano fresco, both of which are similar to the Gulbenkian Collection's drawing, raising the possibility that this sanguine could have been kept in studio of the Luinis', where it may have served as a model for various compositions. ¶ However, Maria Teresa Binaghi disagrees and believes that Cesare da Sesto (1477–1523) may have been the author of the Gulbenkian drawing[8]. Her view is based on a comparison with the frescos that the artist created in 1512 to decorate the Episcopio, the palace of Cardinal Raffaele Riario in Ostia. ¶ Supporting the idea that the drawing should not be attributed to Luini is the theory expressed by Jonathan Bober, Curator of Prints and Drawings at the College of Fine Arts at The University of Texas at Austin[9]. In his opinion, although the composition's structure has some similarities with that of the Lugano fresco and also that of another work, *Preparation for the Departure from Egypt*, which was painted for the Villa Pelluca in the early 1520s, its expression is more superficial, its contours are less spontaneous, and it has a less sensitive character than that expressed in Luini's art in general and in his red chalk drawings in particular. Analysis of the artistic expression of the female figure and the child walking by her side in the Gulbenkian drawing points to several slightly clumsy graphic solutions that are absent from other compositions by Luini, such as the magnificent *Head of a Young Woman*, owned by the Fogg Art Museum at Harvard (fig. 3.1). This discrepancy has led Bober to believe that the Gulbenkian drawing cannot possibly be the work of Luini and is in fact a sixteenth-century Milanese copy of a work by the artist that was later lost. The elegant signature in the style of Luini may have been added later by a sixteenth-century collector. ¶ More recently, thanks to the endeavours of the Florentine specialist Angela Dillon Bussi and of Giorgio Marini, the Curator of the Department of Drawings

7. BANDERA, FIORIO, 2000, p. 87, fig. 35a. I would like to thank Anna Forlani Tempesti for sharing her opinions with me on the subject (2001).

8. Cesare da Sesto, one of the most important artists to emerge from Leonardo's Milanese circle, together with Bernardino Luini and Marco D' Oggine, also worked in Rome and Naples where he painted religious themes in numerous churches. I would like to thank Maria Teresa Binaghi for sharing her opinions on the possible authorship of the Gulbenkian drawing (1987).

9. I would like to thank Jonathan Bober for sharing with me his opinions on the subject (1989).

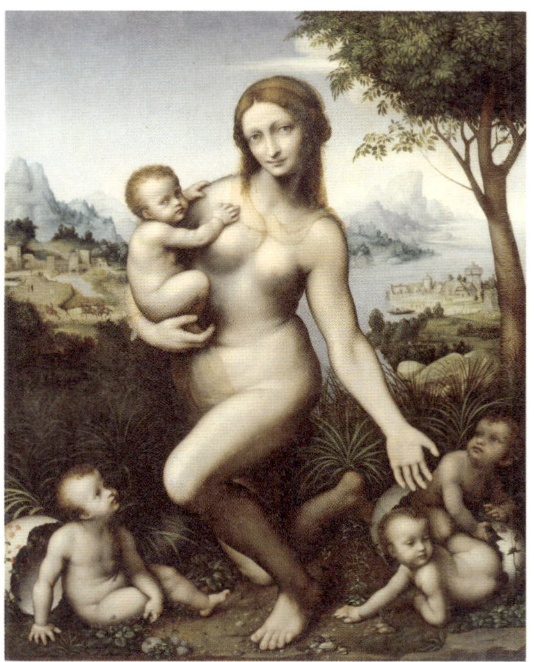

– fig. 3.2 –
Giampetrino (act. 1495/1549) and Cesaro Bernazzano (act. ca. 1530), *Leda and Her Children*, 1520–30. Oil on panel, 128 × 105,5 cm. Kassel, Museumslandschaft Hessen Kassel, Gemäldegalerie Alte Meister. Painting on panel, 128 × 105.5 cm, inv. GK 966. ©2012 Photo Scala, Florence / BPK, Bildagentur für Kunst, Kultur und Geschichte, Berlin

and Prints at the Uffizi[10], both of whom have carefully studied the question of the drawing's authorship, it seems that it may be possible to attribute it to another Leonardesque artist, Giampietrino (Giovanni Pietro Rizzoli – act. 1495–1549)[11], a member of the generation of Lombardian painters who were deeply influenced by Leonardo's long stays in Milan. This theory is based on a comparison between the drawing and the artist's painting *Leda and her Children*[12] (fig. 3.2), which was inspired by a work by Leonardo that is now missing. In comparing the two works, both painting and drawing show numerous similarities, particularly in the handling of the female figures' arms and left shoulders, in the shading and form of the faces, and in the contours of the hair. Additionally, the composition of the right hand that holds the robe and the way in which the figure carries the child are very similar in both. ¶ The authorship of the Gulbenkian drawing therefore remains at a crossroads of many possibilities. However, it is certainly a product of the Italian *Cinquecento* and is unquestionably the work of one of the many Lombardian artists who, after learning of the new Renaissance properties from Leonardo, then embraced the Milanese master's creative principles and adopted much of his pictorial repertoire.

10. I would like to thank both experts for their generosity in sharing their study of this work (2011).

11. He painted large altarpieces, mythological and religious figures which tend to reflect the style of Leonardo.

12. Gemäldegalerie Alte Meister, Kassel, inv. GK966.

PROVENANCE

Marquess of Lansdowne Collection. Acquired by Calouste Gulbenkian at the sale of this collection, through Colnaghi, at Sotheby's, London, on 25 March 1920, lot no. 39 (repr.).

•

EXHIBITIONS

LISBON, 1985, no. 22, p. 22, p. 147 (repr.).

[4]

Attributed to

ANTON VAN DYCK

Antwerp, 1599 – London, 1641

STUDY OF ARMOUR

Antwerp (1627–32)

Black ink and black chalk with grey
and red-chalk washes on paper.
40.5 × 24 cm
Mark of the Prosper Henry Lankrink Collection on the recto – PHL (Lugt 2090);
Mark of Charles Sackville Bale Collection on the verso – C.S.B (Lugt 640);
Mark of John Postle Heseltine Collection on the verso – J.P.H. (Lugt 1507).
Inv. 141

Van Dyck was gifted with a prodigious talent that, from an early age, he expressed through his drawings and paintings. He was still only an adolescent when he left the studio of Hendrick van Balen (1575–1632), where he first trained to start painting on his own. Already a qualified Master, at the age of nineteen (1618) he began working with Rubens (1577–1649), who called him "my best student"[1], even though, right from the start, Van Dyck was more of a collaborator than a disciple. ¶ The painter's vast body of work shows, on the one hand, Rubens' influence in the assimilation of Baroque aesthetics and, on the other, the mark of the Venetian *Cinquecento* pictorial tradition, in particular that of Titian, whom he had always admired. It is important to stress that Van Dyck did not just copy the old masters; he was inspired by their works, having revived and modernized them. ¶ Van Dyck painted historical, mythological, and religious themes and had a great international reputation as a portrait painter, especially among the ruling classes in Flanders, Italy and England. In his portraits he created a unique image of the aristocracy and wealthy bourgeois whose social successes were also consecrated in his paintings. Not satisfied with merely expressing the likeness of his models, he also worked to capture the character which gave them their own specific physiognomy. Thus, the figures portrayed are shown to be aware of their own distinction. The numerous portraits that he painted over the course of different periods in his career, all of which reflect his chronological and geographical[2] life-experiences, include a number of figures wearing armour. Whether portraying royalty, as in *Charles I on Horseback with M. de St Antoine* in the Royal Collection[3], or military nobles, as in *James Hamilton, 3rd Marquess and later 1st Duke of Hamilton* in the collections of the Prince of Liechtenstein, in Vaduz[4], these individuals are portrayed as warriors. The armour, the feathered helmets and the insignia, as well as the weaponry that they often held, all serve to reinforce the image of power and determination, elegance and distinction. ¶ While these portraits, whether full-length, three-quarter-length or on horseback, show

1. Reference made by Rubens in a letter to Dudley Carleton, on 28 April 1618, in which he mentions the painting *Achilles Among the Daughters of Lycomedes* as having been painted "by my best student". Although he does not actually refer to Van Dyck by name, he was then his main collaborator. Cf. BARNES, DE POORTER, MILLAR, VEY, 2004, p. 1.

2. Van Dyck's paintings are usually set in four periods that correspond chronologically with his stays in the major places in which he worked: the first Antwerp period continued until 1620, with a short sojourn in England (1620–21); the Italian period was between 1621 and 1627; the second Antwerp period was from 1627 to 1632; short sojourn in England from 1632 to 1634, when he returned to Antwerp; finally there was the late period in England between 1635 and 1641.

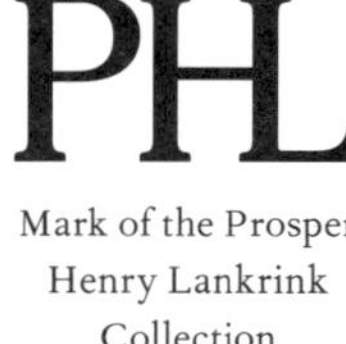

Mark of the Prosper Henry Lankrink Collection

C.S.B

Mark of the Charles Sackville Bale Collection

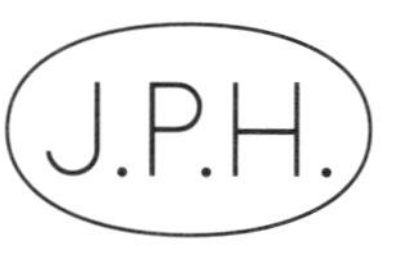

Mark of the John Postle Heseltine Collection

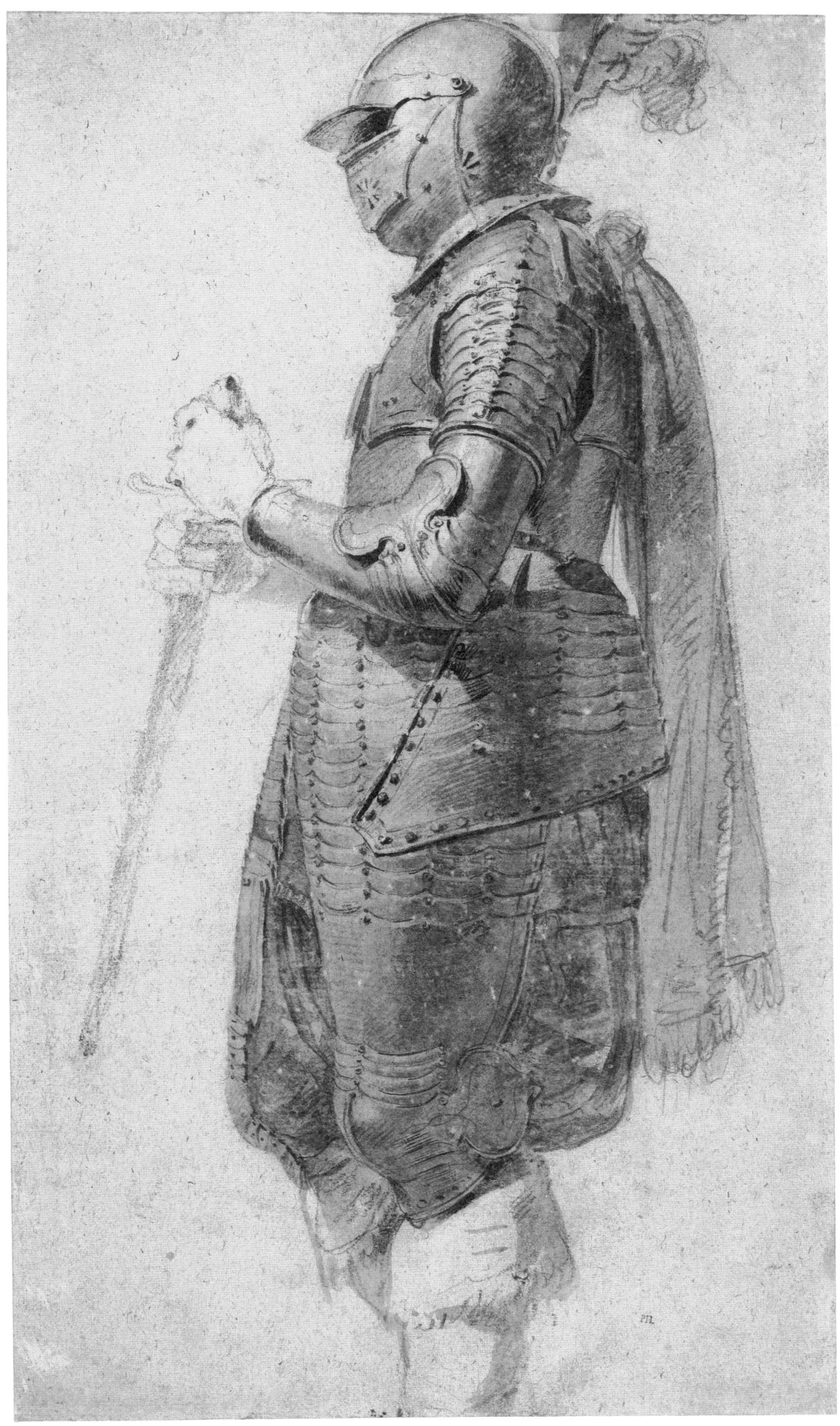

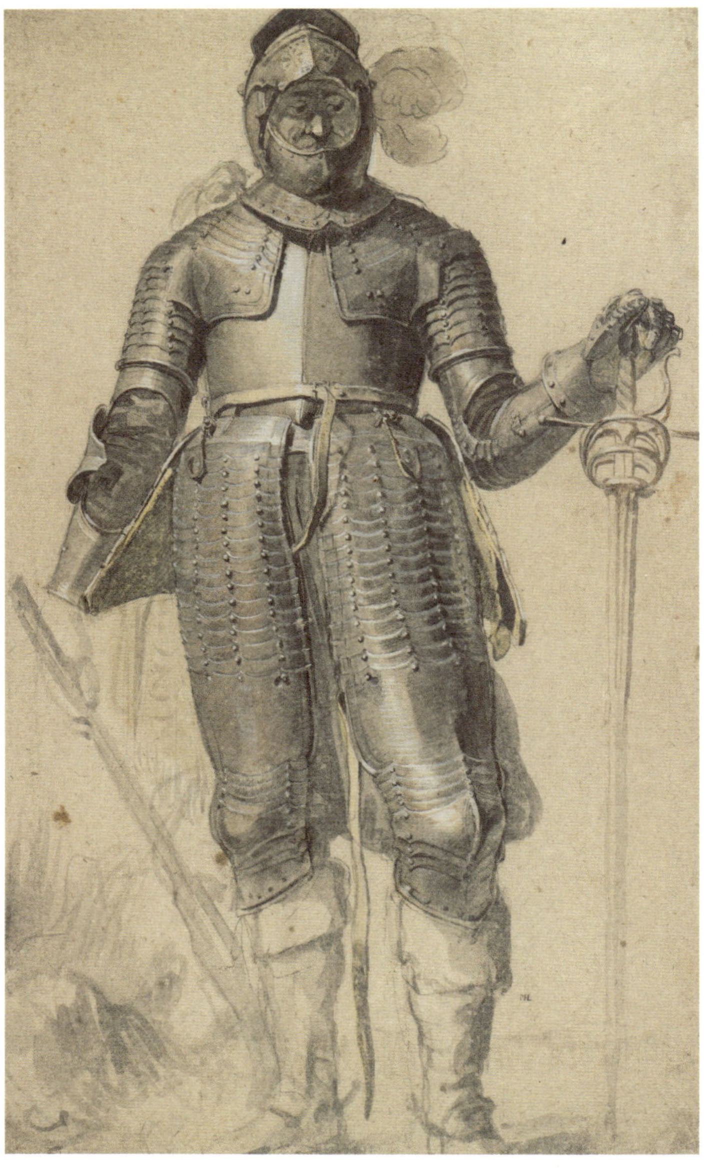

– fig. 4.1 –
Attributed to Anton van Dyck (1599–1641), *A Man in Armour.* Black ink, gray and brown wash, white, gray and yellow gouache, and black and red chalk on laid paper, 42.6 × 26.1 cm. Harvard Art Museums / Fogg Museum, Harvard Art Museums / Fogg Museum. Gift of the Honorable and Mrs. Robert Woods Bliss, 1936.122. Photo: Imaging Department © President and Fellows of Harvard College

the figures wearing their armour, there are also several paintings, such as *Robert Rich, 2nd Earl of Warwick* in the Metropolitan Museum of Art, New York[5], which portray the figures in civilian dress but surrounded by pieces of armour, indirectly evoking their bellicose inclinations. ¶ The representation of so much armour in the portraits painted over the course of Van Dyck's artistic career supports Horst Vey's[6] hypothesis that the painter used extremely detailed studies as models, or that he had them done for him by specific collaborators. The *Study of Armour*, acquired by Calouste Gulbenkian as a work by Van Dyck at the sale of the collection of Max Bonn (1877–1943) in 1922[7], has therefore always been attributed to the artist and is associated with two other studies currently belonging to the Fogg Art Museum in Cambridge, Massachusetts[8] (fig. 4.2). Interestingly, all three drawings were part of the Prosper Henry Lankrink Collection (1628–1692) and are authenticated by his collection mark on each. ¶ In these three studies, the same armour

3. See BARNES, DE POORTER, MILLAR, VEY, 2004, pp. 462–64, p. 463 (repr.).

4. *Ibidem*, pp. 517–18, p. 517 (repr.).

5. See WHEELOCK, BARNES, HELD, 1991, pp. 266–68, p. 267 (repr.).

6. See VEY, 1962, vol. 1, pp. 39–40.

7. The loss of some of the pictorial quality of this drawing is due to the 1967 floods mentioned previously.

8. Inv. 1936.122, and 1954.126. See VEY, 1962, vol. 1, pp. 39–40, and LISBON, PORTO 2000–2002, pp. 174–75, no. 77 (repr.).

– fig. 4.2 –
Attributed to Anton van Dyck (1599–1641), *A Suit of Armour.* Black ink, gray and green wash, and white, gray and yellow gouache over black and red chalk on paper, 38 × 25,3 cm. Harvard Art Museums / Fogg Museum. Gift of Meta and Paul J. Sachs, 1954.126. Photo: Imaging Department © President and Fellows of Harvard College

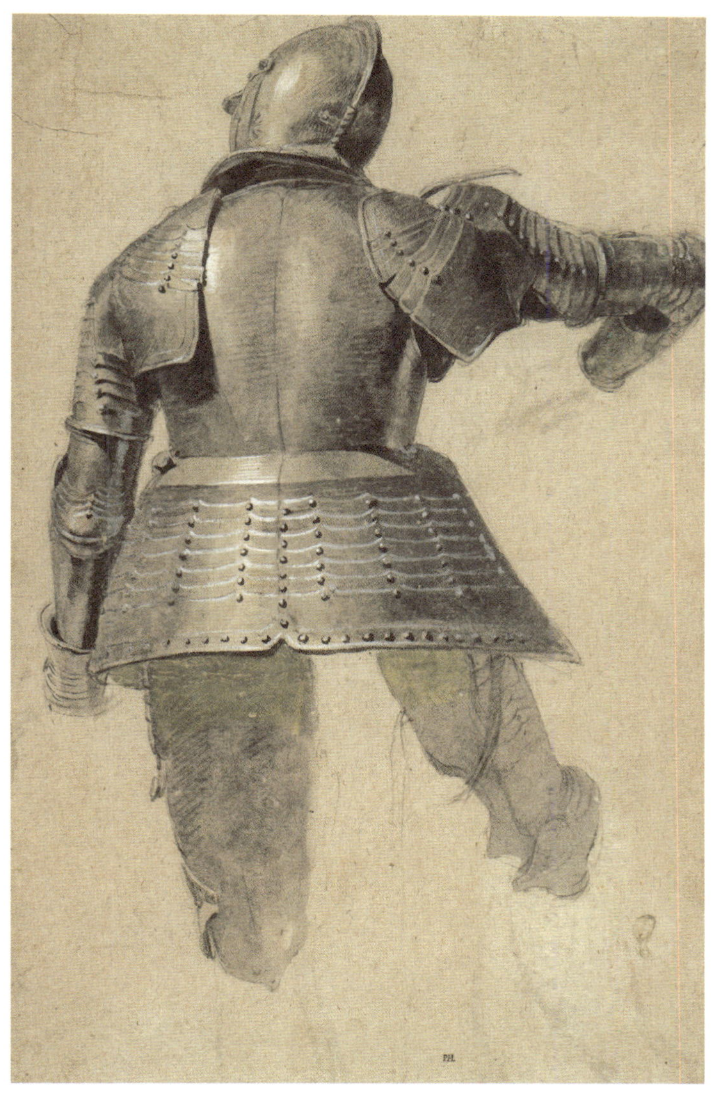

is shown from different angles: the front and back are shown in the Fogg drawings and the Gulbenkian study shows it in profile. According to Walter J. Karcheski from the Higgins Armory Museum in Worcester, it shows a cuirassier armour of Flemish or German origin, dating from around 1625–35. The sword depicted is a wide-bladed rapier, probably dating from around 1625–30[9]. ¶ In contrast to the Cambridge drawings, the Gulbenkian Museum's *Study of Armour* shows the helmet with the visor down, covering the soldier's face. Another difference is that one of these drawings shows a full-length figure and the other shows the figure with its legs just lightly sketched in; however, the figure in the Gulbenkian study is cut off just below the knee. Common to all three works is the use of the same pictorial technique to depict the structure of the armour and its articulations in tiny detail, while the soldiers' hands and weapons are merely sketched. This technique, which is skilfully used, enabled the artist to depict the metallic shine of

9. *Ibidem*. However, Vey dates the armour between ca. 1620 and ca. 1640–45, suggesting the south of Germany as its probable origin. See VEY, 1962, vol. 1, p. 40.

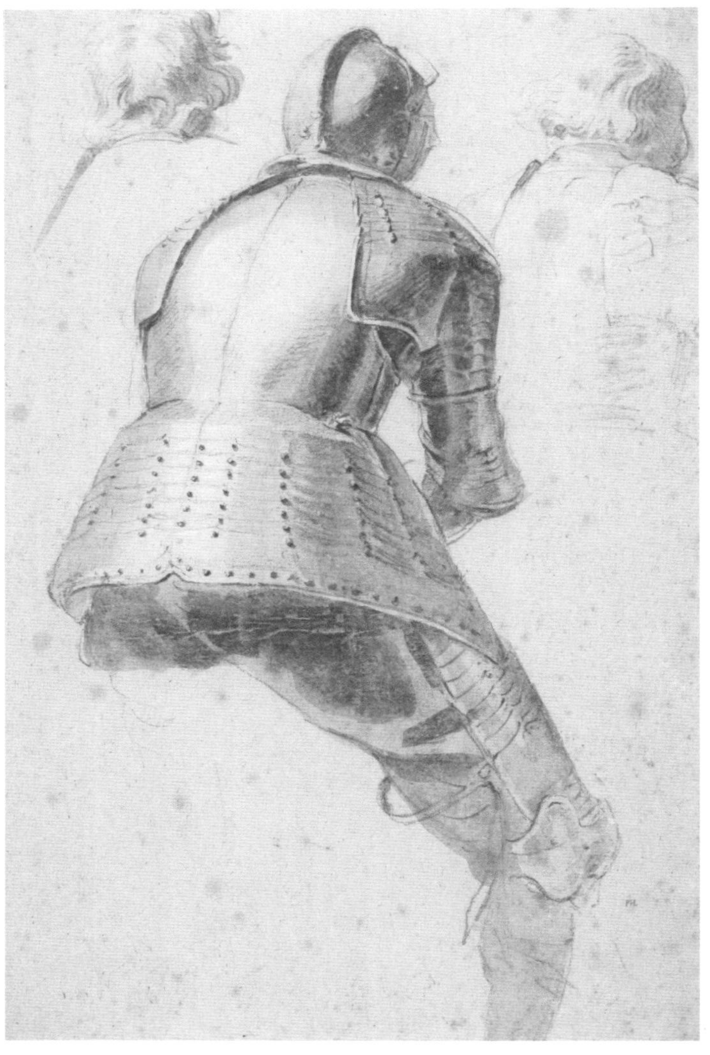

– fig. 4.3 –
Formerly attributed to Anton van Dyck (1599–1641), now attributed to Nicolaes Vienghels (?), *A Curassier Seen from the Back, and Two Details of an Officer's Head.* Black chalk and grey wash with touches of red and white chalk, 38.1 × 25.4 cm. From the Castle Howard Collection. Catalogue no.: Old Master Drawings 062. Reproduced by kind permission of the Hon. Simon Howard.

the armour. ¶ Castle Howard in York possesses another drawing, also from the Lankrink Collection, which shows a rear view of a suit of armour worn by a man on horseback (fig. 4.3). This is another unfinished study made using the same technique as the drawings already mentioned. Although there is an inscription on its back which names Van Dyck as its author, its actual authorship remains problematic[10]. ¶ This type of very precise and meticulous drawing, which also includes completed preparatory studies for some of the portraits included in the *Iconography*[11], differs greatly from the drawings that Van Dyck produced in his youth. In these, the artist expressed his varied compositional forms with an almost frantic energy, using short, quick, often imprecise lines and with the most important lines emphasised by dark-coloured brush strokes. ¶ It has not yet been possible to connect the Calouste Gulbenkian Collection's *Study of Armour* or the Cambridge drawings with any of Van Dyck's known paintings. It is, however, interesting to recall the Hamlet Winstanley (1698–1756) print that was supposedly made after a composition by Snyders (1579–1657) and Van Dyck. Entitled *Amor scientiarum*, the print dates from around ca. 1728–29 and depicts the same kind

10. Castle Howard Collection, catalogue no.: Old Master Drawings 062. I would like to thank Anna Louise Mason for her information on this work (2011).

11. A collection of prints of portraits of illustrious persons (sovereigns, politicians, captains, scholars, artists and collectors) that were painted or drawn by Van Dyck. The initiative for this major undertaking, which was financed by the Master, began in Antwerp after his return from Italy in 1627 and occupied him until the end of his life. The first edition was published by the publisher Gillis Hendricx four years after the painter's death, in 1645.

of armour[12]. ¶ The notable graphic quality of the study under discussion is characteristic of the exquisite work produced by Van Dyck, which should not make it hard to accept its authorship. However, attributing it to the Master is not unproblematic, especially if one considers the increasingly diffuse style and features that the artist used in his drawings, particularly in later life. Is this meticulous and precise drawing actually from the Master's hand, or is it a product of his studio, made by one of his more talented collaborators or by one of the artists from Van Dyck's circle?[13] The question remains unanswered.

12. See VEY, 1962, no. 182, p. 252.

13. I would like to thank Alexis Merle du Bourg for sharing his opinions on the subject (2008).

PROVENANCE

Prosper Henry Lankrink Collection. Posthumous sales in London, 1693 and 1694; Charles Sackville Bale Collection. Sold at Christie's, London, 1881, lot no. 2484; John Postle Heseltine Collection. Sold at Colnaghi, 1912; Colnaghi's, London; Max J. Bonn Collection. Acquired by Calouste Gulbenkian at this sale, through Colnaghi, at Sotheby's, London, on 15 February 1922, lot no. 7.

•

EXHIBITIONS

LISBON, 1976, no. 49; LISBON, 1985, no. 5, p. 20, p. 127 (repr.); CAMBRIDGE, 2000, no. 77, pp. 174–75, p. 175 (repr.); LISBON, PORTO, 2000–2002, no. 77, pp. 174–75, p. 175 (repr.); MADRID, 2002, no. 51, pp. 124–25, p. 125 (repr.).

•

LITERATURE

WAAGEN, 1857, p. 118; VEY, 1962, vol. 1, p. 39 (as *van Dyck*); KELLY, SCHWABE (1931), 1972, pp. 78–79 (repr).

[5]

JACOB VAN RUISDAEL
Haarlem, 1628/1629 – Amsterdam, 1682

FORD IN A WOODED LANDSCAPE
Holland, 1650–55

Black chalk, black ink, and grey washes on paper.
16.2 × 26.2 cm.
Signed monogram lower centre: *JR*.
Inv. 861

1. STECHOW, 1968, p. 71.

Jacob van Ruisdael was the most versatile of all the seventeenth-century Dutch landscape painters. He depicted nature through nearly every kind of landscape in a vast body of work comprising over seven-hundred paintings, a much smaller number of drawings, and some etchings. ¶ Of all his subjects – woods, forests and mountains, rivers and torrents, dunes and sandy paths, landscapes featuring ruins, castles and churches, watermills and windmills, meadows, cabins and cottages, winter landscapes, coastal scenes, seascapes, waterfalls and panoramic views – it is the forest in its multiple forms that is present throughout his work, from his earliest pieces created in the 1640s until the end of his career. ¶ According to Wolfgang Stechow, "It can be assumed that his very first serious attempts at painting, at the age of seventeen, led him first to the edge of the forest and afterwards into the thicket itself"[1]. Initially, he reflected the realism and meticulous observation of the Dutch tradition and was particularly influenced by Cornelis Vroom (1590/1591–1661) in his representation of dense twisted foliage and in his evocation of a meditative tranquillity. He focused on the landscapes near Haarlem and, through his monumental trees, leafy woods, dunes with winding paths, dense bushes and lush vegetation along the banks of ponds or water courses, he created a magnificent vision of nature in his own style. In the 1650s and '60s, while he retained the monumentality imparted by the large, solid trees, his compositions became more expansive and included spaces with clearings that allowed him to create dramatic effects of light and shade between the different compositional planes and also to glimpse distant landscapes that stretched out to the horizon. In the following decades, Ruisdael would focus on wider, more open, spatial effects and would concentrate on panoramic views which balanced and contained the vast plains that stretched as far as the eye could see and were topped by skies that sometimes took up more than half of the composition. ¶ Landscapes were one of Calouste Gulbenkian's favourite subjects and occupy a prominent place in his collection. It is therefore no surprise that he acquired four of Jacob van Ruisdael's

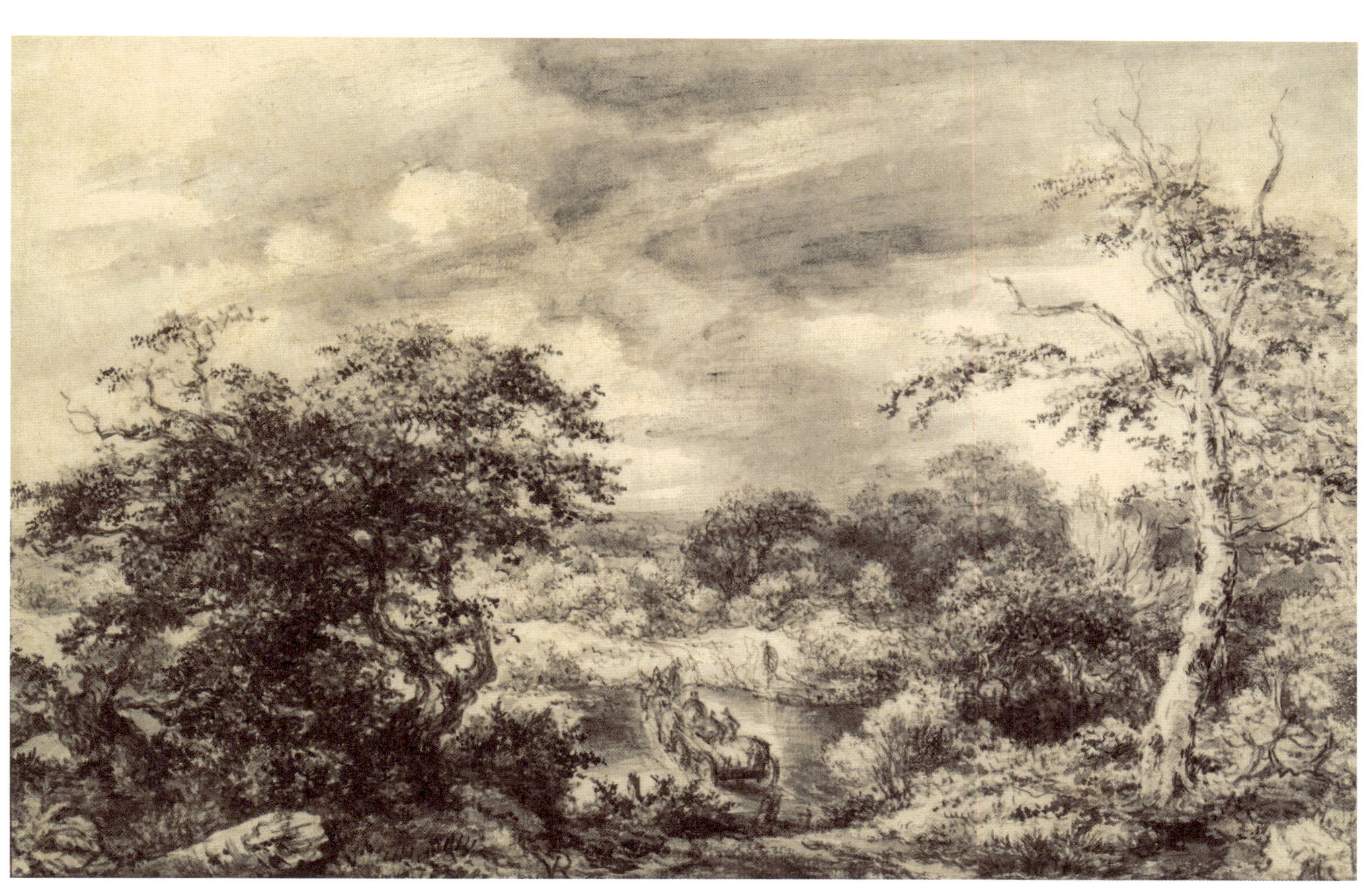

works: three paintings that illustrate different aspects of his output namely a seascape, a forest scene, and a *Haarlempje* (panoramic view of Haarlem)[2] and the drawing under discussion. ¶ *Ford in a Wooded Landscape* dates from the first half of the 1650s[3] and was made after the painter's journey with his friend and collaborator Nicolaes Berchem (1620–1683) to the mountain region between Holland and Germany. It was perhaps his most ambitious trip, as he never again strayed far from his homeland. ¶ Unrelated to any known painting, this work by Ruisdael is one of his completed independent drawings. Around thirty such works are known to exist, some of which, like *Oak Trees at the Edge of a River*[4], were finished in watercolour. Only a few dozen of his drawings can be considered to have served as preparatory studies for the several hundred paintings that Ruisdael produced. One such drawing is *A Water Mill*[5], which served as the model for the painting *Water Mill at the Edge of a Wood*[6]. However, as a careful observer of nature, the painter drew constantly, making quick records of places which he would later use in future compositions. This resulted in large numbers of preliminary drawings that can be considered as *aides-mémoires* or even *premières-pensées*[7]. ¶ In this drawing, as in his early works, a group of leafy trees stands in the foreground on the left with strong intertwined branches and foliage depicted in tiny detail with almost calligraphic strokes. There is also an old broken tree trunk, a decorative but symbolic element that is common in the painter's landscapes. However, Ruisdael's stylistic evolution towards more expansive views is also expressed here as the elements soften on the right of the composition, where a more slender tree is the harbinger of lighter vegetation which then opens into a clearing around a stream and ford. With its strongly contrasting shades, it is clear that we are looking at a

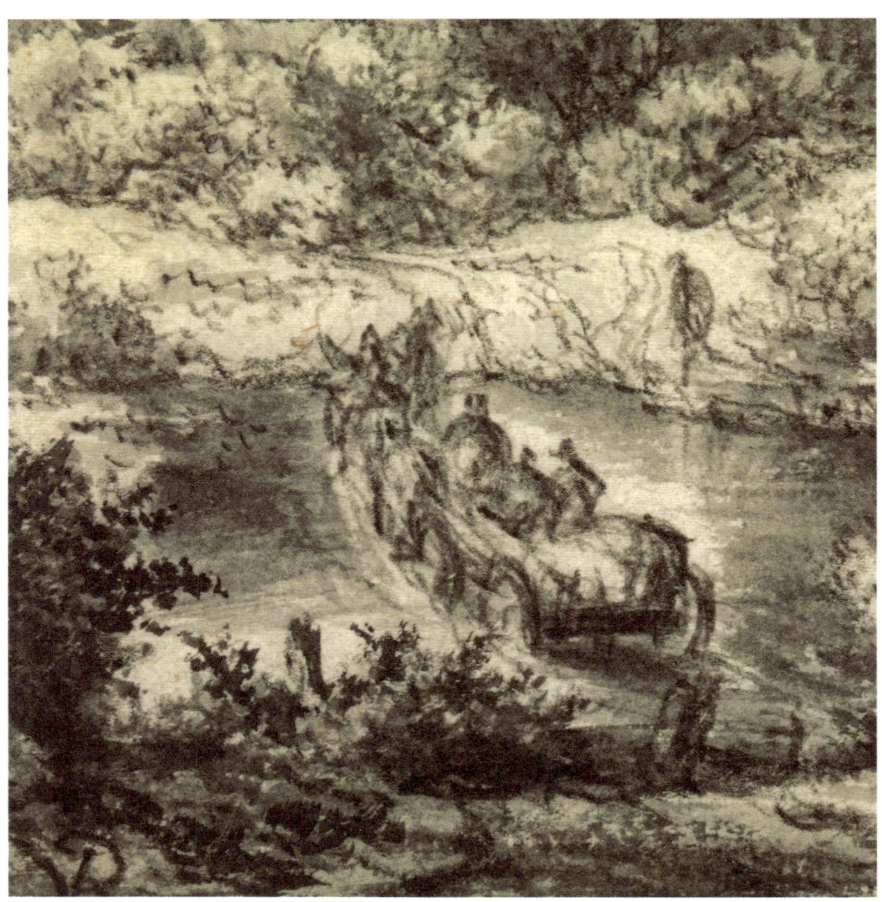

– fig. 5.1 –
Detail.

2. Attributed to Ruisdael on the date of the Calouste Gulbenkian purchase, this painting (*Landscape near Haarlem*, inv. 501) is now considered to be a copy of an original by the author. See SAMPAIO, 2009, pp. 66–67.

3. The dating is suggested by several authors. See SIMON, 1930, pp. 84–85 (dated at the start of the 1650s); GILTAY, 1980, pp. 141–208, p. 155; no. 73 (repr.) (dated ca. 1650–53); SLIVE, 2001, pp. 550–51, no. D78 (repr.) (dated from the first half of the 1650s).

4. Chantilly, Musée Condé inv. 369 bis, SLIVE, 2001, pp. 522–23, no. D40, p. 522 (repr.)

5. Amsterdam, Rijksmuseum, Rijksprentenkabinet, inv. A 1392. SLIVE, 2001, pp. 496–97, no. A6, p. 496 (repr.)

6. Toledo, The Toledo Museum of Art inv. 75.86. SLIVE, 2001, pp. 142–43, no. 124, p. 142 (repr.).

7. See *Ibidem*, pp. 491–92.

heroic forest scene, one whose thematic drama is reinforced by the dark colours and the pulses of light enacting a constant counterpoint in the middle distance and background. ¶ In his encounter with nature, Ruisdael shows a meditative pleasure in the silent immobility of the landscape and the tranquil solitude that it suggests. For this reason the representation of human figures as fragile silhouettes integrated into his work is of little importance[8], an aspect of his oeuvre that distances him from the picturesque scenes with lively groups created by Isaac van Ostade (1621–1649) or the similar scenes depicted by Philips Wouwerman (1619–1672), both of whom were his contemporaries[9]. ¶ In the Gulbenkian drawing the solitude and stillness of the landscape are disturbed by the presence of moving human figures. A cart driven by two men and pulled by two pairs of horses is crossing the ford at full speed (fig. 5.1). In a diagonal line that unfolds the perspective into several panoramic views, it rushes towards the opposite bank, where there is a hunched man striding away. It seems that they all are keen to escape the approaching storm, which is indicated by the dark clouds depicted with grey washes in a sky that takes up nearly half the drawing. ¶ Although many of the places that Ruisdael painted and drew are easily identifiable, a fact which lends verisimilitude to the artist's relationship with nature, the place depicted in the Gulbenkian drawing is not familiar and is therefore an excellent example of his imaginative flair. ¶ Signed with his monogram in the lower centre of the composition, the authorship of *Ford in a Wooded Landscape* has always been accepted. Before Calouste Gulbenkian acquired it in 1920, it had belonged to several collectors and was the most valuable drawing at the sale of the Neyman Collection in Paris in 1776, where it was one of a group of sixteen pieces attributed to Ruisdael[10].

8. While in some paintings figures do play a greater role, these were supposedly added by other artists such as Nicolaes van Berchem (1620–1683) and Adriaen van de Velde (1632–1672).

9. THE HAGUE; CAMBRIDGE MA, 1981–1982, p. 186, no. 72 (repr.).

10. SLIVE, 2001, pp. 550–51, no. D78 (repr.).

PROVENANCE

Neyman Collection, Amsterdam, Paris sale, 8–11 July 1776, lot no. 768; Christiaan Josi Collection; Ch. Philipe Collection, London, 1802 (acquired from C. Josi – See JOSI, 1821); Marquess of Lansdowne Collection. Acquired by Calouste Gulbenkian at the sale of this collection, through Colnaghi, at Sotheby's, London, 25 March 1920, lot no. 67, (repr.).

•

EXHIBITIONS

THE HAGUE, CAMBRIDGE MA, 1981–1982, no. 72 (repr.); LISBON, 1985, no. 17, p. 21, p. 142 (repr.); CAMBRIDGE, 2000, no. 78, pp. 176–77, p. 177 (repr.); LISBON, PORTO, 2000–2002, no. 78, pp. 176–77, p. 177 (repr.); MADRID, 2002, no. 52, pp. 126–27, p. 127 (repr.).

•

LITERATURE

ROSENBERG, 1928, p. 114, no. 53; SIMON, 1930, pp. 84–85; GILTAY, 1980, pp. 141–208, p. 155, cat. no. 73, no. 22 (repr.); SLIVE, 2001, pp. 550–51, no. D78 (repr.).

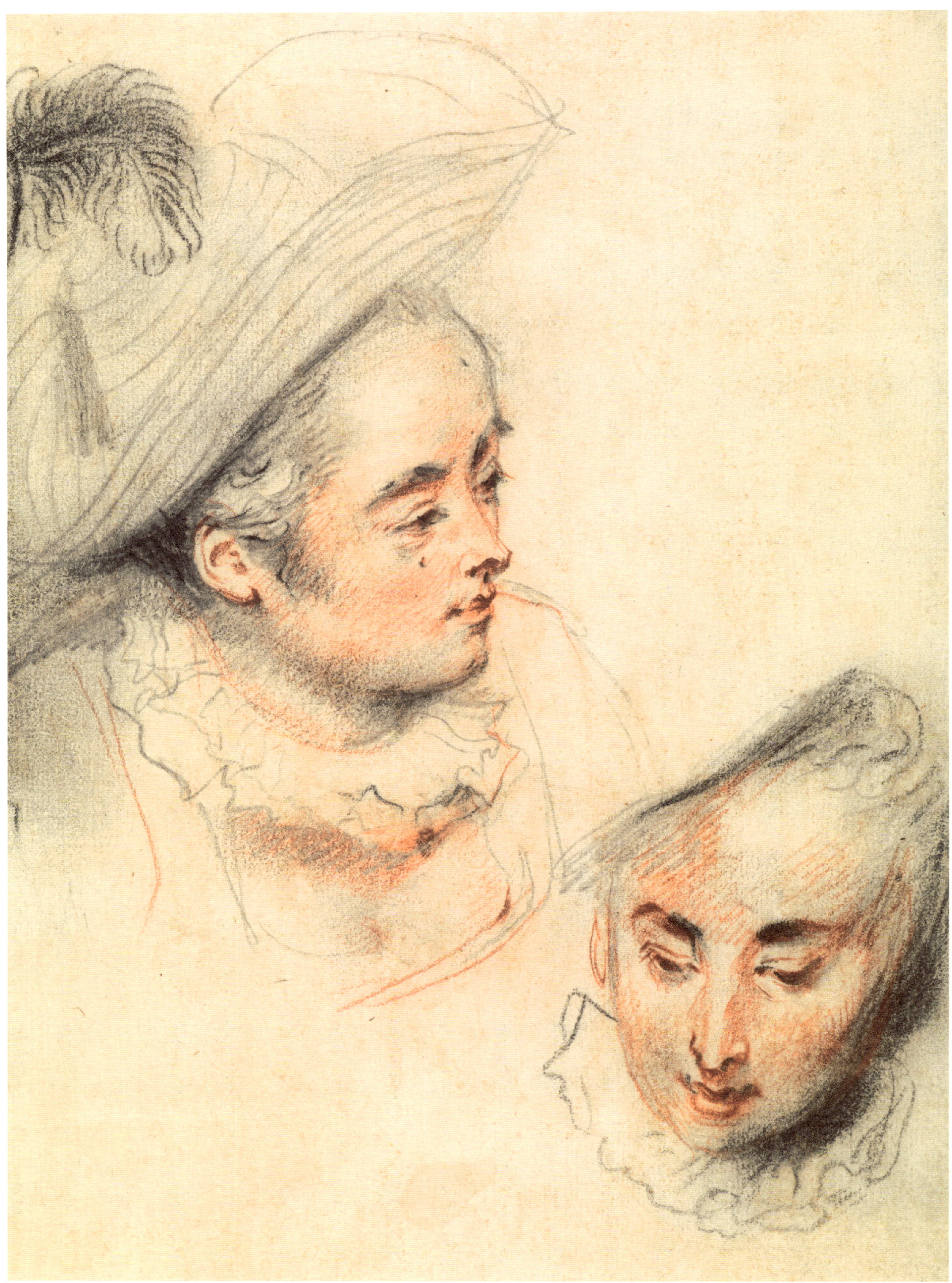

EIGHTEENTH CENTURY

[6]

WILLEM VAN MIERIS
Leiden, 1662–1747

TARQUIN AND LUCRETIA
Leiden, ca. 1700–10

Black chalk and stumping on parchment
41.4 (41.6) × 36.3 (36) cm.
Unidentified mark on lower right-hand corner:
the letter "G" inside an empty circle[1].
Imperceptible inscription on the lower left-hand corner.
Inv. 518

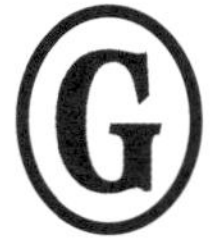

1. This mark is not mentioned in Fritz Lugt's, *Les marques de collections de desseins & d' estampes*, but see in this work, nos. 1128 a and 1131.

2. See BROOS, 1992, pp. 89–95. I would like to thank Ben Broos for sharing his views with me on the subject (1989).

3. For more on these two painters see LEIDEN, 1988, pp. 152–68 and THE HAGUE, WASHINGTON, 2005–2006.

4. This title was given to the Dutch Golden Age painters who, between 1630 and 1710, depicted scenes of everyday life with great realism and meticulous technical skill in highly refined and frequently small-scale paintings. Gerrit Dou (1613–1675), Frans and Willem van Mieris and Adrien van der Werff (1659–1722) were among the most successful Dutch Baroque painters of this genre.

Calouste Gulbenkian acquired this drawing, entitled *Rapt de Lucrece*, without any reference to author and to its previous ownership. The Collector's archives also contain no information on the place and time of its acquisition. ¶ Following several contacts carried out by the Calouste Gulbenkian Museum with the Mauritshuis Museum (The Hague), a study in 1992 by Ben Broos[2], the Dutch museum's then curator, answered some of the most relevant questions related to this drawing for the first time. ¶ The painter and draughtsman Willem van Mieris (1662–1747) is the likely author of this drawing in the Gulbenkian Collection, which still carries the signs of the signature and date on the lower left-hand side. The fact that they are now illegible was reinforced by the effects of the aforementioned floods of 1967. ¶ Willem always worked in Leiden. The son and pupil of Frans van Mieris the Elder[3] (1635–1692), one of the greatest Dutch genre painters of the seventeenth century and one of the most celebrated *fijnschilders*[4], Willem was inspired by his father's themes and style, although he never achieved the same level of virtuosity in his own work. In his genre scenes he depicts with great realism family and everyday life in shops, kitchens or in serene corners at home. His artistic language was full of life and his greatest attribute was his meticulous attention to detail. In the style of Gerrit Dou (1613–1675), who had been his father's master, many of these scenes are framed by a stone window, the base of which could be adorned with a bas-relief. Willem also specialised in portrait and landscape painting and a feature of his artistic work was the exploration of religious, historical and classical themes. ¶ In the Gulbenkian drawing, Willem van Mieris uses black chalk on parchment to evoke two episodes from the legendary history of Ancient Rome. One of these is the central subject of the composition and unfolds in a space dominated by a classical architectural structure. This is *Tarquin and Lucretia*, a story told by Ovid (43 BC-18 AC) in the *Fasti* and by Livy (59 BC-17 AD) in *Ab Urbe Condita Libri*. ¶ The painter portrays the dramatic moment when Sextus Tarquinius, son of the King of Rome, Tarquinius Superbus, is about to

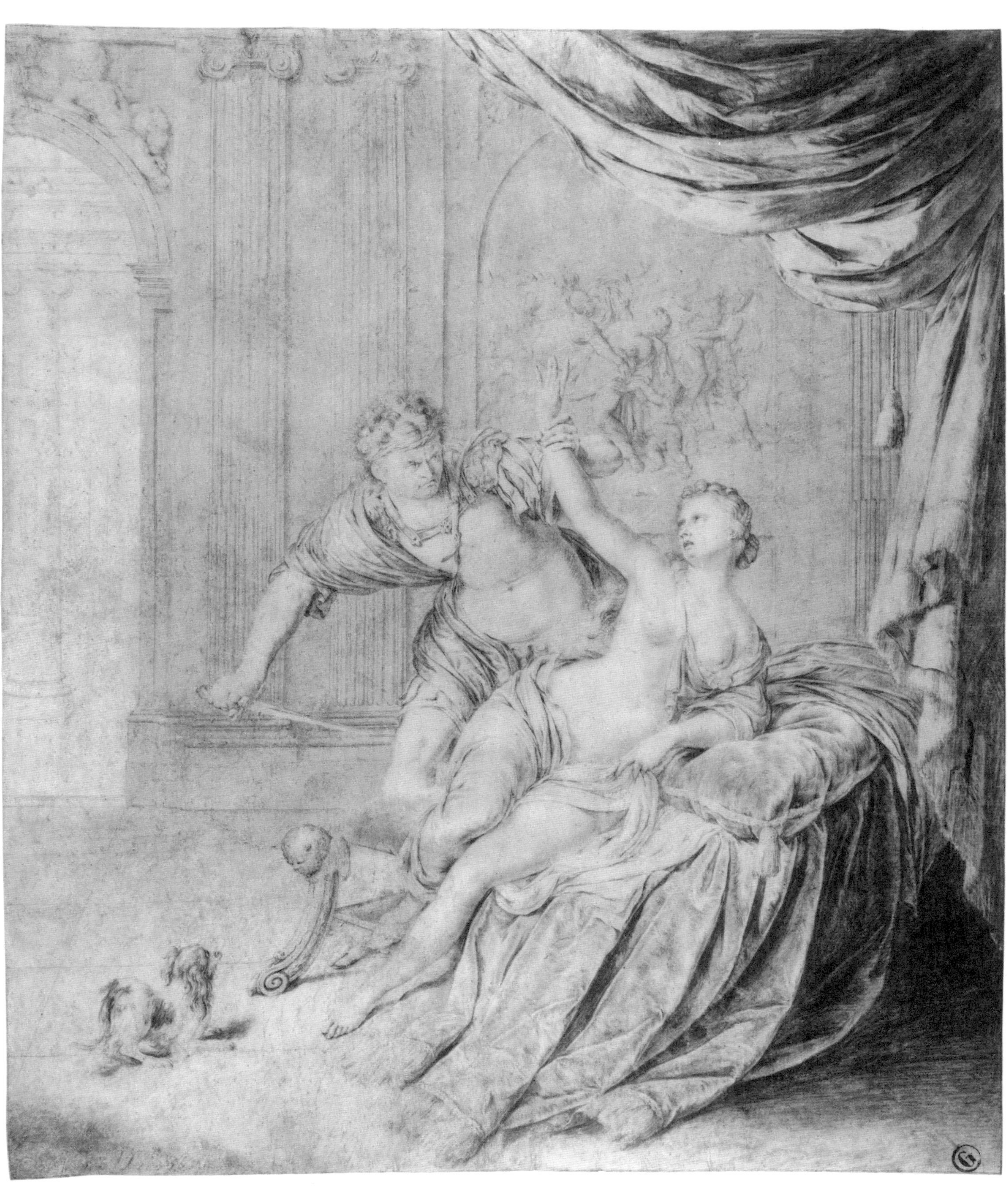

5. This episode from the legendary history of Rome as told by Livy and Plutarch occurred soon after it was founded by Romulus.

6. I would like to thank Albert J. Elen, for his valuable information on this drawing (2012).

7. Flemish sculptor trained in Antwerp and Brussels. After a sojourn in Italy where he developed a strong interest in classical culture, he settled in Amsterdam where he became well-known for his ivory bas-reliefs.

8. VAN BREUGEL, 1992, pp. 12–24; I would like to thank Christian Theuerkauff for sharing his views on the subject (1993).

rape Lucretia, the beautiful wife of Lucius Tarquinius Collatinus, who was known for her chastity and virtue. After telling her father and husband of the violent act, Lucretia then kills herself. With the aid of Lucius Junius Brutus, Collatinus incites a revolt against the royal family and expels it from Rome. Then, with the support of the people who made Lucretia a heroine, the monarchy is overthrown and the Roman Republic is founded in 509 BC. Brutus and Collatinus became its first two consuls. ¶ To reinforce the classical elements of the drawing a representation of a bas-relief is featured in the background architecture. With its theme of *The Abduction of the Sabine Women*[5], it emphasises the eroticism of the first representation, which is marked by the nudity of both figures and by Tarquin's criminal lustfulness. The depiction of this story was very popular, and many artists worked on the theme on a range of supports. Willem van Mieris himself depicted it in another of his drawings, entitled *Rape of the Sabine Women*, which now belongs to the Metropolitan Museum of Art, New York, inv. 2007.276.2[6]. Mieris may have been inspired by an ivory by Francis van Bossuit (1635–1692)[7] that was probably made around 1680–90, the composition of which is identical in every detail to the 'painted' bas-relief in the drawing (fig. 6.1)[8]. ¶ In an essay published in 1985, Emke Elen-Clifford Kocq van Breugel[9] singled out ten drawings that were directly related to other paintings by the artist. The Gulbenkian sheet, a finished drawing in its own right, can be added to this group as it was also a preparatory study for a painting on the same theme which only differs from the original in a few details, such as the position of the columns (which are further to the left),

9. VAN BREUGEL (1985) [Delft 1987], pp. 147–64.

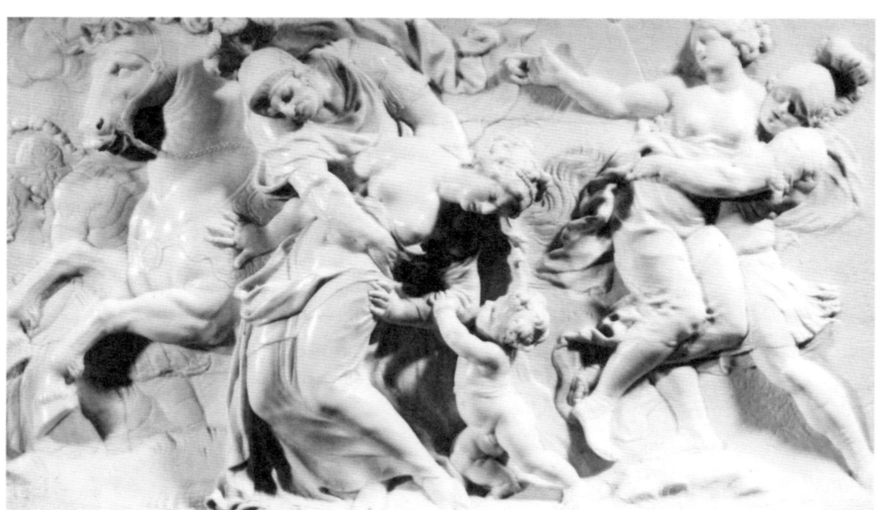

– fig. 6.1 –
Francis van Bossuit (1635–1692),
The Rape of the Sabine Women, ca. 1680–90 (?).
Ivory, 14.9 (15.1) × 27.7 (28) cm.
Germany, private collection.
Rights reserved

and the head of Sextus (which is set more artificially on the character's shoulders) (fig. 6.2). Interestingly, there is another Mieris drawing in Amsterdam's Rijksmuseum collections which, despite having a very similar composition to that of the Gulbenkian piece and the painting, was made before either work. In the Rijksmuseum drawing, however, it is not possible to identify the subject of the sketched bas-relief in the background (fig. 6.3)[10]. ¶ According to previous studies, this painting was sold at successive public sales and was presented by the London art dealers Verner Amell Ltd in Maastricht at the European Art Fair in 1991[11]. Curiously, at an auction held at Christie's of London on 7 July 2010, a painting by Willem van Mieris on this same subject was listed under lot no. 121. This piece

10. See ELEN, 2012, pp. 534, 538, no. 7.

11. BROOS, 1992, pp. 90–1.

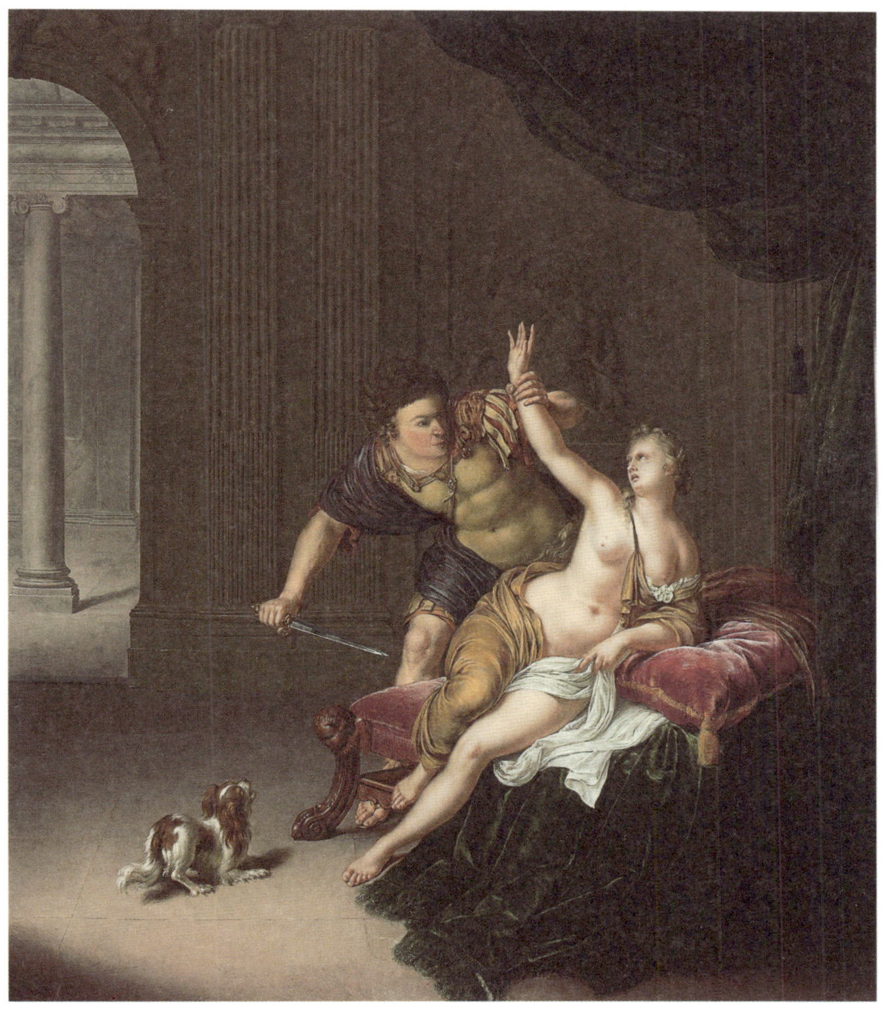

– fig. 6.2 –
Willem van Mieris (1662–1747),
The Rape of Lucretia. Oil on panel.
© Christie's Images Limited (2013)

12. Benjamin Peronnet of Christie's, to whom I am grateful for all of the information that he provided on the subject (2012), told me that the painting was not actually sold at this auction.

13. THE HAGUE, WASHINGTON, 2005–2006, pp. 207–9, ill.

was identical to the drawing[12] and may therefore have been the work displayed in 1991. ¶ Painters and writers find in the story of Lucretia an inexhaustible source of inspiration for their works. Titian, Tintoretto, Rubens, Cranach, Veronese and Rembrandt, among others, depicted it in their paintings, and Shakespeare himself tackled it in his narrative poem *The Rape of Lucrece*, which was published in 1594 and dedicated to one of his patrons, Henry Wriothesley, the Earl of Southampton. There are therefore numerous sources that may have inspired Van Mieris. We may recall that his father, although not habitually a painter of historical subjects, had in 1679 made a painting entitled *The Death of Lucretia*[13] which now belongs to a private collection in New York. However, it was most likely Titian's paint-

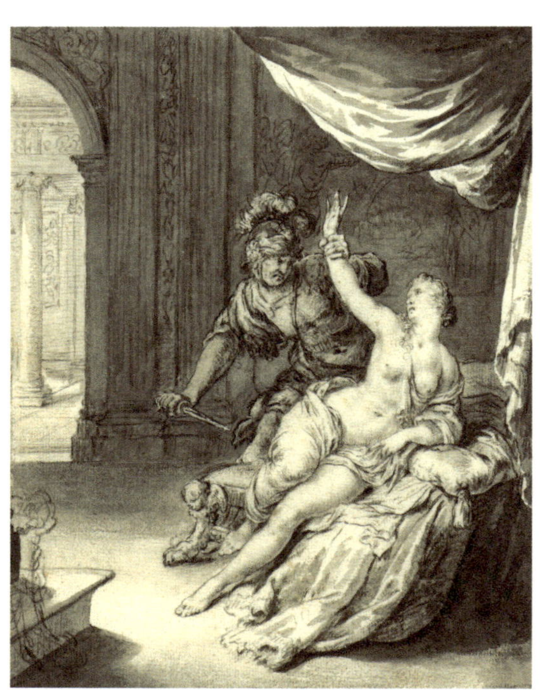

– fig. 6.3 –
Willem van Mieris (1662–1747),
The Rape of Lucretia. Black chalk and grey wash on paper, 22.9 × 18.4 cm. Rijksprentenkabinet, inv. RP-T-1957-331. Collection Rijksmuseum, Amsterdam. Purchased with the support of the F.G. Waller-Fonds

ing of the subject that stirred Willem's interest, via the print made by Cornelis Cort (1533–1578) in 1571[14]. ¶ The coherence of Willem van Mieris' style over the course of his artistic career makes it hard to date the Gulbenkian drawing and the painting that is so similar to it, especially as the inscription is partially erased in both works. Thus, the date currently attributed to it (ca. 1700 -10) is based somewhat arbitrarily on the date (1706) inscribed on the painting *The Drinker*[15], which, like the drawing *Tarquin and Lucretia,* includes the same representation of the *Abduction of the Sabine Women* in the decoration of the wall in the background.

14. HOLLSTEIN, 1949, vol. IV, p. 56, no. 193 (repr.).

15. Painting in Leiden, Stedlijk Museum De Lakenhal, inv. 1202. See BROOS, 1992, p. 94.

PROVENANCE
Unknown.

•

LITERATURE
BROOS, 1992, pp. 89–95;
ELEN, 2012, pp. 533–38, 35 (repr.).

[7]

JEAN ANTOINE WATTEAU

Valenciennes, 1684 – Nogent-sur-Marne, 1721

THREE STUDIES OF A YOUNG WOMAN'S HEAD

France, ca. 1716–17

Three chalks (black, red and white chalk) with stump on paper.
23.2 × 31 cm.
Mark of Thomas Dimsdale Collection
on the lower left of the verso – TD (Lugt 2426).
Inv. 2300

1. See WASHINGTON, PARIS, BERLIN, 1984–1985, pp. 17–30.

This drawing was made by Jean Antoine Watteau when his artistic production had reached full maturity. ¶ Considered to be one of the greatest French painters of the turn of the eighteenth century, Watteau was active over the last few years of Louis XIV's reign and the Regency period, creating a completely innovative body of work that conveyed the aesthetic ideals of the Rococo through a new pictorial genre known as *fête galante*. ¶ He was born in Valenciennes, where he first began to learn about painting. However, it was in Paris that he came into close contact with other artists who helped him to develop his artistic skills. Through his first master, Claude Gillot (1673–1722), he came into contact with the world of the theatre, particularly the *commedia dell'arte*, which became one of the most common themes in his work. Claude III Audran (1658–1734), a skilful decorator who, at the time, was responsible for the Luxembourg Palace in Paris, took him in afterwards as a student and collaborator, offering him, on the one hand, a chance to study the great Flemish masters (particularly Rubens) and Venetian masters (primarily Titian) which were on display there and, on the other, to experience the landscape of the surrounding park and the aristocratic society that visited it[1]. ¶ Despite his premature death, Watteau left a body of work that was extremely influential in a wide range of cultural and aesthetic fields. Over the centuries, his paintings have fascinated generations of writers, painters, poets, musicians and film-makers. However, Watteau's biographers and experts on his work, both his contemporaries and those who came afterwards, unanimously agree on the artist's passion for drawing. ¶ Watteau drew for the sheer pleasure of it, without any specific purpose in mind. He saw every free moment as an opportunity to observe the surrounding world and record it in his notebooks. These became the repositories of forms and models which he then used in his paintings. Those close to him said that he was a reserved and restless man, solitary yet afraid of loneliness and given to a melancholy that drove him to move constantly from place to place, as if he were in fear of losing the freedom that he valued so highly. Perhaps this is why

Mark of Thomas Dimsdale Collection

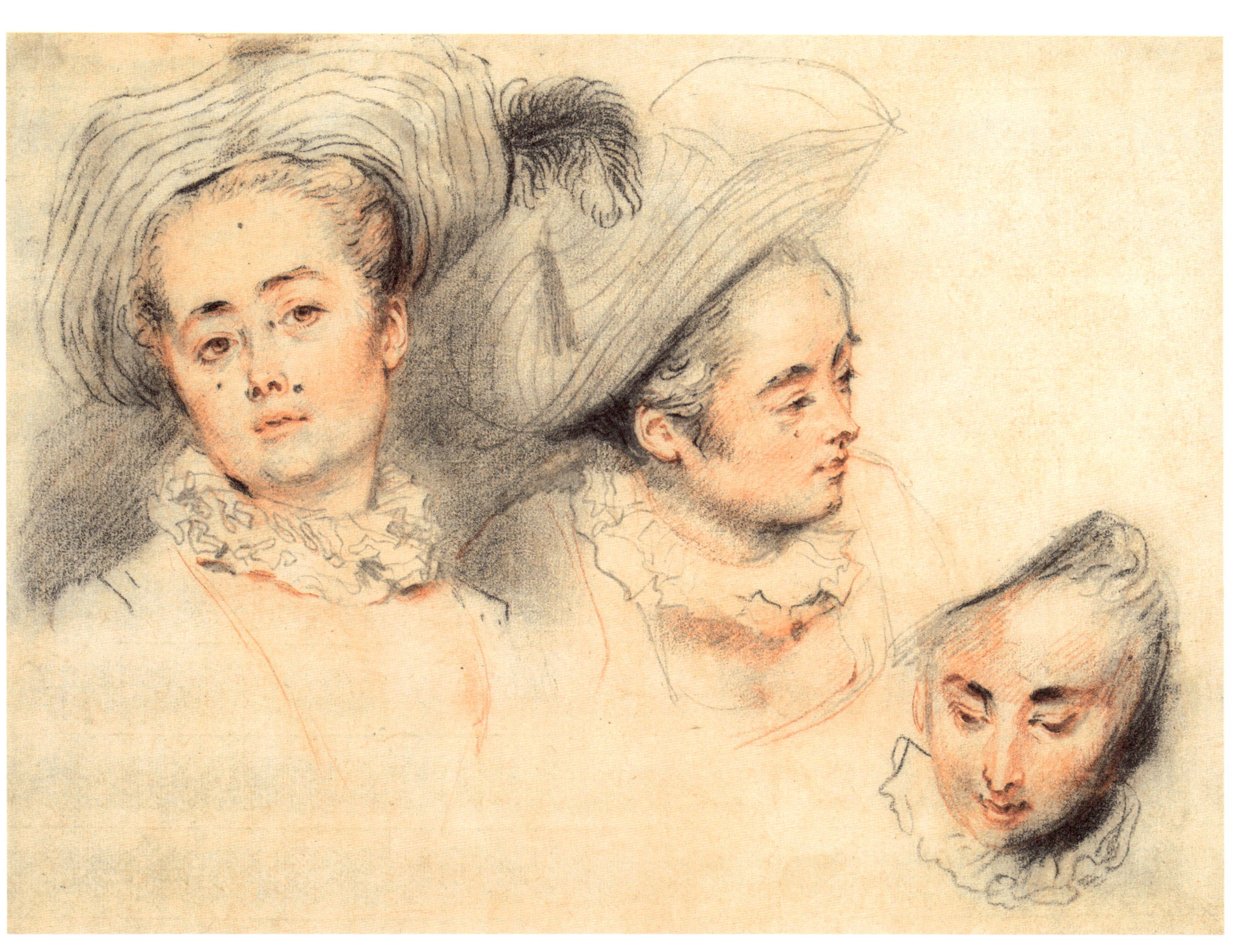

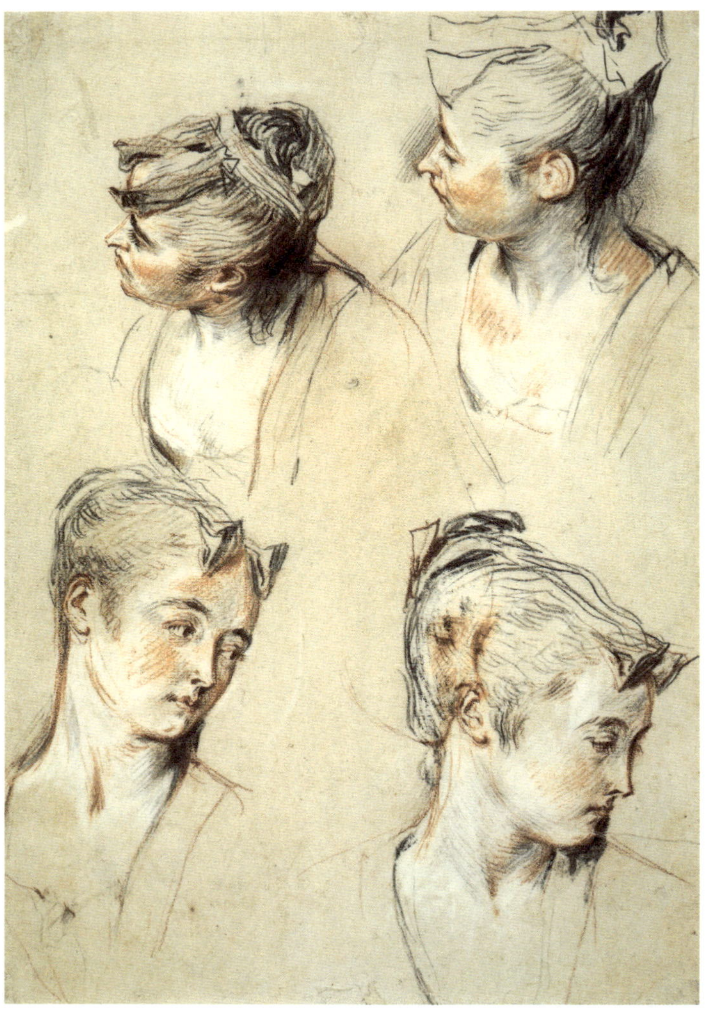

– fig. 7.1 –
Antoine Watteau (1684–1721), *Five Studies of a Young Woman's Head*, ca. 1716–17. Black, red and white chalk (*trois crayons*), red wash and white gouache highlights on cream paper, 33.9 × 23.8 cm. London, The British Museum, inv. 1895.09.15.941. © 2012 The Trustees of the British Museum c/o Scala, Florence

he loved drawing so much, as its immediacy and speed of execution were best suited to his nervous temperament. ¶ But this generally gloomy outlook, which was heightened by his ill health, was not reflected in his drawings or paintings. On the contrary, Watteau's work transports us to a happy and healthy world filled with the *joie de vivre* of the society of the times and has a timeless sense and dreamlike quality. The everyday lives of the aristocracy that were the models for his compositions are seen by the spectator through his magical and poetic eye; eternal evocations of love, ephemeral theatrics, joyous moments spent dancing to the sound of music all take place in pastoral, idyllic, and romantic scenes that are sometimes lightly touched by a gentle mist. Nevertheless, a fleeting and enigmatic nostalgia can sometimes be seen in the eyes of some of the figures that inhabit his compositions. ¶ Several of Watteau's friends and protectors[2] left accounts commenting on the artist's relationship with drawing. Edme-François Gersaint (1694–1750), one of his first biographers and closest friends wrote that "[...] Watteau was more satisfied with his drawings than with his paintings. He had more pleasure out of drawing than out of painting. I often saw him feeling discouraged in spite of himself, because he could not convey in painting the spirit and truth that he knew how to convey using his crayon"[3]. Another loyal friend, the collector Jean de Jullienne (1686–1766), wrote enthusiastically that "[Watteau's

2. For more on Watteau's friends who were related in some way to the evolution of his work see PARMANTIER, Nicole – "Les Amis de Watteau", *in* WASHINGTON, PARIS, BERLIN, 1984–1985, pp. 33–52.

3. "Watteau était plus content de ses dessins que de ses tableaux [...]. Il trouvait plus d'agrément à dessiner qu'à peindre. Je l'ai vu souvent se dépiter contre lui-même, de ce qu'il ne pouvait point rendre, en peinture, l'esprit et la vérité qu'il savait donner à son crayon." See "Préface du Catalogue raisonné [...] de la Collection de M. Angran, vicomte de Fonspertuis, Paris, Prault et Barrois, 1747", *in* ROSENBERG, PRAT, 1996, tome I, pp. XVI–XVII.

drawings] have a new taste, a beauty so connected with the spirit of the author that we might say they are inimitable"[4]. ¶ Concerning changes that would have to be made to one of Watteau's paintings, he wrote in a letter to Julienne dated 2 September 1720 that he would only be able to do the work later because at the time he "was busy with his thoughts with red chalk"[5]. ¶ Of the numerous subjects that Watteau drew, those of greatest interest are his studies of heads. The artist's extraordinary talent as a portraitist of human physiognomy shines through in these works. At times he shows the same model in different poses, as in the Gulbenkian drawing. In these cases, the composition is magnificent and meticulous and nothing in the arrangement of the different faces is left to chance. In other cases, in which several models appear, male and female heads, either bareheaded or wearing hats, seen in profile, from behind, or looking straight at the spectator, obsessively invade the blankness of the page, as if it did not suffice to contain everything that his hand was able to produce. ¶ The drawing studied here, which dates from ca. 1716–17, is a wonderful piece that is contemporaneous with the painting *Pèlerinage à l'Île de Cythère*, the masterpiece that gained him membership of the French Royal Academy in 1717[6]. The stylistic maturity and technique that Watteau displays in these works, in both the drawing and the painting, is echoed in two other very similar studies of female heads dating from the same period, one of which belongs to the British Museum[7] in London (fig. 7.1) and the other to a private collection currently held in New York[8]. ¶ The Gulbenkian sheet shows three bust-length studies of the same woman with a feathered hat and fringed collar in different poses. The three sketches are harmoniously arranged along a diagonal line that runs from the upper left-hand corner, where the first model is seen from the front with her head slightly to one side, to the second study, which is shown in profile, down to the final pose in the lower right-hand corner, where she is seen from above with her eyes lowered. This composition recalls Watteau's slightly later drawing at the Haarlem Teylers Museum, which, in addition to the three heads, also contains the study of an arm (fig. 7.2)[9]. ¶ In the relationship between the three studies in the Gulbenkian work, it is interesting to note that the first is drawn in great detail and has an admirable depth and volume arising from the shaded background against which it stands out, while the last study is much more sketchily done. However, all bear the mark of Watteau's tremendous expressiveness. ¶ The beauty of the composition, achieved through his skilled use of the three-chalk technique in black, red, and white chalk, is emphasised by the range of shades, by the contours of the face, whose volumes are accentuated by the diagonals and the stumping, by the details that highlight her expression and, finally, by the soft and luminous atmosphere that surrounds her. ¶ For many years, experts on the artist have attempted to establish the identity of the woman portrayed in the Gulbenkian drawing and to find her as a model in some of Watteau's subsequent paintings. In the catalogue for the sale of the Sarah Ann James Collection, which took place in London in 1891, this work is referred to as "Three studies of the Head of Madame Duclos, of the Comedie française". Three years later, at the sale of the H.H.A. Josse Collection in Paris, which was held in 1894, the name of the actress had disappeared from the title of the drawing[10]. According to Parker and Mathey, the lack of similarity between the woman depicted and other known portraits of this actress from the Comédie-française, and the fact that Mlle. Duclos was born in 1665, make it unlikely that she would have posed for this drawing[11].

4. "Ils sont d'un goust nouveau, ils sont des grâces tellement attachées à l'esprit de l'auteur qu'on peut avancer qu'ils sont inimitables". JULLIENNE, J. – "Abrégé de la vie d'Antoine Watteau", préface aux Figures de différents caractères, de Paysages et d'Études dessinés d'après nature par Antoine Watteau, Paris, [1726] vol. I, *in* DACIER, VUAFLART, HÉROLD, 1929, tome II – *Historique*, p. 6.

5. "[...] je m'occupe des pensées à la sanguine". See GONCOURT, GONCOURT, 1880, p. 27.

6. Currently in the Musée du Louvre in Paris, inv. 8325.

7. See LONDON, 2011, pp. 154–55, no. 68 (repr.).

8. *Four Studies of a Woman's Head*. See *Ibidem* pp. 152–53, no. 67 (repr.).

9. See *Ibidem*, pp. 182–83, no. 84 (repr.).

10. See ROSENBERG, PRAT, 1996, tome III, pp. 1452–53, and 1454–55.

11. PARKER, MATHEY, 1957, tome II, p. 345, no. 777 (repr.).

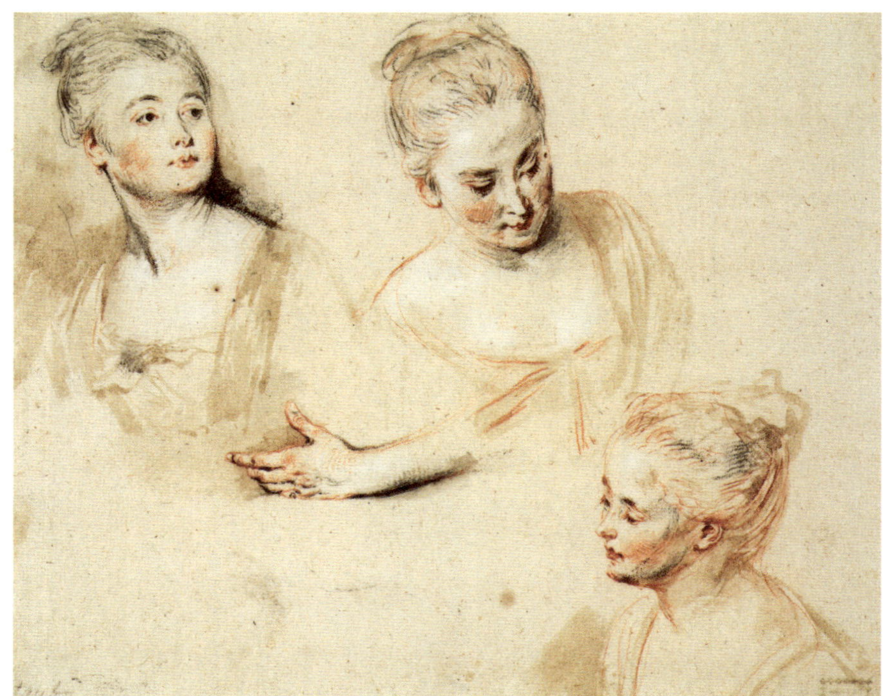

– fig. 7.2 –
Antoine Watteau (1684–1721), *Three-bust Length Studies of a Woman; Study of a Left Forearm*, ca. 1718–19. Black, red and white chalk (*trois crayons*), with brown, grey and red washes on cream paper, 26.5 × 34.6 cm. Teylers Museum, Haarlem, The Netherlands, inv. M14.

This opinion is supported by Rosenberg and Prat in their *Catalogue Raisonné* of Watteau's drawings[12]. Regarding the relationship between the figure in the drawing and others that appear in the artist's works, several experts have established a connection between the head on the left and the actress depicted in the centre of the composition *Les Habits sont Italiens*[13]. Also according to Rosenberg and Prat, the face in the lower right-hand corner of the sheet is similar, although inverted, to the one seen in the drawing in the British Museum, *Deux études de têtes féminines...* dating from ca. 1716 (inv.00-11-262)[14]. ¶ Although Watteau is known to have produced a vast number of drawings, it is not known how many drawings were left in the estate that he bequeathed when he died on 18 July 1721 at a friend's home in Nogent-sur-Marne. In his work *Abrégé de la vie d'Antoine Watteau*, published in 1744[15], Gersaint mentions that some time beforehand, Watteau had appointed him custodian of the drawings in his possession, which were to be divided between four of his most loyal friends: Jean de Jullienne, Abbot Haranger (the Canon of St-Germain-l'Auxerrois), Nicolas Hénin, and Gersaint himself. Jean de Jullienne was not indifferent to this demonstration of friendship[16]. ¶ After the artist's death, Pierre Crozat (1665–1740), an important banker and art collector, and also a patron and protector of Antoine, wrote in a letter dated 11 August to the painter Rosalba Carriera (1675–1757), who painted one of Watteau's last portraits, now in Treviso at the Museo Civico Luigi Bailo: "We have lost poor Vateau, who finished with a brush in his hand. His friends must provide the public with a speech on his life and rare talents..."[17].Jean de Jullienne, one of the heirs to Watteau's drawings and the Director of the Manufacture des Gobelins since 1718, responded to this plea by financing a work that would honour the memory of his

12. See ROSENBERG, PRAT, 1996, vol. II, pp. 880–81, no. 523 (repr.).

13. DACIER, VUAFLART, HEROLD, 1929, vol. III, no. 130, pp. 64–65 and tome IV (1), fig. no. 130.

14. See ROSENBERG, PRAT, 1996, vol. II, pp. 770–71, no. 463 (repr.).

15. GERSAINT, E. F., "Abrégé de la vie d'Antoine Watteau", *Catalogue raisonné des divers curiosités du cabinet de feu M. Quentin de Lorangère* (Paris, 1744), *in* DACIER, VUAFLART, 1929, vol. I, pp. 142–45.

16. For more on the questions raised by Gersaint's information on the number of Watteau's drawings, see ROSENBERG, PRAT, vol. I, pp. XII-XIX.

17. "Nous avons perdu le Pauvre Vateau qui a fini le pinsseau à la main. Ses amis doivent donner au public un Discours sur sa vie & sur ses rares talens...", *in* DACIER, VUAFLART, HÉROLD, 1929, tome II – *Historique*, p. 2.

friend by publishing prints of his drawings and paintings made by the best artists of the time. This huge undertaking, known as *Recueil Jullienne*, took about fifteen years and consists of four volumes in two large publications: the two volumes of *Figures de différents caractères de Paysages et d'Études dessinées d'après Nature*, published respectively in 1726 and 1728, and the two volumes of *L'œuvre d'Antoine Watteau, peintre du Roy en son academie roïale de peinture et sculpture. Gravé d'après les tableaux et dessins originaux tirez du Cabinet du Roy et des plus curieux de l'Europe, par les soins de M. de Julliene*, published in 1735[18]. The Calouste Gulbenkian Collection owns a copy of the latter collection (inv. LA124).

18. For more on the "Recueil Jullienne", see DACIER, VUAFLART, HEROLD, 1929, vols. I–IV (2).

PROVENANCE

Thomas Dimsdale Collection, London; Samuel Woodburn Collection, sold 4th June 1860, lot no. 1067; Andrew James Collection (d. before 1857); Sarah Ann James Collection (daughter of Andrew James), London (up until 1891); sold at Christie's, London, 22–23 June 1891, lot no. 340, acquired by Asher Wertheimer, *art dealer*; H.H.A. Josse Collection, sale after his death at Galerie Georges Petit, Paris, 28–29 May 1894, lot no. 44; Comte de Greffulhe Collection. Acquired by Calouste Gulbenkian at the latter's sale (by order of the Comtesse de Greffulhe and the Duke and Duchess of Gramont), through Hans Stiebel, at Sotheby's, London, 22 July 1937, lot no. 52 (plate XVI).

•

EXHIBITIONS

LONDON, 1878, no. 7; PORTO, 1964, no. 65 (repr.); OEIRAS, 1965, no. 231 (repr.); LISBON, 1976, no. 55 (repr.); LISBON, 1985, no. 13, p. 21, p. 138 (repr.); NEW YORK, 1999, no. 46, pp. 96–97 (repr.); CAMBRIDGE, 2000, no 90, pp. 202–03, p. 203 (repr.); LISBON, PORTO, 2000–2002, no. 90, pp. 202–03, p. 203 (repr.); MADRID, 2002, no. 58, pp. 140–41, p. 141 (repr); LONDON, 2011, no. 70, pp. 158–59, p. 158 (repr.).

•

LITERATURE

PARKER, [1931], pp. 22, 44, no. 43; PARKER, MATHEY, 1957, no. 777 (repr.), p. 345; ROSENBERG, PRAT, 1996, no. 523, p. 880.

[8]

FRANÇOIS BOUCHER
Paris, 1703–1770

PASTORAL SCENE
France, ca. 1745

Black, red, and white chalk,
with blue and yellow
pencil highlights on paper.
32 × 33.9 cm.
Signed on the lower right-hand side:
F. Boucher.
Inv. 66

François Boucher lived in a period of peace and prosperity. The *Grand Siècle* and Louis XIV's stifling control had given way to new codes of conduct, and this change, which had a tremendous cultural impact, became even more influential after the Court and the ruling class left Versailles for smaller scale Parisian palaces. The arts blossomed and reflected the wealth and new tastes of their patrons; the social gatherings and exchange of ideas taking place in private *salons* increased; there were dances and masked balls, theatre, opera, the *Comédie-Française*, and the pantomimes of the *commedia dell' arte*, all of which responded to the elite's constant quest for pleasure and entertainment. The interiors of these quarters reflected this new spirit of gallantry and small Parisian apartments were designed to offer comfort and intimacy and were decorated with cheerful themes intended to appeal to the senses. ¶ Boucher's art corresponded fully to the artistic tastes of the period, with the charm of most of his works being tempered by a gentle voluptuousness and sensual abandonment. According to Pierre Rosenberg, Boucher's work conveys "a careless world, a young world, the happiness in an idyllic nature which overlooks winter, a spring full of hope, a summer without heat waves, an autumn marked by abundance, where all that is needed to harvest is to stretch out one's hand, a world which banishes all kinds of effort..."[1] ¶ Boucher's *rocaille* work created a world in which reality was illusory; a world populated by gods, nymphs, *putti* and timeless shepherds. In mythological, pastoral and rural scenes, most of which were a pretext for numerous representations of the female nude, Boucher flexed his astonishing imaginative power in the paintings and panels that he created for the Parisian elite; in the drawings that he did for collectors; in his compositions for the Beauvais[2] and Gobelins workshops[3]; in the subjects that he developed for the Vincennes and Sèvres workshops[4]; and in his decorative drawings for prints and for the decorations of fountains, vases, carriages, screens, theatre decor, book illustrations and a succession of small decorative objects (boxes, fans, etc.). ¶ Thus, according to Edmond and Jules Goncourt,

1. «[...] un monde insouciant, un monde jeune, la joie de vivre dans une nature idyllique qui ignore l'hiver, un printemps riche en espérances, un été sans canicule, un automne d'abondance où il suffit de tendre la main pour cueillir, un monde qui bannit tout effort...», cit. *in* VERSAILLES, 2004, p. 13.

2. Boucher was invited to collaborate with the Manufacture de Beauvais by Oudry, its director, in 1734. The first tapestries created after drawings by Boucher, *Fêtes Italiennes*, were woven in 1736.

3. After Oudry's death in 1755, Boucher broke off his collaboration with Beauvais and became inspector of the Manufacture des Gobelins, which also produced tapestries from his designs.

4. The porcelain workshop that was founded in Vincennes in 1738 and transferred to Sèvres in 1756 used designs conceived or inspired by Boucher for the decoration of its pieces.

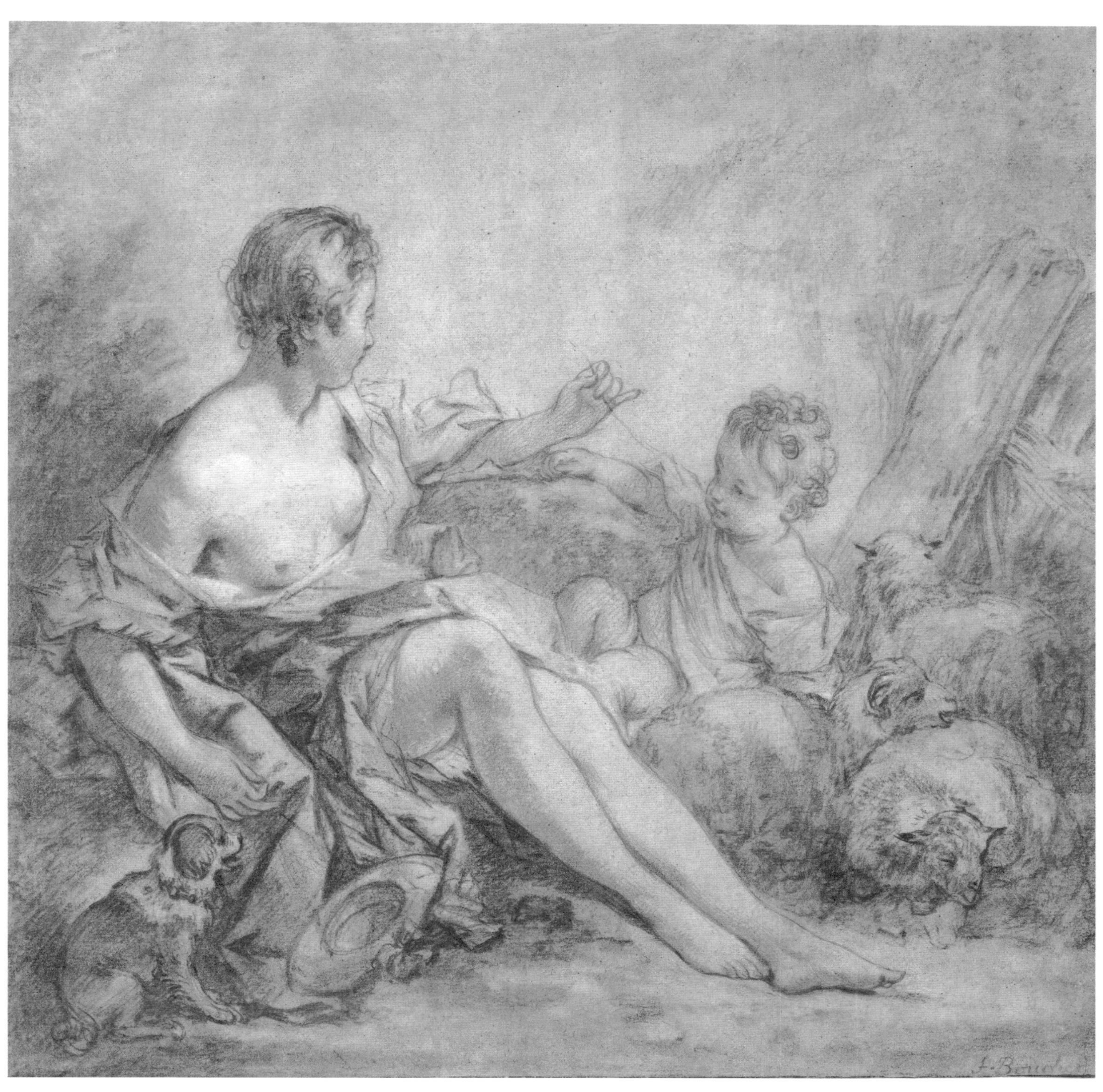

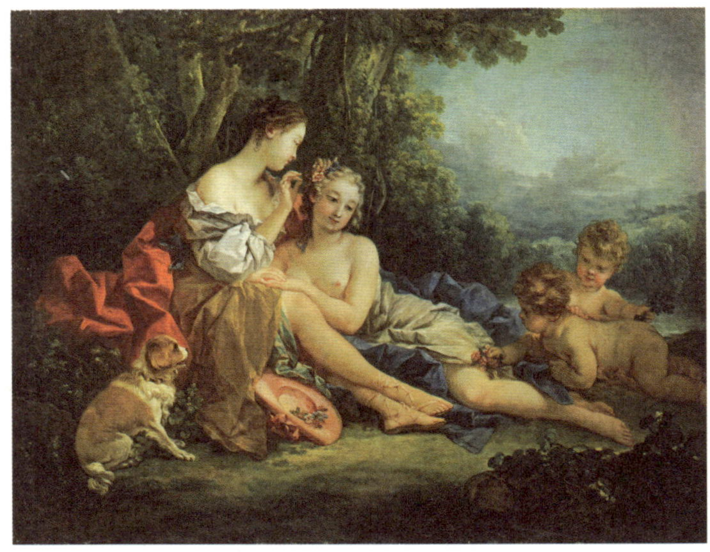

– fig. 8.1 –
François Boucher (1703–1770),
Spring, 1745.
Oil on canvas, 98.5 × 132 cm.
London, Wallace Collection, inv. P445.

writers who, in the nineteenth century, helped to rebuild the reputation of the painter, which had suffered criticism since the mid-eighteenth century for the frivolity and amorality of his works[5], "Boucher is one of the men who represent the taste of a century, that express, personify and embody it. The French taste in the eighteenth century manifested itself in him in terms of its unique nature: Boucher will remain its painter, as well as its witness, representative, its prototype"[6]. ¶ Of the group of François Boucher's drawings acquired by Calouste Gulbenkian, the work shown here, commonly known as *Shepherdess and Cupid*[7], is an example of the pastoral genre that brought the artist his greatest success and to which he dedicated himself until his final years. ¶ Boucher allowed himself to be seduced by this subject, with its long literary and artistic tradition and roots dating back to classical antiquity. In it he depicts an idealised vision of rural life in Arcadia, a kind of Paradise Lost, in which shepherds and shepherdesses lived in virtuous simplicity. In Boucher's pastoral scenes the characters often mingled with the gods of Olympus in joyous celebrations that were as pleasing to the artist as they were to his clientele. Influenced by his friend Charles-Simon Favart of the Théâtre de la Foire, which began using pastoral backdrops in 1730, Boucher reinvented the genre while adhering to the playwright's intention to create a more French atmosphere by setting the action on the outskirts of Paris and not in Arcadia, as had been done previously, and also by depicting figures with truly rustic characteristics after 1746–47. ¶ The pastoral scene shown here was the last work by Boucher to be acquired by Calouste Gulbenkian, in 1923[8]. It shows a rural scene containing three sheep, which lend a sense of realism, and a young woman who is tickling a child's plump face with a straw. This same game is repeated in other works by Boucher, such as the painting *Le Sommeil interrompu*, signed and dated 1750[9]. ¶ In the Gulbenkian drawing, the painter yet again surpassed himself in the portrayal of the female body which so delighted his patrons' sense of frivolity: the loose garments open languidly to reveal round breasts, shapely legs and delicate feet. ¶ Signed by the author on the lower right-hand side, there is no clear indication of the date on which the work was made. However, it can reasonably be dated from around 1745 given that many of its details allow it to be related to two of the four pastoral scenes that the artist made the same year to serve as decorations above door lintels[10]. The Gulbenkian drawing mirrors two of these paintings: *Le Printemps* (recorded under the title *La toilette pastorale*) (fig. 8.1), in which the

5. La Font de Saint-Yenne and Diderot were two of François Boucher's severest critics. At the *Salon* of 1765, the latter stated "I do not know what to say about this man. The degradation of taste, colour, composition, characters, and the expression of drawing has gradually served the depravation of moods" [«Je ne sais que dire de cet homme-ci. La dégradation du goût, de la couleur, de la composition, des caractères, de l'expression du dessin a servi pas à pas la dépravation des mœurs»]. See PARIS, SYDNEY, OTTAWA, 2003–6, p. 19.

6. «Boucher est un de ces hommes qui signifient le goût d'un siècle, qui l'expriment, le personnifient et l'incarnent. Le goût français du XVIII siècle s'est manifesté en lui dans toute la particularité de son caractère: Boucher en demeurera non seulement le peintre, mais le témoin, le représentant, le type." In GONCOURT, GONCOURT, 1880 ("Boucher"), p. 135.

7. I would like to thank Alastair Laing for generously providing me with information on Boucher's drawings (2011). Laing states that the nudity of the female form and her hairstyle are not actually those of a shepherdess but are more likely to be the representation of a nymph, meaning that the drawing could also be called *Nymph Tickling the Nose of a Small Boy with a Straw*.

8. In addition to the artist's drawings referred to in this catalogue, Calouste Gulbenkian also bought the painting *Cupid and the Three Graces* (inv. 433), in London in 1917. This work was created in 1738 as a version of the theme used to decorate the apartment of Marie-Sophie de Rohan, Princess of Soubise, at the Hôtel de Soubise. See SAMPAIO, 2009, no. 29, pp. 78–79, p. 79 (repr.).

9. Metropolitan Museum of Art, New York, inv. 49.7.46.

10. Despite numerous studies of these paintings, the place for which the paintings were intended is not known. See BUROLLET, 1980, no. 11, pp. 46–50; WILDENSTEIN, 1976, vol. 1, nos. 279-82, pp. 390–95 (drawing reproduced on p. 395, fig. 835); DETROIT, PARIS, 1986, pp. 222–25.

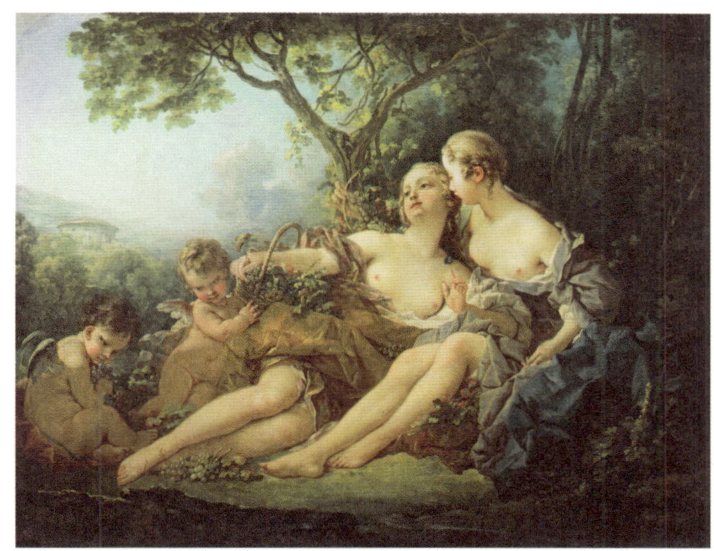

– fig. 8.2 –
François Boucher (1703–1770), *L'Automne*, 1745. Oil on canvas, 99 × 134.5 cm. London, Wallace Collection, inv. P447. ©2012 by kind permission of the Trustees of the Wallace Collection, London / Scala, Florence

dog that watches the scene unfold and the upturned hat are shown in the same position (the details of the dog and hat are recurring elements in Boucher's pastoral scenes); and *L' Automne* (in the print entitled *Erigone Vaincue*) (fig. 8.2), in which the nymph on the far right is an exact reproduction of the figure in the Gulbenkian drawing, having the same position and movement of the head, the same hairstyle, the same garments and the same style of nudity. The series of four paintings is completed by another conventional pastoral scene in *Les confidences pastorales*[11] and the return to mythology is undertaken in *Le retour de chasse de Diane*, also known as *Le repos des nymphes au retour de la chasse*[12]. ¶ These four paintings were made into rectangular prints by Claude Duflos the Younger (1700–1786). Duflos is certain to have worked from the drawings rather than the paintings, as the final result differs in several details. In February and May 1751, the *Mercure de France* announced the publication of the prints accompanied by titles and verses which alluded to the different contents[13].

11. Los Angeles County Museum of Art, inv. 47.29.17.

12. Paris, Musée Cognacq-Jay, inv. 10.

13. JEAN-RICHARD, 1978, nos. 917–22, pp. 238–39.

PROVENANCE

Max and Maurice Rosenheim Collection. Acquired by Calouste Gulbenkian at the sale of this collection, through Colnaghi, at Sotheby's, London, 2 May 1923, lot no. 51.

•

EXHIBITIONS

LONDON, 1913, no. 29, no. XVI (repr.); PORTO, 1964, no. 59 (repr.); OEIRAS, 1965, no. 112; LISBON, 1976, no. 48; LISBON, 1985, no. 6, p. 20, p. 130 (repr.); CAMBRIDGE, 2000, no. 93, pp. 208–09, p. 209 (repr.); LISBON, PORTO, 2000–2002, no. 93, pp. 208–09, p. 209 (repr.).

•

LITERATURE

WILDENSTEIN, 1976, vol. I, nos. 279–82, pp. 390–95, p. 395, fig. 835; BUROLLET, 1980, no. 11, p. 50.

[9]

MARIE-MADELEINE IGONET

(act. 1744–60)
Copy after François Boucher
Paris, 1703–1770

RURAL SCENE
or
FILLETTE APPÂTANT DES POULETS

France, ca. 1752

Black chalk on paper.
16 × 21.3 cm.
Signed on the lower left-hand side:
F. Boucher (?).
Inv. 865

This small drawing in black chalk shows a rural scene. The rustic atmosphere of the setting is transmitted by the tools used to work the land and by the sleepy cat, the haystacks, the freshly laid eggs, and the vine climbing over the porch. In the front yard in the foreground, a country girl is busy feeding the chickens, scattering grain for them from a basket hung from her waist. Further away is an old dovecote overlooking the leafy landscape beyond. ¶ When it became part of the Calouste Gulbenkian Collection in 1917, this drawing, which is of unknown provenance, was known as *Fillette appâtant des poulets* and was attributed to Jean-Baptiste Huet (1745–1811)[1]. However, in the schematic lines of the composition and in the tiniest details, a clear link can be established to the theme portrayed by Boucher in his painting *La Petite Fermière*[2], which is signed and dated 1752 (fig. 9.1). In addition, despite the slight wear suffered by the surface of the drawing in the aforementioned floods of 1967, careful scrutiny reveals the signature *F. Boucher* on the lower left-hand side. ¶ The possibility of the work being Huet's having been discarded, it becomes necessary to attempt to find the relationship between the Gulbenkian drawing and Boucher's painting. Ananoff[3] refers to the Gulbenkian drawing neither in his 1966 *Catalogue raisonné* nor in the extensive work that he published ten later years together with Daniel Wildenstein[4]. ¶ This latter publication provides information on the painting *La Petite Fermière*, which includes three prints related to it: *Jeanette*, printed by J. H. Eberts in the eighteenth century, is dedicated to "Monsieur F. Boucher, peintre du Roy"[5] and depicts a theme that is closer but different in the composition; another print by Claude Duflos (1704–1772) in a different format, entitled *La Petite Fermière* and accompanied by a poem[6]; and lastly, a print by Marie-Madeleine Igonet with the title *La petite ménagère*[7] (fig. 9.2). ¶ The Gulbenkian drawing has been the focus of several expert studies. Alexander Ananoff and Daniel Wildenstein[8] consider this piece to be the work of Boucher, who made it with the intention of producing a print. Pierrette Jean-Richard[9], an expert on the artist's prints, compares

1. See the catalogue for the sale, through Agnew, at Christie's, in London, 9 July 1917, lot no. 213.

2. ANANOFF, WILDENSTEIN, 1976, vol. II, no. 413, pp. 102–03, p. 102 (fig. 1164).

3. ANANOFF, 1966, vol. I.

4. ANANOFF, WILDENSTEIN, 1976.

5. *Ibidem*, vol. I, no. 255/3, p. 371 (fig. 768); JEAN-RICHARD, 1978; vol. I, no. 950, p. 102 (repr.), pp. 243–44.

6. ANANOFF, WILDENSTEIN, 1976, vol. II, no. 413/2, pp. 102–03, fig. 1165; JEAN-RICHARD, 1978, vol. I, no. 938, p. 242 (repr.)

7. ANANOFF, WILDENSTEIN, 1976, vol. II, no. 413/4, pp. 102–03, fig. 1166; JEAN-RICHARD, 1978, vol. I, no. 1196, p. 294.

8. I would like to thank these experts for sharing their information on the Gulbenkian drawing in the early 1980s. After contacting Alexander Ananoff, Daniel Wildenstein said that they both considered the Gulbenkian drawing to be Boucher's and that it would be included in the following volume, tome III, of the artist's paintings as one of the analogies with *La Petite Fermière*.

9. I would like to thank Pierre-Jean Richard for sharing information with me on the Gulbenkian drawing (1982).

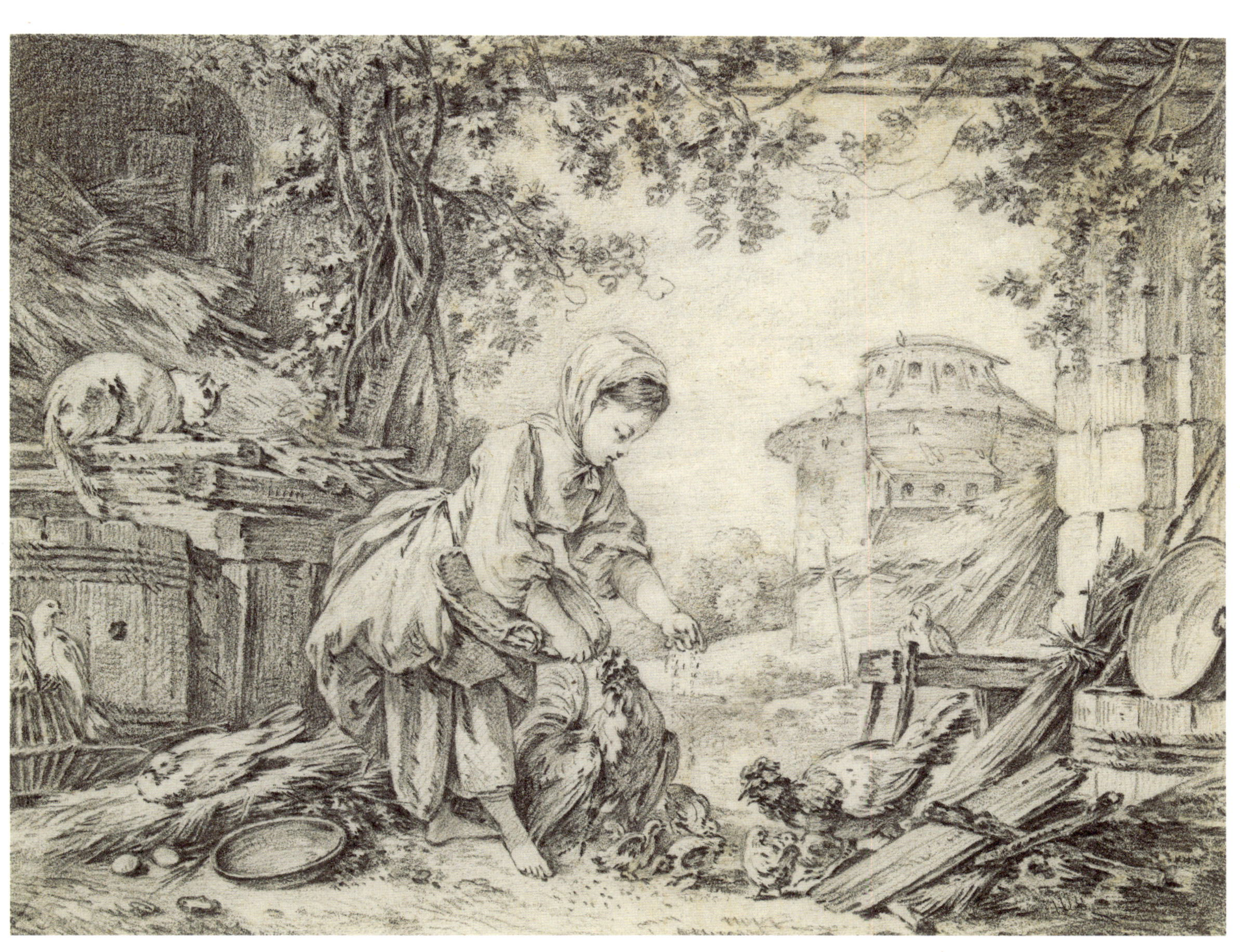

the Gulbenkian drawing with Igonet's print and points out that both show the same "gaucheness" in certain aspects, particularly in the way that the girl's hand is depicted. The author also posits that the information conveyed by the letters in the print (Boucher inv. and not *pinx.* or *del.*) may suggest that the print was not created from a painting or a drawing by the artist but was an interpretation of Boucher's theme made by one of his followers or by the printer herself. For Alastair Laing[10], the comparison between the Gulbenkian drawing and the drawing[11] that is linked to another of Boucher's paintings, *La Petite Fermière* or *Le Bol de Bouillie*[12], led him to conclude that the latter, due to its superior quality, was probably the Master's work, while the former may have been made by Mlle. Igonet to interpret the print. ¶ Marie-Madeleine Igonet, a printer working in Paris in the mid-eighteenth century, used the etching and burin technique to depict the subject of the Gulbenkian drawing in great detail but in reverse. This print, like the one by Duflos, lacks only the scene of the rooster and chicken that appears in the painting, giving it an unmistakable touch of frivolity. ¶ In the face of all this, the question of the Gulbenkian drawing's authorship remains problematic. ¶ A highly productive painter, Boucher depicted pastoral scenes, mythological scenes, children's games and small love scenes, and devoted a fair proportion of his work to creating rural scenes that celebrated the simplicity of country life and rural environments. ¶ Influenced by Dutch genre scenes, particularly those of Abraham Bloemaert (1566–1651), whose original drawings he interpreted in prints in 1735, Boucher dedicated himself to this genre (which was much in demand by Parisian collectors) from a young age, even prior to his trip to Italy in 1728, and he continued to work it even in his last years of artistic production. In the intimate interior scenes and the depictions of rural exteriors in which he recorded the picturesque contours of the French country landscape, he showed his more spontaneous and naturalistic creative side, inspired by the direct observation of nature. ¶ In these works, however, the aim is not, as in Dutch painting, to express the protagonists' social reality but rather to show the relationships established between them. The painter does not depict the untamed side of rural life, as this would have displeased his elite clientèle. In contrast to Chardin's realistic depictions and Greuze's moralistic paintings, Boucher's characters are eternally young (gardeners, cooks, milk-maids, country folk, fishermen, washerwomen), and are peacefully resigned to their daily chores in an idyllic unchanging world, where there is sometimes a place for gallantries, as in *La Belle Cuisinière*[13], a work currently owned by the Musée Cognacq-Jay in Paris. The Calouste Gulbenkian Museum owns a copy of the print in which Pierre Aveline (1702–1760) conveyed Boucher's theme in etching and burin, and which dates from around 1735.

10. I would like to thank Alastair Lang for generously sharing information on the Gulbenkian drawing when I was preparing this book (2011).

11. ANANOFF, 1966, no. 5, pp. 24–25; "réproductions", n.p., fig. 1.

12. ANANOFF, WILDENSTEIN, 1976, vol. II, no. 414, pp. 103–04, fig. 1168.

13. NEW YORK, DETROIT, PARIS, 1986–1987, no. 21, pp. 150–53, p. 151 (repr.).

PROVENANCE

Acquired by Calouste Gulbenkian through Agnew & Sons, at Christie's, London, 9 July 1917, lot no. 213.

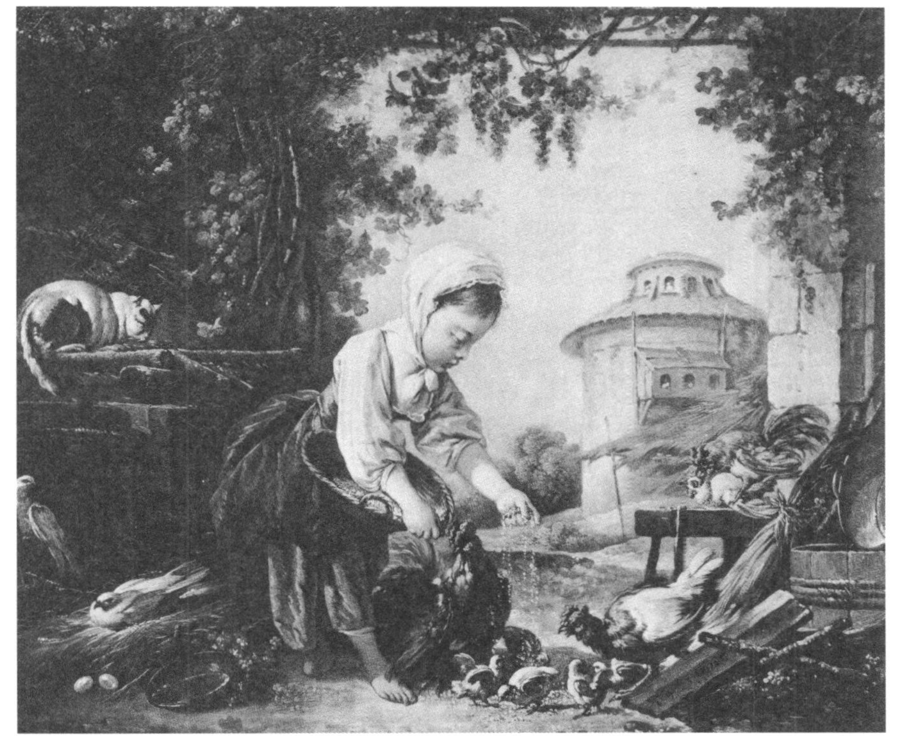

– fig. 9.1 –
François Boucher
(1703–1770),
La Petite Fermière, 1752.
Oil on canvas, 52 × 63 cm.
Whereabouts unknown.

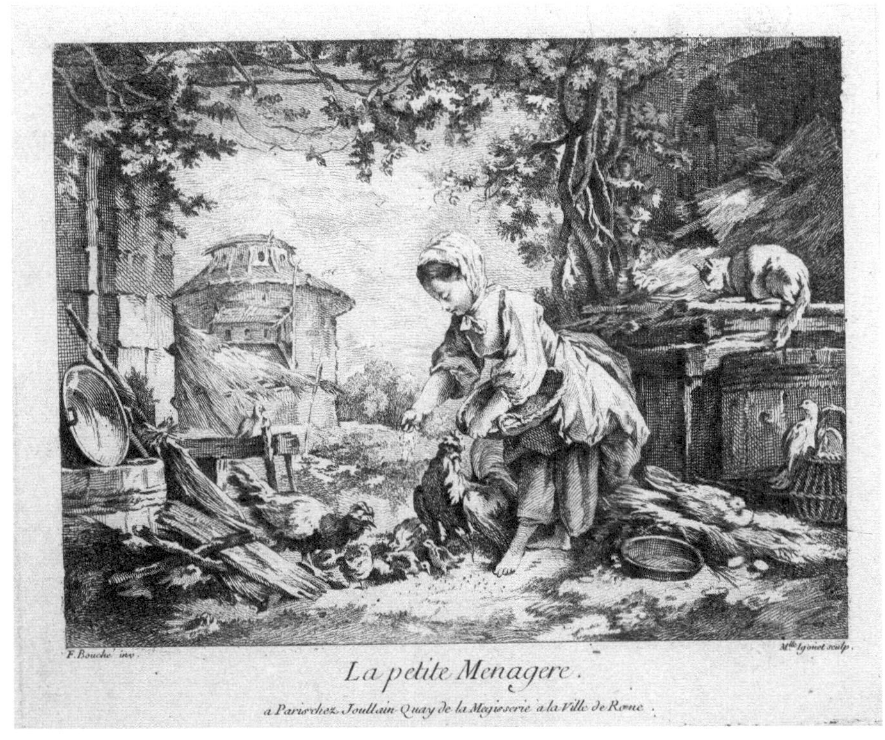

– fig. 9.2 –
Marie-Madeleine Igonet
(act. 18th century),
La petite ménagère,
after François Boucher
(1703–1770).
Etching and burin,
16.5 × 21.7 cm.
Paris, Musée du Louvre,
Rothschild Collection,
inv. 18720LR.

[10]

FRANÇOIS BOUCHER

Paris, 1703–1770

RECLINING FEMALE NUDE

France, 1760–65

Black and white chalk with stumping
and touches of red chalk on grey paper.
28.3 × 40.7 cm.
Inv. 515

Boucher's early virtuosity as a painter and his clear understanding of the cultural backgrounds of his age enabled him to create a vast body of work characterized by sensual, idyllic, and joyful compositions in response to his public's taste for pleasant and illusory themes. ¶ The most common of the artist's themes were mythological representations, which recurred constantly throughout his career from his time as a student to the height of his artistic maturity. Paintings, drawings, prints and tapestries depict scenes frequently inspired by literature, in which the protagonists are the gods of Olympus surrounded by their nymphs and love intrigues. Sometimes appearing alongside them are shepherds and shepherdesses shown in scenes that delighted the eighteenth-century French aristocracy. The mythological scenes nearly always gave the opportunity to portray numerous nudes, particularly female nudes. *Le Triomphe de Venus*[1] is a perfect example of these. ¶ The female nude is portrayed in multiple poses: from the front, from behind, outstretched, sitting down, or lying prone, immediately recalling, in the latter case, the painting *L' Odalisque blonde*, 1752[2]. All have a common thread of feminine beauty allied with an air of innocence and eternal youth. None of their faces shows the slightest expression of feeling or emotion. Boucher knew that such expressions would please neither his patrons nor his admirers and so instead he showed figures full of vitality, grace and femininity. ¶ As well as being a painter, Boucher was also an academician[3] for whom drawing preparatory studies from life models was a daily task over the course of a long professorial career. He drew countless studies that were either incorporated into his pastoral and mythological works or that appeared as works in their own right. Boucher's work was particularly appreciated by the numerous admirers of female nudes. Later, in the nineteenth century, the Goncourt brothers revealed themselves to be as enthusiastic about the artist's work as his contemporary admirers had been: "There is nothing more charming than Boucher's academies of women! They are amusing, provocative, a delight to the eyes. [...] And they have so many different postures, constantly renewing this

1. Stockholm, Nationalmuseum, inv. NM770.

2. Munich, Alte Pinakothek, inv. 1166

3. Brought into the Royal Academy of Painting and Sculpture in 1731 as a history painter, Boucher was accepted as an academic in 1734 with his painting *Renaud et Armide*. See NEW YORK, DETROIT, PARIS, 1986–1987, no. 26, pp. 164–66.

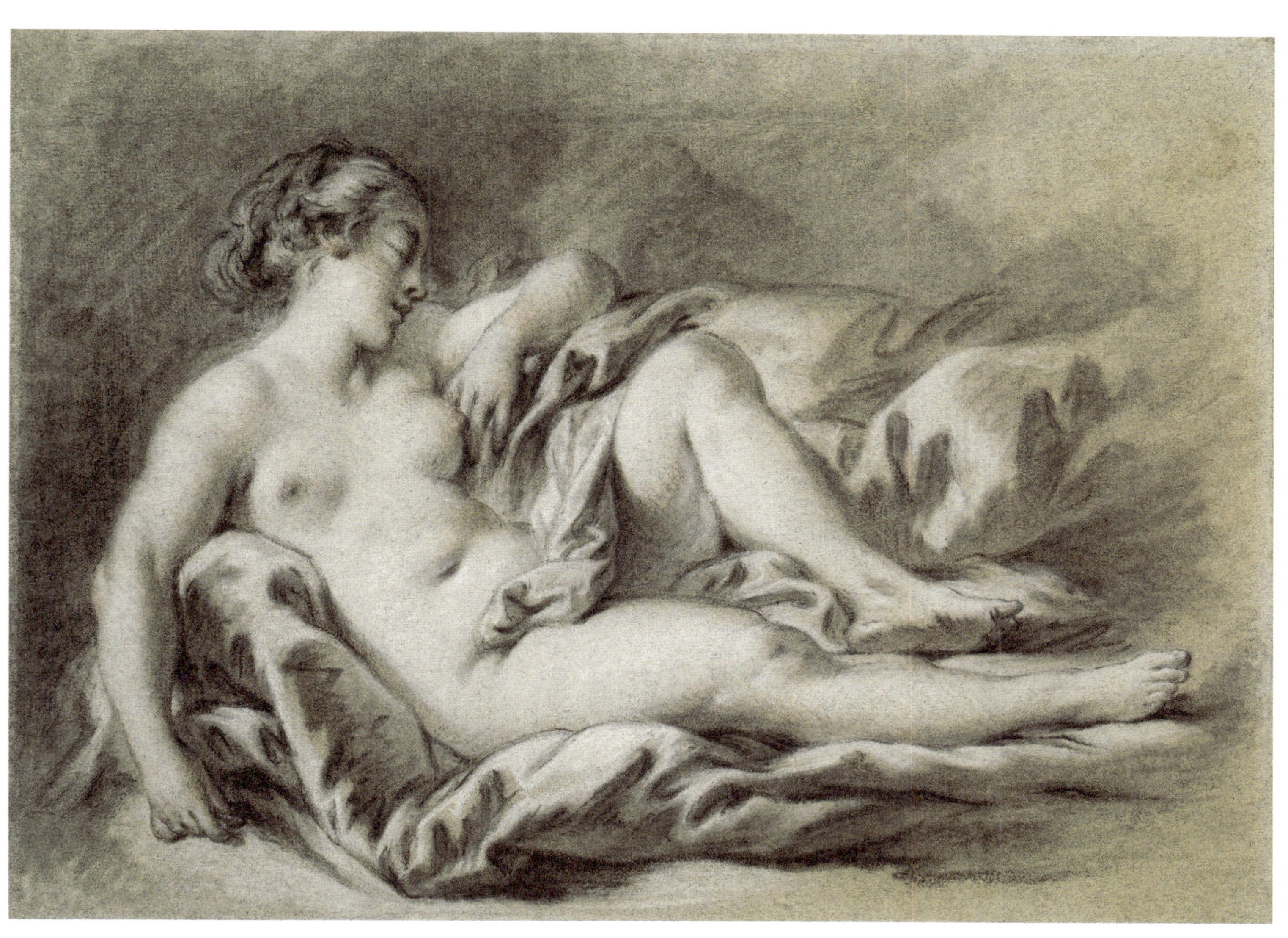

4. "Quoi de plus charmant que des académies de femmes de Boucher! Elles amusent, elles provoquent, elles chatouillent le regard. [...] Et quelle variété, quelle diversité de postures, renouvelant sans cesse ce poème de la nudité agaçante!", *in* GONCOURT, GONCOURT, 1880, p. 151.

5. Paris, Musée du Louvre, inv. 2723.

6. New York, The Metropolitan Museum of Art, inv. 49.7.46.

poem on the annoying nudity!"[4] ¶ In many of these studies, as in this drawing, the figures are portrayed in a peaceful somnolence, wearing mysterious smiles and exuding a dream-like quality. From time to time, Boucher varied the meaning of the scene by including, for example, an onlooker admiring the beauty of the vision presented (*La Bergère endormie*)[5], an innocent game showing a shepherd tickling a young woman's neck with a straw (*Le Sommeil interrompu*)[6], or a moment of sweet romance (*Daphnis et Chloé*) (fig. 10.1). ¶ The Gulbenkian Collection drawing *Reclining Female Nude* shows a young woman lying on her right side on a cloth that completely covers the seat supporting her. Her hair is held up and tied with a ribbon from which a few unruly curls escape, and her head hangs tranquilly over her left shoulder. Her eyes are closed, her lips innocently parted, and the flaccidity of her loose arms, the abandonment of her legs, with the right leg outstretched and the left leg bent, all help to create the impression that she is succumbing to a deep and languid sleep. ¶ In this black-chalk drawing the artist uses the stump to accentuate the volume and uses white gouache to highlight and create points of light under the body which contrast with the dark background, particularly

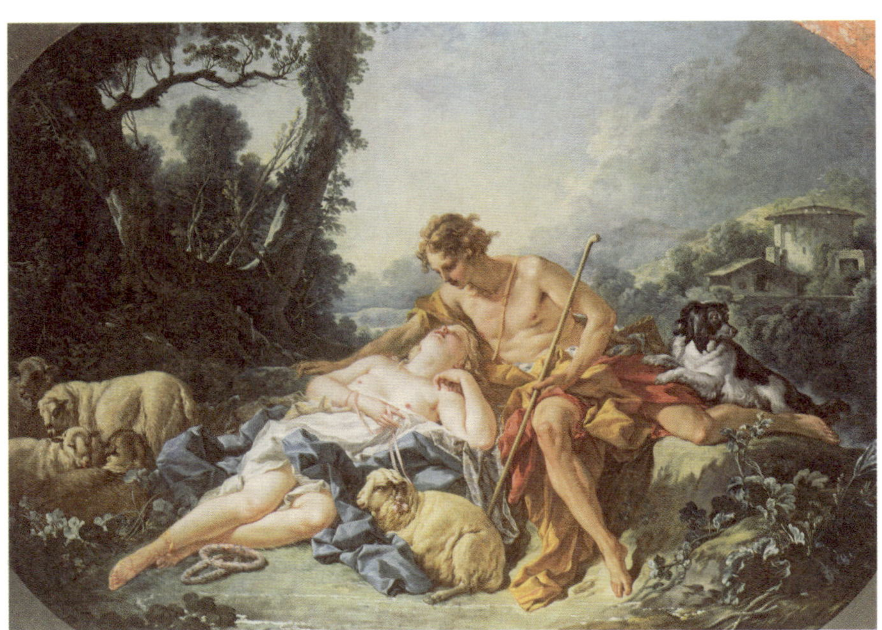

– fig. 10.1 –
François Boucher (1703–1770), *Daphnis et Chloé*, 1743. Oil on canvas, 109.5 × 154.8 cm. London, Wallace Collection, inv. P385.

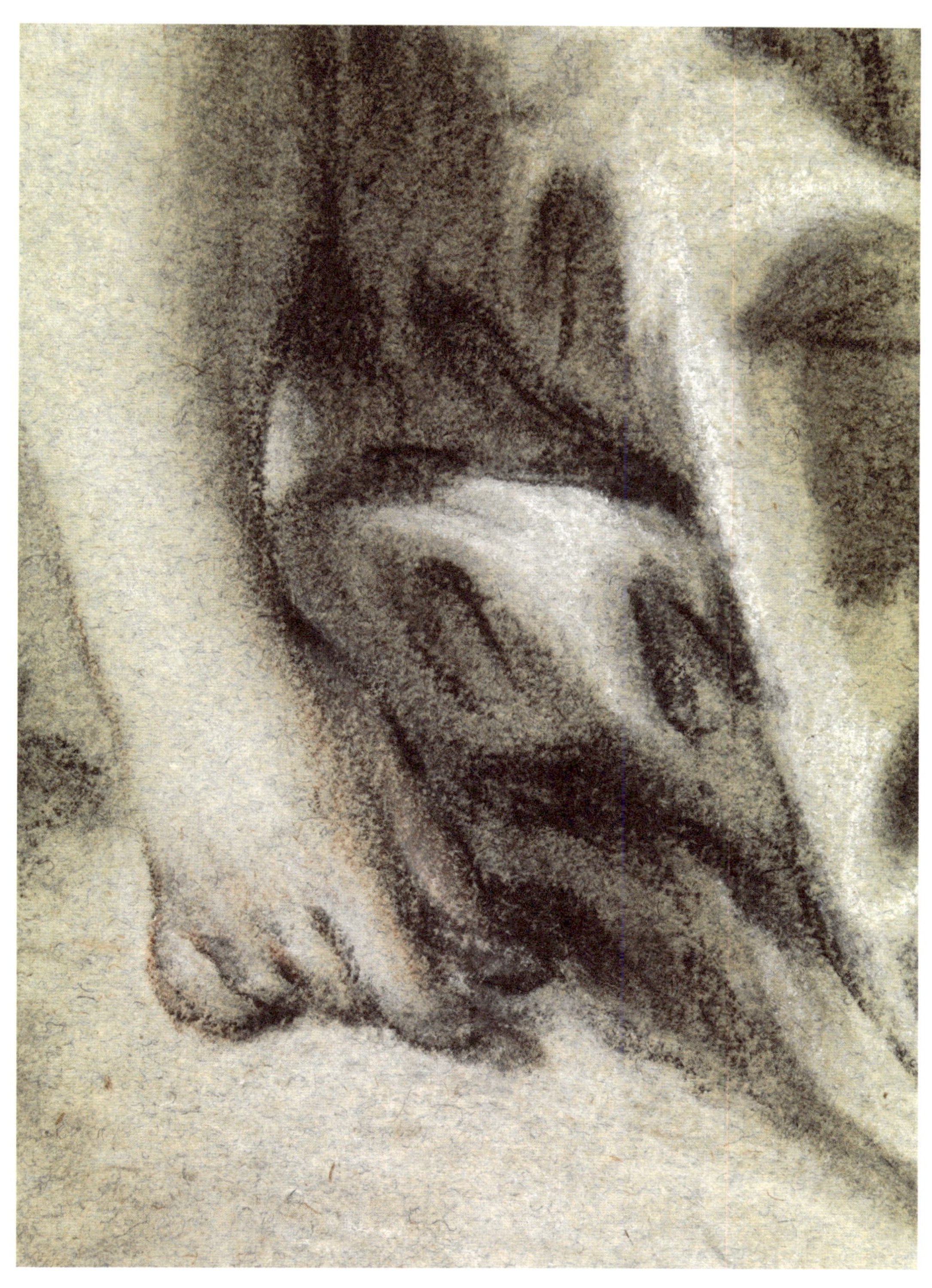

– fig. 10.2 –
Detail of [10].

7. I would like to thank Alastair Laing for his kind collaboration studying this drawing (2011).

8. *Oskar Reinhart Collection*, 2005, no. 46, pp. 256–57, note 6.

behind the head. Some of the folds in the cloth are in watercolour and some of the details of the young woman's body are accentuated in red chalk to better convey their sensuality. ¶ Boucher drew this work after he had gained greater mastery in his portrayal of the female body, which lends it greater naturalness. Whether working from a life model or from memory, the artist depicted a voluptuous and perfectly proportioned figure that may have dated from the first half of the 1760s[7]. ¶ A common feature of all stages of Boucher's career, this genre of drawing represents a variety of nymphs and goddesses, particularly Diana and Venus, although this fact was not considered relevant to this Gulbenkian work due to the absence of these divinities' usual attributes. However, a more careful look reveals the tip of a small arrow in the figure's right hand which continues behind, ill-defined but perceptible (fig. 10.2). This makes it possible to identify the figure with one of the two goddesses who are so often the subject of the artist's work. ¶ This drawing was part of the famous collection of the Marquess of Lansdowne that was sold at an auction held at Sotheby's in 1920, where it was bought by Calouste Gulbenkian. In this collection, the drawing was paired with another, *Reclining Nude*[8] (fig. 10.3) which showed a figure from behind. This drawing was used by Boucher as a preparatory study for more than one of his works. According to the

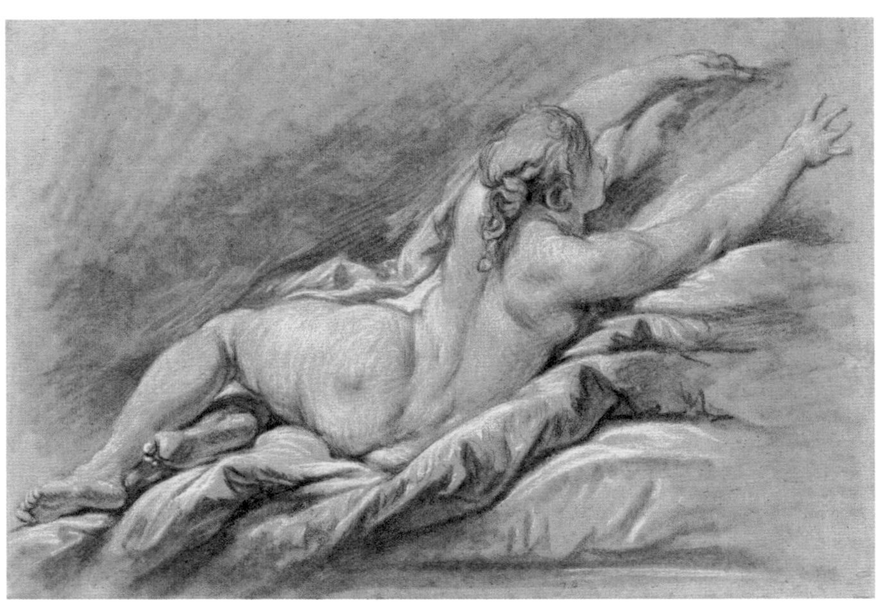

– fig. 10.3 –
François Boucher (1703–1770), *Reclining Nude*, ca. 1750–53. Black and white chalk on blue paper, 26 × 36 cm. Collection Oskar Reinhart "Am Römerholz" Winterthur, inv. 1926.3

Lansdowne Collection's sale catalogue, both drawings were "framed by Glomy", a reference to Jean-Baptiste Glomy, an eighteenth-century frame specialist and manufacturer whose work was greatly valued by collectors of the time. ¶ Ananoff and Wildenstein state that the Gulbenkian drawing is one of those related to the subject of the painting *Le Repos de Diane*[9], a painting dating from 1722 which has now disappeared. Among other works, this reference also mentions a print[10] by Jean Pelletier (ca. 1736-?) with the same title, and a gouache[11] by Jacques Charlier (ca. 1705–1790), entitled *Le Faune*, which has a very similar composition to the former. Louis-Marin Bonnet (1736–1793) interpreted one of Boucher's drawings in a pencil-style print[12] entitled *Le Sommeil de Venus*, which was mentioned by the paper *Avant-Coureur* in December 1771, and in which the goddess' pose is very similar to that seen in the Gulbenkian Museum drawing.

9. ANANOFF, WILDENSTEIN, 1976, vol. 1, 1976, no. 6, pp. 161–62.

10. *Ibidem*, no. 6/1, pp. 161–62, fig. 190.

11. *Ibidem*, no. 6/1, bis, p. 162, fig. 191.

12. JEAN-RICHARD, 1978, no. 361, p. 117 (repr.).

PROVENANCE

Marquess of Lansdowne Collection. Acquired by Calouste Gulbenkian at the sale of this collection, through Colnaghi, at Sotheby's, London, 25 March 1920, lot no. 8 (repr.).

•

EXHIBITIONS

PORTO, 1964, no. 62 (repr.); OEIRAS, 1965, no. 111; LISBON, 1976, no. 51 (repr.); LISBON, 1985, no. 7, p. 20, p. 131 (repr.).

[11–12]

FRANÇOIS BOUCHER

Paris 1703–1770

PAIR OF CUPIDS WITH A BASKET OF FLOWERS

France, late 1760

Black chalk with white chalk highlights on light-brown paper.
30.4 × 15.4 cm.
Inv. 172 A/B

Calouste Gulbenkian bought these two works in 1914 at the sale of the collection of the Marquis de Biron, a collector of French and Italian drawings and a connoisseur of frames. This fact may explain why these works were sold along with Louis XV carved and gilded wooden frames with girded sides that are ornamented at the corners with shells and garlands of foliage, the outside being encircled by an egg trim[1]. These features add to the *rocaille* feel of the drawings, with their asymmetries, irregular shapes and excessive ornamentation. ¶ Unlike the previous drawing [10], in this piece Boucher uses a sketch-like visual language that was to become typical of his later drawing work, comprising rapid movements that set out the volumes and include only those elements necessary for inserting the figures, without paying much heed to the finer details. A less obvious reading of the surface of these two drawings might discern that both sheets were damaged in the flooding of 1967. However, Alastair Laing[2] points out their obvious quality, linkening them to another drawing by Boucher, *Fountain with Tritons and Dolphins*, which belonged to the Albert Meyer Collection. ¶ Boucher's work is characterised by a penchant for decorative elements, leading to the inclusion of ornamental motifs in his interior decoration projects and all other types of work, including paintings and tapestries which feature fountains, groups of statues and bridges in the background, as well as prints or even book illustrations, as in the famous edition of *L'Œuvre de Molière*, created in 1734–35[3]. ¶ These two apparently similar drawings form a pair that share the same subject but contain a large number of differences in their details. In the first drawing (172A), two *putti* stand with their arms aloft, supporting a basket full of flowers, on top of which two birds flit atop a flower-covered, standing on a cone-shaped plinth with fluted sides and eggs around the base. On a ledge behind the plinth, against a backdrop of abundant flowers, are the symbols of Bacchus: a jug on one side and a tambourine on the other. In the second drawing (172 B) the pedestal appears smooth and rounded, with a circular rim at the base. Again, the *putti* are holding a basket of flowers that

1. Reference in the sale catalogue to the Biron Collection, Paris, 1914, lots 7 and 8.

2. I would like to offer my sincere thanks to this expert for generously sharing his opinions on these drawings (2011).

3. The Art Library established by Calouste Gulbenkian contains the six volumes from this edition, which brings together a number of specific features (inv. LA 247 A/F). See LISBON, 2006a, no. 37, pp. 143–45, p. 143 (repr.).

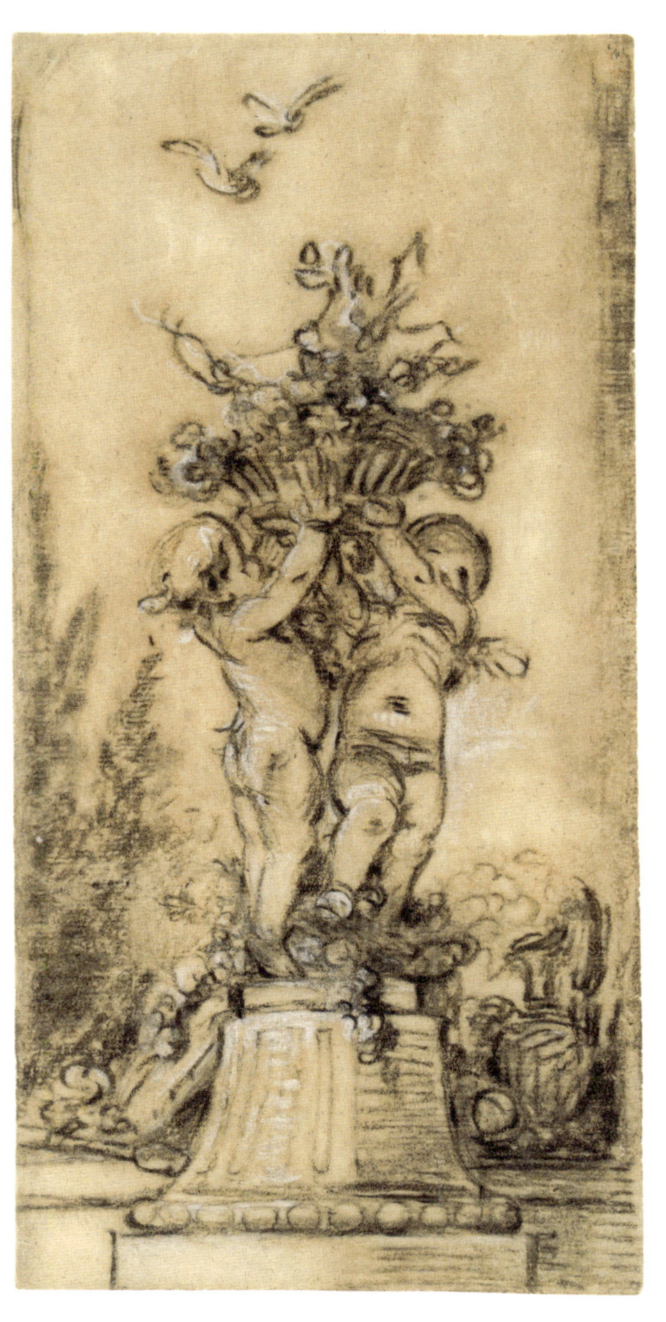

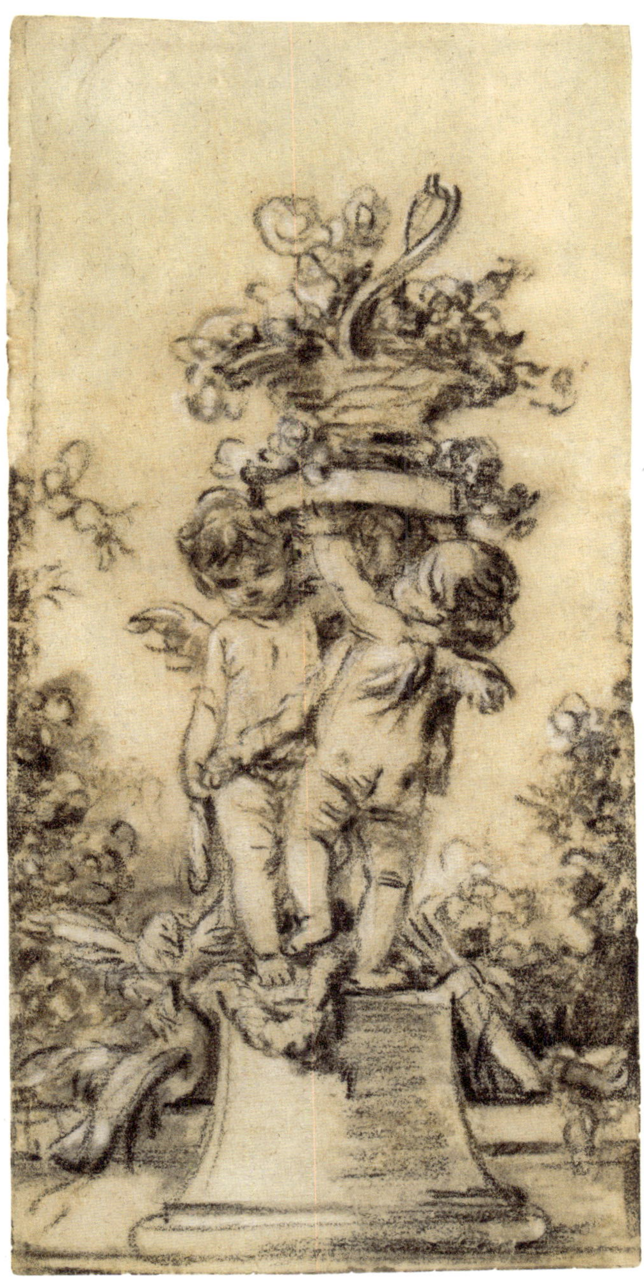

4. ANANOFF, 1966, nos. 841 and 842, p. 217, "réproductions," n.p.: figs. 136 and 137.

5. Alastair Laing disagrees with this attribution, as the initials E.G. appear at the bottom of the drawing, on the left-hand side, suggesting that it might be the work of Edmond de Goncourt. Laing identifies it as belonging to the collection of Emil Wolf, New York. For this drawing see ST PETERSBURG, FL, 1982, p. 15, no. 28 (repr.), and fig. 11–12.1.

6. This drawing was a study for a vase shown in a lost painting, recorded by Aliamet as *La Bergère prévoyante*, exhibited at the 1763 *Salon*. See ANANOFF, 1966, no. 974, p. 251, "réproductions," n.p.: fig. 158; ANANOFF, WILDENSTEIN, 1976, vol. II, no. 574/4, p. 227, fig. 1551.

is identical to the one in the first drawing, but this time one of them keeps one hand free to hold a garland of flowers. On the low wall behind the pedestal are the symbols of Venus, with Cupid's quiver and arrows on one side, and two doves – also symbols of love – on the other. ¶ According to the sale catalogue, these drawings were intended as decorative drafts for a series of garden sculptures, an opinion stated again in the *Catalogue raisonné* by Alexander Ananoff[4]. However, Alastair Laing believes that such a purpose is not supported by the inclusion of the features next to the base of the pedestals; instead, he considers that thee drawings may be studies for interior wall decorations, probably identical to those covering the walls of the Salon Desmarteau at the Musée Carnavalet in Paris. Laing points out that a drawing attributed to Boucher, Garden Urn and Statues, lent to the exhibition "Fragonard and His Friends" in St Petersburg, Florida, reproduced the two drawings from the Gulbenkian Collection, along with a garden vase decorated with a satyr's mask and a frieze depicting *putti* (figs. 11–12.1)[5]. This vase also appears in another drawing belonging to the Biron Collection (no. 6) and, previously, to the collection of the Goncourt brothers (1897)[6]. ¶ Boucher was just as fond of depicting *putti* or simply children in everyday scenes as he was of portraying pastoral or mythological scenes, as is evident in his very earliest works. Classical literature and art were a frequent source of inspiration for this type of piece during the Renaissance, in particular when tackling decorative and allegorical themes.

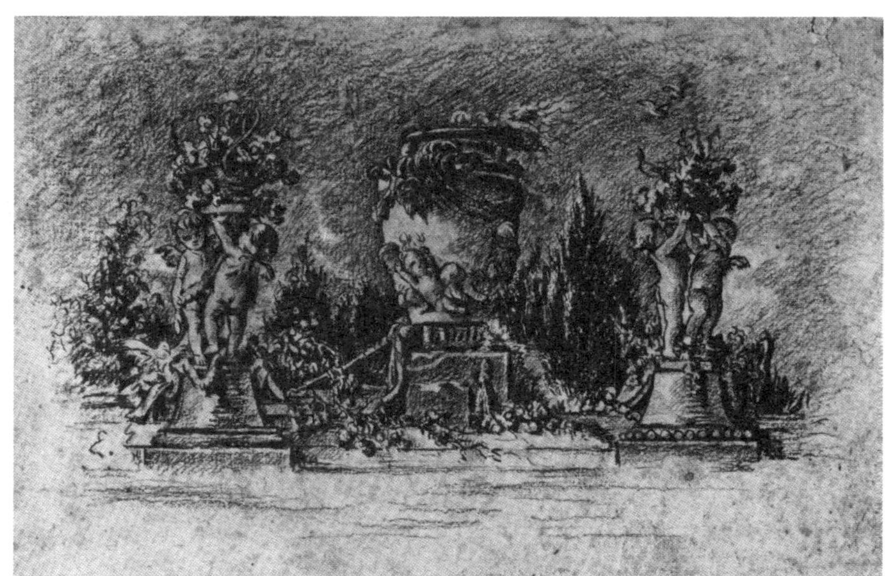

– fig. 11–12.1 –
François Boucher (1703–1770), *Garden Urn and Statues*
Red chalk on graphite, 21.08 × 31.75 cm.
Private collection.
Whereabouts unknown.

Boucher appears to have been a forerumers in this area, raising the portrayal of cupids to that of a separate genre. His penchant for depicting *putti* must have started in Italy; in 1728 he travelled to Rome to stay at the French Academy, which at that time was under the directorship of Nicolas Vleughels[7]. From 1731 onwards, Boucher's work increasingly comprised either whole compositions dedicated to cupids, in which they are the main figures, or pieces in which they are included, mainly to emphasise feminine sensuality. By giving free rein to his imagination, the painter created an infinite repertoire of *putti* in a wide range of contexts: sleeping or awake; playing or lying in a woman's lap. ¶ Between 1735 and 1740 Boucher sketched out drawings for several books in the series *Groupes d'enfants*, which was published by Gabriel Huquier le Vieux and engraved by Aveline, Huquier le Jeune and Louis-Félix de la Rue. These compositions are lacking in decorative backgrounds and the figures appear as though suspended in the air, reclining on the light clouds that surround them like cushions. These chubby children with rumpled hair are normally depicted in small groups, sometimes holding the symbols of the god of love. On other occasions they are portrayed as allegories of drawing, music and painting, while sometimes they may merely be small children engaged in everyday tasks, appearing as little gardeners, shepherds or peasants[8]. ¶ Almost all of Boucher's works featuring cupids or small children have become coveted items among collectors. Madame de Pompadour (1721–1764), who came to the French court in 1745 as a favourite of King Louis XV, became a fervent admirer of this genre and had such images reproduced in various media, in particular Sèvres porcelain, Beauvais and Gobelins tapestries, and on various small ornaments. ¶ The allegorical and youthful aesthetic favoured in the eighteenth century explains the popularity of Boucher's compositions depicting children. Like other works by the artist featuring nymphs and shepherdesses, such pieces make poetic and visually pleasing allusions while appealing to the senses.

7. NEW YORK, DETROIT, PARIS, 1986–1987, p. 21.

8. See BRUNEL, Georges – "Boucher : le corps et le décor», *in* PARIS, SYDNEY, OTTAWA, 2003–2006, p. 89.

PROVENANCE

Marquis de Biron Collection. Acquired by Calouste Gulbenkian, in the sale of this collection, through Agnew & Sons, at Galerie Georges Petit, in Paris, 9 June 1914, lot nos. 7 and 8.

•

EXHIBITIONS

PORTO, 1964, no. 57 (repr.).

•

LITERATURE

ANANOFF, 1966, vol. 1, nos. 841–42, p. 217, figs. 136, 137.

[13]

CHARLES-NICOLAS COCHIN, THE YOUNGER

Paris, 1715 – 1790

BIRTH OF LOUIS XV

France, 1753

Graphite on paper.
33.5 × 22.9 cm.
Signed and dated:
C. N. Cochin filius delineavit. 1753
Mark of the Alfred Beurdeley Collection
on the right-hand corner of the recto – AB (Lugt 421).
Inv. 459

Calouste Gulbenkian began his small but significant collection of European drawings with two acquisitions from the sale of the Alfred Beurdeley Collection in Paris, March 1905, where he had the opportunity to buy Cochin's work *Birth of Louis XV*, the work now being discussed. ¶ Charles-Nicolas Cochin, the Younger was one of the brightest names in French art in the second half of the eighteenth century[1]. His work shows his natural gift for drawing and printmaking and he was fortunate also to have been born into a family of artist-printmakers; according to the Goncourt brothers, "He grew-up amidst this neighbourhood of printers"[2]. He received rigorous training from his father, Charles-Nicolas Cochin (1688–1754), first learning the art of burin engraving and then moving on to etching, which he preferred. His drawing skills led him to complete his training with Jean Restout II, (1692–1768) and he also, on occasion, discreetly visited the studio of J.-P. Le Bas (1707–1783), who helped him develop his art. Cochin was only twelve-years-old when he completed his first print on a religious theme – *Sainte Famille*[3] – and at sixteen he had already started to draw Parisian street scenes filled with small groups of common people[4]. ¶ As a draughtsman and engraver, one of his most fundamental contributions to French art was his work as an illustrator[5], which he probably first attempted at the invitation of Charles-Antoine Jombert (1712–1784), who, besides being a printer and bookseller, was also the young Cochin's long-standing friend and the publisher of the catalogue of his work[6]. The most beautiful editions of eighteen-century illustrated *rocaille* books included the artist's work, which initially involved the use of decorative elements (frontispieces, fleurons, vignettes, *culs-de-lampe)* and also thematic prints which were later expressed in a more allegorical language or in narratives directly related to the text. ¶ With his solid artistic training, and his intelligence, culture and talent, Cochin began to garner respect in the 1730s before reaching the peak of his abilities between 1751–70. The public, and even the often critical Diderot, loved his work[7], and he received numerous commissions. Working as draughts-

1. For more on this, see MICHEL, 1993.

2. "Il grandit au milieu de ce quartier de la gravure...". GONCOURT, GONCOURT, 1882, VOL. II, p. 52.

3. *Ibidem*, p. 52, note 1.

4. *Ibidem*, p. 54.

5. For more on this subject, see MICHEL, 1987.

6. See C.A. Jombert, *Catalogue de l'œuvre de Ch. Nic.Cochin fils.* Paris, 1770, quoted *in* MICHEL, 1987, p. 415.

7. Diderot was on good terms with Cochin and admired his talent and spirit. Despite this affection, the philosopher still on occasion heavily criticised the artist's work and theories, as happened with Cochin's drawings for President Hénault's (Charles-Jean-François Hénault, 1685–1770) *L'Abrégé chronologique de l'Histoire de France* that were presented at the 1767 *Salon*. See PORTALIS, 1877, VOL. I, pp. 106–07.

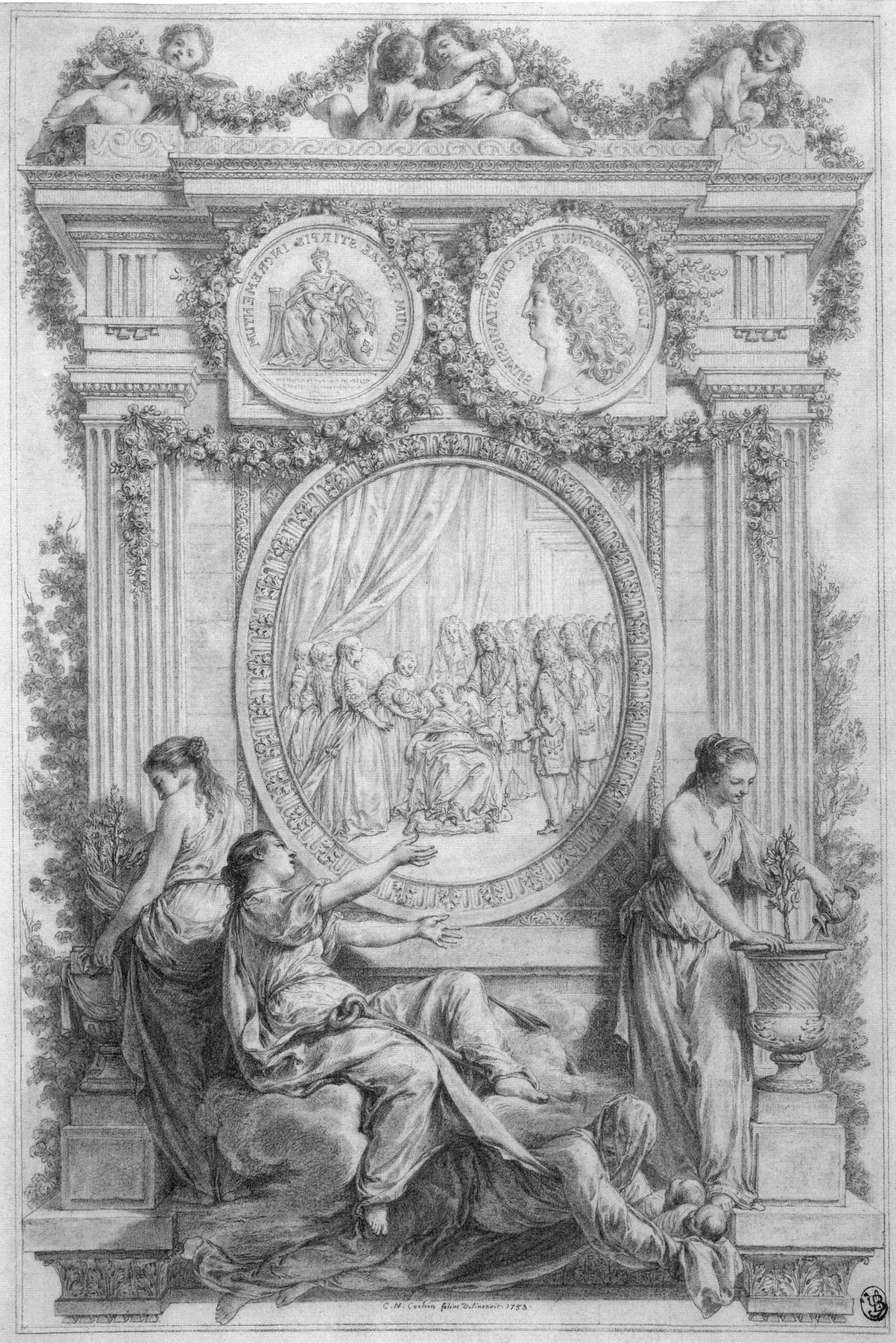
C.N. Cochin filius Delineavit. 1753.

man for the King's *Menus-Plaisirs* between 1736 and 1751, he made his own large prints, showing scenes depicting the festivities and official ceremonies of the court (firework displays, marriages, funerals, dances, etc.) as well as the related decorations and ephemeral architecture. He was an influential member of the Royal Academy of Painting and Sculpture where he held various positions[8] and played a considerable role in fostering the arts. In his attempt to better understand art and its relation with artists he became a theoretician and inspired Neoclassicism in his country[9]. The talent that he had shown from an early age earned him a place under the wing of Madame de Pompadour and her brother, the Marquess of Marigny, to whom he became a trusted confidante[10]. His worldly ways made him a regular guest at high-society parties and dinners and he was an eminent figure in the cultural *Salons* of Madame Geoffrin (1699–1777). ¶ According to the Goncourt brothers, Cochin

> "[...] was the artist sought after, requested by the court and the town at the time, tormented by the organizers of festivities, and by book printers for all types of drawings and engravings, at the time so associated with luxury. His ability to respond is a triumph over time, of the number of orders, of the variety and multiple works. The hour will come where vignettes will no longer be named vignettes, but rather *Cochin's*"[11].

After his return from Italy he reached maturity as an artist; the numerous positions that he held meant that he did not have as much time for the art of printmaking as he once had, and so he opted to execute drawings which could then be made into prints by other artists, while also managing a variety of other undertakings connected with printmaking. However, in 1752 he did not hesitate to accept a royal commission for a collection of fifteen prints on *L'Histoire de Louis XV par Médailles*[12], which was similar to the work carried out by Sébastien Leclerc (1637–1714)[13] for Louis XIV. In contrast to Leclerc, who had limited himself to recording the monarch's medals within allegorical cartouches, Cochin drew and recorded more complex compositions which historically and allegorically evoked the themes of the medals included. In a style which showed his evolution towards Neoclassicism, he drew eight of the main compositions, five of which he also made into prints, as well as undertaking nine decorations for the pages of text. This publication, which also involved the work of other artists[14], was never completed. ¶ *Birth of Louis XV*, the drawing discussed here, was the first work in this collection to be planned and printed in 1753 by Cochin and exhibited at the 1755 *Salon* together with the three following compositions:*Death of Louis XIV*, (fig. 13. 1); *The Ascension of Louis XV to the Throne*, (fig. 13.2), and *The Declaration of the Regency, 1715*[15]. ¶ In this work, the artist depicted the birth of Louis XV on 15 February 1710. Inside an oval cartouche within a classical architectural structure is the image of Marie-Adélaide de Savoie, the Duchess of Burgundy, taking into her arms her new-born son, Louis, Duke of Anjou, and future King of France, known as *le Bien-Aimé*. The still-exhausted mother is watched over by her husband Louis de France (1682–1712) and by several members of the court. At the bottom of the composition are four allegorical figures which reinforce the importance of the event and symbolize the contrast between Life and Death, past

8. He became an associate member in 1741 and a full member by unanimous vote in 1751 after his return from Italy; then, after the death of Coypel, he was named guard of the King's drawings (1752), and was given an apartment in the Louvre. After the death of Lépicié, who had held the position of Secretary at the Academy, he was chosen to replace him as secretary and historian (1755); he also became the official counsellor of the arts bureau after Carle Van Loo had resigned.

9. See for example the text with which he intended to put paid to the decorative excesses of the *rocaille*: "Supplication aux orfèvres, ciseleurs, sculpteurs en bois pour les appartements et autres, par une société d'artistes", *Mercure de France*, December 1754, pp. 178–87.

10. See [15].

11. "[...] devient l'artiste couru, demandé, recherché par la cour et la ville, tourmenté par les intendants des menus et les libraires pour toutes les grandes et les petites choses du dessin et de la gravure, alors si mêlés au luxe courant de la vie sociale. Sa facilité, son abondance, triomphent du temps, du nombre des commandes, de la variété et de la multiplicité des travaux. L'heure va venir où les vignettes ne s'appelleront plus des vignettes mais des *Cochin.», in* GONCOURT, GONCOURT, 1882, VOL. II, p. 52.

12. MICHEL, 1993, p. 71, pp. 94–98, figs. 9.1, 9.2, 9.3.

13. Sébastien Leclerc had been his father's master and was an inspiration for the young Cochin from the start of his career, capturing the elegance of his *en petit* prints. MICHEL, 1993, pp. 43, 94, 391.

14. Joseph-Marie Vien (1716–1809), Jean-Jacques Lagrenée (1740–1821), François Boucher (1703–1770) and Nöel Hallé (1711–1781) drew the other compositions, which were made into prints by several artists. Pierre-Philippe Choffard (1730–1809) created twenty frames for the pages of text.

15. The first two belong to the Speed Art Museum, Louisville, Kentucky, and the third was put up for sale at Artemis Fine Arts in Paris, January 2004.

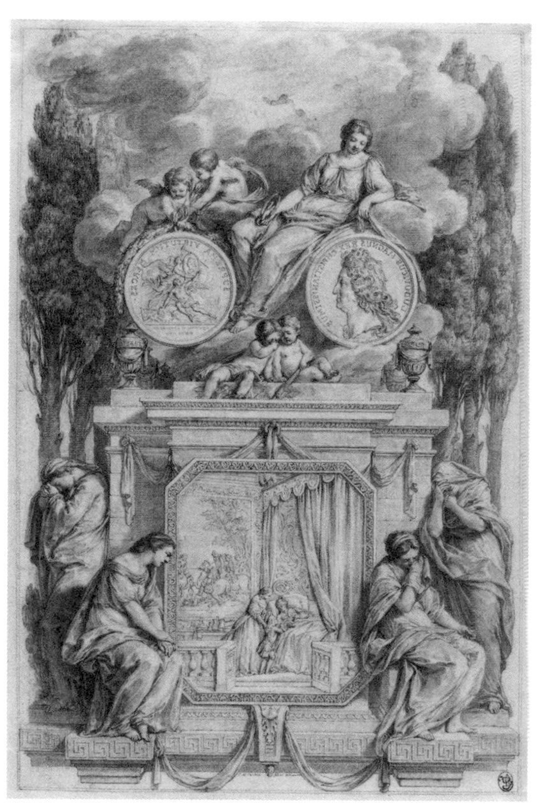

– fig. 13.1 –
Charles-Nicolas Cochin (1715–1790),
The Death of Louis XIV, 1753. Graphite on paper,
33.7 × 22.9 cm. Gift from the Preston Pope Satterwhite Collection,
inv. 1941.97. Collection of the Speed Art Museum,
Louisville, Kentucky

and present, hope and disillusionment. In the centre is a young woman with an anchor who represents the fresh hope brought by the new prince and who defeats the figure of Death, who had taken the future king's two older brothers. The figure on the left has its back to the onlooker and is wrapping two cypress trees in shrouds (an allusion to the premature death of the two princes). A contrast to this sombre past is provided by the figure on the right, who faces the onlooker and is tending to a young plant to ensure that it grows healthy, representing what should

16. Information provided by Jean Belaubre, Curator at the Musée de Monnaies et Médailles, *in* PARIS (1989).

happen with the new-born child. Above the composition is the inverse representation of the two faces of the commemorative medal for the event, designed by the French medallist Thomas Bernard (1650–1713)[16]. The front of the medal on the right shows the bust of Louis XIV encircled by the inscription "Ludovicus Magnus Rex Christianissimus" (Louis the Great, most Christian King) and the back of the medal on the left shows a crowned female figure symbolizing France and holding the young newborn prince in her arms. Around the edge is the inscription "Novum Regiae Stirpus Incrementum" (A new child of royal lineage). ¶ This graphite drawing is an example of the finished piece and contains minutely detailed depictions throughout the composition. While Cochin shows François

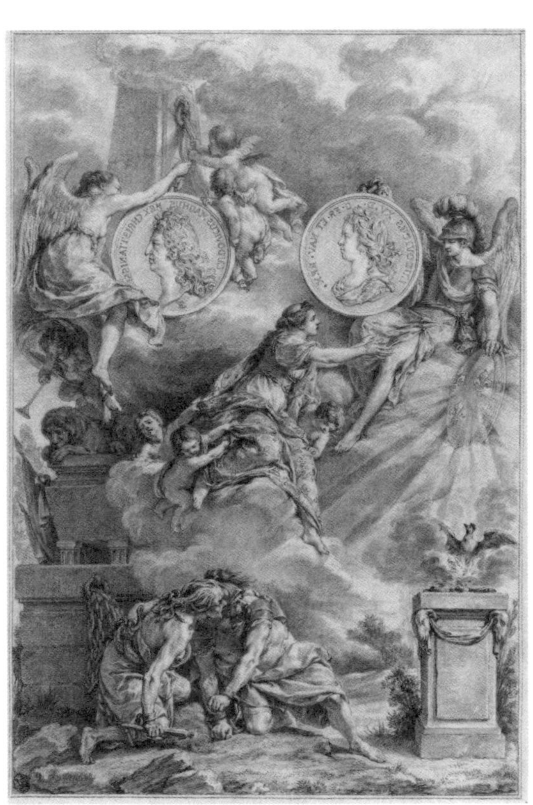

– fig. 13.2 –
Charles-Nicolas Cochin (1715–1790),
Accession of Louis XV to the throne, 1754.
Graphite on paper, 33.5 × 22.9 cm.
Gift from the Preston Pope Satterwhite Collection,
inv. 1941.98.Collection of the Speed Art Museum,
Louisville, Kentucky

Boucher's influence in his recourse to the *putti* that decorate the top of the architectural cornice with a wreath, the dominant features of this work – fluted pillars, friezes of waves, triglyphs and metopes, acanthus leaves and ribbed vases – show the work as a precursor of the so-called *goût a la grecque* that was popular in France between 1750 and 1775. It should be noted that Cochin began this series of drawings and prints two years after returning from Italy, where he acquired a taste for classical culture. ¶ Aware of the quality of the drawings for this publication, Cochin decided to bequeath some of them to the *Cabinet de Dessins du roi* "[...] so that are left in this deposit some memories of [his] faint talents"[17]. However, it is now known that these drawings were never actually sent to the office.

17. "[...] et ce afin qu' il reste dans ce dépôt quelque mémoire de [ses] faibles talens." See MICHEL, 1993, p. 97.

PROVENANCE

Alfred Beurdeley Collection. Acquired by Calouste Gulbenkian at the sale of this collection, through Graat et Madoulé, at Galerie Georges Petit, Paris, 13 March 1905, lot no. 26 (repr.).

•

EXHIBITIONS

PARIS, Salon 1755, no. 165, IV, p. 35; ROUX, 1946, V, p. 107, no. 353; PORTO, 1964, no. 6 o (repr.); OEIRAS, 1965, no. 226; LISBON, 1976, no. 50; LISBON, 1985, no. 9, p. 20, p. 133 (repr.); CAMBRIDGE, 2000, no. 96, pp. 214–15, p. 215 (repr.); LISBON, PORTO, 2000–2002, no. 96, pp. 214–15, p. 215 (repr.); MADRID, 2002, no. 62, pp. 148–49, p. 149 (repr.); LISBON, 2006b, no. 14, pp. 126–27, p. 127 (repr.).

•

LITERATURE

MICHEL, 1993, pp. 71, 95, 97, fig. 9.1 (repr.).

[14]

CHARLES-NICOLAS COCHIN, THE YOUNGER

Paris, 1715 – 1790

FEMALE FIGURE

Study for the drawing "Birth of Louis XV"

France, 1753

Black chalk on paper.
37.4 × 23.2 cm.
Signed on the bottom right-hand side: *C.N. Cochin.*
Inv. 2872

The collection put together by Calouste Gulbenkian, which is exhibited in a museum designed especially to house it, has only rarely been enlarged through subsequent acquisitions. Use of this practice has only been made when the new works deepen our scientific knowledge of the pieces bought by the collector during his own lifetime, as in the case of this drawing. ¶ This is a preparatory study for one of the female figures featured in the drawing *Birth of Louis XV* [13], which was discussed previously. We recall that, in this work, the figure appears in the lower part of the composition, on the left-hand side, with her back to the viewer. Allegorically, she turns back to the past, draping funerary veils around two cypresses which represent the brothers of Louis XV, who died in 1705 and 1712 respectively. This figure contrasts with the one on the right-hand side, who faces the viewer and, metaphorically, the future. She is shown watering a young plant, symbolising the long and healthy life desired for the newborn prince. ¶ For a composition as complex as that of the *Birth of Louis XV*, brought to life through minute attention to detail, Cochin would have felt the need to carry out separate studies of the various components of the theme without, however, losing sight of his overall vision for the drawing. The sketch in question conveys the 'first idea', evoking the position of the aforementioned figure, from the lowered head and moving arms to the slightly bent legs that support her body weight. However, Cochin uses only light traces to indicate the visible, naked part of the female body. Here, he is more concerned with the garments around her. He uses black chalk to delineate the folds in the draped material, to bring out the shadows, and to translate de modelling by the use of the chiaroscuro. ¶ After returning from his trip to Italy, where he had the opportunity to study works by Italian artists, Cochin abandoned the stereotypes to which he had previously been attached and looked to nature for inspiration for his models[1]. Thus, with the compositions designed for *L'Histoire de Louis XV par Médailles* particularly in mind, he produced several preparatory studies[2] (such as the one acquired by the Gulbenkian Foundation) and representations of academy figures. In these latter studies, the model is rigorously followed and the depiction very faithful to real life. One of these academy figures[3], produced in 1753 and engraved by Prévost (ca. 1735–1809) in 1764 to be included in Diderot and Alembert's *Encyclopédie*, is associated with the sketch in question and was used in the preparation of the finished drawing found in the Gulbenkian Collection [13]. This link is nevertheless hard to recognise. The rough, barren qualities which characterise the study were overcome in a timely manner in the final work, giving way to graceful and delicate handling.

1. MICHEL, 1993, pp. 413–14.

2. The Louvre Museum's Graphic Art Department has a collection of fifty studies of figures and drapes for this work (inv. RF 5472–5525). Cf. *Ibidem*, p. 413, note 54.

3. *Ibidem*, p. 414, fig. 49.

PROVENANCE
Acquired by the Calouste Gulbenkian Foundation at Paul Prouté Gallery S.A., Paris, in June–July 2003, lot no. 14.

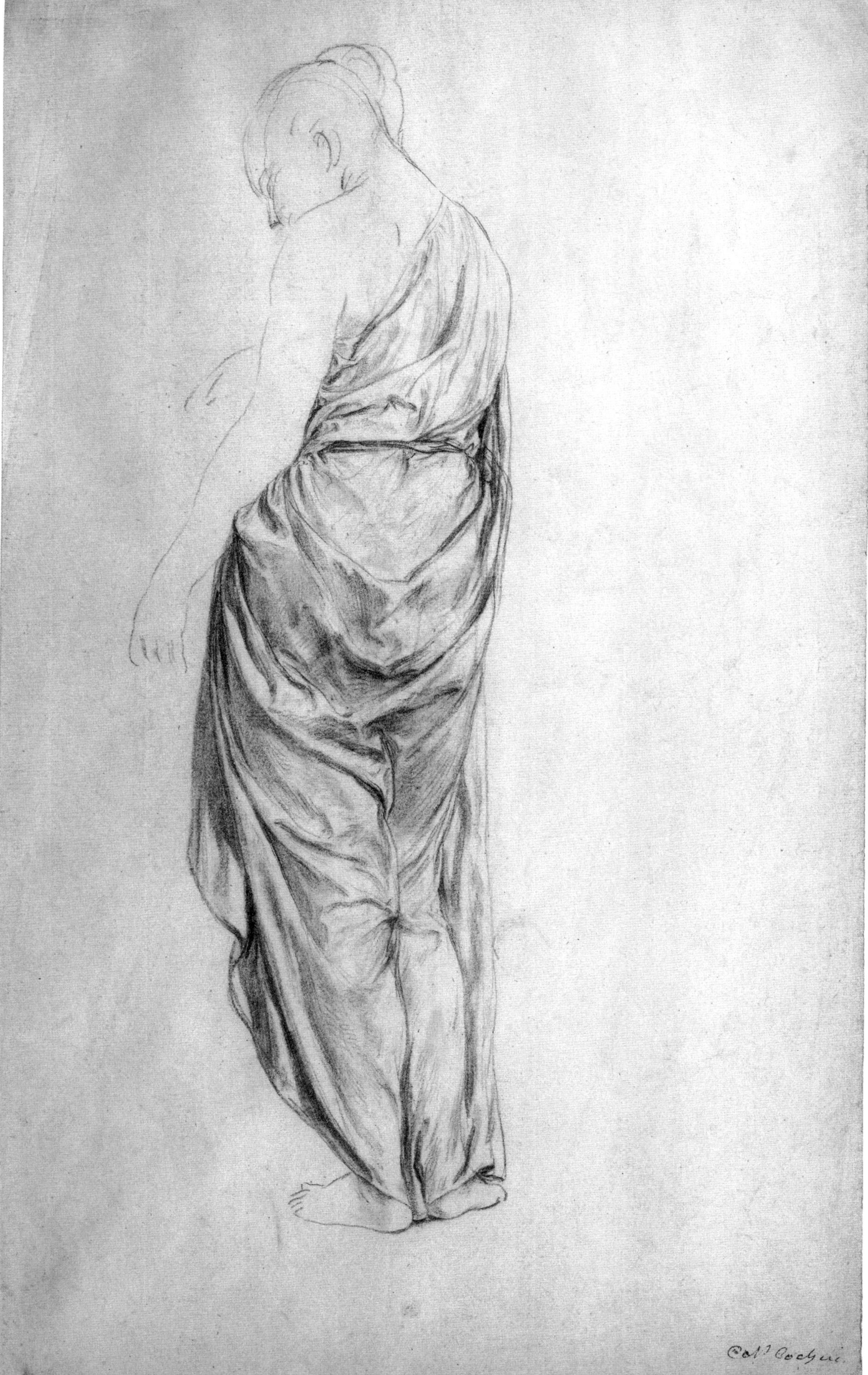

[15]

CHARLES-NICOLAS COCHIN, THE YOUNGER

Paris, 1715–1790

PORTRAIT OF THE MARQUIS DE MARIGNY

Paris, 1781

Black chalk on paper.
13.7 × 8.8 cm.
Signed and dated: *C. N. Cochin f.[ilius] delin.[eavit]. 1781.*
Inv. 458

This drawing shows the portrait of the Marquis de Marigny, the youngest brother of Jeanne-Antoinette Poisson (1721–1764), Louis XV's official mistress from 1745, who was given the title Marquise de Pompadour. She had been born into a wealthy bourgeois family, and her beauty and wit, together with her excellent education, opened doors for her to the court where, until her premature death in 1764, she influenced the political and cultural life of the times. ¶ In 1746, the *maîtresse en titre* ensured the future of her youngest brother Abel-François Poisson (1727–1781) by introducing him to court, giving him the titles Monsieur de Vandières and Marquis de Marigny, and making him the future successor of Lenormant de Tournehem (1684–1751), the then Director-General of the King's Buildings. ¶ This meant that it was important to culturally prepare this young man, who was only nineteen-years old, for the role that awaited him. His first experiences were at the Royal Academy of Painting and Sculpture under Charles-Antoine Coypel (1694–1752), the first-painter to the King, and Charles-Nicolas Cochin the Younger (1715–1790) who introduced him into the circle of the most influential artists of the time. The most significant moments of Vandières' education came with his stay at the French Academy in Rome and his *Grand Tour* of Italy and Southern France, a journey that lasted from December 1749 to September 1751. He was accompanied by three men who were crucial to his education: the aforementioned Cochin[1], who was responsible for his artistic education; the architect Jacques-Germain Soufflot (1713–1780); and the abbot Jean-Bernard Le Blanc (1707–1781), a man of letters and historiographer. Summoned to Paris in 1751 after the death of Tournehem, Vandières finally took up his post as Director--General of the King's Buildings, a role that he held until 1773 (fig. 15.1). ¶ Marigny was one of the first patrons to react against the excesses of the Rococo and was also one of the earliest and most stalwart supporters of the "rediscovery of good taste"[2], aligning himself with the "goût grecque" that characterized the rise of Neoclassicism in France in the late eighteenth century. The vast collection of art

1. Cochin, who had already shown an interest in writing and art criticism, brought back a huge number of notes and reflections from the journey, and these were published in 1758 by Jombert under the title *Voyage d'Italie ou recueil de notes sur les ouvrages de peinture et de sculpture qu'on voit dans les principales villes d'Italie*, Paris, 1751, 3 volumes.

2. GORDON, 2003, p. 125.

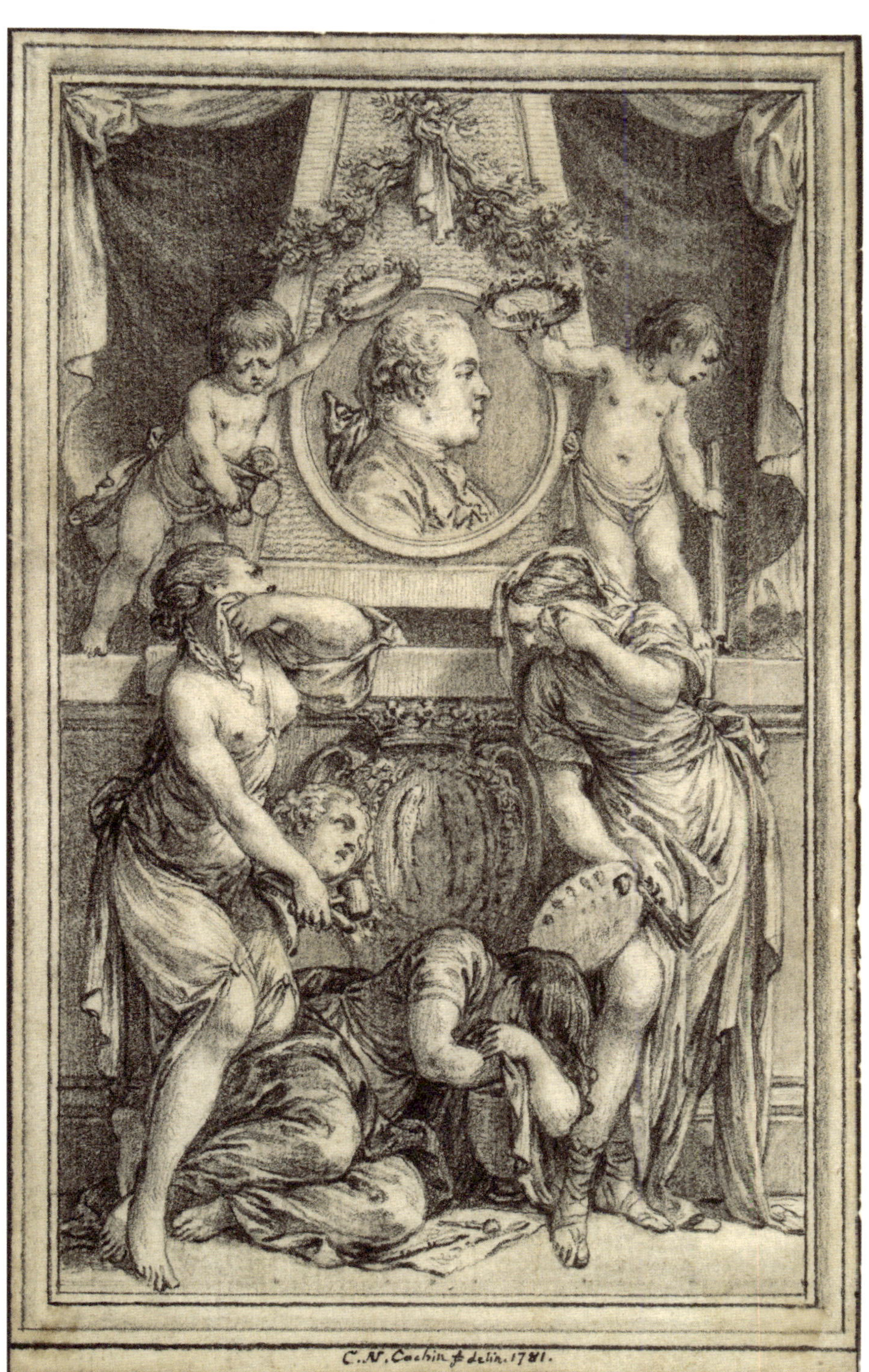
C. N. Cochin f. delin. 1781.

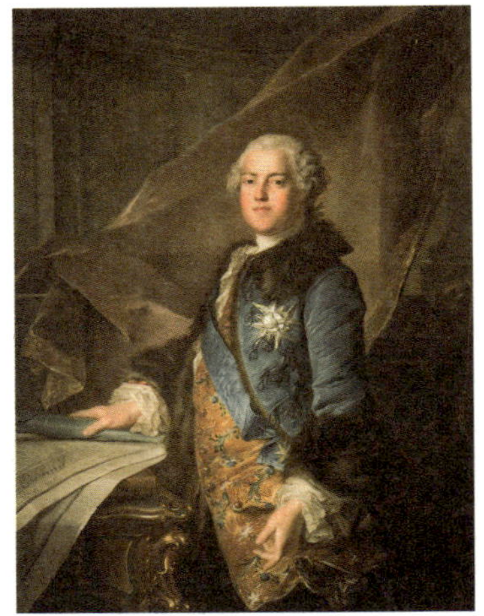

– fig. 15.1 –
Louis Tocqué (1696–1772), *Portrait of Abel-François Poisson, Marquis de Marigny*, ca. 1750–60. Oil on canvas, 136 × 106 cm. Paris, Musée Carnavalet, P 2322. © 2012 White Images / SCALA, Florence

that he accumulated over his life, which was dispersed throughout his numerous residences, clearly showed the evolution of his artistic tastes[3]. ¶ Charles-Nicolas Cochin, the author of the two aforementioned drawings (cats. 13 and 14), was more than just a travel companion for Marigny; he also became a great friend and an invaluable official advisor on all questions pertaining to the arts. The Marquis relied so strongly on his support in all areas that he affectionately referred to him as *mes yeux*[4]. It was with Cochin (as well as the writer and his personal secretary Jean-François Marmontel) that Marigny made a second journey abroad, this time to Flanders and Holland in 1767. ¶ The Marquis de Vandières, de Marigny and de Ménars (he was given this last title in 1778), Director-General of the King's Buildings, Gardens, Arts, Academies and Manufactures, and, no less importantly, the brother of Madame de Pompadour, died on 10 May 1781. Cochin's deep affection for the Marquis de Marigny endured beyond his death, as reflected in the obituary written for his friend that was published in the *Journal de Paris* on 1 June 1781, as well in his collaboration on the inventories for his existing collections at the time[5]. In the catalogue produced by François Basan and François-Charles Joullain *fils*, published in 1781, Cochin was responsible for the written introduction, the tribute to Marigny and the drawing for the frontispiece that was printed by Benoît-Louis Prévost (ca. 1735–1809) and is the object of this study (fig. 15.2). ¶ Acquired by Calouste Gulbenkian in 1921, this small but exuberant preparatory study for Prévost's print clearly shows Cochin's deep dismay at the loss of his friend and protector. The composition, which is conveyed in a formal pictorial format conventional for the late eighteenth century, exudes a predominantly elegiac and yet laudatory quality inspired by the pagan rituals of Antiquity. The tombstone, an imaginary monument adorned with the Marquis' coat-of-arms, is topped by a pyramid, at the base of which there is a portrait of Marigny set in a circular plaque. This kind of bust, showing the protagonist in profile and with the natural features depicted in detail, is characteristic of Cochin's work[6]. (Note the expression of the face, the waves of the hair, and the details of the neck scarf and hair-tie). Several different figures, all with an air of despair, complete the composition: two children who offer the Marquis crowns of flowers, and three female figures who are allegories of the arts to which Marigny was so dedicated: Painting holding a palette, Sculpture showing a sculpted head (which, curiously, also bears an expression of pain) and finally, Drawing and Printmaking, which are suggested by several tools of the trade. ¶ The small dimensions of the drawing

3. LISBON, 2008, pp. 116–19.

4. See PORTALIS, 1877, first part, p. 109.

5. *Catalogue des différens objets de Curiosités dans les Sciences et Arts, qui composoient le Cabinet de feu M. le Marquis de Menars, Commandeur des Ordres du Roi…, Directeur & Ordonnateur-Général des Bâtimens du Roi, Jardins, Arts, Académies & Manufactures Royales…* See GORDON, 2003, no. 167, p. 343.

6. Cochin portrayed numerous figures of the period and left a gallery of life-like profile portraits, all of which were as meticulously rendered as that of the Marquis de Marigny, shown here. See PORTALIS, 1877, pp. 99–101.

are in contrast to the grandiloquent tone that Cochin gave it, using a meticulously detailed visual language founded on short, firm lines and touches of black chalk. Within well-defined contours a sense of volume develops that is marked by areas of light and shade, lending the composition a feeling of movement and enriching its expressiveness.

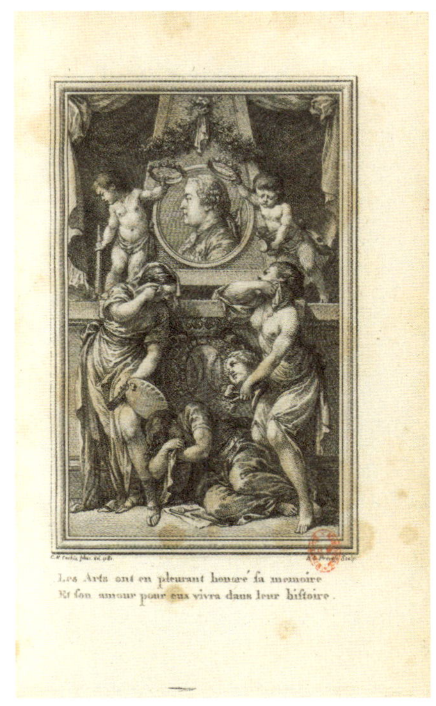

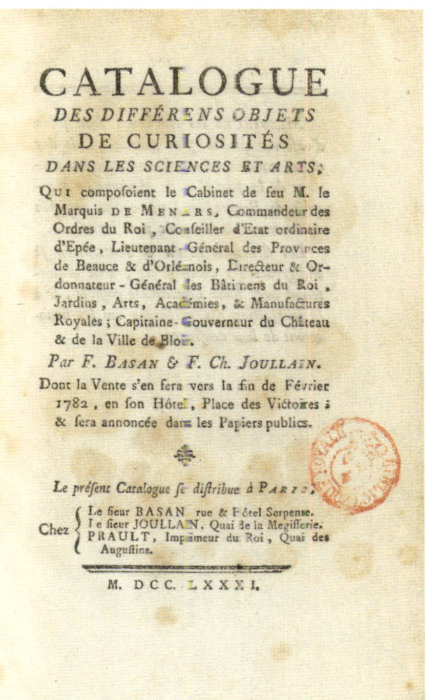

CATALOGUE
DES DIFFÉRENS OBJETS
DE CURIOSITÉS
DANS LES SCIENCES ET ARTS;
Qui composoient le Cabinet de feu M. le Marquis DE MENARS, Commandeur des Ordres du Roi, Conseiller d'Etat ordinaire d'Epée, Lieutenant-Général des Provinces de Beauce & d'Orléanois, Directeur & Ordonnateur-Général des Bâtimens du Roi, Jardins, Arts, Académies, & Manufactures Royales; Capitaine-Gouverneur du Château & de la Ville de Blois.
Par F. Basan & F. Ch. Joullain.
Dont la Vente s'en fera vers la fin de Février 1782, en son Hôtel, Place des Victoires; & sera annoncée dans les Papiers publics.

Le présent Catalogue se distribue à Paris,
Chez { Le sieur BASAN rue & Hôtel Serpente. / Le sieur JOULLAIN, Quai de la Megisserie. / PRAULT, Imprimeur du Roi, Quai des Augustins.

M. DCC. LXXXI.

– fig. 15.2 –
Frontispiece and title page. Basan et Joullain, *Catalogue des différens objets de Curiosités dans les Sciences et Arts, qui composoient le Cabinet de feu M. le Marquis de Menar...* Paris: Basan, Joullain & Prault, 1781. © Bibliothèque nationale de France, 2013

PROVENANCE

Guyot de Villeneuve Collection, Paris, sale on 28 May 1900, lot no. 10; Le Breton Collection. Acquired by Calouste Gulbenkian at the sale of this collection, through Graat et Madoulé, Paris, on 6 December 1921, lot no. 49.

•

EXHIBITIONS

PORTO, 1964, no. 61 (repr.); OEIRAS, 1965, no. 227; LISBON, 1985, no. 8, p. 20, p. 132 (repr.); LISBON, 1999, no. 38, pp. 126–27, p. 127 (repr.); CAMBRIDGE, 2000, no. 97, pp. 216–17, p. 217 (repr.); LISBON, PORTO, 2000–2002, no. 97, pp. 216–17, p. 217 (repr.); MADRID, 2002, no. 63, pp. 150–51, p. 151 (repr.); MADRID, 2007, no. 3, pp. 140–41, p. 141 (repr.); LISBON, 2008, no. 3, pp. 140–41, p. 141 (repr.); ATHENS, 2009, no. 7, pp. 144–45, p. 145 (repr.).

•

LITERATURE

GORDON, 2003, fig. 3.

[16]

JEAN-HONORÉ FRAGONARD

Grasse, 1732 – Paris, 1806

QU'EN DIT L'ABBÉ? or LA LEÇON DE DANSE or LE MAÎTRE DE DANSE

France, ca. 1770

Brush brown ink and brown washes,
with red and black chalk tracing on paper.
23.6 × 36.6 cm.
Inv. 2297

One of the singularities of Fragonard's creative genius is the variety of themes that his work encompasses and the range of techniques that he used to achieve them. ¶ One of the greatest painters in the Rococo tradition, Fragonard created a gallery of portraits, mythological and religious scenes, genre and family scenes, landscapes[1], allegories and copies of the great masters, some of whom left an indelible mark on his style[2]. However, in the context of his work as a whole, it was Fragonard's drawing skills that Portalis, in his study of the artist, described so definitively: "Drawing is the triumph of Fragonard. He was adorable with the brush on his hand, but irresistible when he holds the crayon"[3]. The Goncourt brothers also agreed: "His paintings do not reveal much about him: in his paintings he is Fragonard, whereas in his drawings he is less and more: he is entirely and simply *Frago*"[4]. ¶ Fragonard's education was shaped by such renowned artists as Chardin, with whom he took his first steps as a painter; Boucher, who took him into his studio in 1748 and who, recognizing his undeniable talent, later encouraged him to take part in the Grand Prix de Rome de l'Académie royale de Peinture[5]; Carle van Loo (1705–1765), the director and professor of the École Royale des Élèves Protégés, in Paris, the institution from which he graduated before going on to Rome; and also Charles-Joseph Natoire (1700–1777), the mythological and historical painter and director of the French Academy in Rome, which took him on a scholarship in 1756. This training was consolidated by his two trips to Italy, the first of which took place between 1756 and 1761 and the second between 1773 and 1774, largely as a result of the intervention of the Abbé de Saint-Non[6] and of the collector Bergeret de Grancourt[7]. ¶ On his return to Paris, about to start a promising painting career in the style of the Academy[8] and for state commissions, Fragonard decided not to take this path[9]. Due to his optimistic personality and delight in pleasure, he gave in to the requests of his clientele of aristocrats, high-flying financiers, *fermiers-généraux* and private collectors and dedicated himself to representing *fête galante* scenes that reflected the tastes and habits of his time: the deliciously sensual and enchanting eighteenth

1. Fragonard's famous landscape *Ile d'Amour*, ca. 1770, is part of the Calouste Gulbenkian Collection (inv. 436). See ROSENBERG, Pierre, *in* PARIS, NEW YORK, 1987–1988, no. 168, pp. 355–57, p. 356 (repr.); SAMPAIO, 2009, pp. 92–93 (repr.).

2. In addition to the masters who contributed to his artistic training, Fragonard also had the opportunity to study the works of Italians such as Pietro da Cortona, Tiepolo, Baroccio, as well as those of Rubens, Rembrandt and Ruisdael.

3. «Le dessin, voilà le triomphe de Fragonard. Adorable le pinceau à la main, quand il tient le crayon il est irrésistible.» *In* PORTALIS, 1889, p. 187.

4. «Ses tableaux n'en disent pas autant sur lui: dans sa peinture, il est Fragonard; dans ses dessins il est moins et plus: il est *Frago* tout court et tout intimement.» *In* GONCOURT, GONCOURT, 1882, p. 347.

5. However, Fragonard had not followed the Academy courses, and this meant that he was not eligible to enter the contest. "It does not matter, you are my pupil" ["Ça ne fait rien, tu es mon élève"], clarified Master Boucher. Fragonard finally won first prize in 1752 with the painting *Jéroboam sacrifiant aux Idoles* (currently in Paris, École nationale supérieure des Beaux-Arts).

6. Jean Baptiste Claude Richard de Saint-Non (1727–1791), a cultured lover of the arts, was one of Fragonard's most loyal friends and protectors. They met in Rome in 1760 and formed a close professional and personal relationship.

7. Pierre-Jacques-Onésyme Bergeret de Grancourt (1715–1785), Saint-Non's brother-in-law (see note 6), who held an influential position in finance (*fermier-général*), was an Associate of the Academie des Beaux-Arts and an influential art collector. He sponsored

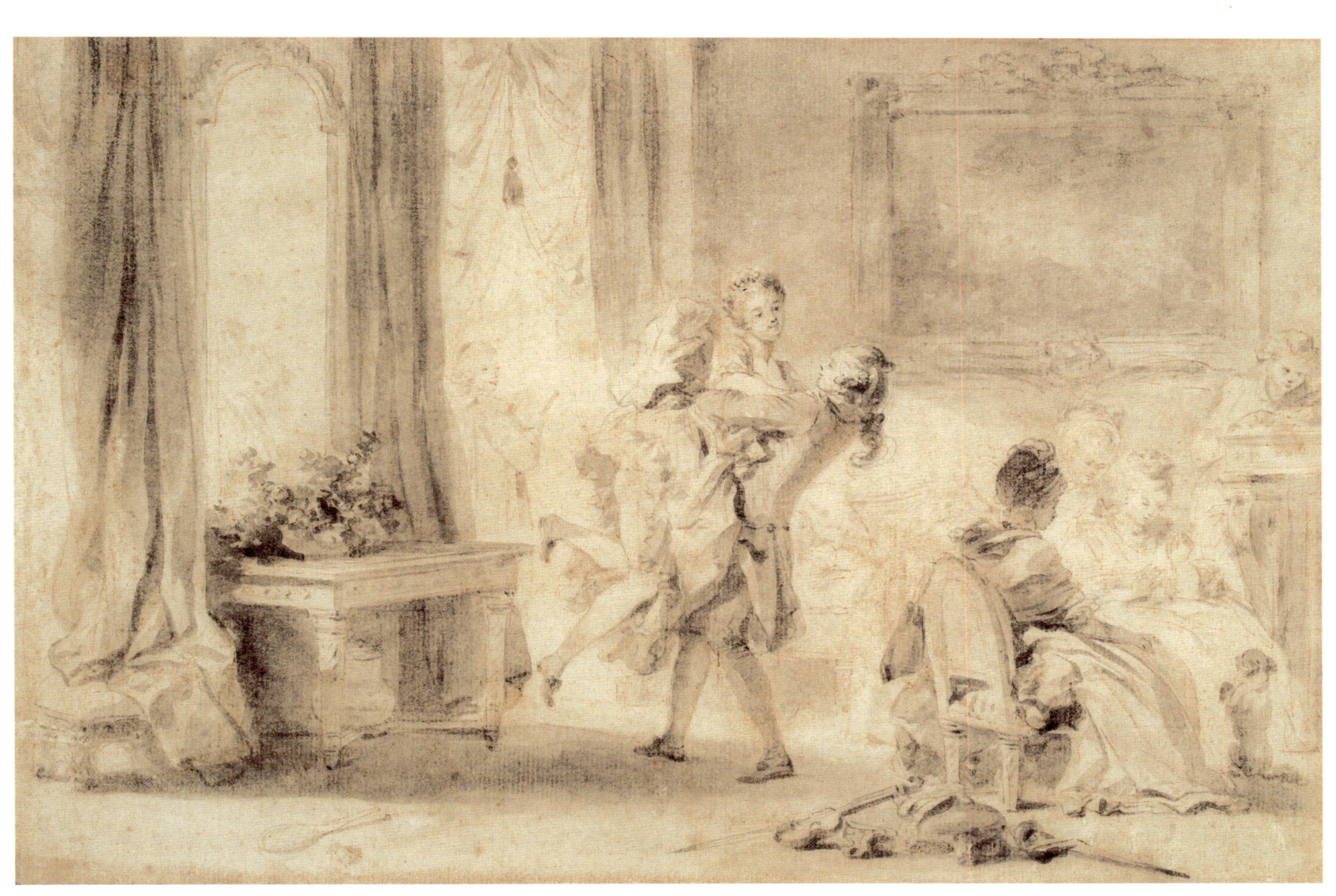

Fragonard's second trip to Italy in 1773–74. See L'ISLE-ADAM, GRASSE, 2001–2002.

8. Fragonard was accepted as an Associate of the Academy in 1765 with his painting *Corésus se sacrifie pour sauver Callirhoé*, (Musée du Louvre, inv. no. 4541). Afterwards, his official commissions multiplied, although he never managed to complete several of them for a variety of reasons.

century. ¶ Despite the damage caused by the aforementioned floods of 1967, the different styles of the two drawings by Fragonard that were acquired by Calouste Gulbenkian in 1937 are testimony to both his extraordinary ability and spontaneity as a draughtsman and to the freedom of his imaginative nature. ¶ *Qu' en dit l' Abbé?*, the drawing discussed here, dates from around 1770[10], a period in which Fragonard created many other *galante* subjects such as *The Servant Girl's Dormitory* (which Rosenberg compares with the Gulbenkian drawing, fig. 16.1), *Les pétards*[11], and *Les jets d' eau*[12]. In all of these works, the artist reveals an unrivalled ability to depict seemingly innocent scenes in which young, seductive women, watched by strangers in the intimacy of enclosed spaces, abandon themselves in voluptuous poses or unexpectedly and unintentionally reveal their most intimate secrets. At the centre of this subtle language is play, surprise, the veiled allusion; there is an erotic and malicious sensuality, but never a lack of modesty, and this teases the onlooker, lending a sense of voyeurism to the contemplation of the work. The cunning positioning of the shafts of light further enhance the seductive nature of these scenes of gallantry. ¶ Prior to this, Fragonard created two extraordinary paintings in the same genre which made him tremendously successful with his clientele at the time. These were *Les Hasards Heureux de l'Escapolette*[13] and *Jeune Fille faisant danser son chien sur son lit*, better known as *La Gimblette*[14]. ¶ The inventive and audacious *Qu' en dit l' Abbé?*, also known as *La leçon de danse* or *Le maître de danse*, shows the precise moment in which the dance master spins his young student up and around, lifting her skirts and giving the priest, who is close by reading his breviary, an unexpected view . ¶ Fragonard shows the subject of this drawing in a black-chalk composition with subtle red-chalk tracing and finished with strokes of brown wash. In a parlour decorated in the most sober taste of the last quarter of the century, three young people are shown playing with a little dog that, to their delight, manages to balance on its hind legs while another figure leans against the chimney breast engrossed in reading. In the centre the dance lesson is reflected in the elegant mirror above a table on which there is a flowered jug, quietly observed by a priest whom the painter has carefully placed a

9. There are many possible explanations for Fragonard's decision to give up portraying the major themes of history. His personal leaning towards scenes in the *fête galante* style, his dislike of the violent criticism levelled at him after his participation in the 1767 *Salon*, and his difficulties in making ends meet with the invariably late payments from state commissions may all be seen as contributory factors. Cochin see [13, 14 and 15], his close friend, explained: "He is forced, due to necessity, to engage himself in works which are not in keeping with his genius." [«(il est) obligé par le besoin de se livrer à des ouvrages peu confomes à son génie]. See WILDENSTEIN, 1960, p. 15.

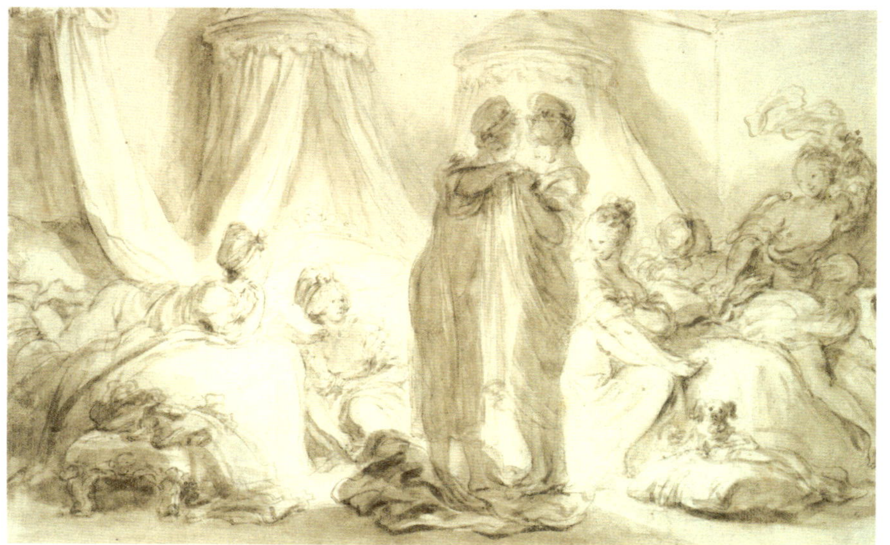

– fig. 16.1 –
Jean-Honoré Fragonard (1732–1806), *The Servant Girl's Dormitory*, ca. 1770. Brown wash over black chalk on cream laid paper, 23.9 × 36.7 cm. Harvard Art Museum / Fogg Museum, Gift of Charles E. Dunlap, inv. 1954.106. Photo: Imaging Department © President and Fellows of Harvard College

little to one side. The decoration of the room is completed with a large landscape painting on the opposite wall and several objects scattered over the floor which allude to the activities of the young people: a racquet and shuttlecock, a violin, and a sword. ¶ In their work on the study of Fragonard, Edmond and Jules Goncourt describe this drawing in the Calouste Gulbenkian Collection and draw attention to Fragonard's delight in representing desire and sensuality in such a refined and sublime way: "Fragonard amuses himself: beware, he is going to debauch! Behold him putting a dancing master in a salon typical of that period. While ladies amuse themselves, near the chimney, with a dog which rolls over, next to the stool where the pouch laid, the charming young master, lifting and swirling his beautiful pupil in his arms, inadvertently shows a part of her beautiful legs to the shrewd abbot who is reading his breviary back there, on the window frame. That is delightfully ambiguous! The brush has the liveliness of the gesture and of the flight of the scene: a little water, a little brown, a helping hand and the move is complete!"[15] ¶ In 1862 Jules de Goncourt created an etching of the central motif of this drawing. The print, entitled *Le maître à danser*, was used to illustrate the 1865 edition of the two brothers' study of Fragonard.

PROVENANCE

Varanchan de Saint-Geniès Collection, sale in Paris, 29–31 December 1777, lot no. 62; Hubert Robert Collection, sale after the artist's death, Paris, 5 April 1809, lot no. 172; Amédée Constantin Collection, sale in Paris, 29 March 1830, lot no. 91; Saint Collection, sale in Paris, 4 May (actually took place on 30 May) 1846, lot no. 16; Émile Norblin Collection, sale in Paris, 16–17 March 1860, lot no. 5 of the supplement; Camille Marcille Collection from 1862, sale in Paris, 6–7 March 1876, lot no. 78, p. VII; H.H.A. Josse Collection from 1889, sale after his death, at Galerie Georges Petit, Paris, 28–29 May 1894, lot no. 11, repr.; Marquis de Biron Collection, Paris, from 1899; Mme de Polès Collection, Paris, 1927; David David-Weill Collection, Neuilly-sur-Seine, 1921. Acquired by Calouste Gulbenkian from Wildenstein, London, April–May 1937.

EXHIBITIONS

PARIS, 1884, no. 275; PARIS, 1921, no. 157, p. 48; PORTO, 1964, no. 62, (repr.); OEIRAS, 1965, no. 228; LISBON, 1976, no. 53 (repr.); LISBON, 1985, no. 11, p. 21, p. 136 (repr.); PARIS, NEW YORK, 1987–1988, no. 114, pp. 239–41, p. 240 (repr.); CAMBRIDGE, 2000, no. 98, pp. 218–19, p. 219 (repr.); LISBON, PORTO, 2000–2002, no. 98, pp. 218–19, p. 219 (repr.); MADRID, 2002, no. 64, pp. 152–53, p. 153 (repr.).

LITERATURE

GONCOURT, GONCOURT , (1865), 1882, vol. 2, pp. 348–49; PORTALIS, GONCOURT, 1889, p. 194, 195, 221–22, 307, repr. between p. 192 and 193; HENRIOT, 1928, III, pp. 173–74; REAU, 1956, repr. p. 36, p. 197; ANANOFF (1961, 1963, 1968, 1970), vol. IV, pp. 39–40, no. 1992, fig. 544.

10. I would like to thank Eunice Williams for the information on this drawing and the following one, [17] (2011). See also ROSENBERG, Pierre, *in* PARIS, NEW YORK, 1987–1988, no. 114, pp. 239–41; p. 240 (repr.).

11. Boston, Museum of Fine Arts, inv. 44.815.

12. Williamstown, Sterling and Francine Clark Art Institute, inv. 1955.1967.

13. London, the Wallace Collection, inv. P430. Fragonard came to paint this work through a stroke of chance. In 1767, the collector M. de Saint-Julien commissioned the painter Doyen to paint a work showing his lover being pushed on a swing by a bishop, with Saint-Julien himself in a position from which he could see the legs of his young lover as the swing swept upwards. Feeling that his reputation as an historical painter would suffer, Doyen suggested Fragonard for the job. The artist seized the opportunity and the work became his first great success.

14. Munich, Alte Pinakothek Bayerische Hypotheken-und Wechsel-Bank Sammlung, inv. HUW35. This painting is dated around 1770, and shows Fragonard's preference for the *fete galante* style with its themes of seduction, eroticism and playful *joie de vivre*.

15. «Fragonard s'amuse: prenez garde, il va polissonner! Le voilà qui jette un maître de danse dans un salon du temps. Tandis que les dames s'amusent, auprès de la cheminée, d'un petit chien qui fait le beau, à côté du tabouret où pose la pochette, le ravissant petit-maître, enlevant et faisant pirouetter entre ses bras sa belle élève, montre, sans le vouloir, un peu de ses jolies jambes au fin matois d'abbé lisant son bréviaire, là-bas, dans l'embrasure de la fenêtre. Et que cela est délicieusement troussé! Le pinceau a la vivacité du geste et de l'envolée de la scène: un peu d'eau, un peu de bistre, un coup de main, – et le tour est fait!» GONCOURT, GONCOURT, 1882, vol. II, pp. 348–49.

[17]

JEAN-HONORÉ FRAGONARD

Grasse, 1732 – Paris, 1806

INTERIOR OF A ROMAN PARK

France, mid 1770s

Pen and brush, brown ink and brown wash;
black chalk tracing on paper.
34.3 (6) × 45.2 cm.
Inv. 2299

Fragonard's interest in landscape arose due to the encouragement of Charles-Joseph Natoire (1700–1777), director and teacher of drawing at the French Academy in Rome when the artist was staying at the Mancini Palace as a *pensionnaire*. At that time Fragonard was struggling with a creative block[1] and Natoire encouraged him to draw *en plein air*, creating a personal style in his depiction of nature. Equally important was the support and friendship of Hubert Robert (1733–1808), another student at the Academy who also favoured the landscape as a subject for his work. The two artists would work together outdoors, drawing side by side, often in the same spots, although Robert tended to seek out themes that referenced Antiquity. ¶ Fragonard's interest in the Italian landscape, and the parks and gardens of Roman villas in particular, grew even stronger when he accepted the invitation of the engraver and collector Jean Baptiste Claude Richard (1727–1791), the Abbot of Saint-Non[2], to spend the summer of 1760 at the Villa d'Este[3] in Tivoli. There, amid the picturesque gardens left to become overgrown with lush vegetation, affording glimpses of fountains, statues, staircases and marble vases, Fragonard rediscovered his flair as a painter and poet. His imagination sharpened his gaze and each corner of the garden chosen for his pieces was captured through almost palpable sensations brought about by the light flickering through the foliage, the murmuring of water gushing from fountains into calm pools, the blowing of the wind at the top of old cypresses and oaks, and the scorching heat hanging in the air, suggested by the shadows of the trees lining the paths. ¶ On his return to Paris in 1761 with his patron, Fragonard continued to draw and paint views of Italian gardens and landscapes which reveal the influence of the skies painted by Jacob van Ruisdael (ca. 1628/29–1682) or plays of light and shadow in the manner of Rembrandt (1606–1669). His interest in the Italian landscape was reawakened on a second trip to Italy in 1773–74, in the company of his new patron, Bergeret de Grancourt[4]. ¶ This drawing from the Calouste Gulbenkian Collection dates from the mid-1770s and was created following this journey with Bergeret. With

1. Overwhelmed by the greatness of the masters, in particular the great painters of the Renaissance, and the art of Antiquity, Fragonard underwent a major crisis which he described as follows: "The energy of Michael Angelo frightened me; I experienced a feeling that I could not convey; seeing the beauties of Raphael, I was moved to tears, and the crayon fell off my hands. I remained a couple of months in a state of indolence I was not able to overcome, until the moment when I finally devoted myself to the study of the painters who gave me the hope of competing one day with them. It was thus that Baroccio, Pietro de Cortona, Solimena and Tiepolo caught my attention" ["L'énergie de Michel-Ange m'effrayait; j'éprouvais un sentiment que je ne pouvais rendre. En voyant les beautés de Raphaël, j'étais ému jusqu'aux larmes, et le crayon me tombait des mains. Enfin, je restai plusieurs mois dans un état d'indolence que je n'étais pas maître de surmonter, lorsque je m'attachai à l'étude des peintres qui me donnaient l'espérance de rivaliser un jour avec eux, c'est ainsi que Baroche, Piètre de Cortone, Solimène et Tiepolo fixèrent mon attention»]. See LENOIR, A. – «Fragonard, (L.G. Michaud), *Biographie des hommes vivants*..., XV, 1816, cit. by ROSENBERG, Pierre, *in* PARIS, NEW YORK, 1987–1988, p. 61.

2. See [16]. note 6.

3. The Villa d'Este in Tivoli was built in the sixteenth century by Pirro Ligorio (ca. 1510–1583) for Ippolito d'Este, and belonged in the eighteenth century to the Duke of Modena, Francesco III d'Este (1698–1780). The beautiful estate gradually became dilapidated through lack of investment by its owners. Saint-Non was able to rent it as a result,

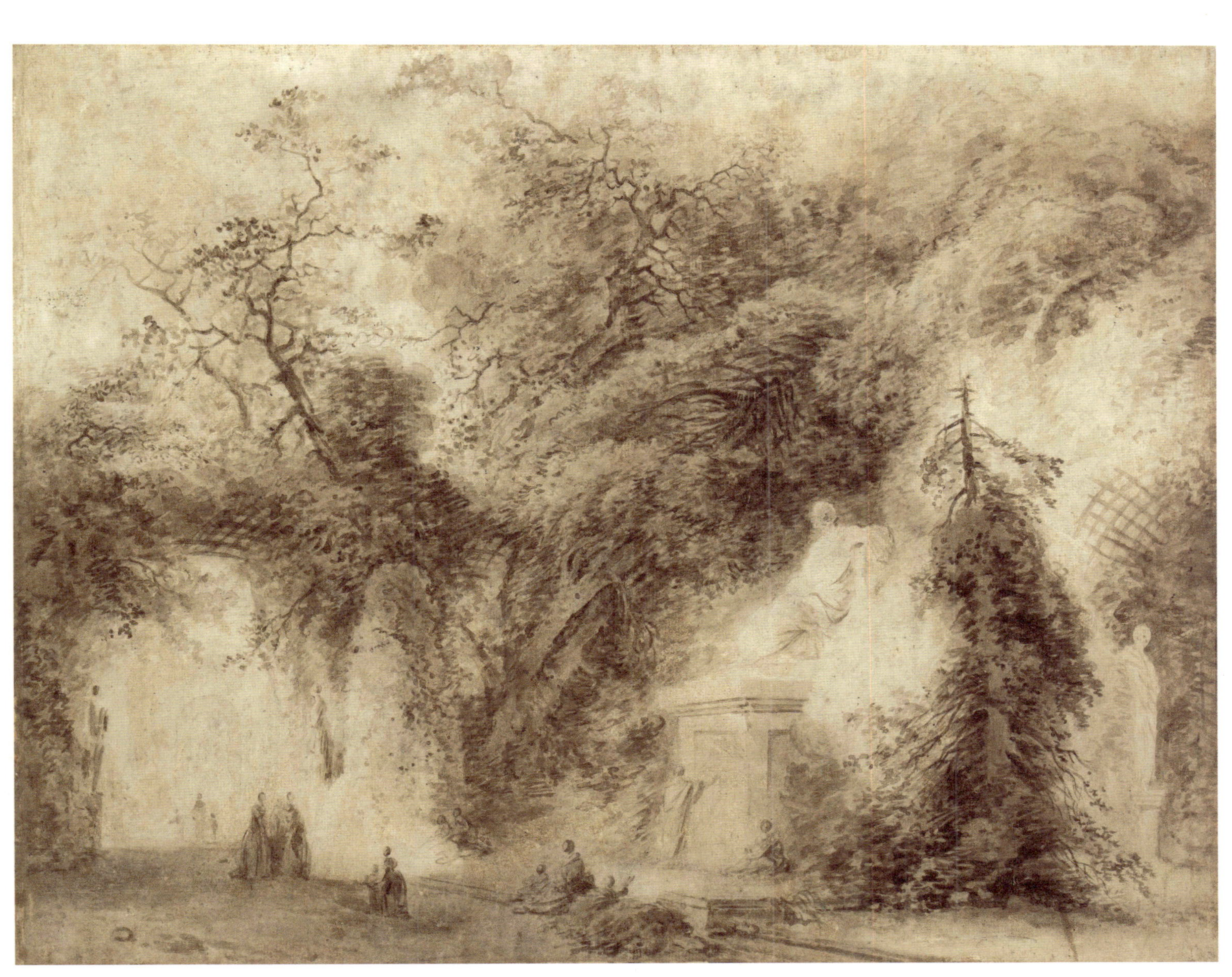

and spent the Summer months of 1760 here with Fragonard, who made numerous drawings of the grounds for his patron. See ROSENBERG, Pierre, *in* PARIS, NEW YORK, 1987–1988, pp. 94–97.

4. See [16], note 7.

5. ROSENBERG, Pierre, *in* PARIS, NEW YORK, 1987–1988, pp. 383–93.

the exception of a set of drawings marked "Rome 1774"[5], the vast majority of Fragonard's works were undated. In addition, many of his landscapes were drawn in his studio from memory or his imagination, or on the basis of sketches previously made by the artist, so that they do not contain any reference to the actual places they depict, making the dating process all the more difficult. ¶ Despite the effects of the flooding in 1967, the technical excellence of the Gulbenkian drawing reveals a level similar to that attained in the aforementioned set of works. As in those drawings, here Fragonard forgoes the use of red chalk[6] and instead opts for lightly applied black chalk to set out his composition before going over it with a brown wash, using a paintbrush. This approach is similar to that used for the drawings *Parc romain avec une fontaine* (fig. 17.1) and *Parc romain aux cyprès* (inv. 12.737) from the Graphische Sammlung Albertina in Vienna[7], the former drawing being identified by the aforementioned inscription ("Rome 1774"). Like those works, the drawing from the Gulbenkian Collection makes superlative use of the wash, which captures the effects of the contrasts between light and shadow and in particular the way in which it renders the lush foliage using subtle strokes. ¶ This drawing, acquired by Calouste Gulbenkian in 1937, appeared in the sale catalogue under the title *Un coin des Jardins de Tivoli* and has continued to be

6. The musée des Beaux-Arts de Besançon has ten views of Tivoli drawn in red chalk during Fragonard's first sojourn in Italy, which are among his most accomplished works and among the most beautiful in the history of drawing. See *Ibidem*, pp. 94–114, nos. 24, 25, 27, 28, 29, 30, 32, 33, 34 and 35.

7. *Ibidem*, pp. 384–85, nos. 181 and 182 respectively.

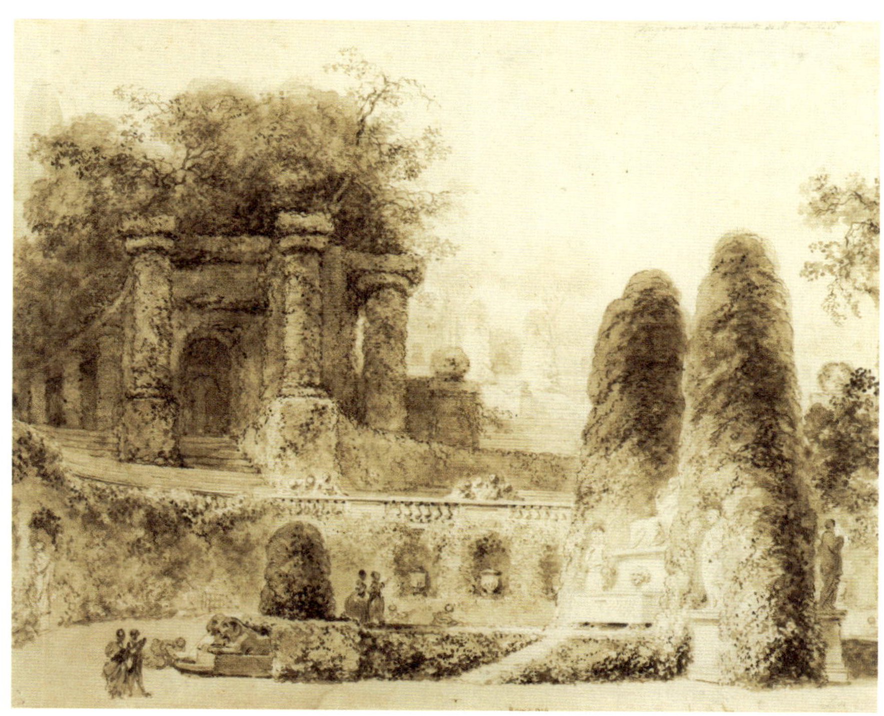

– fig. 17.1 –
Jean-Honoré Fragonard (1732–1806),
Parc romain avec une Fontaine, 1774.
Bistre wash over black chalk on paper, 28.9 × 36.8 cm.
Viena, Graphische Sammlung Albertina, inv. 12736

named as such in the records of the Gulbenkian Collection. However, exhibitions held in previous years referred to it as *Paysage d'Italie*[8], while more recent studies have identified it as *Intérieur de Parc*[9] or *Interior of a Roman Park*[10]. Identifying the specific setting has, however, remained problematic. Although Bergeret and Fragonard visited Tivoli together, the collector was apparently not particularly enamoured of the park, and it is likely that the image shown here does not correspond to a particular place but is the result of the artist's imagination, albeit based on reality – an example of the "poetic idealisation" referred to by Rosenberg[11]. ¶ The Gulbenkian drawing may evoke the sort of beautiful Roman gardens that were much sought-after by the foreign visitors who flocked to Italy in the eighteenth century. The dense foliage of the massive trees, stretching into the distance, allow patches of intense sunlight to pass through the branches, contrasting with more shadowy areas. By using this alternating chiaroscuro effect through the gradation of the washes and small brushstrokes, Fragonard gives the foliage the illusion of space and volume. Fountains and statues on pedestals stand out from the surrounding greenery, evoking Classical sculpture. On both sides of the composition, pillared structures are swathed in vegetation, forming decorative arches. In the foreground, low down within the image, a promenade stretches into the distance on the left, bustling with people. Indeed, the spontaneous, exuberant and profuse depiction of nature does not dispense with human presence. Rather, it is offered up for the enjoyment of the family groups seen taking a stroll, talking, playing with their children or simply sitting wrapt in thought. However, these slender, elegantly dressed figures are of secondary importance for Fragonard. He makes them so small that they are merely accessories to the imposing trees that tower over the whole area shown in the drawing; nature remains all-pervasive.

8. PARIS, 1921, no. 187, p. 54.

9. ANANOFF, (1961, 1963, 1968, 1970), mentioned in vol. I, no. 371, p. 160,

10. Name used by Eunice Williams. See [16], note 10, in this catalogue.

11. Cf. ROSENBERG, Pierre, *in* PARIS, NEW YORK, 1987–1988, no. 183, p. 386.

PROVENANCE

Mahérault Collection, sale in Paris, 27–29 May 1880, lot no. 49; Vicomte Greffulhe Collection (ca. 1889); Comte de Greffulhe Collection. Acquired by Calouste Gulbenkian at the sale of the latter collection (ordered by the Comtesse de Greffulhe and by the Duc and Duchesse de Gramont), through Hans Stiebel, at Sotheby's, London, 22 July 1937, lot no. 19 (pl. VI).

•

EXHIBITIONS

BERLIN, 1910, no. 177; PARIS, 1921, no. 187, p. 54; PORTO, 1964, no. 63 (repr.); OEIRAS, 1965, no. 229; LISBON, 1976, no. 54; LISBON, 1985, no. 10, p. 20, pp. 134–35 (repr.).

•

LITERATURE

ANANOFF, (1961, 1963, 1968, 1970), vol. I, no. 371, pp. 159–60.

[18]

UNKNOWN AUTHOR

GALLANT SCENE

France, second half of the eighteenth century
(ca. 1770–80?)

Pen and black ink with grey and blue wash,
and touches of red on paper.
12.5 × 9.4 cm.
Mark of Alferd Beurdeley Collection,
on the lower right corner – AB (Lugt 421).
Inv. 2226

1. FUHRING, Peter, *in* LISBON, 2005, no. 98, pp. 256–57 (repr.).

This small-scale drawing shows a *scène galante*, a theme depicting the irreverent pleasures of youth, flirtation, the awakening of sensuality, and the surrendering to voluptuous des ire. In this drawing the scene unfolds in intimate surroundings, in a room where two young lovers are caught off guard in their tryst. On a bed that occupies the centre of the composition, accentuated by the convergence of the decorative motif of the carpet, a sensual young woman reclines on the cushions, giving herself over to her companion's charms. These evocative themes of love and fantasy are portrayed with a lascivious mischief and reflect the tastes and habits not only of an eighteenth-century society hungry for distraction and easy pleasures but also of a clientele of collectors and aristocrats who were interested in the arts. ¶ The room in which the scene takes place is elegant and luxurious; it is filled with the neoclassical features that were so popular in the second half of the eighteenth-century, although some of the details still contain elements that reflect earlier artistic styles[1]. The new styles are depicted both in the architectural structures as well as in the furniture. The double doors, with rectangular panels decorated with grotesques and garlands of leaves and the six-leaf screen also shown are topped with the representation of an oval portrait carried by two *putti*. The walls are more simply decorated with fabric-covered panels ornately framed by wave scrolls. The ceiling is delineated with a cornice of egg moulding. The structure of the bed and the partially visible seat convey architectural elements and ribbed cylindrical-conical legs. The bedhead is reminiscent of Louis XV style although the decorative scrolls and acanthus leaves are more aligned with classical tastes. However, the decorative fringing of the canopy affixed to the wall is closer to the style of Louis XIV. ¶ This drawing was executed in pen in tiny detail. It is the subtle touch of the sometimes almost imperceptible black ink that is most responsible for conveying the spirit and sensuality of the subject. The delicate blue and grey wash both shades the surrounding spaces and highlights certain elements of the composition, thus strengthening its internal dialogue with small

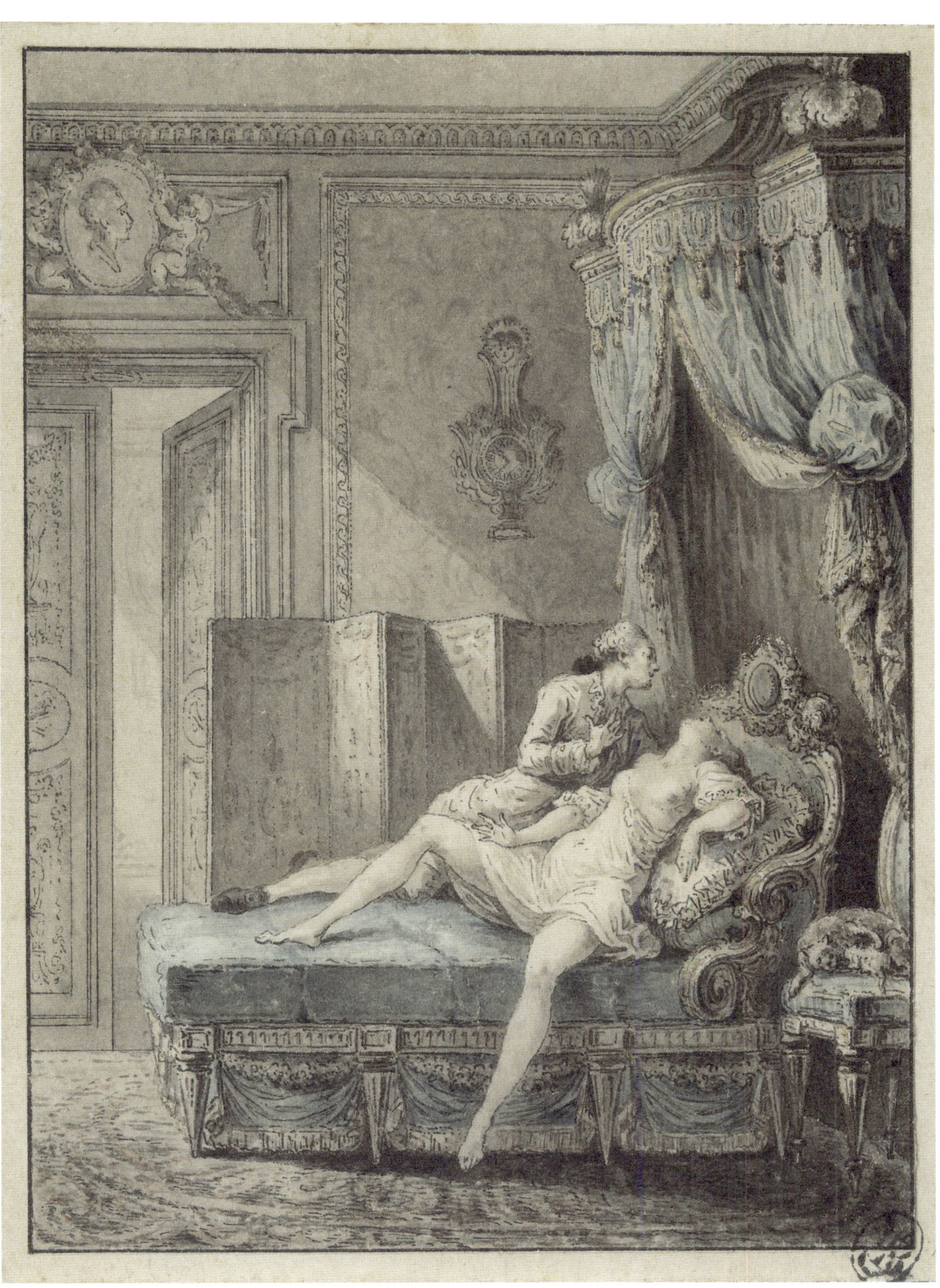

2. TURNER, Nicholas, *in* CAMBRIDGE, 2000; LISBON, PORTO, 2000–2002, no. 102, pp. 226–27 (repr.); MADRID, 2002, no. 68, pp. 160–61 (repr.).

3. I would like to thank David Scrase, Curator of the museum, for the interest that he showed in the problem of the authorship of the Gulbenkian Collection drawing (2001).

4. See note 1.

5. FONTAINE, Docteur Jean-Paul – *Des origines à nos jours – Le Livre des Livres*. Paris: 1994, pp. 86–103.

touches of red. ¶ When Calouste Gulbenkian acquired this drawing in 1932 at the sale of the Boerner Gallery in Leipzig, its authorship was unknown. Since then several possible names have been suggested, including Gabriel de Saint-Aubin (1724–1780), Jean-Michel Moreau the Younger (1741–1814), and even Clément-Pierre Marillier (1740–1808). The possible attribution to this last illustrator came after the exhibition organized by Nicholas Turner, "European Master Drawings from Portuguese Collections"[2], which was shown at the Fitzwilliam Museum in Cambridge in May 2000. This institution owns two drawings by Marillier[3], both signed and dated 1771, which depict a similar environment and are on a similar scale to the Gulbenkian drawing. These are *Les Faux-amis* (inv. PD 93–1961) and *L'Indigent* (inv. PD 84–1961), works that appear to have been intended for prints to be used to illustrate one of the many popular books published in the eighteenth century. This suggestion is lent further credence by the fact that some of the decorative motifs in the Gulbenkian piece (the door, panel and clock) also appear in a drawing by Marillier which was engraved by Pierre-Adrien Le Beau (1744/48-ca. 1817) for *Turcaret*, a comedy by Alain-René Lesage (1668–1747)[4]. ¶ All of the artists suggested here worked in the field of illustration and contributed to it with the elegance of their drawings, which were then reproduced in intaglio by the most skilled engravers. There were, however, numerous talented illustrators whose compositions graced the literary works of the time, which were also decorated with vignettes, *culs-de-lampe* and other kinds of typographical ornamentation that contributed to making the eighteenth century, in terms of book production, the "era of the perfect book"[5]. ¶ The fact that so far the research has not indentified an eighteenth-century illustrated edition containing a printed image of the Gulbenkian drawing means that not only its authorship but also its intended purpose remains open.

PROVENANCE

Alfred Beurdeley Collection. Sale at Galerie Georges Petit, Paris, 13–15 March 1905. Acquired by Calouste Gulbenkian, through Wildenstein, at a sale at C. G. Boerner Gallery, Leipzig, 9 May 1932, lot no. 34.

•

EXHIBITIONS

CAMBRIDGE, 2000, no. 102, pp. 226–27, p. 227 (repr.); LISBON, PORTO, 2000–2002, no. 102, pp. 226–27, p. 227 (repr.); MADRID, 2002, no. 68, pp. 160–61, p. 161 (repr.); LISBON, 2005, no. 98, pp. 256–57, p. 257 (repr.).

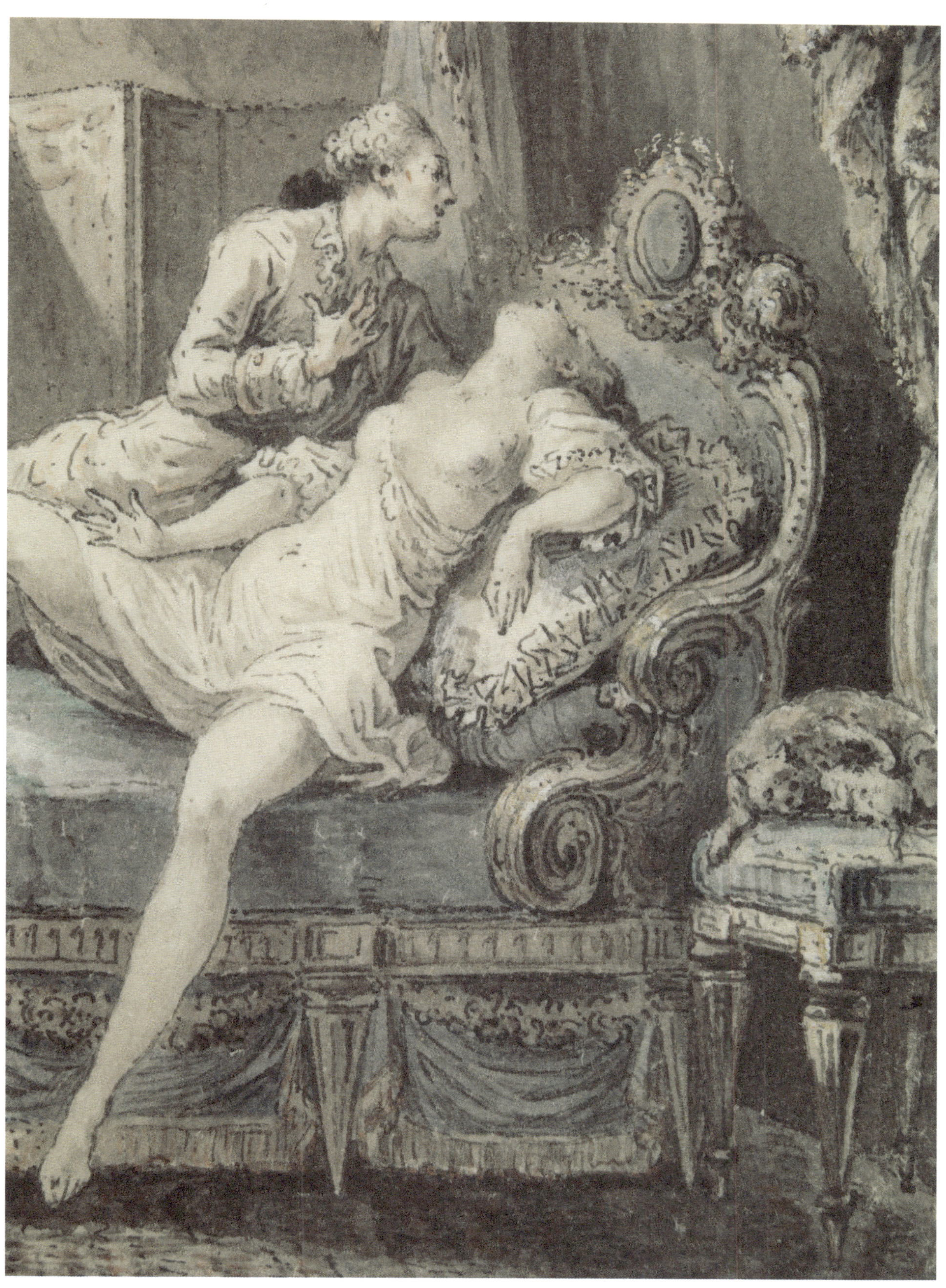

[19]

After CLAUDE MICHEL, known as

CLODION

Nancy, 1738 – Paris, 1814

SATYRS

France, second half of the eighteenth century

Black and white chalk
with stump on paper.
41.8 × 52 cm.
Inv. 2298

Calouste Gulbenkian acquired this drawing in 1937 at the sale of the D. David-Weill Collection. This drawing, entitled *Petits satyres*, was described in the sale catalogue as being the work of Clodion and, as if attempting to dispel any future doubt, stated: "We know the extreme rarity of Clodion's drawings. We have noted he has 'a charm, a flexible modelling which make his use of terracotta so remarkable'."[1] The prestigious collections to which this drawing belonged to are also referred in the same sale catalogue. ¶ Severely damaged in the aforementioned floods of 1967, this work was restored some years later by specialists in the Conservation Department at the Calouste Gulbenkian Museum[2]. ¶ This drawing is one of a group of works that were initially attributed to Claude Michel, better known as Clodion[3], mainly on the basis of the subject matter rather than the style of the piece[4]. Clodion was one of the most versatile sculptors of the second half of the eighteenth century, and his creations, while still showing signs of the *galante* style and traces of the French Rococo, also reflect his great admiration for the aesthetics of Classical Antiquity. The literary and artistic models of Greco-Roman civilization are a recurring theme in French art and are the foundations of French Classicism, which continued to be cyclically influential between the seventeenth and the nineteenth centuries. ¶ Clodion began his artistic training in Paris under the tutelage of his uncle Lambert-Sigisbert Adam (1700–1759), a respected academician and sculptor[5], in whose studio he discovered the art of the Antiquity through Adam's extraordinary collection of *antiques*[6] and his library, both of which brought him closer to Classical culture and literature. His first stay in Italy, between December 1762 and March 1771, brought him into contact with "ancient art" and provided him with countless sources of inspiration. According to Guilhelm Scherf, Clodion's knowledge of the classical world allowed him to recreate the spirit of Arcadia, the odes of Anacreon, the idylls of Theocritus, the eclogues of Virgil, the pastorals of Ovid and the historical themes of Homer, who was one of his favourite authors[7]. He returned to Paris in the

1. "On connait l'extrême rareté des dessins de Clodion. On a justement remarqué dans celui-ci 'le charme, la souplesse dans le modelé, qui rendent si remarquables ses terres cuites'".

2. See "Introduction", pp. 18–19.

3. This was to distinguish him from one of his older brothers.

4. I am deeply grateful to Guilhem Scherf, the Curator of the Department of Sculpture at Musée du Louvre and an expert on the work of Clodion, for sharing his information and opinions on the current drawing (2011).

5. For more on the Adam family, see THIRION, 1885.

6. After being awarded the "Grand Prix de Rome" in 1723, Adam went that same year to Italy where he soon came under the protection of Cardinal de Polignac (1661–1741), a collector of Greek and Roman antiquities. Adam was so seduced by classical art that he eventually built up his own collection, which included some works that had belonged to the cardinal. In 1755, when Clodion began to live with his uncle, Adam published a work entitled *Recueil de sculptures antiques grecques et romaines, trouvées à Rome dans les ruines des Palais de Neron et de Marius*, with prints of old marbles made from his own drawings.

7. PARIS, 1992, p. 36.

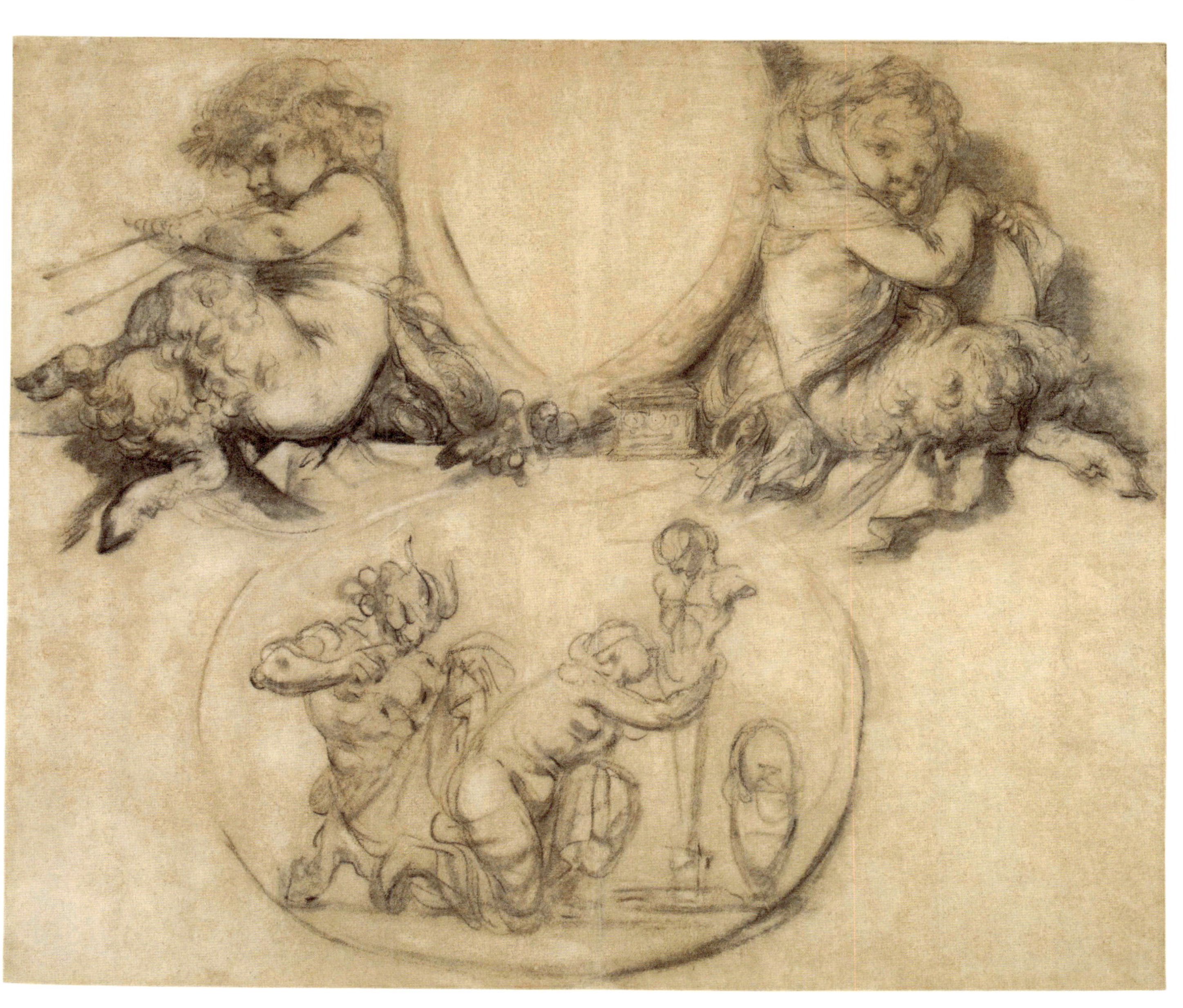

spring of 1771[8] at a time when the quality of his works in terracotta and marble was already widely recognized by a refined clientele who were guaranteed to buy his pieces[9] before they were even finished. Clodion was accepted as an associate of the Academy in 1773 and his classical training was consolidated with a second sojourn in Italy between December 1773 and July 1774[10]. ¶ Clodion had dedicated himself to making small-scale sculptures, generally in terracotta, with themes and motifs taken from antiquity such as offerings and sacrifices, representations of bacchantes, satyrs, "Greek youths," nymphs, vestal virgins and fauns, among other classical figures that satisfied the demands of private collectors. ¶ No documents have been found from the period that testify to the existence of any finished drawings or studies for later works by Clodion, a situation which does not apply to most of the sculptors who were his contemporaries. However, it is known that Clodion did not tend to make sketches or preliminary studies for his carved and sculpted works. This methodology may in part be explained by the advice given by Natoire (1700–1777), the director of the French Academy in Rome, who encouraged sculpture students to put aside drawing and copy the old models in plaster[11]. This being the case, Clodion would have drawn infrequently, making it even more difficult to confirm that he was indeed the author of drawings that were initially attributed to him. However, the Metropolitan Museum of

8. On 27 February 1771 Natoire wrote the following in a letter to Marigny: "Le sr Claudion se determine enfin de s'en retourner en France après neuf années de séjour à Rome; c'est un sculpteur qui, partout où il se trouvera, se fera estimer avec distinction par son talent" ["Mr. Claudion finally decides to return to France after nine years living in Rome; he is a sculptor who, wherever he is, makes himself loved with distinction thanks to his talent"] (*Corresp. Directeurs*, 1902, p. 324). See *Ibidem*, 1992, p. 54.

9. "On recherchait ses charmantes productions, les unes inspirées par l'antique, et les autres par ce goût qui lui était naturel pour le genre aimable et gracieux. Elles étaient achetées avant même qu'il les eût finies. Des amateurs français, italiens, anglais, allemands et russes s'empressèrent de l'occuper [...] Son génie fécond multipliait les sujets aimables, sans se répéter ni se copier [...] Il savait rendre intéressans jusqu'aux sujets les plus simples." ["People sought after his charming works, some inspired by ancient times and others by the taste, which came naturally to him, for the kind and graceful gender. His works were bought even before they were finished. French, Italian, English, German, and Russian admirers hastened to occupy his time [...] His fertile genius multiplied the kind subjects, without repetitions and without copying himself [...] He knew how to render interesting even the most simple themes."]. See DINGÉ, [1814], pp. 1–2.

10. Clodion travels to Italy, more specifically to Rome and to Carrara on an official mission to procure marble for the King's Buildings and for the decoration of the pulpit at Rouen Cathedral.

11. PARIS, 1992, p. 19.

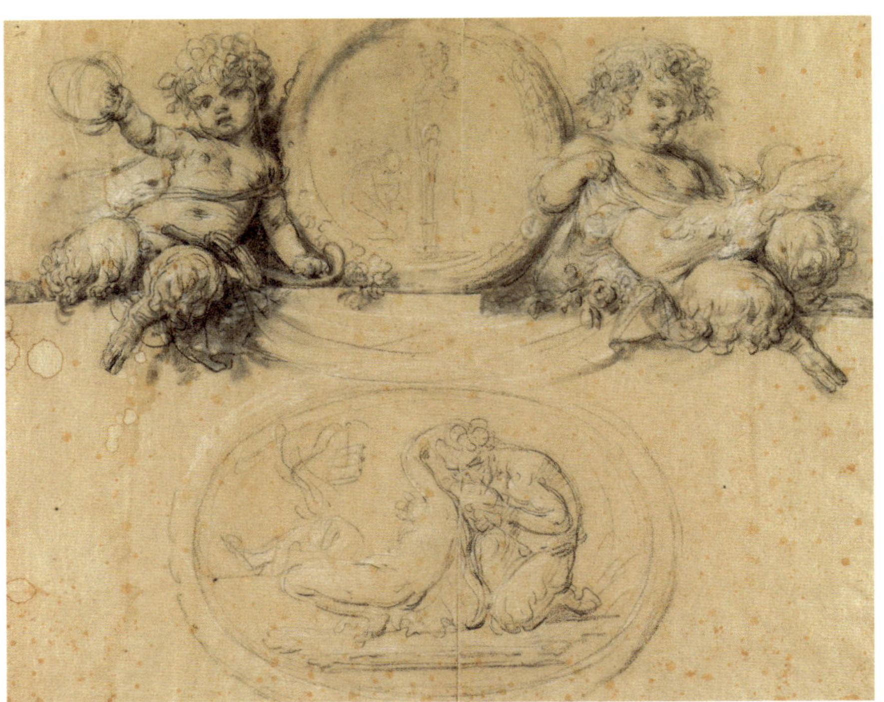

– fig. 19.1 –
Claude Michel, called Clodion (1738–1814),
Deux satyres enfants tenant un médaillon; une nymphe et un satyre,
second half of the 18th century. Black chalk with white chalk highlights on paper, 42.4 × 52 cm, inv. 608.
© Bayonne, musée Bonnat-Helleu
Photo A. Vaquero

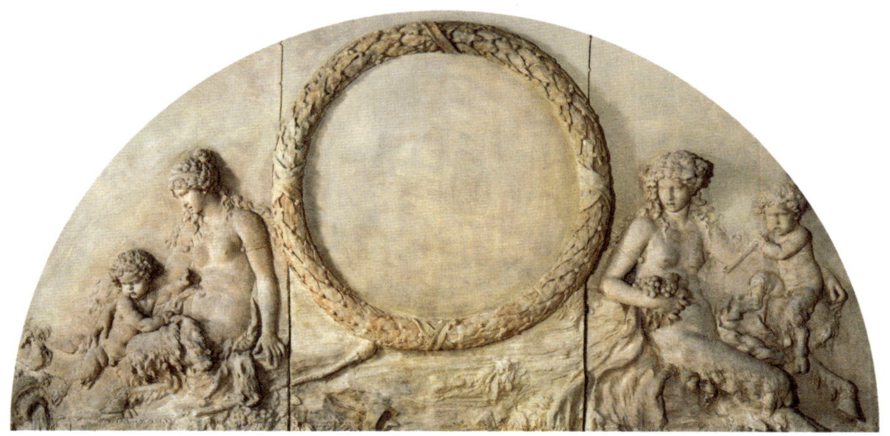

– fig. 19.2 –
Claude Michel,
called Clodion
(1738–1814),
Satyresse jouant avec un satyre enfant, de part et d' autre d' une guirlande ayant entouré un oeil-de boeuf.
Plaster relief,
205 × 410 × 11 cm.
Paris, musée du Louvre,
département des Sculptures,
inv. R.F. 3424.

Art in New York owns a drawing by Clodion entitled *Two Putti with Grapes and an Overturned Pitcher* (inv. 59.104), which, in its handling of the figures, has been likened to the Gulbenkian drawing. At the Bonnat Museum in Bayonne, there are two drawings that are also attributed to the master, entitled *Un amour et un satyre* (inv. 1616) and *Deux satyres enfants tenant un médaillon; une nymphe et un satyre* respectively (fig. 19.1). The latter has an almost identical theme and composition to the work shown here, featuring as it does the same two differentiated parts and the same protagonists doing similar things. Additionally, the dimensions of this study are very similar to those of the Gulbenkian Collection's drawing[12]. ¶ These facts raise, however, serious doubt about the authorship of the Gulbenkian drawing, and all of this leads one to believe that it is the work of another artist who was seduced and inspired by Clodion's themes and style. However, this means that the identity of its author remains unknown to us. ¶ The study shows a clearly unfinished decorative composition, divided into two sections. In the upper section two young satyr musicians are shown sitting against an empty oval medallion with traces of decoration on the surrounding frame. The satyr on the left, in profile, is playing a double flute while the one on the right is looking at the spectator and holding a tambourine. On the same plane as these elements, in the space between the figures, a decorative box and an indistinct pair of doves can just be made out. The image of the two satyrs shows the strong influence of François Boucher. They are depicted as charmingly plump children and are adorned with ribbons tied around their arms and wound around their backs, as they are in so many of the painter's works. Interestingly, this type of composition, with figures leaning against a medallion, can also be seen in Clodion's works, namely his stucco bas-relief *Satyresse jouant avec un satyre enfant, de part et d' autre d' une guirlande ayant entouré un oeil-de boeuf*[13] (fig. 19.2). ¶ In the lower section, a bacchanal is depicted within a cartouche: a kneeling adult satyr voluptuously unveils the naked body of a young woman, who kneels adoringly before a bust of Priapus, next to which is a winged vase. This Greek divinity was the protector of gardens, vineyards, flocks and bees. He was also considered to be the god of fertility and the reproductive force of nature. The representation of Priapus is not infrequent in Clodion's works, particularly in the sculptural group *L 'Offrande à Priape*, a terracotta piece which now belongs to the J.P. Getty Museum[14]. The figure of the kneeling adult satyr, with his strong physique and smiling face, has horns, a beard and goat's legs which are clearly visible and characteristic of the kinds of mythological figures that are so common in Clodion's work. ¶ The Calouste Gulbenkian Collection's

12. I would like to thank Sophie Harent, the Director of the Musée Bonnat for providing information on the works in the museum.

13. PARIS, 1992, no. 39, pp. 214–15 (repr.).

14. LOS ANGELES, The J. Paul Getty Museum, Malibu. See PARIS, 1992, no. 65 (pp. 311–15), p. 312, fig. 157 and 158.

drawing shows a recognizable technical and stylistic quality and its subject matter reveals the sources that inspired its author. However, many of the questions raised by analysis of the work remain unanswered. Who was its author and when was it made? What is the relationship between the two parts? Is it a preliminary study for a single decorative composition or for different compositions? Further research on the drawings attributed to Clodion, however scarce these may be, might shed some light on these questions.

PROVENANCE

Mahérault Collection, sale in Paris, 27–29 May 1880, lot no. 20 (reproduced in the auction catalogue, p. 11, engraved by Campollion); Guyot de Villeneuve Collection, sale in Paris, 28 May 1900, lot no. 12; Marquis de Biron Collection, first sale in Paris, 9 June 1914, lot no. 14 (reproduced in the auction catalogue, p. 11); David David-Weill Collection, Neuilly-sur-Seine, 1921. Acquired by Calouste Gulbenkian from Wildenstein, London, April–May 1937.

•

EXHIBITIONS

PORTO, 1964, no. 64 (repr.); OEIRAS, 1965, no. 230; CAMBRIDGE, 2000, no. 101, pp. 224–25, p. 225 (repr.); LISBON, PORTO, 2000–2002, no. 101, pp. 224–25, p. 225 (repr.); MADRID, 2002, no. 67, pp. 158–59, p. 159 (repr.); LISBON, 2006b, no. 53, pp. 194–95, p. 195 (repr.).

•

LITERATURE

HENRIOT, 1928, III, pp. 49–50.

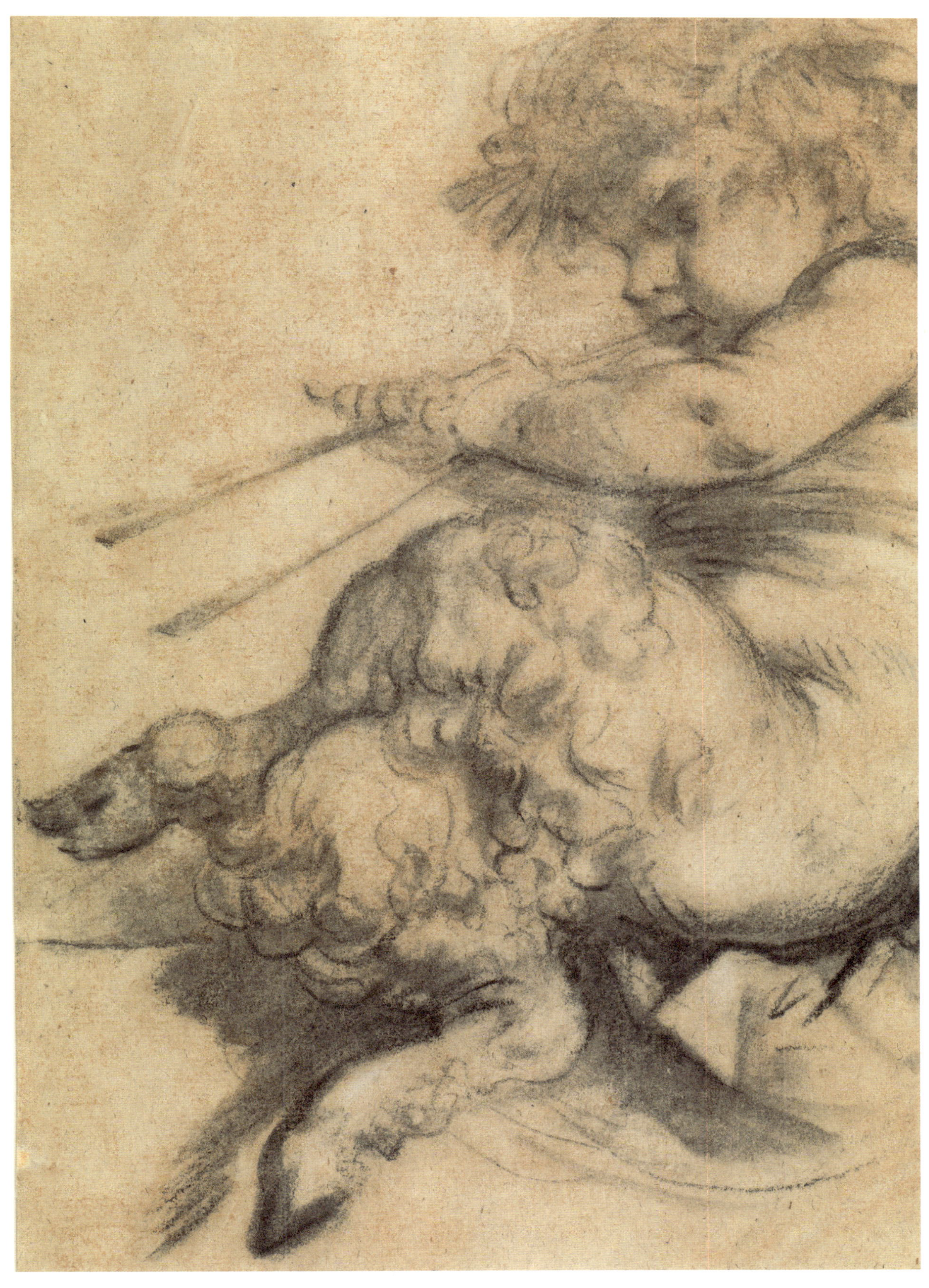

Detail of composition [19].

[20]

FRANCESCO GUARDI

Venice, 1712–1793

CAPRICCIO WITH ROMAN RUINED ARCH AND CIRCULAR TEMPLE

Venice, ca. 1770–80

Pen and brown ink with grey wash on paper (recto);
pen and brown ink, with graphite tracing (verso).
23.1 × 14.7 cm.
Verso: Interior with columns.
Inv. 2871

Between 1907 and 1921, Calouste Gulbenkian purchased a series of twenty paintings by Francesco Guardi, nineteen of which can be found in the permanent exhibition in his museum in Lisbon[1]. The pieces in this group (*vedute*, *capricci* and *feste*) are unique in their quality and thematic range and attest to the Collector's admiration for the pictorial work of the Venetian artist. Although Guardi was also a reputable draughtsman, Gulbenkian was not attracted by his graphic work, which mostly consisted of preparatory studies for paintings. ¶ However, being keenly aware of the importance of drawing in studying the pictorial work of an artist as unique as Guardi (in the words of Simonson, it is in drawing that "[...] one sees [...] his simplest formulae of artistic expression stripped of the attribute of colour")[2], the Calouste Gulbenkian Foundation decided to purchase this piece[3], which have formely been in the collection of the Duke of Talleyrand, at a public sale held in New York in 2002. Experts have always believed the work to be a preparatory study for one of the paintings bought by Calouste Gulbenkian. ¶ Indeed, a close relationship exists between the drawing now under discussion and the painting *Capriccio* (inv. 531), which has belonged to the Gulbenkian collection since 1919[4] (fig. 20.1). The two works, which are both late-period pieces created at the height of the artist's maturity, contain a recurring theme in Guardi's oeuvre, that is, an imagined view of a ruined double arch above a watercourse that extends diagonally, passing out of sight. Through the second arch, part of a temple with a circular dome can be seen in the background. ¶ This *mise-en-scène* varies, however, in the number and distribution of the figures that enliven the composition. In the painting, the foreground is occupied by two fishermen and a dog suggesting movement along the riverbank as well as by a second group of small figures who appear to be looking for something on the ground under one of the arches. In the drawing, however, the dog do not appear and only three of the above-mentioned figures are shown, although their poses are the same as those in the painting. ¶ The back of the sheet contains a study of an interior space featuring columns and some

1. The group of paintings by Francesco Guardi has been studied in its entirety by several experts, including PALLUCHINI, 1965; MORASSI, 1984; MURARO, 1993.

2. SIMONSON, 1904, p. 58.

3. MORASSI, 1958, pp. 9–10 and no. 72, p. 31; MORASSI, 1984, vol. III, no. 639, p. 188 (il. 620).

4. PALLUCHINI, 1965, Tav. XII (repr.); MORASSI, [1973], p. 279, p. 483, no. 934 (fig. 831); BORTOLATTO, 1974, no. 524, p. 121, p. 119 (repr.); MORASSI, 1984, VOL. I, p. 279, no. 934, p. 483, and vol. II, fig. 831; MURARO, 1993, no. 6, pp. 26–27 (repr.); SAMPAIO, 2009, no. 65, pp. 150–51 (repr.).

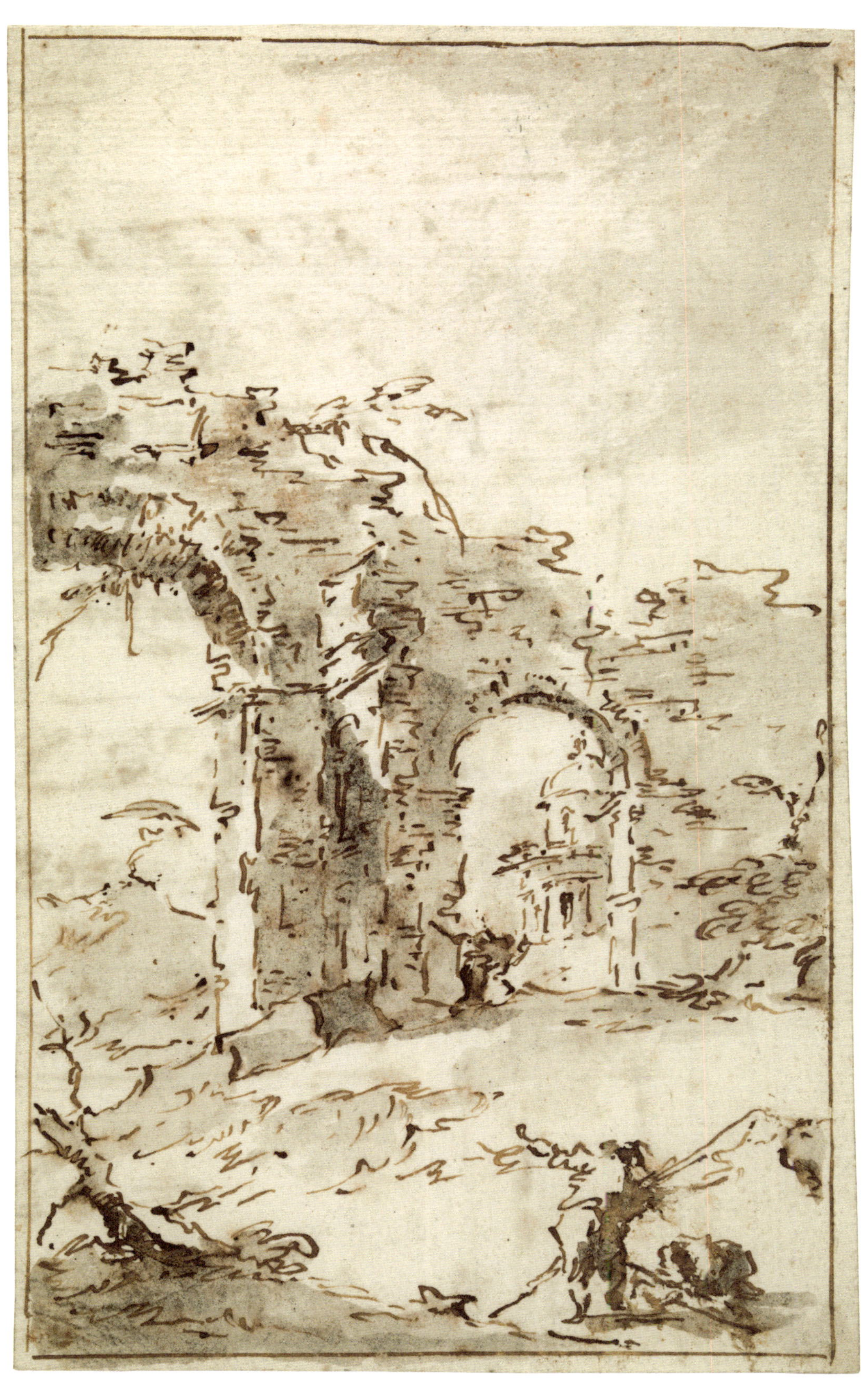

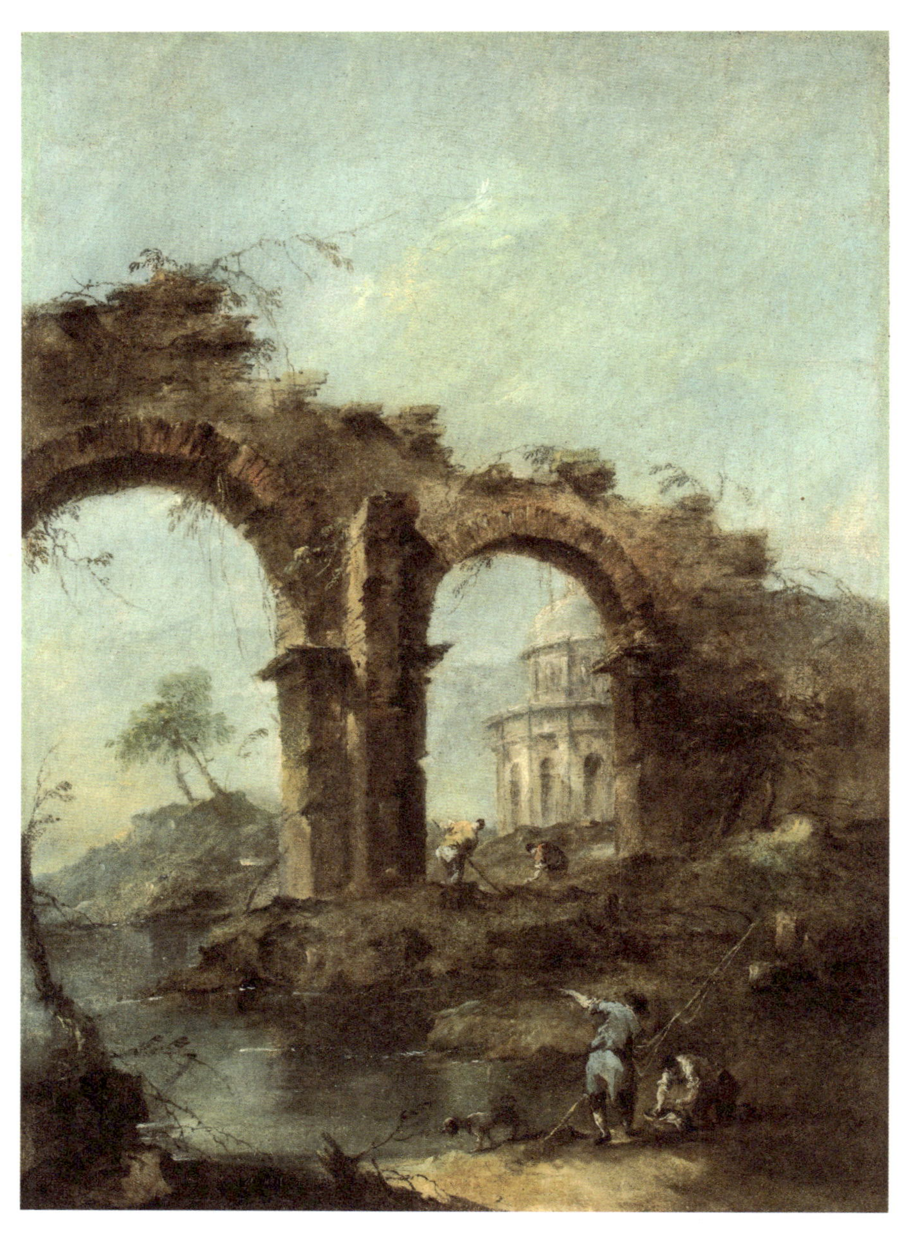

– fig. 20.1 –
Francesco Guardi (1712–1793),
Capriccio, ca. 1770–80. Oil on canvas,
46 × 34 cm. Lisbon, Calouste Gulbenkian Museum, inv. 531.

Photo: Catarina Gomes Ferreira

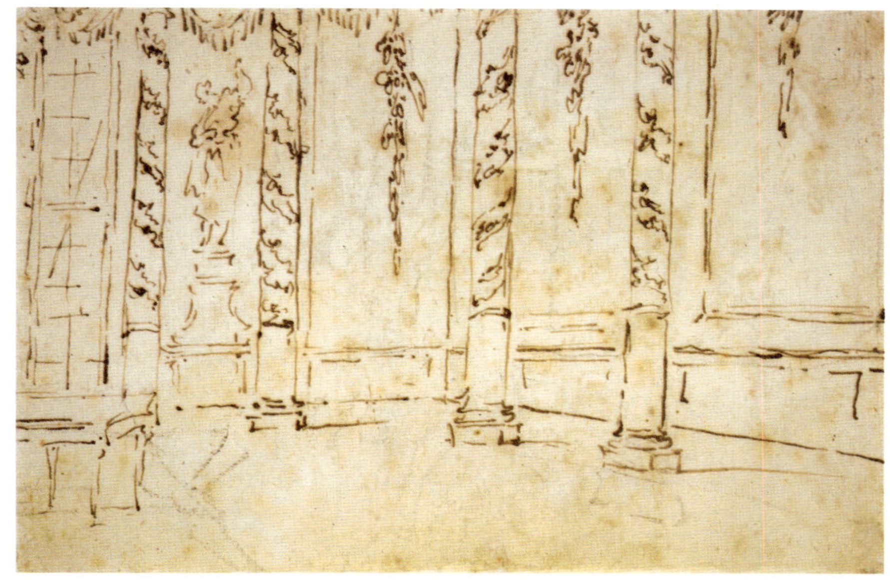

[20] verso

5. MORASSI, 1984, vol. III, no. 472, p. 162, il. 475.

6. *Ibidem*, vol. III, no. 318, p. 134, il. 317.

7. SHAW, 1951, pp. 29–32.

8. *Ibidem*, p. 39.

Louis XVI-style decorative elements including garlands, wreaths, a sculpture on a pedestal, a mirror and a table. This composition resembles the drawing *Projetto di decorazione con Colonne*, which belonged to the J. Scholz Collection and later offered to the Pierpont Morgan Library in New York[5] (fig. 20.2) and was one of the preparatory studies for the watercolour drawing *Il Banquetto per le nozze del duca di Polignac nella Villa dei Gradenigo a Carpenedo*. The latter work, which depicts a ceremony celebrated on 6 September 1790, is now owned by the Correr Museum in Venice[6] (fig. 20.3). ¶ Using different artistic media specific to both painting and drawing, Guardi obtained the same harmonious effect in these works. In the painting, which according to Byam Shaw, could be considered "romantic capricci"[7], the use of an almost monochrome palette dominated by greenish hues, of diluted brushstrokes producing transparent effects and dissolved outlines, as well as the quality of light and shade with contrasts between the different planes, creates an atmosphere of great romantic intensity. In the drawing, the same result is achieved by the use of short broken lines drawn with a pen. These lines are broken off and then frenziedly restarted, while the wash emphasizes and enhances the structural elements of the composition and allows the transitory nature of the gestures and emotions to be captured. ¶ Guardi's drawings, like his paintings, feature a wide range of themes. They include sketches for figures and studies for religious, mythological and historical scenes as well as for Venetian views or festivals and *capricci*. The variety of his themes is matched by the broad range of techniques that he used[8], although it must be acknowledged that Guardi made most frequent use of the pen and washes, which allowed him to express himself more freely and capture the transitory atmosphere of eighteenth-century Venice more immediately. ¶ Although little is known of the graphical work that Guardi produced when employed as a youth in the family workshop under the direction of his eldest brother Giovanni Antonio, or Gian Antonio (1698–1760), it was early in his career that he adopted the broken and angular lines, quick and tremulous

9. Venice, which had dominated the seas and maintained its independence for centuries, succumbed to the invasion of Napoleon Bonaparte (1769–1821) in 1797. With its independence lost and the last doge deposed, a series of political agreements (the Treaty of Campo Formio) brought Venice under the rule of the Austrian Empire and the Republic was abolished.

10. PALLUCHINI, 1965, p. 10.

11. "[...] est l'homme du temps qui fuit, des formes qui se font et se défont." *In* BRION, 1976, p. 46.

touch, and contrasts between light and shade that would characterise his drawings as an independent artist. ¶ The change that took place in Guardi's style can be seen in both his graphical work and in his painting, which evolved from the initial precision of the early years to the unsettled atmospheres and light effects seen in his later drawings. While his early religious or merely decorative works were created in his studio, the drawings that reveal the influence of Canaletto were faithful portraits characterised by greater topographical rigour that were executed *in situ* after a period of detailed observation. At the height of his maturity, the artist often returned to studio work. At this stage, his output was dominated by imagined scenes, the characteristic sites of Venice or idealised landscapes whose blurred outlines are transformed in the shimmering of the lights reflected in the waters of the lagoon, creating a fantastic, quasi-magical yet also elegiac interpretation. In this way, he also captured the historical moment of the decline of the Venetian Republic, which had been heralded by weaknesses in its political, economic, social and moral structures[9]. ¶ As Palluchini writes, in the *capricci* "the frenetic rhythm [of Guardi's] style eliminates allboundaries between reality and fantasy'[10]. In effect, it is in these imagined or idealised views that the painter best expresses his inner disquiet. In many of these works, decayed ruins, such as the arch in the Gulbenkian drawing, signal the irreversible passage of time, to which the grass that has invaded its stones already bears witness. Classical architectural structures, such as the circular temple, symbolise the memory of an age that has past. This discontinuity is highlighted by the presence of stagnant waters and figures who, although in motion, also appear to be suspended in an age without meaning. For Francesco Guardi, the theme of most of his *capricci* is therefore the solitude and silence emanating from the history of Venice in the late eighteenth century. The last European painter of the rococo period, Guardi "is the man of the time that vanishes, of the shapes which are formed and undone"[11]. ¶ The drawing now

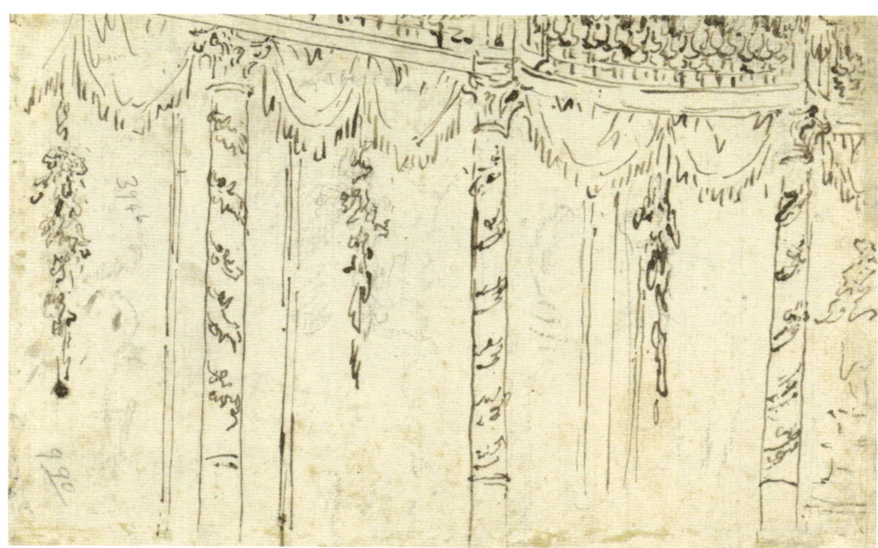

– fig. 20.2 –
Francesco Guardi (1712–1793), *Sketch for a Decoration with Column, Festoons, and a Loggia* (verso), 23.2 × 14.5 cm. [*View with an Obelisk and Figures*, recto]. The Pierpont Morgan Library, New York, inv. 1977.54. Gift of Mr. Janos Scholz

under discussion served as a study not only for the Gulbenkian painting but also for the other two versions that the artist also produced. One of these versions, owned by the former Broglio Collection of Paris[12], features variations in the foreground details and in the distribution of the figures, while the second version[13], which is oval in shape, formed part of the former Fauchier-Magnan Collection and was subsequently sold at Christie's in London in 1957 under lot number 46. A copy of the Gulbenkian drawing, which had previously belonged to the W.G. Mather Collection, was attributed to Giacomo (1764–1835), Guardi's youngest son. However, in 1937 it was presented at the Museum of Fine Arts in Springfield, Massachusetts, as the work of Francesco Guardi himself[14]. ¶ When the artist died in 1793, his son and close collaborator owned thousands of drawings by his father, a large number of which were sold to Count Teodoro Correr in 1829 and now form part of the Correr Museum's estate in Venice[15].

12. MORASSI, [1973], no. 935, p. 483, fig. 830; BORTOLATTO, 1974, no. 525, p. 121, p. 119 (repr.).

13. MORASSI, [1973], no. 948, p. 486; BORTOLATTO, 1974, no. 124bis, p. 121.

14. MORASSI, 1984, vol. III, p. 188, no. 639.

15. BYAM SHAW, 1951, p. 13, n. 2 and pp. 14–15.

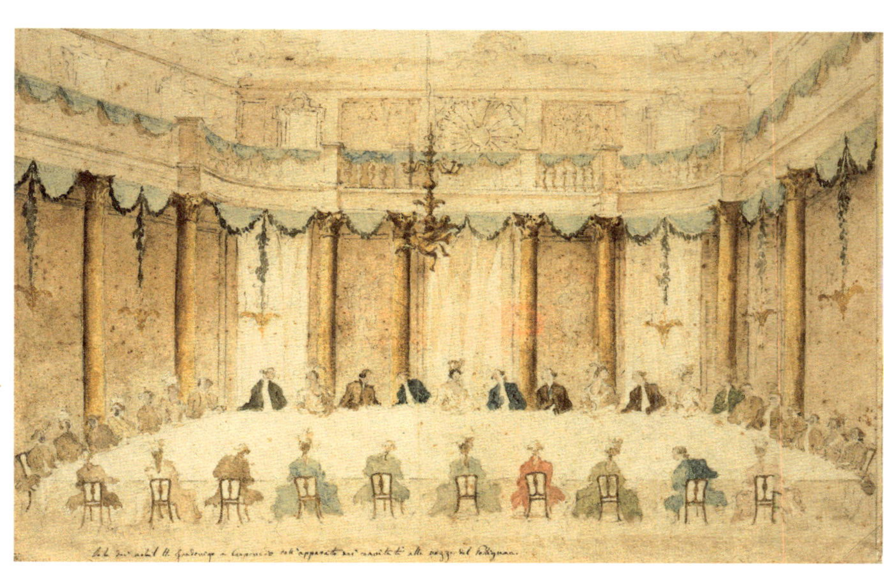

– fig. 20.3 –
Francesco Guardi (1712–1793), *Banquet for the Wedding of the Duke of Polignac in Gardenigo Villa at Carpenedo.* Watercolour, 27.5 × 41.9 cm. Venice, Museo Correr, inv. 29. ©2012 DeAgostini Picture Library / Scala, Florence

PROVENANCE

Former Fauchier-Magnan Collection, Paris, sale at Sotheby's, London, 4 December 1935, lot no. 29;
Duke of Talleyrand Collection. Acquired by the Calouste Gulbenkian Foundation, at Christie's, New York, 23 January 2002, lot no. 51.

•

LITERATURE

MORASSI, 1958, no. 72, p. 31 (repr.).

[21]

JOSEPH MALLORD WILLIAM TURNER
London, 1775–1851

RUINS OF TINTERN ABBEY
England, ca. 1794

Watercolour with pencil tracing on paper.
33.3 × 24 cm.
Inv. 375

1. Indianapolis Museum of Art, inv. 72.166. See SHANES, Eric, *in* LONDON, 2000, no. 1, p. 60.

2. The Calouste Gulbenkian Museum owns two key paintings by the master, *Shipwreck of a Cargo Ship*, inv. 260, and *Quillebeuf, Mouth of the Seine*, inv. 2362.

3. London, Tate Britain, inv. TO1585. See WARRELL, Ian, *in* LISBON, 2003, p. 14 (repr.), p. 16.

4. See SHANES, Eric, *in* LONDON, 2000, p. 11.

Turner was only fifteen years' old when he exhibited his first watercolour at the Royal Academy in 1790. The work in question was *View of the Archbishop's Palace, Lambeth*[1], in which the influence of Thomas Malton (1748–1804) and Edward Dayes (1763–1804) can be seen in the architecture and the figures that inhabit the composition, respectively. In fact, the artist's first works were exclusively rendered in watercolours and, even when he had become an outstanding oil painter[2], he continued working intensively as a watercolourist. Only six years later, at the Royal Academy in 1796, he exhibited his first oil painting, *Fishermen at Sea*[3], a dramatic moonlit scene that opened the way to a long and brilliant career as a painter of seascapes. ¶ The sketches contained in the small notebooks that he carried with him on the fifty-or-so trips that, since childhood, he had undertaken in Great Britain and the European continent bear witness to his passion for drawing and the important role that these notes played in the creation of more elaborate compositions. Further proof of this passion is provided by the multiple series of watercolour landscapes that he painted both in response to patrons' commissions and for his own enjoyment. ¶ In the 1780s, following in the footsteps of skilled English artists such as Edward Dayes (1763–1804), Thomas Hearne (1744–1817) and John Robert Cozens (1752–1797), Turner adopted the watercolour genre, the characteristics of which – transparency, spontaneity and immediacy – particularly favoured the interpretation of atmospheric effects. From this point onwards, Turner became the great master of a specific genre of drawing, that is, the finished watercolour[4]. These works, created in response to commissions placed by his patrons, were shown to the wider public at the Royal Academy (until 1830) and in commercial galleries as well as through reproductions published by printers and publishers such as W.B. Cook, Charles Heath and Thomas Lupton. ¶ An outstanding landscapist, Turner's exposure to the work of masters such as Claude Lorrain (ca. 1604/5–1682), Willem van de Velde the Elder (1611–1693), Willem van de Velde the Younger (1633–1707), and Claude-Joseph Vernet (1714–1789)

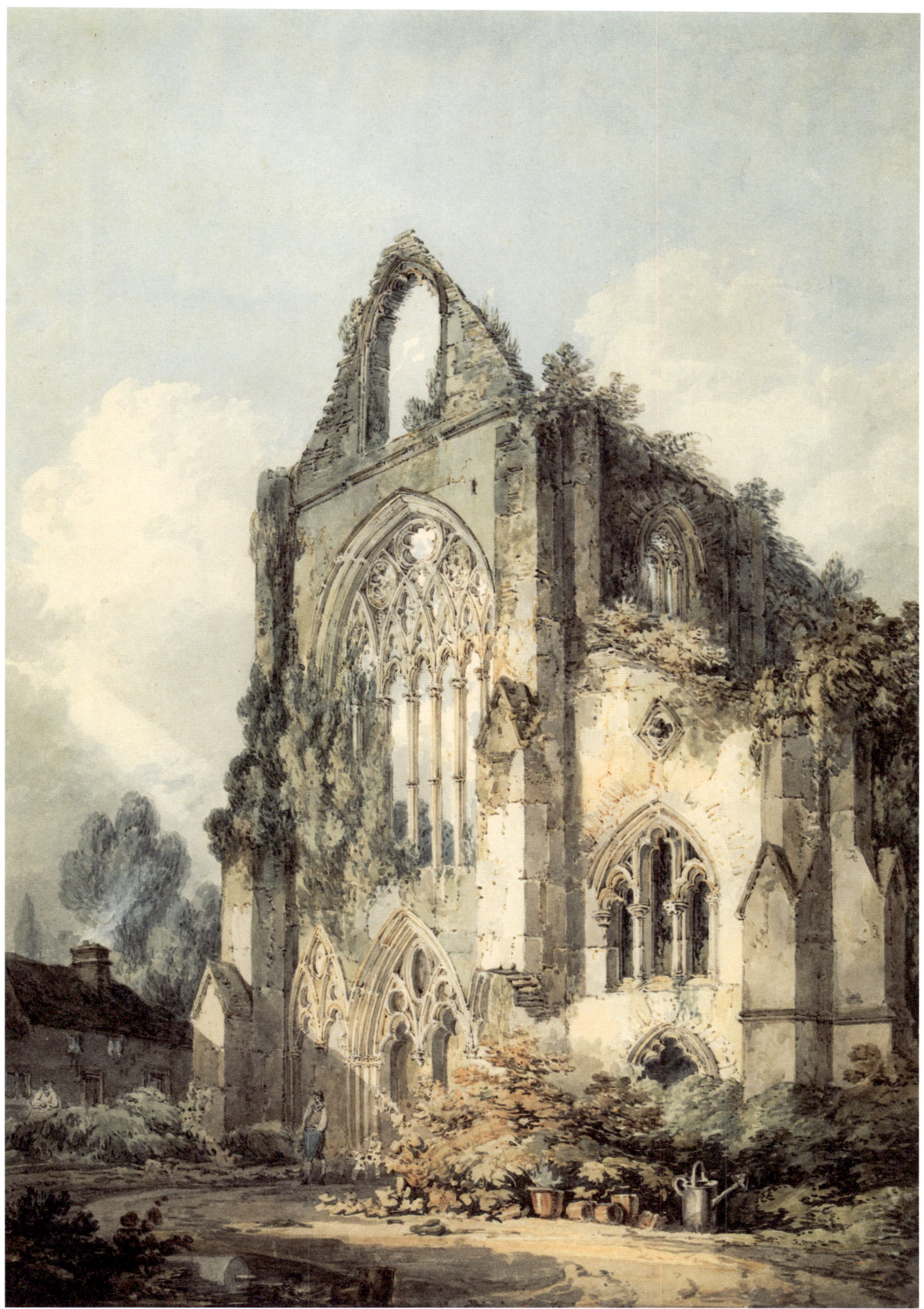

proved to be particularly important in his artistic training. In his youth he created meticulously detailed works that were essentially topographical and were inspired by trips that, at this stage of his life, were limited to regions around the west coast of Britain, Wales and the Isle of Wight, as well as the more frequently visited parts of Kent and Sussex. When he reached maturity he largely sought to employ a visionary imagination in order to express the grandeur and sublimity of the landscape under the dramatic effects of light and atmosphere, an approach which led to real forms becoming gradually dissolved to the point of absolute abstraction. ¶ The watercolour *Ruins of Tintern Abbey* was painted around 1794, two years after the artist visited Wales for the first time. The beauty of the ruins of this Cistercian abbey, which was founded in the twelfth century, served as an inspiration to several painters, particularly after the publication of William Gilpin's (1724–1804) work *Observations on the River Wye and several parts of South Wales, etc. relative chiefly to Picturesque Beauty; made in the summer of the year 1770* (London, 1782). The building also naturally attracted the attention of Turner, who depicted it in several topographical views, one of which, owned by the British Museum (inv. 1878, 1228.41), closely resembles the Gulbenkian Collection's. It is

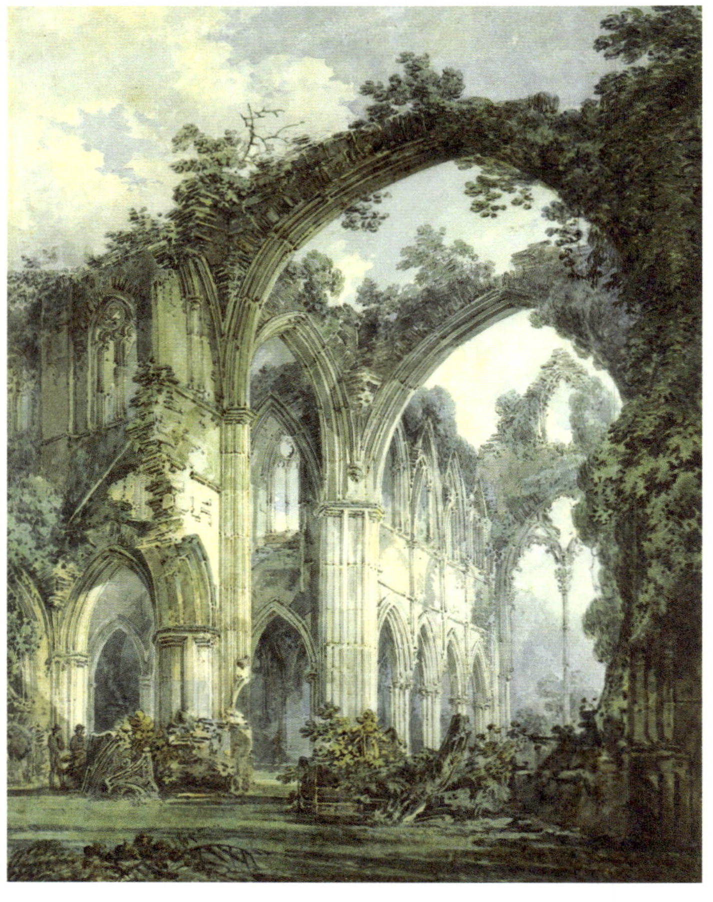

– fig. 21.1 –
Joseph Mallord William Turner (1775–1851), *The Inside of Tintern Abbey, Monmouthshire*, ca. 1794. Watercolour, 32.1 × 25.1 cm. London, Victoria and Albert Museum, inv. 1683-1871. ©2012 Photo Scala, Florence / V&A Images / Victoria and Albert Museum, London

no surprise that the romantic poet William Wordsworth (1770–1850) visited the area around the same time and, in 1798, published the poem *Lines Written a Few Miles above Tintern Abbey.* ¶ The many representations of Tintern Abbey that Turner produced show the various façades, the insides of the structure, or its situation in the surrounding landscape. Of these works, a more complex composition of the ruined building can be seen in the watercolour *The Inside of Tintern Abbey, Monmouthshire*[5], a piece owned by the Victoria and Albert Museum (fig. 21.1) that may have been presented by Turner at the Royal Academy exhibition in 1794, under number 402[6], at a time when his participation was lauded by the critics. ¶ In the watercolour owned by the Gulbenkian Collection, the western façade of the Abbey is shown with ogee arches in which can clearly be seen the delicate tracery of windows that had once held beautiful stained glass. This Gothic church, which is situated among the hills of the Wye Valley, close to Chepstow, was rebuilt in the thirteenth and fourteenth centuries before falling into ruin after Henry VIII gave the order to dissolve the monasteries in 1536. Turner evokes what remains of the construction's beauty through meticulous, almost miniaturist, brushstrokes with smooth and luminous shades that demonstrate his skill in playing with effects of light and shade. The different hues in which he painted the stones reveal the influence of the watercolourist Michael Angelo Rooker (1743–1801), whose works Turner had studied and copied. The grandeur of the monument, which rises out of the observer's sight, is accentuated by the use of subtle pictorial processes applied to the treatment of perspective, specifically in relation to the diagonal view of the building (emphasized by the winding path leading towards the entrance), the adoption of a viewpoint situated on a lower plane, and the inclusion of small human figures. ¶ A picturesque architectural landscape created in the taste of the time, this watercolour reveals Turner's precocious instinct for capturing the sublime in nature that was so cherished by the romantic generation to which he belonged. Among the stones that remain standing, evoking the historic nobility of the abbey, tufts of vegetation appear, bearing witness to the ephemeral and inevitable passage of time. ¶ But it is mainly the present, enveloped in a sense of total harmony, which Turner evokes: a man calmly leaves the abbey, various gardening tools lie waiting to be used, another figure appears behind some nearby bushes, and smoke emerges from the chimney of the cottage in the background, a sign of the human life taking place there.

5. A very similar watercolour to this one (inv. TB XXIII A; D00374), made after a pencil drawing, also belongs also to Tate Britan (TB XII E).

6. The studies of this work that have been carried out to date have failed to resolve this question. See WARRELL, Ian, *in* WASHINGTON, DALLAS, NEW YORK, 2007–2008, no. 1, p. 26 (repr.).

PROVENANCE

Acquired by Calouste Gulbenkian through Agnew & Sons, at Christie's, London, 30 June 1916, lot no. 60A.

EXHIBITIONS

LISBON, 1973, no. 5, pp. 38–39, p. 39 (repr.); LISBON, 1976, no. 19; LISBON, 1985, no. 20, p. 22, p. 145 (repr.).

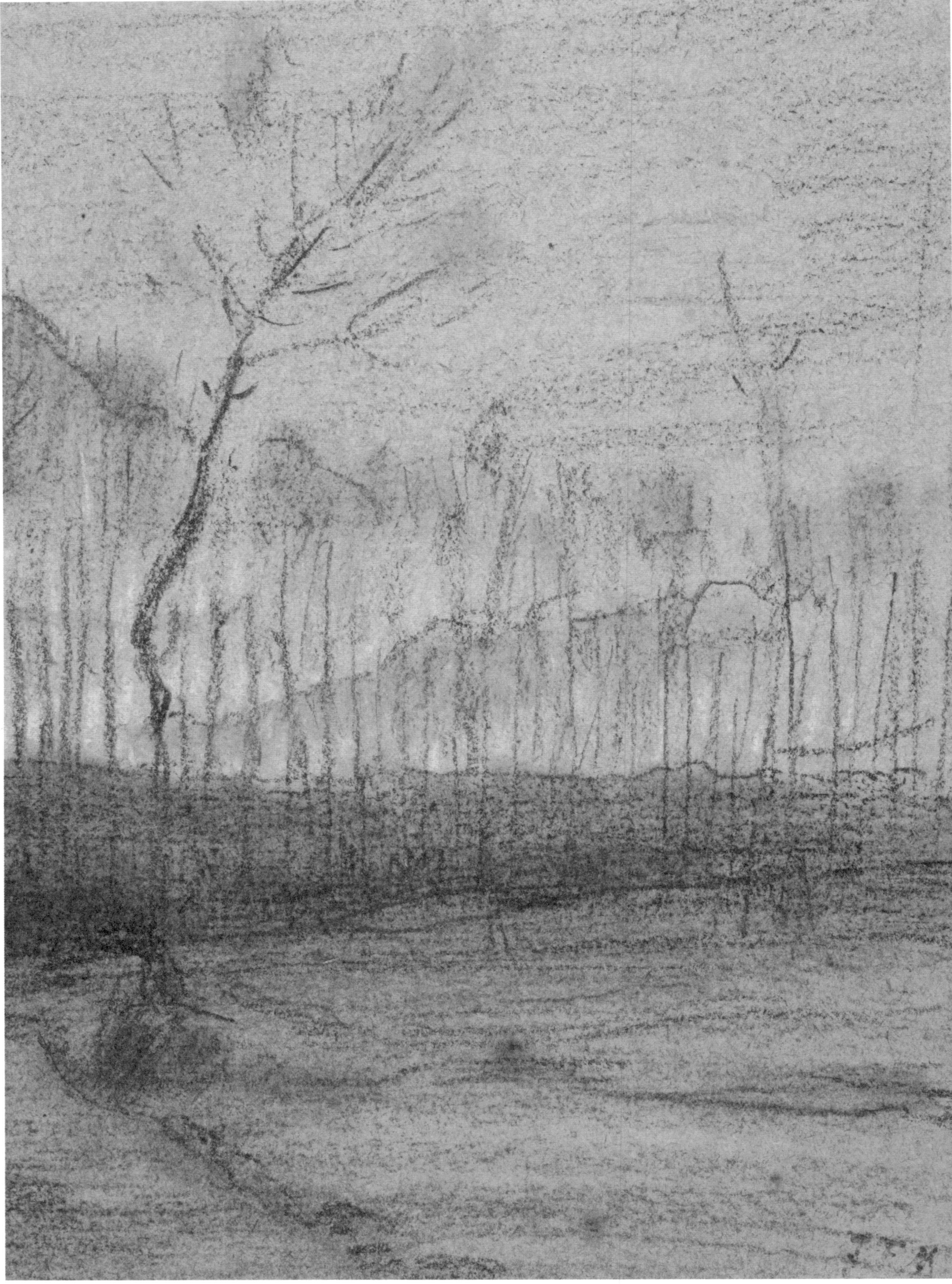

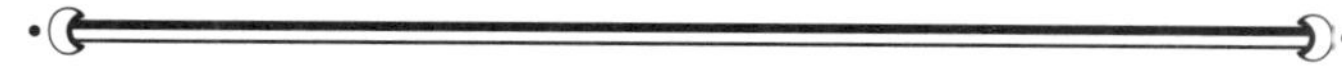

NINETEENTH CENTURY

[22]

JOSEPH MALLORD WILLIAM TURNER
London, 1775–1851

PLYMOUTH WITH A RAINBOW
England, ca. 1825

Watercolour with touches of gouache on paper.
16.4 × 24.7 cm.
Inv. 374

1. See SHANES, 1981. However, the dates of each series vary slightly from author to author.

Turner's art developed through the practice of watercolour. Using this technique, he began by creating landscape views characterized by an objective depiction of reality that still retained strong ties to eighteenth-century traditions. As he matured, however, his relationship with nature gradually came under the sway of a more introspective, poetic and dramatic vision, particularly after he had fully grasped the effects of light and the use of colour. In his later years, Turner made full use of the resources of the watercolour: the landscape, immersed in an atmospheric haze, becomes little more than a sublime and at times magical space made of light and touches of colour that are sometimes tumultuous and sometimes crystalline. ¶ Together with Turner's creative power and inventive capacity, his control over the pictorial process won him a host of loyal admirers and patrons from whom he received numerous commissions. In the 1810s he started to work on series of finished watercolours for printer-publishers who wanted to turn them into etchings and publish them in collections with specific themes. Over the artist's career, this led to series such as *Liber Studiorum* (1807–19), *Views in Sussex* (1810–23), *Picturesque Views on the Southern Coast of England* (1811–25), *The Rivers of England* (1822–26), *Marine Views* (ca. 1822–24), *The Ports of England* (1825–28), and *Picturesque Views in England and Wales* (1827), among others, which portray landscapes from the sketches he made on his trips[1] away. ¶ The Gulbenkian's watercolour *Plymouth with a Rainbow* belongs to one of these collections, *The Ports of England*. While still working on *The Rivers of England* for William Bernard Cooke (1778–1855), Turner was invited to produce twenty-five watercolours for a new maritime-themed series sponsored by Thomas Lupton (1791–1873), a master engraver with a wealth of experience in the studios of the Cooke brothers, William Bernard and George Cooke (1781–1834). Of the total number of planned watercolours, Turner produced only thirteen, including one for the frontispiece, the preliminary drawing of which currently belongs to the Fitzwilliam Museum in Cambridge. Six of these watercolours were published in May 1826; however,

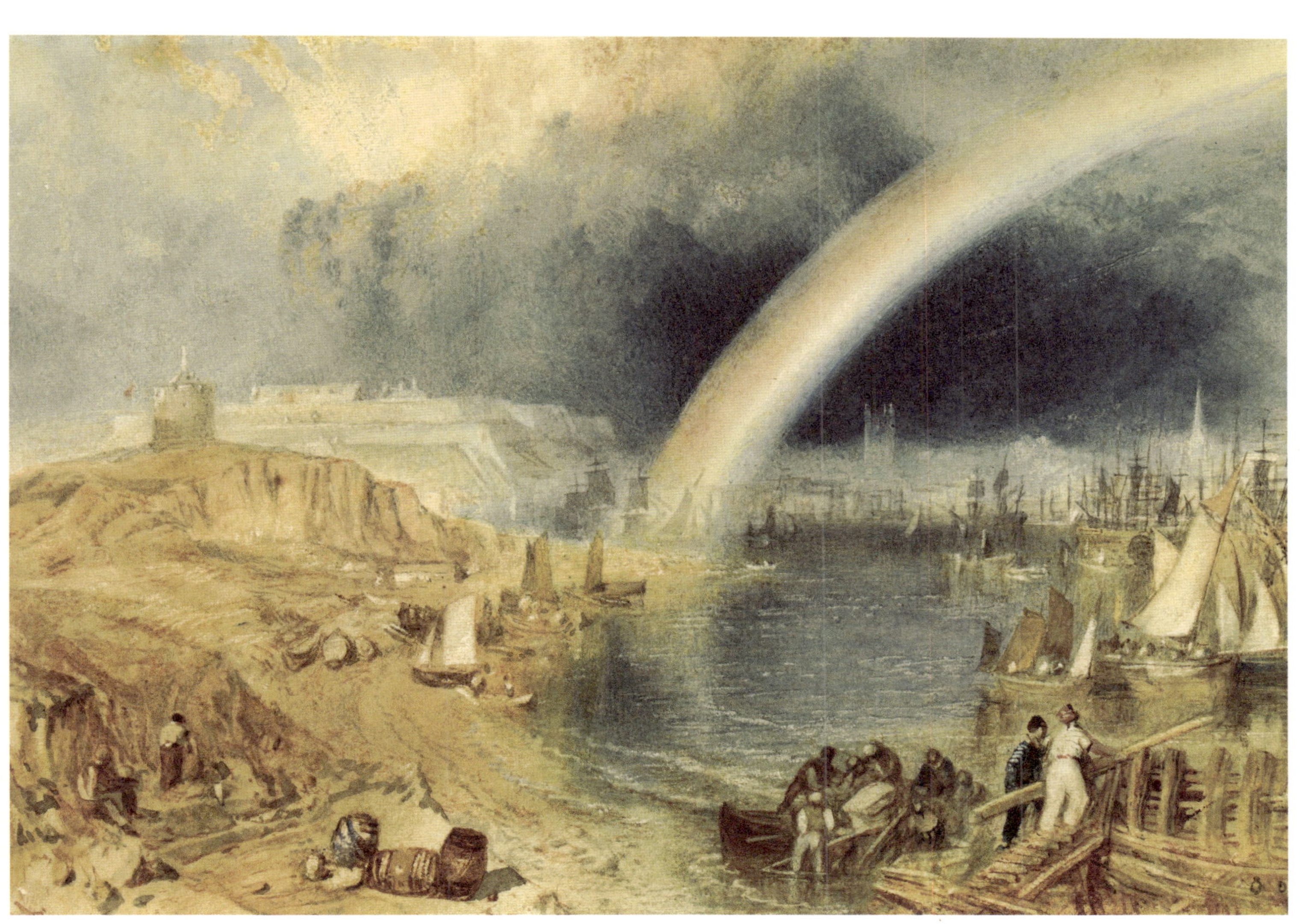

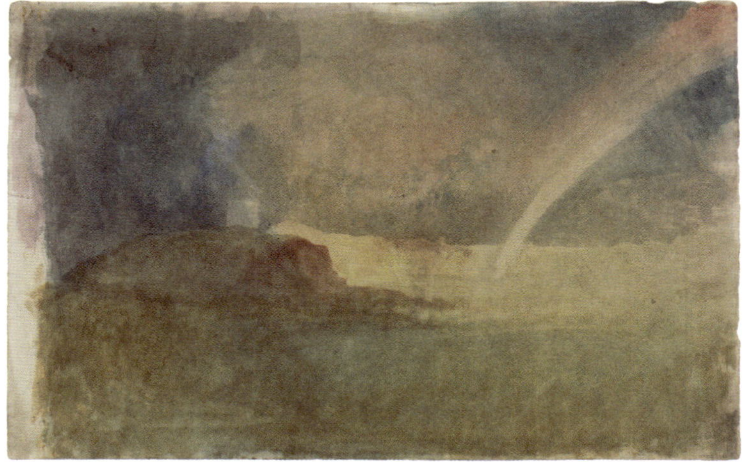

– fig. 22.1 –
Joseph Mallord William Turner (1775–1851), *Preliminary Study for 'Plymouth'*, ca. 1825. Pencil and watercolour, 30.6 × 46.8 cm. London, Tate, Turner Bequest CCLXIII 150-D25272 © Tate, London 2012

2. London, Tate Britain, inv. T.B. CXXXI. See LONDON, 1974, no. 173, p. 80.

3. Turner achieved this effect by scraping the paper with a nail that he allowed to grow for this purpose. See LISBON, 2003, p. 62.

due to the breakdown in relations between Turner and Lupton in 1828, the others remained unfinished and were only published in 1856, five years after the painter's death, when the whole group was republished under the new title *The Harbours of England*. John Ruskin (1819–1900), a collector and scholar of Turner's work, wrote a critical piece for the publication, which Thomas Lupton dedicated to King George IV. ¶ Lupton used a mezzotint technique to translate the features of these watercolours into prints and to transmit the tiny brushstrokes used for atmospheric effect and the meticulous depiction of the compositional detail. This enabled him to create subtle velvety textures and tonal gradations by using steel plates that, being more resistant, could be used to produce large numbers of copies. For his part, Turner also took great care over the quality of this work, following its execution through each stage of the technical process. ¶ The watercolour here shows a view of the town and port of Plymouth, a city located on the south coast of England, around 300 km from London, on the estuary of the Plym and the Tamar rivers. The area, where Turner spent some time, was the subject of several works painted at different times for which numerous studies were made in the sketchbook *Plymouth, Hamoaze*, now owned by the Tate[2]. ¶ In the 1825 version in the Gulbenkian Collection, the full expanse of Plymouth is shown from Turnchapel over Cattewater: the imposing citadel precedes the small fort on Mount Batten; the houses of the city are in the centre background; the fleet of typical Plymouth vessels is shown sailing along the edges and further out to sea; and, lastly, in the foreground, the sandy beach is populated with figures going about the business of the port. ¶ When he made this work, Turner was interested not only in interpreting the surrounding reality but also in capturing the subtleties of the landscape. Thus he gave free rein to his visionary imagination: he enveloped the entire scene in an atmosphere in which one can sense the bright humid light left after the rain; he used a broad palette of warm colours to strengthen the drama of the composition; he sprinkled the surface of the paper with fleeting white dots that suggest the dance of light on the water's surface[3]; and he makes the rainbow that hits the coast into the protagonist of the scene. Above all, Turner saw nature as a setting against which human life unfolded; for this reason the foreground of the watercolour is inhabited by figures who inimitably express the spirit of the place. ¶ In preparing for this work, Turner made a preliminary sketch (as he had done since the 1820s) in pencil and watercolour that currently belongs to the Tate (fig. 22.1). This can be classed as one of the so-called "colour beginnings," or initial studies in which

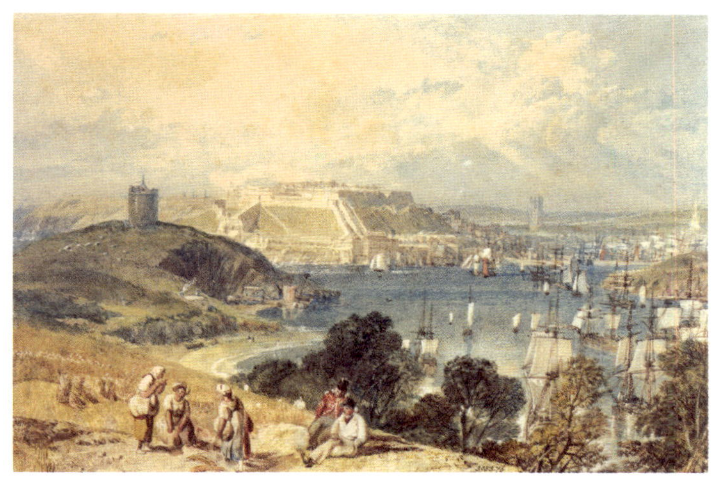

– fig. 22.2 –
Joseph Mallord William Turner (1775–1851), *Plymouth with Mount Batten*, ca. 1816. Watercolour, 14.6 × 23.5 cm. London, Victoria and Albert Museum, inv. 3035-1876. ©2012 Photo Scala, Florence / V&A Images / Victoria and Albert Museum, London

stains of pure colour already determine key areas of the future composition. In the Tate study it is also the rainbow that imposes itself between the stains of colour that determine the organizational layout of the final work. ¶ The Victoria and Albert Museum in London owns a watercolour entitled *Plymouth with Mount Batten* (ca. 1816) (fig. 22.2) which depicts a view that is similar to that of the Gulbenkian watercolour[4] but was perhaps made from a closer and lower vantage point. Comparing both compositions allows us to understand how Turner's art evolved over little less than a decade. In the first composition, the artist evokes the port's activity on a warm afternoon that is interpreted through clear tones; in the Gulbenkian watercolour, the author showed little interest in the surrounding nature. What interested him was capturing the atmospheric effects produced by the passing rain, including the humidity of the air, the light sparkling on the water's surface and, particularly, the dramatic force of the rainbow appearing in the distance among the boats and touching the tip of Mount Batten. ¶ The depiction of the rainbow as a natural atmospheric phenomenon can be seen in several of Turner's works over his career. He was fascinated by its real form, and, as can be seen in the Gulbenkian watercolour, it allowed him to grant aesthetic primacy to atmospheric effects of light and colour. In John Ruskin's opinion, this work "[...] contains the brightest rainbow he [Turner] ever painted [...] not the best, but the most dazzling. [...] It is very like one of Turner's pieces of caprice to introduce a rainbow at all as a principal feature in such a scene; for it is not through the colours of the iris that we generally expect to be shown eighteen-pounder batteries and ninety-gun ships"[5].

4. SHANES, 1981, pp. 37–38, no. 78.

5. RUSKIN, 1904, p. 55.

PROVENANCE

John Dillon; Foster & Son sale, 7 June 1856, lot no. 143; C. Langton (loaned to "Manchester Art Treasures Exhibition", 1857, no. 324); John Farnworth, sale at Christie's, May 1874; William Quilter, sale at Christie's, 4 July 1913, lot no. 107. Acquired by Calouste Gulbenkian from Agnew & Sons, London, 12 February 1914.

•

EXHIBITIONS

MANCHESTER, 1857, p. 188, no. 324; LISBON, 1973, pp. 82–83, no. 27; LONDON, 1975, p. 80, no. 173; LISBON, 1976, no. 18; LISBON, 1985, p. 22, no. 19, p. 144 (repr.); LISBON, 1998, p. 234, no. 233 (repr.); LISBON , 2003, p. 62, 69, no. 25 (repr.); ST IVES, 2006, pp. 38–39, (repr. p. 39 and cover); LONDON, 2013, pp. 94–95, no. 47 (repr.).

•

LITERATURE

RUSKIN, (1904), p. 55; ARMSTRONG, 1902, p. 271; SHANES, 1981, p. 37–38, no. 78.

[23]

HENRY EDRIDGE

London, 1769 – 1821

PORTRAIT OF TWO YOUNG LADIES

England, ca. 1816 (?)

Graphite and watercolour with grey wash on paper.
30.5 × 37.8 cm.
Signed on the lower left-hand side: *Edridge*.
Inv. 864

1. See HARDIE, 1969–1971, vol. III, p. 1–4.

Henry Edridge began his career as a painter of miniatures and portraits before moving on to landscapes and architectural views, which are of equal interest in the wider context of his artistic production. These compositions, which show a deep understanding of nature through his harmonious use of colour, were precursors of the picturesque scenes that subsequently became so characteristic of English painting. ¶ The son of a Westminster tradesman, Edridge first learnt about the arts in his apprenticeship to the painter and engraver William Pether (1738–1821)[1]. He went on to study at the Royal Academy in 1784, where he was taken under the protection of Sir Joshua Reynolds (1723–1792), the institution's first president. There he became skilled in painting miniatures, which became the main focus of his artistic activities. In the landscape genre, Edridge further developed his studies over the course of two trips to France (Normandy and Paris) in 1817 and 1819 respectively. ¶ He began as a portraitist by painting friends and colleagues such as Thomas Girtin (1775–1802) and Thomas Hearne (1744–1817), his companions on trips that allowed him to practise the art of drawing. Edridge became known for his full and three-quarter length portraits, sometimes showing the figures in formal poses against the backdrop of a landscape, as in the graphite and wash drawing of Anne, Countess of Sheffield (1764–1832) (fig. 23.1). He portrayed the royal family (George III, Queen Charlotte and their daughter, the Princess Mary) and enjoyed great success among the elite, with whom he was on intimate terms. The many figures that he painted include the Duchess of Hamilton, Mrs Crutchley, the daughter of Lady Burell, Francesco Bartolozzi, William Wordsworth, the Marquess of Lansdowne, Lord Nelson and the Prime Minister William Pitt. ¶ He often used graphite to create his compositions, which he then enriched by applying soft coloured washes. The heads and faces of the figures were shown in minute detail and were then meticulously finished in watercolours, while the rest of the composition often remained a mere sketch. ¶ The drawing reproduced here, *Portrait of Two Young Ladies*, is an example of the kind of portrait in which Edridge

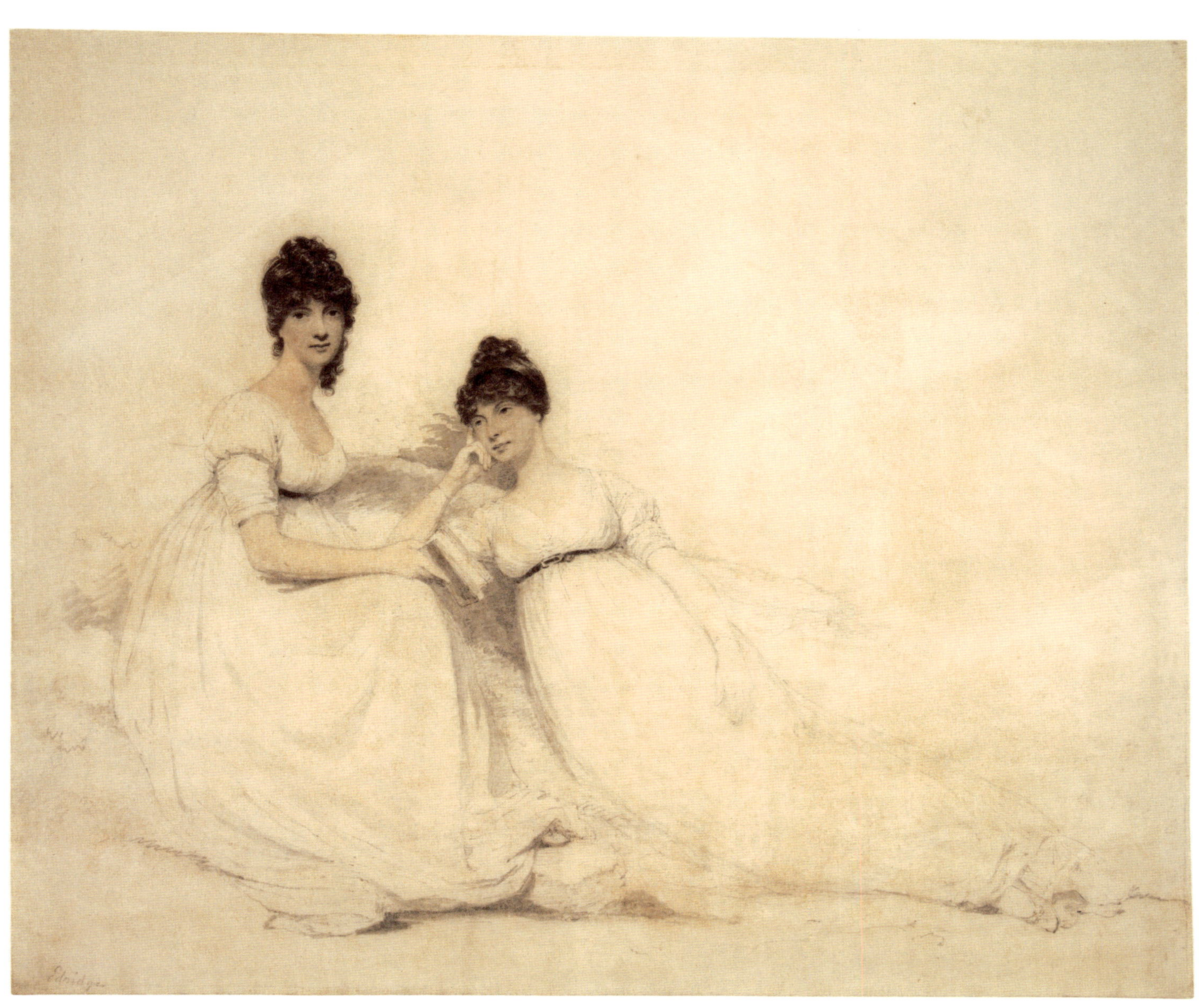

specialised, revealing as it does his neo-classical references. Made around 1816, during his mature period, Edridge depicts an intimate family reading scene in which are depicted two young ladies, whose identities are unknown. ¶ The artist shows the precise moment at which one of the young women, the reader seated on the left with her foot resting on a cushion, breaks off from reading, lowers the book in which she has marked her place with a thumb, and looks straight at the observer with a thoughtful air conveyed by a slight smile. The young listener beside her is more distant; with her head resting on her hand, she appears to ignore the onlooker and her eyes gaze into the distance. Both young ladies are seated on a sofa that is only partially suggested and are wearing similar empire-line dresses, differing only in the shape of the necklines, with high waists accentuated by coloured ribbons. ¶ Curiously, while in his portrayal of the young reader Edridge created a delicate composition with the combined movement of the body and the slight inclination of the head, in that of the listener the lower part of the body seems out of proportion, with excessively elongated legs, causing a sense of unease. In this

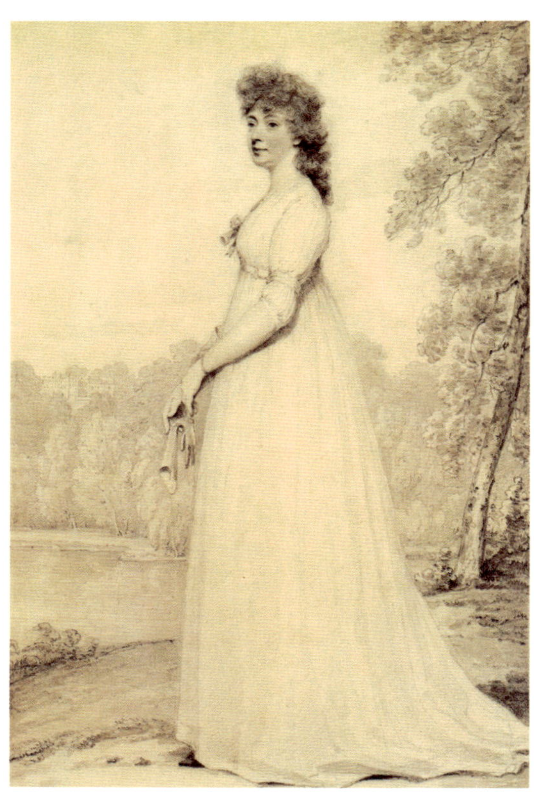

– fig. 23.1 –
Henry Edridge (1769–1821),
Anne (North), Countess of Sheffield, 1798.
Graphite and wash on paper, 26.7 × 18.4 cm.
London, National Portrait Gallery, inv. 2185a.
© National Portrait Gallery, London

example, the protagonists are not shown against the customary landscape but in an interior setting, in which Edridge simply depicts them against the white background of the paper, that is, the wall of the room that they are in. ¶ As in many of his portraits, the faces and hairstyles of the two figures are meticulously described, with rich detail and subtle nuances introduced by his use of watercolour. Loose curls fall over the foreheads of both girls while the rest of their hair is held up; however, there are subtle differences between them that, in a certain sense, reveal their different moods: the hair of the reader, who appears to be more open, is loose at the nape of her neck, while the hair of the other girl, who is shown in a more static position, is impeccably tied back with a ribbon. Edridge also extended his use of grey wash to the folds of the clothing and the shaded areas of the seat and wall, in some way compensating for the sketchiness of the rest of the composition. ¶ In November 1820 Henry Edridge was elected an associate of the Royal Academy, where he had shown his work for so long. This public recognition of his talent came only shortly before the artist died in London in April 1821.

PROVENANCE

Marquess of Lansdowne Collection. Acquired by Calouste Gulbenkian at the sale of this collection, through Colnaghi, at Sotheby's, London, 25 March 1920, lot no. 139 (repr.).

•

EXHIBITIONS

LISBON, 1999, no. 72, pp. 182–83, p. 183 (repr.).

[24]

JEAN-FRANÇOIS MILLET
Gruchy, 1814 – Barbizon, 1875

LANDSCAPE AT DUSK
France (Barbizon), ca. 1851–52

Black and white chalk on paper (recto); black chalk (verso).
18.6 × 24.7 cm.
Cachet of the artist's studio, on the lower right-hand side – J.F.M. (Lugt 1460).
Inv. 867

Millet used both sides of the sheet discussed here: on the recto he drew a landscape and on the verso a sketch of a peasant woman[1]. This work is emblematic of the artist's production as it depicts the two subjects to which he was closest: nature and the human figures that inhabited it. ¶ Jean-François Millet was born in 1814 into a relatively wealthy land-owning family that lived in the small village of Gruchy, "a forgotten place of Cotentin, between Cherbourg and La Hague"[2]. For the first twenty years of his life, the young Millet worked on his family's land and was proud of his familiarity with a wide range of rural occupations; at the same time he also received a well-rounded education. While still a child he learnt Latin from the village priests, who were his first teachers, and developed a keen interest in reading the Bible and the works of Virgil and other classical writers. One of the most erudite artists of his time, he was acquainted with the work of Shakespeare, Milton, Byron, Dante, La Fontaine, Victor Hugo, and Chateaubriand, among others. ¶ Displaying a rare appetite for drawing, he began studying in Cherbourg in 1835 under the most skilled local painters and, two years later, the municipality awarded him a grant to complete his training in Paris. As a country man, Millet found it hard to adapt to the big city, where, in his own words, "There were moments when I wished to leave Paris and return to my town, as I was so bored with the solitary life I led"[3]. He loved to visit the Louvre, where he discovered the works of the artists that most influenced his creations, including Mantegna, Michaelangelo, Poussin and Rembrandt. He studied at the École des Beaux-Arts under Paul Delaroche, where he developed his natural skill for drawing in the academic discipline that was to formally characterize his artistic work. He then began a conventional professional career, painting mythological and biblical scenes and also creating portraits and representations of *galante* idylls and nudes. ¶ With the political conflicts triggered by the 1848 Revolution, and the outbreak of cholera that made life in the big city even more unbearable, Millet decided to leave Paris and move south of the capital towards the forest of Fontainebleau, following in the footsteps of artists such as

1. The information provided by Professor Robert L. Herbert greatly helped with the study of this drawing (1974–1975).

2. "un coin perdu du Cotentin, entre Cherbourg et la Hague". *In* MOREAU-NELATON, 1921, vol. 1, p. 1.

3. "Il y avait des moments où j'avais grande envie de quitter Paris et de retourner à mon village, tant je m'ennuyais de la vie solitaire que je menais.", *in* SENSIER, 1881, p. 54.

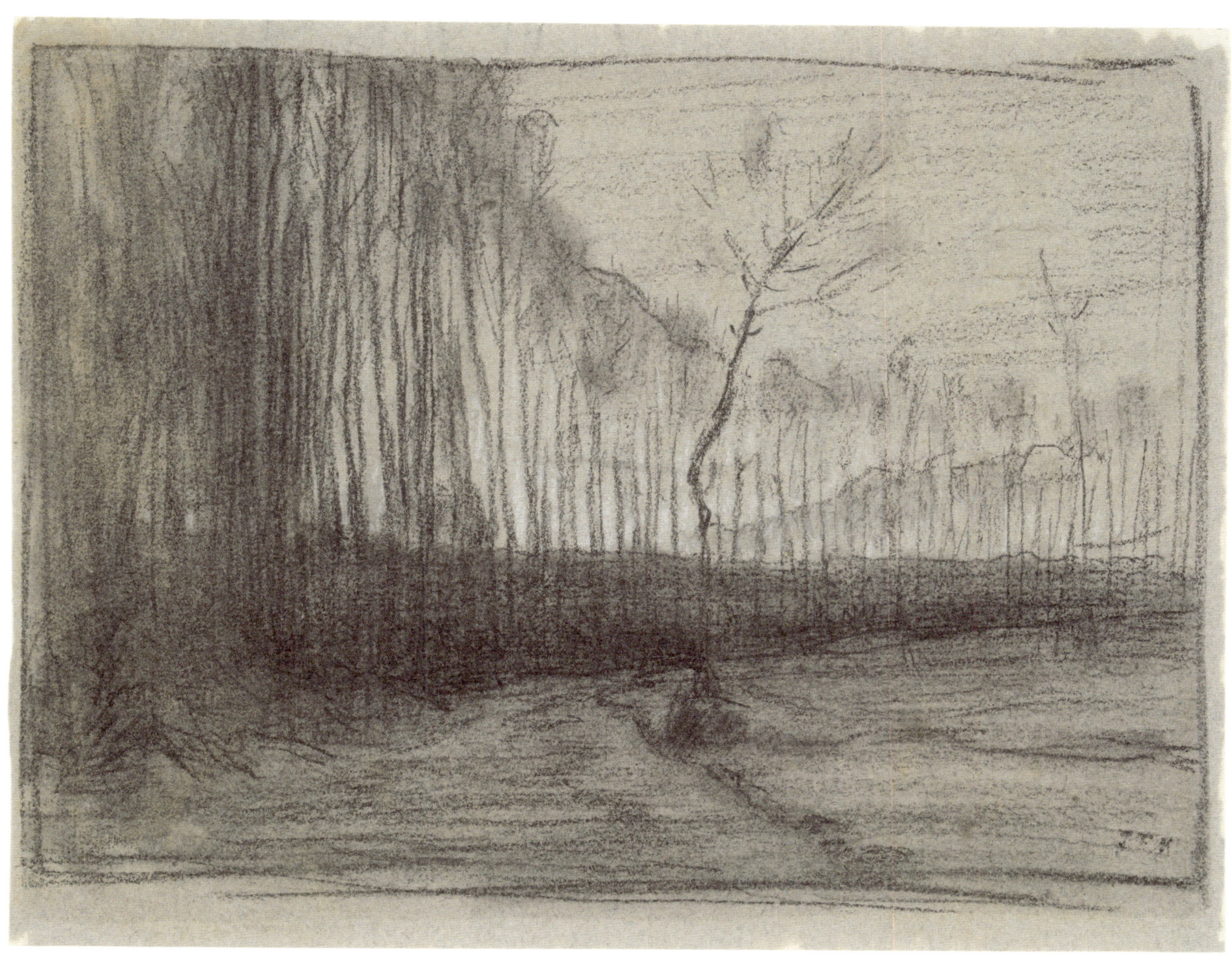

[24] verso

Rousseau, Corot, Daubigny, Diaz de la Peña, Jacque and Troyon. In 1849 he moved with his family[4] to Barbizon (the "painters paradise", as Moreau-Nélaton called it)[5], where, aside from a few short trips away, he remained until the end of his days. ¶ Of all the artists that settled in Barbizon, Millet was the only one whose journey from the city to the country involved a return to the nature that would become the preferred theme of all his works. In a letter to Alfred Sensier[6], dated 1851, Millet shared his feelings: "If only you could see how beautiful the forest is! I run there sometimes at the end of the day, after my day of work, and I return home always overwhelmed. It has such a dreadful peacefulness, a magnificence ambiance, to the extent that I surprise myself feeling true fear. I do not know what those begging trees talk between themselves, but they say something we cannot understand, because we do not speak the same language, [...]"[7]. Life in Barbizon, which was close to the forest, the wide plains, and the fields in which sombre, hard-working country folk laboured, took him back to his days in his village in Normandy and led him to declare: "I am a peasant and nothing more than a peasant"[8]. ¶ Thus, starting in 1848, the year in which he showed his painting *Le Vanneur* at the Salon[9], Millet dedicated himself entirely to the realistic portrayal of rural themes. As he confessed to Sensier in February 1851, "[...] it is the human aspect, truly human, that moves me the most in art ; and, if I could do whatever I wanted, or at least try it, I would only do something that would be the result of impressions conveyed by nature, whether in landscapes or in figures. And it is never the joyful aspect that appears before my eyes. I do not know where it is: I have never seen it. What I know that is more cheerful it's this calm, this silence that one enjoys so delightfully

4. In 1841 Millet married Pauline-Virginie Ono (born in 1821) who died in April 1844. That same year he met Catherine Lemaire (1821–1894) again in Cherbourg, with whom he lived and had nine children. When they left for Barbizon the couple had already had their third child.

5. See MOREAU-NELATON, 1921, pp. 80–81.

6. Alfred Sensier (1815–1877), a loyal friend of Millet from 1846–47 up until the artist's death, was his first biographer, a great collector of his works and acted as middle-man for the sale of his creations.

7. "Si vous voyiez comme la forêt est belle! J'y cours quelque fois à la fin du jour, après ma journée, et j'en reviens, à chaque fois écrasé. C'est d'un calme, d'une grandeur épouvantables : au point que je me surprends ayant véritablement peur. Je ne sais pas ce que ces gueux d'arbres-là se disent ; mais ils se disent quelque chose que nous n'entendons pas, parce que nous ne parlons pas la même langue, [...] ». Letter from Millet to Sensier, 25 January 1851. See MOREAU-NELATON, 1921, p. 89.

8. "Je suis un paysan et rien qu'un paysan". See MOREAU-NELATON, 1921, p. 1.

9. LONDON, National Portrait Gallery, Inv. NG 6447. See HERBERT, Robert L., *in* PARIS, 1975, no. 42, pp. 73–75.

– fig. 24.1 –
Jean-François Millet (1814–1875), *Garden Scene*, 1854. Oil on canvas, 17.1 × 21.3 cm. Bequest of Maria DeWitt Jesup, from the collection of her husband, Morris K. Jesup, 1914. inv. 15.30.24. © The Metropolitan Museum of Art / Art Resource / Scala, Florence

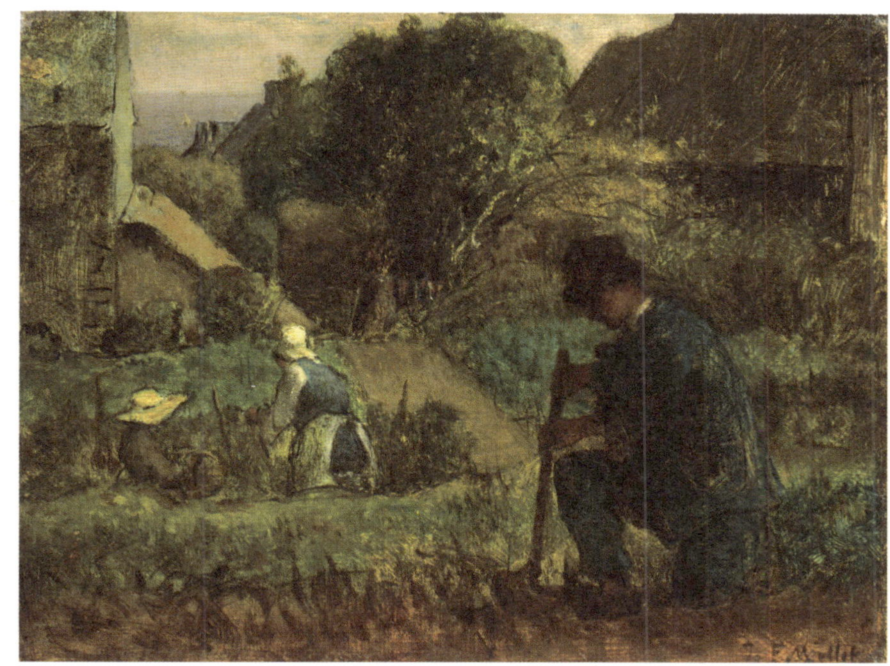

in forests or in ploughed places [...]"[10].¶ During the 1850s and 60s he produced his most famous works – *Le Semeur*[11], *Le Greffeur*[12], *Les Glaneuses*[13], *L'Angelus*[14], and *L'Homme à la Houe*[15] in which his naturalist language clearly expresses his attitude to the social conditions of rural life. These works depict male and female country folk; men and women who were humble characters, being for the most part simple, uneducated, unaware, unselfconscious, resigned, and always occupied with heavy, monotonous work. Nevertheless, these characters were not the expression of a revolutionary zeal against the established social order, as many critics of the time suggested. Rather, they were a sincere and realistic representation of country folk who were destined to live humbly in nature; protagonists of the simplest of human activities whose moral greatness Millet conveyed with a profound, epic, and almost symbolic human meaning. ¶ When conceiving a work, Millet drew numerous sketches in the open air and made studies in his studio to prepare his more ambitious themes. He also made many finished drawings that satisfied the demands of the collectors who had become his faithful customers. ¶ Curiously, the Gulbenkian drawing exemplifies both of these categories. The landscape, which was executed in black and white chalk in the early 1850s, probably between 1851 and 1852, is not related to any known painting by the artist. However, it is most certainly a view of Barbizon that was familiar to the painter, a spot near the small house and garden where he and his family lived, a stone's throw from the easily accessible forest. This idea is supported by the letter he wrote to Sensier on the subject of his friend's next visit: "Although the weather is not good, the country is beautiful. The narrow paths bordered by poplars, which we can find at the end of Barbizon, leave a charming

10. "[...] c'est le côté humain, franchement humain, qui me touche le plus en art ; et, si je pouvais faire ce que je voudrais, ou tout au moins le tenter, je ne ferais rien qui ne fût le résultat d'impressions reçues par l'aspect de la nature, soit en paysage, soit en figures. Et ce n'est jamais le côté joyeux qui m'apparaît; je ne sais où il est: je ne l'ai jamais vu. Ce que je connais de plus gai, c'est ce calme, ce silence dont on jouit si délicieusement ou dans les forêts, ou dans les endroits labourés [...]". Letter from 1 February 1851. See MOREAU-NELATON, 1921, p. 90.

11. Boston, Museum of Fine Arts, (*The Sower*), inv. 76,441.

12. Munich, Neue Pinakothek, inv. VD6096.

13. Paris, Musée d'Orsay, inv. R. F. 592.

14. Paris, Musée d'Orsay, inv. R. F. 1877.

15. Los Angeles, J. Paul Getty Museum, inv. 85.PA.114.

16. "Quoique le temps ne soit pas beau, la campagne est belle. Les petits chemins bordés de peupliers, qui se trouvent au bout de Barbizon, sont d'une impression charmante, d'une fraîcheur vraiment idyllique. Il y aurait à faire, avec cela, les plus beaux tableaux du monde. Vous verrez." Letter from Millet to Sensier, 22 May 1851, see MOREAU-NELATON, 1921, p. 94.

17. Included in a sale at Christie's, New York, 24th October 1990.

impression and have a truly idyllic freshness. One should do with that the most beautiful paintings in the world. Just wait and see"[16]. ¶ This beautiful drawing clearly reflects his stated intention. It is a landscape untouched by humankind, showing a path that opens out in the foreground, flanked by a row of poplars that are denser near the spectator and subtler in the distance. The elegantly delineated trees, with their narrow vertical and parallel lines, can be seen in numerous works by Millet, including the drawing *The Edge of the Woods*[17] (fig 24.2) from a private collection, and in the pastel *La Nuée de Corbeaux*, from ca. 1866 (Frick Art and Historical Center, Pittsburgh). On the right of the composition a wide plain opens up in the middle of which stands an isolated, slightly broken tree. The entire composition is enveloped in a half-light that suggests that the spot has been captured at a particular moment at dusk. The artist achieved this crepuscular shade by covering the entire area of the sky with light homogeneous lines that lend a shadowy and poetic veil to the atmosphere and the surface. ¶ As mentioned above, the back of the Gulbenkian work contains a sketch that is lightly executed but extraordinarily expressive. With just a few strokes Millet delineates and characterizes the figure

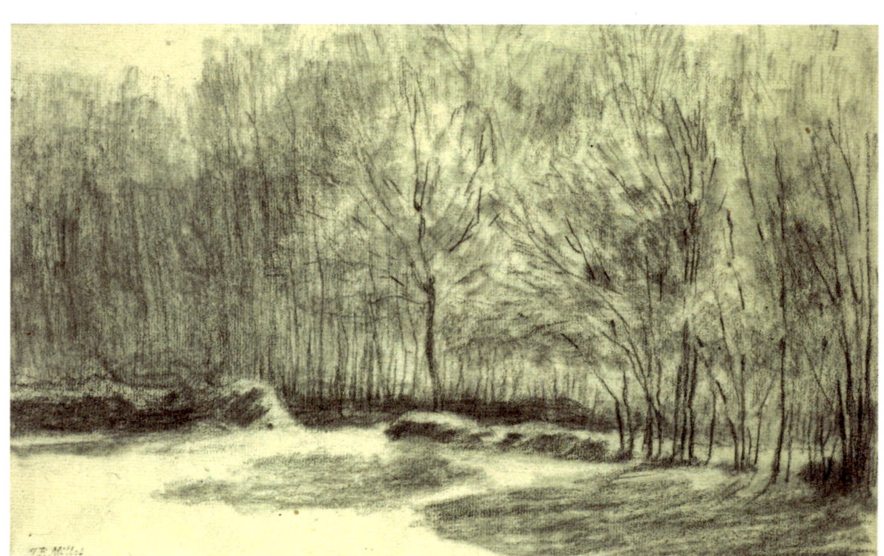

– fig. 24.2 –
Jean-François Millet (1814–1875),
The Edge of the Woods, early 1850s.
Charcoal on paper, 22.5 × 36.1 cm.
Private collection.

of a woman. It shows a peasant in traditional dress, slightly bent and showing the signs of advancing age. In contrast to the independent landscape on the front, this figure is a study for one of the characters in the painting *Garden Scene*, which belongs to the New York Metropolitan Museum of Art (fig. 24.1). This oil painting dates from 1854, the year that Millet returned to Gruchy to spend the summer with his family and to revisit the places he knew and remembered so well from his childhood. The New York painting shows one of these settings, with a garden depicted between the traditional granite houses of the village, behind which can be glimpsed the distant ocean. ¶ Millet was one of the main exponents of the Barbizon school, whose followers advocated the direct study of nature and whose repertoire included truthfully and realistically portrayed themes. From the mid-1860s he concentrated on painting landscapes that are never remote from the lives of the people and that evolved to encompass formal qualities and a visual language that preceded the chromatic experimentation carried out by the Impressionists of the next generation.

PROVENANCE

Sale at the artist's studio, Paris, organized by Durand-Ruel, 10–11 May 1875. Acquired by Calouste Gulbenkian from Colnaghi, London, 24 November 1915.

•

EXHIBITIONS

LISBON, 1976, no. 52; LISBON, 1985, no. 15, p. 21, p. 140 (repr.).

[25]

FÉLIX ZIEM

Beaune, 1821 – Paris, 1911

THE ENTRANCE OF THE OLD PORT OF MARSEILLE

France, ca. 1862

Pen, ink and brown washes on paper.
18.7 × 33.9 cm.
Signed on the lower right-hand side: *Ziem*
Inscription on the verso:
'Ce dessin faisait partie d'un album de 40 commandes par Monsieur Roux Traissinet de Marseille à Monsieur Ziem en 1862'.
Inv. 373

Besides being a painter of recognized merit, Félix Ziem was a draughtsman and watercolourist whose talent is confirmed by the many pieces of graphical work that he produced. While he satisfied the commissions of discerning patrons and clients with an extraordinarily vast pictorial repertoire (which included representations of flowers and animals, still lifes, portraits and, above all, landscapes), Ziem's drawings were kept in his studio for strictly personal use, possibly to serve as studies for future works. They reveal a more intimate side of his character and were not intended to be sold. At most, he might have offered them to special friends, as shown by the dedications written on some of them. His graphical work came to be better known and studied in greater depth thanks to a donation made by Lil Treilles-Ziem, the painter's granddaughter, to the Ziem Museum in Martigues in 1993. ¶ Ziem's relationship with the art of drawing began long before he discovered his vocation as a painter, an activity which he only took up once he had completely mastered the watercolour technique. In fact, while still a young student at the School of Fine Arts in Dijon, he produced several watercolour drawings in which he depicted views of the city and its main monuments. ¶ In 1839 he left Burgundy for Rome, stopping in Marseille on the way to complete his artistic training. His liking for the Provencal city, the acclaim received by the drawings that he exhibited in several shops, and regular sales of watercolours conceived as finished works led him to extend his stay until 1841. Eventually, he set up a studio in the city from which to teach the art of drawing and the watercolour. From this point onwards, Marseille was to serve as one of his main inspirations throughout his career and the starting point for the endless journeys that he tirelessly embarked on until the end of his days. In 1860, reflecting at the age of forty on the many journeys that he had undertaken, Ziem wrote in his journal: "I have devoted my youth to a feverish and hasty work. I have experimented with several paths [...]. Midi has impressed me for the first time. I am there. [...]. Now I will go to Venice, but my heart loves my country – the country

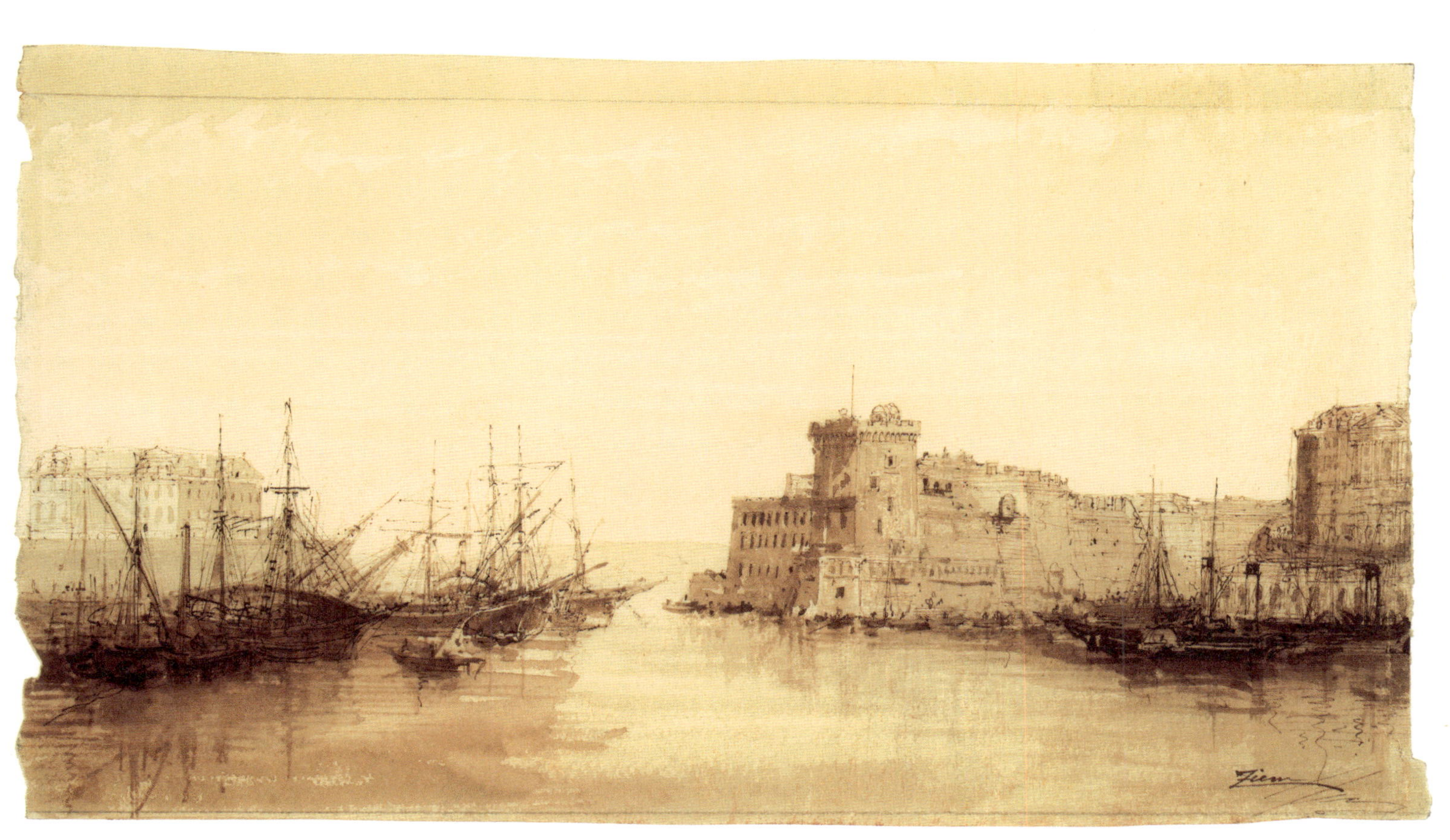
Ziem

of my first impression, the place where I felt myself a painter for the first time in my life. I am going to Martigues, Marseille; [...]"[1].¶ The artist's graphical work consisted of drawings on loose sheets, watercolours, sketches on wood or card and, above all, hundreds of drawings that he set down in his travel journals. In fact, as a perennial painter-traveller, Ziem never embarked on a journey without his notebooks, in which he drew, *in situ*, the places that impressed him, creating both more elaborate works and detailed studies that served as an aide-memoir for future compositions. These pieces, which are of outstanding artistic quality, give us an accurate picture not only of the artist's travels but also of his aesthetic and stylistic development. ¶ The themes of his graphical work are centred on places that are also naturally represented in his paintings: the south of France, particularly Marseille and Martigues; Italy, particularly Venice (his adopted homeland); views of Constantinople and Egypt in the east; and the Netherlands and Russia. It is curious to note that Barbizon, where he kept a caravan-studio, appears with greater frequency in his drawings then it does in his paintings. Possessing an overwhelming interest in maritime themes from an early age, Ziem mostly drew landscapes, including urban views. But as he approached maturity, he mainly became interested in representing the effects of light and the atmosphere on the calm flat waters of the Venetian lagoons, the Bosporus Strait, and areas around the coast or the banks of the Martigues lakes. ¶ An insatiable draughtsman, Ziem explored a range of different techniques including pencil, charcoal, Conté pencil, pens dipped in ink, washes, chalk or gouache highlights and watercolours. The drawings that he produced in his youth are well-defined compositions featuring short, serrated and parallel lines. By the 1850s and '60s, however, he had moved towards broader compositions that reveal a more subjective approach and less precise outlines. In later periods, he focused on playing with of light on architectural surfaces and representations of natural light and the transparency of water. With regard to his skill as a watercolourist, the words of the critic Théophile Gautier clearly reveal the heights that Ziem reached: "We are aware that Mr. Ziem has long ago been considered to be among the most illustrious «painters of water's colours», as the English say, to whom watercolour is greatly renowned [...] His glory goes hand in hand with that of the Turner, Bonington, [...] and other celebrities alike"[2]. ¶ Although his pictorial output sometimes became stereotyped as a result of his great commercial success, the authenticity of the artist, who was always inspired by the real world around him, is clearly revealed in his drawings and watercolours. At the end of his life his real vocation, drawing, ceased to be a means of producing studies and became a technique that rivalled painting in its importance. ¶ The drawing now being presented, one of six works by the artist that the Collector acquired between 1899 and 1926[3], represents a view of Marseille and its old port, a theme that is repeated in two of the paintings in the aforementioned series. Calouste Gulbenkian's memories of the time that he spent as a student in the Provençal city would have kept him alert to the beauty of the place and must have played a part in his decision to buy these works. ¶ Ziem's drawing notebooks bear witness to the importance of the city of Marseille in his graphical output. The city, where he discovered light and the sea for the first time, appears in many of his works, represented through its monuments, alleys, and people engaged in everyday activities. But it was the old port, with all its bustle, that most attracted him. In 1839, Ziem wrote in his diary: "I stayed at Marseille, on the quay of channel no. 1, [...] from the window ... I could see the old shortened port

1. "J'ai employé ma jeunesse à un travail fièvreux et hâtif. J'ai essayé plusieurs chemins [...]. Le Midi m'a impressionné pour la première fois : j'en suis. [...]. J'irais maintenant à Venise. Mais mon cœur aime ma patrie – la patrie de ma première impression, là enfin, où je me suis senti peintre pour la première fois. Je vais à Martigues, Marseille; [...]." *Journal*, 20 October 1860. See MIQUEL, 1978, vol. 1, p. 97.

2. "On sait que M. Ziem est compté depuis longtemps parmi les plus illustres des 'painters of water's coulours, comme disent les Anglais, chez qui l'aquarelle est en grand honneur [...] Sa gloire va de pair avec celle des Turner, des Bonington, [...] et autres célébrités du genre". In 1868, Ziem asked this critic to write the preface to the catalogue for the sale at auction of a series of thirty-four watercolours. The sale took place in the Drouot Hotel on 21 December of the same year. See BIASS-FABIANI, *in* MARTIGUES, 1995 (*œuvre graphique*) p. 23.

3. Four paintings (inv. 137, 354, 366 and 397), one drawing (inv. 373) and one watercolour (inv. 426-420). It is known that Gulbenkian bought another watercolour by Ziem in 1908 that was subsequently given away in 1935.

with its thousand ships designed against the setting sun as a forest of firs lost amidst the fog of the atmosphere"[4]. It is this air that is breathed in the Gulbenkian drawing *The Entrance of the Old Port of Marseille*. The boats are moored and human figures are only barely suggested by minute traces, leaving the observer with the tranquil port landscape with its broad, reflective water opening up in the foreground. Interrupting this flat expanse, which extends to the distant horizon and the vastness of the sky, is a line comprised of boats and buildings, the most notable of which are the forts of St Nicholas and St John, situated at the entrance. ¶ Where the style of the work is concerned, the inscription on the back: "*This drawing was part of an album of 40 orders of Mr. Roux Traissinet from Marseille to Mr. Ziem in 1862*"[5] – situates it in the artist's mature period, in which he devoted himself to capturing the effects of light glimmering on the calm surface of the water. The landscape of lines and delicate contours, subtly drawn in pen, is shaped by the use of brown washes that enhance the slight variations in atmospheric effects and allow the architectural forms and surrounding boats to be reflected in the mirror of the water. ¶ Most of Ziem's representations of the port of Marseille show it from the outside, from the immensity of the sea looking towards the narrower space of the port basin. By contrast, in composing this drawing, he represented the entrance to the port from an interior perspective. As a result, the work resembles the painting *Le Port de Marseille*

4. "Je logeai à Marseille sur le quai du canal nº 1, [...] de la fenêtre ... je voyais le vieux port en raccourci avec ses milliers de navires se détachant sur le soleil couchant comme une forêt de sapins perdue dans la brume de l'atmosphère." See MIQUEL, 1978, vol. 1, p. 33.

5. "Ce dessin faisait partie d'un album de 40 commandes par Monsieur Roux Traissinet de Marseille à Monsieur Ziem en 1862." I am grateful to Sophie Biass-Fabiani, the conservator at the Ziem Museum in Martigues and an expert in the artist's work, for sharing her opinions on the graphical works in the Collection (1996). It was not possible to find any references in Ziem's account book either to the person commissioning the work or to the aforementioned album.

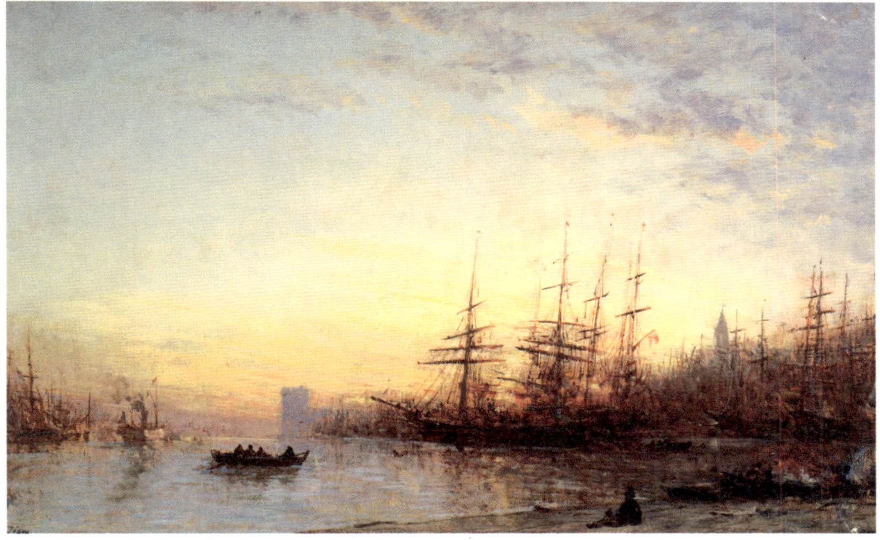

– fig. 25.1 –
Félix Ziem (1821–1911), *Le Port de Marseille au coucher du soleil*. Oil on canvas, 69 × 115.5 cm.
Paris, Musée du Petit-Palais, inv. 216.

6. "[...] De ma fenêtre, je vois le point d'où j'aperçus pour la première fois la mer, à dix-neuf ans; Cette impression est aussi fraîche qu'aujourd'hui'. BIASS-FABIANI, 1994, p. 112. See MARTIGUES, 1995 (*peintures*), p. 83.

au couché du soleil, which Ziem himself gave to the Petit Palais Museum in Paris in 1905 (fig. 25.1). ¶ Marseille and its port, light and sea, as well as the comings and goings of its people, became a dominant and eternally renewed theme in Ziem's life and work, particularly between 1853 and 1868. Besides having a great love for this city, he also felt drawn to Martigues and Nice, where, as in Marseille, he worked in his own studios. The light and colours of the southern Mediterranean became such a necessary part of his life that, in late 1860, Ziem wrote in his diary: " [...] From my window, I can see the point where I saw the sea for the first time, when I was nineteen. This impression is as fresh in my memory as it is today"[6]. ¶ Owing to his decision to work directly in nature (using mobile studios), his ability to enhance and intensify colour, his interest in capturing the visual effects of atmospheric luminosity and the subsequent dissolution of outlines in his work, Ziem, who lived an unusually long life (he died at the age of 90) can be situated in the transition that took place in landscape art during the second half of the nineteenth century, between the Barbizon school and Impressionism.

PROVENANCE

Roux Traissinet of Marseille (inscription on the verso); Ernest Le Roy Collection. Acquired by Calouste Gulbenkian at the sale of this collection, through Graat, Paris, at Galerie Georges Petit, 2 December 1926, lot no. 17.

•

EXHIBITIONS

LISBON, 1985, no. 16, p. 21 and p. 141 (repr.); LISBON, 1998, p. 177, no. 152 (repr.).

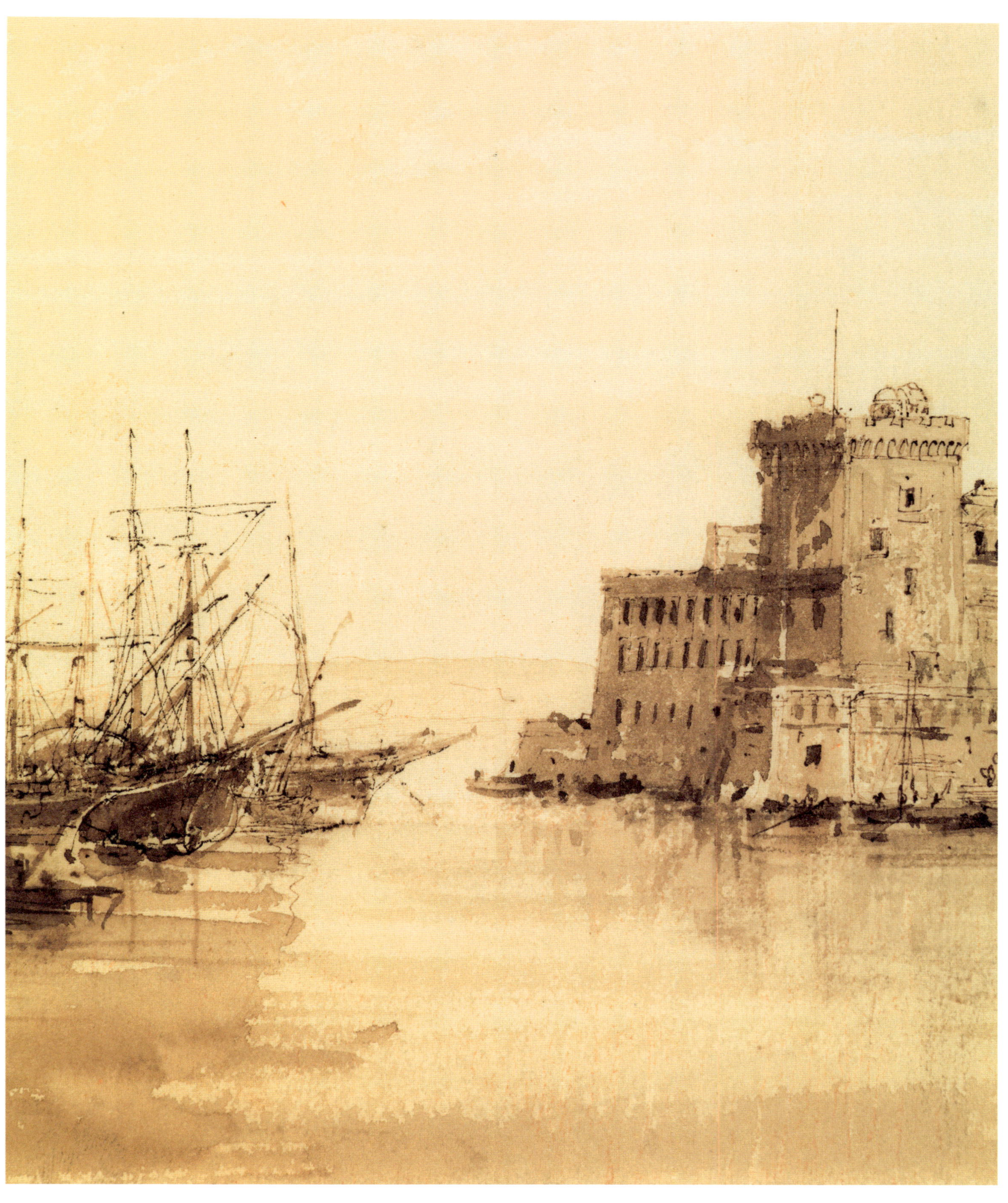

JULES-ADOLPHE--AIMÉ-LOUIS BRETON
Courrières, 1827 – Paris, 1906

FANEUSE AU REPOS
France, 1891

Charcoal and white chalk on brownish paper.
48.1 × 32 cm.
Signed and dated on the lower right-hand side: *Jules Breton; 23 8br 1891*
Inv. 460

This drawing, which was purchased by Calouste Gulbenkian in 1911 at the sale of the works comprising Jules Breton's studio, is a paradigmatic example of the rural themes that the artist continually explored as a painter, poet and writer[1]. ¶ Breton was born in Courrières (Pas-de-Calais) in the north of France in a small village situated in the agricultural region of Artois. In the paternal home, in the bosom of a wealthy, rural bourgeois family, he spent his childhood in an environment enlivened by the healthy, open-air pleasures of country life. From the age of sixteen onwards, the young man's artistic training took place away from home, first in Gand, and then in Antwerp, where he was influenced by the works of the most renowned Flemish artists, particularly Rubens. He finally settled in Paris, where he continued his studies and lived through the 1848 revolution, the ideals of which inspired two of his paintings: *Misère et Désespoir*[2], the first of his works to be presented at the *Salon*, in 1849, and *La Faim*[3], which was exhibited at the *Salon* in 1850. Throughout these years of absence, Breton was tormented by homesickness. In fact, his memories of Artois became so obsessive that he decided to return in the certainty that his native land and its people would henceforth become the protagonists of his work. In 1853, the year in which he painted his first rural scene, he settled in Courrières and, as if discovering his true vocation, devoted himself exclusively to representing themes associated with the lives of the peasants. ¶ Jules Breton loved the tender and simple form of nature that lived in his childhood memories, which were replete with the magic of open-air life, meandering walks, local stories told *en famille*, religious festivals suffused with the poetry of hymns, and the daily work of the country people with whom he mixed[4]. These memories, and his ceaseless observations of nature, gave rise to compositions imbued with an optimistic vision of rural life in which peasants are shown engaging in a wide range of agricultural tasks, taking a short break from work, or enjoying the conviviality of rural or religious festivals. The subservience and harshness of country life are always absent from these scenes. The artist omits any suggestion

1. Jules Breton wrote several works of art criticism and memoirs, including: *La vie d'un artiste: Art et Nature* (Paris, 1890); *Un peintre paysan: Souvenirs & Impressions* (Paris, 1896); *Nos peintres du siècle* (Paris, 1899); *La Peinture: les lois essentielles* (Paris, 1904). He also published several poems in *Les champs et la mer* (Paris, 1875), some of which are dedicated to his friend, the painter Jean-François Millet (1814–1875), whom he greatly admired.

2. Arras, musée des Beaux-Arts.

3. Arras, musée des Beaux-Arts. Painting destroyed in 1915. See LACOUTURE, Annette Bourrut, *in* ARRAS, QUIMPER, DUBLIN, 2002, p. 69, fig. 25.

4. "Jules Breton: Creator of a Noble Peasant Image," *in* STURGES, (1982), ca. 1987, p. 28 and note 12.

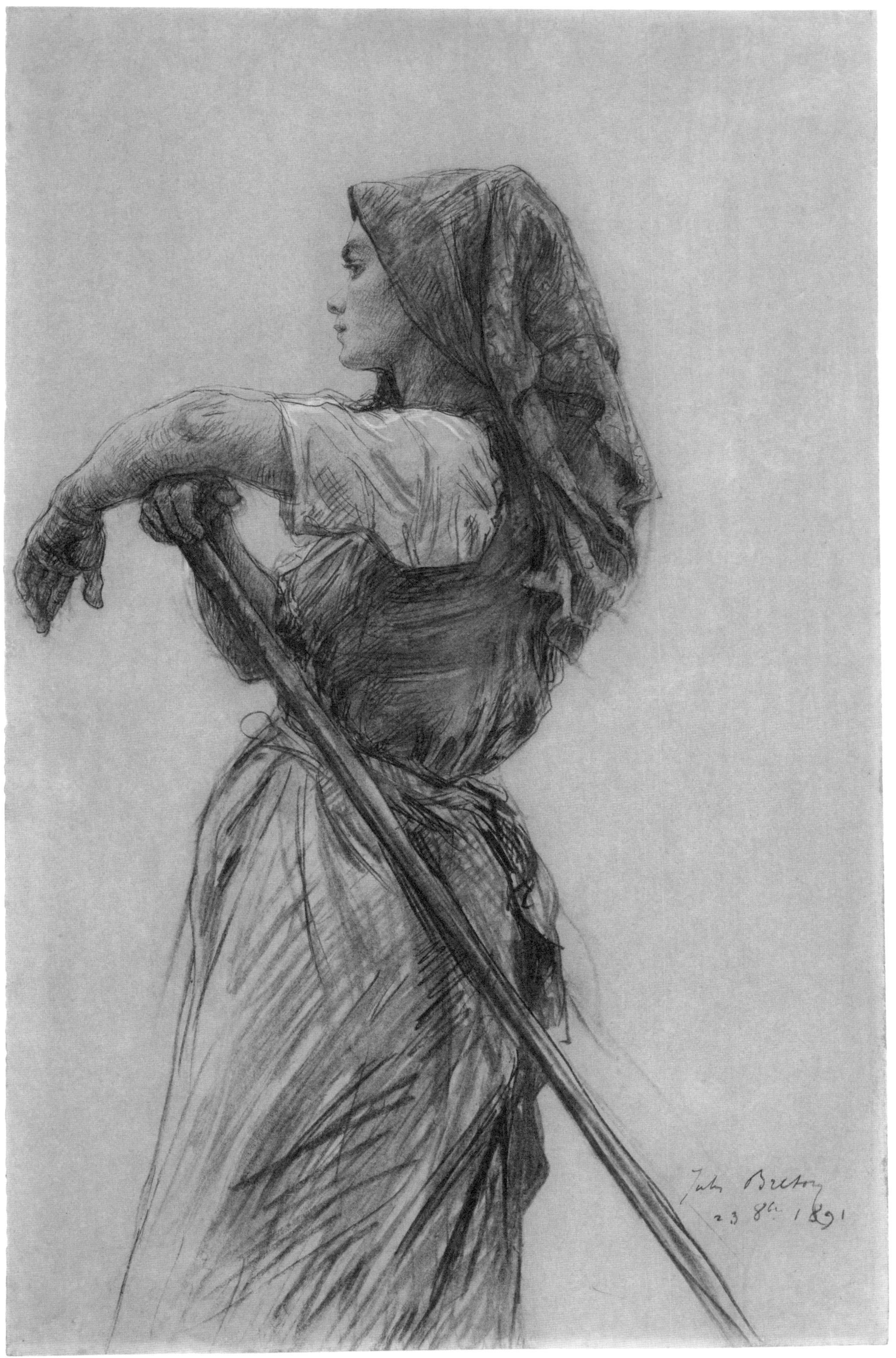
Jules Breton
23 8bre 1891

5. With regard to Breton's painting, *Le Rappel des Glaneuses* (Paris, musée d'Orsay, inv. MI289), which was presented at the 1859 *Salon*, a contemporary critic defined the female models that the painting depicted as being 'belles cariatides rustiques' (beautiful rustic caryatids). See Paris, 1979, p. 314.

6. VACHON, 1899, p. 76.

7. *Ibidem*, hors-texte, n.p. [between p. 68 and p. 69].

of misery, thereby maintaining the social harmony of the traditional agricultural community. Modest, devout and active, Breton's peasants are happy with their lot and grateful for their daily bread. For this reason, while extolling the values that governed their lives, the artist showed his protagonists to be enveloped in an atmosphere of respect, dignity and 'ancient' nobility[5]. ¶ In his monograph on the work of Jules Breton, Marius Vachon places the themes tackled by the artist in four groups: work, rest, country festivals, and religious festivals[6]. The Gulbenkian drawing *Faneuse au repos*, which is reproduced twice in the aforementioned publication[7], belongs to the wide range of compositions that make up the second group. Against a background of brownish shades, a close-up view of a peasant woman in three-quarter profile appears. Her position in life is immediately confirmed by the typical rural clothing that she wears: a white short-sleeved blouse, a tight waistcoat, and an apron tied at the waist, covering her skirt. The scarf that completely covers her hair outlines her face, emphasizing her beauty. With her robust shape and classically perfect features, the young woman leans on the end of an agricultural tool while her vague but proud gaze conveys a serenity that comes from the satisfaction of a job well done. This drawing, and the painting to which it is related, were created at the height of the artist's mature period, when his style became more austere and his compositions less complex, thereby allowing him to focus on creating a nobler and more fitting image of the rural worker. ¶ In his gal-

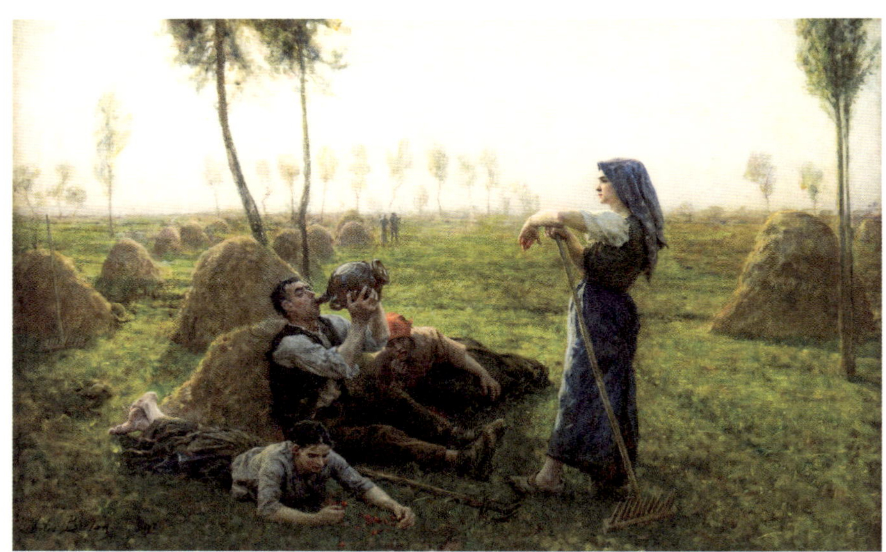

– fig. 26.1 –
Jules-Adolphe-Aimé-Louis Breton (1827–1906), *Juin*, 1892. Oil on canvas, 96.5 × 123.2 cm. Collection of the Arnot Art Museum, Elmira, New York, USA, inv. 98

lery of characters, Breton gave pride of place to women, whose grace and perfect features inspired him. Men are rarely the protagonists of the action, being kept in the background or included as part of collective scenes. His heroines, young peasant women from the Artois region, were beautiful, simple and strong, possessing calm faces and a kind of moral grandeur that came from the pleasure with which they devoted themselves to their work. Breton created realistic scenes of rural life that were an integral part of the broad plains which he knew so well. However, his was an idealised, almost romantic, realism in which there was room only for the good and beautiful side of life. The portrait of this young woman, who has just broken off from her agricultural work, is typical of his work, as is the setting in which she is framed. ¶ *Faneuse au repos*[8] is a preparatory study created in 1891 for one of the central figures in the painting *Juin* (fig. 26.1) which the artist presented the following year at the *Salon des Artistes Français* in Paris[9]. In this painting, which is currently owned by the Arnot Art Museum in Elmira, New York, the young woman represented in the drawing cuts an imposing figure on a broad plain on which stacks of recently harvested hay sit in rows. Her work complete, it is now time to rest. The peasant woman leans on a rake (which is unfinished in the drawing), absently gazing at the horizon, while the two girls accompanying her lie on the hay and a man refreshes himself with water from a canteen (fig. 26.2). ¶ Of all the works by Breton that depict the theme of rest, two paintings stand

8. I would like to thank Annette Bourrut Lacouture for the information that she gave me about the Gulbenkian drawing and the corresponding painting (1989–90).

9. See SALON, 1892, no. 258.

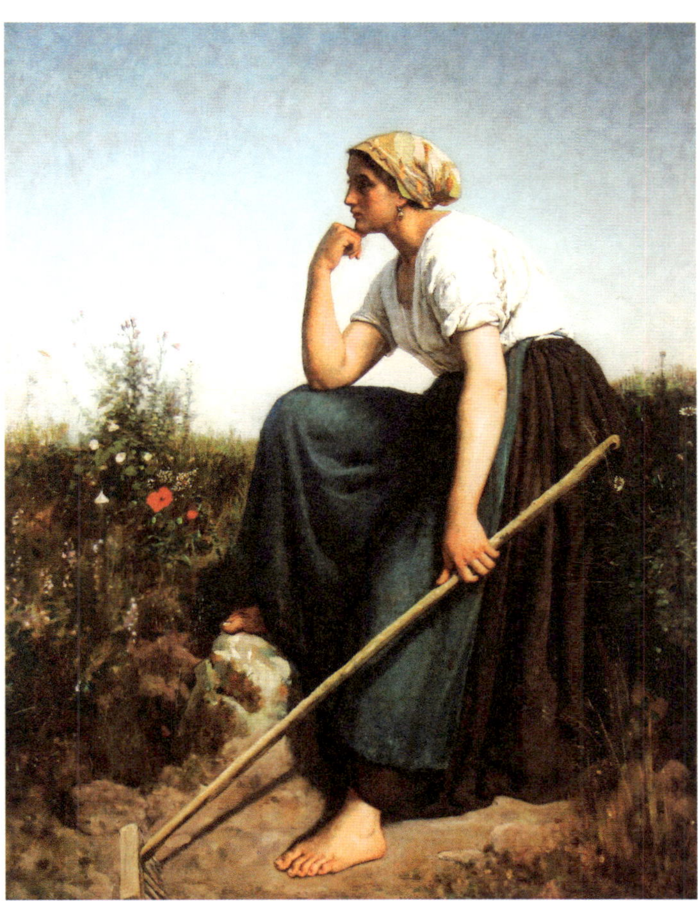

– fig. 26.2 –
Jules-Adolphe-Aimé-Louis Breton (1827–1906), *Le Repos*, 1864.
Oil on canvas, 74 × 60 cm.
© musée des Beaux-Arts d'Arras, inv. 864.2

10. The current location of this painting is unknown. The Walters Art Gallery in Baltimore owns a painting in which the two central figures are represented.

out that best synthesise the artist's philosophical and aesthetic language. These are *Le Repos* from 1864 (fig. 26.2) and *La fin de la journée*[10] (1865). In both, rather than being worn down by the harsh nature of their work, the women cut imposing figures in relation to the other elements in the composition; their faces still bear traces of the gravity of the task that they have carried out but their bodies have already lost the muscular tension demanded by it. What remains is therefore the pictorial record of a serene and dignified acceptance of a completed duty in which, at times, an introspective religiosity can almost be discerned. ¶ For Jules Breton, drawing was mainly a matter of creating an immediate sketch for a project that would later be completed in the form of a painting. For this reason, he drew as many details as he considered necessary for a particular composition and these studies were generally more energetic than the final painted version of the work.

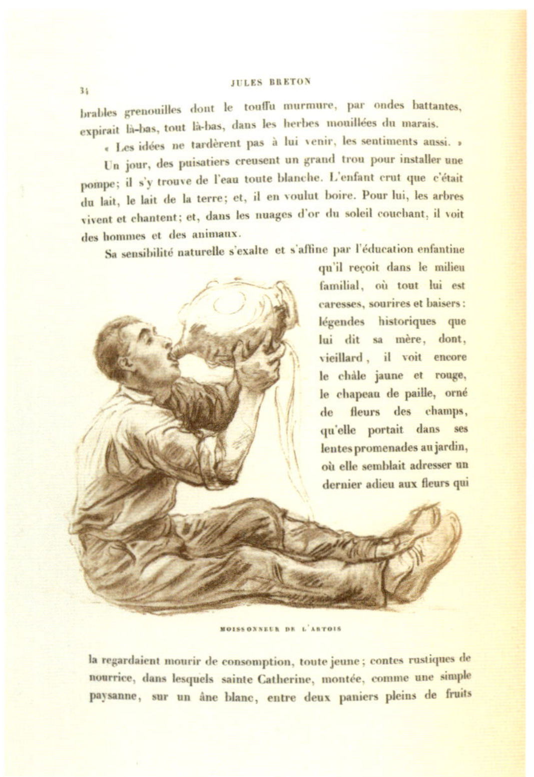

34 JULES BRETON

brables grenouilles dont le touffu murmure, par ondes battantes, expirait là-bas, tout là-bas, dans les herbes mouillées du marais.

« Les idées ne tardèrent pas à lui venir, les sentiments aussi. »

Un jour, des puisatiers creusent un grand trou pour installer une pompe; il s'y trouve de l'eau toute blanche. L'enfant crut que c'était du lait, le lait de la terre; et, il en voulut boire. Pour lui, les arbres vivent et chantent; et, dans les nuages d'or du soleil couchant, il voit des hommes et des animaux.

Sa sensibilité naturelle s'exalte et s'affine par l'éducation enfantine qu'il reçoit dans le milieu familial, où tout lui est caresses, sourires et baisers : légendes historiques que lui dit sa mère, dont, vieillard, il voit encore le châle jaune et rouge, le chapeau de paille, orné de fleurs des champs, qu'elle portait dans ses lentes promenades au jardin, où elle semblait adresser un dernier adieu aux fleurs qui

MOISSONNEUR DE L'ARTOIS

la regardaient mourir de consomption, toute jeune ; contes rustiques de nourrice, dans lesquels sainte Catherine, montée, comme une simple paysanne, sur un âne blanc, entre deux paniers pleins de fruits

– fig. 26.3 –
Jules-Adolphe-Aimé-Louis Breton (1827–1906),
Peasant Drinking from a Canteen (Moissonneur buvant à la gourde), 1891 (?).
Reproduction of the original drawing (whereabouts unknown), published
en texte, *in* Marius Vacon, *Jules Breton*, Paris: A. Lahure, 1899, p. 34.

In the case of the painting to which the Gulbenkian drawing is linked, Breton created another study of the man sating his thirst with fresh water from the canteen[11] (fig. 26.3) and yet another oil-on-canvas, whole-body, sketch of the figure represented in the Gulbenkian drawing[12]. As in the drawing now being analysed, the forms comprising the figure emerge from solid vigorous charcoal lines, visibly intersecting in places, which delimit the contours and create the different shaded textures of the volumes. The composition appears clear and well-defined, free of any superfluous details that might corrupt its harmony, which is formally enriched only by miniscule traces of white chalk. ¶ Breton's work is decidedly subjective. In his approach to nature and the reality of rural life, he sought the answers that were best suited to his temperament. For the reasons already outlined, these answers could only emerge enveloped in a glow of happiness.

11. This drawing is reproduced within the text on p. 34 and on an insert between p. 34 and 35 *in* VACHON, 1899, under the title *Moissonneur de l'Artois*. Its current location is unknown.

12. This work, entitled *The Harvester* (signed and dated 1892), was sold at Christie's in New York on 25 February 1987.

PROVENANCE

Acquired by Calouste Gulbenkian through Graat et Madoulé at the sale of works from the painter's studio at the Georges Petit Gallery, Paris, 3 June 1911, lot no. 265.

•

LITERATURE

VACHON, 1899, no. 52, repr. *hors-texte*.

[27]

MUIRHEAD BONE

Glasgow, 1876–Oxford, 1953

SHIPBREAKING TALMOUTH

England, ca. 1899 (?)

Graphite on paper.
11,2 × 17,7 cm.
Signed on the lower right-hand side: *Muirhead Bone.*
Inv. 2158

1. See TROWLES, Peter, *in* ST ANDREW'S, GLASGOW, 1986–1987.

2. LONDON, 1984, p. 1.

3. Huntarian Art Gallery, University of Glasgow (inv. 25843). See TROWLES, Peter *in* ST ANDREW'S, GLASGOW, 1986–1987, cat. no. 30, ill. no. 3.

4. Huntarian Art Gallery, University of Glasgow (see *Ibid*em,n. 36, ill. no. 5).

There is no reference in the Gulbenkian archives to the addition of this small drawing to the Collection, though it would have interested the Collector because of its maritime theme, which is present in so many other works in his collection. ¶ Muirhead Bone, the author of this drawing, was highly regarded in the field of the graphic arts, and was particularly known for his work as a etcher, draughtsman and watercolourist[1]. ¶ He was born in Partick, an industrial suburb of Glasgow, and initially trained as an architect. His artistic vocation, which he discovered early on, led him to study drawing at the Glasgow School of Art between 1892 and 1894. Having taught himself etching and drypoint engraving, which he started around 1898, he came to be considered the greatest British engraver of his time. According to Sir Kenneth Clark: "for technical skill Bone must be the only one (among British artists) who can be compared with the great Italian Piranesi"[2]. Indeed, much like the eighteenth-century Italian master, Bone was fascinated by the urban changes reflected in the construction of new buildings and in the demolition of architectural edifices surrounded by intricate scaffolding. The monumentality of these compositions is accentuated by the contrast of light and shade, an example of which can be seen in *The Great Gantry, Charing Cross Station*[3], from 1906. ¶ The technical mastery and inventiveness of Bone's work is present in the realism of his chosen themes, which bring together the daily routines of urban life, the architectural aspects of changing cities, portraiture, and landscape. ¶ As well as being an excellent engraver, he was also a prolific watercolourist and draughtsman, doubtless one of the greatest of his generation. He used graphite, charcoal and pen and ink to make sketches and preliminary studies for future prints or independent works created for his personal satisfaction. On occasion the artist's drawings, such as *Queen Street, Glasgow*[4] (1910), were complex studies that expressed the chaotic life of the docks or the big cities with poetic realism. Beside these monochrome works Bone also produced watercolours in which he tested out new ideas and recorded his memories of journeys through Europe (Sweden,

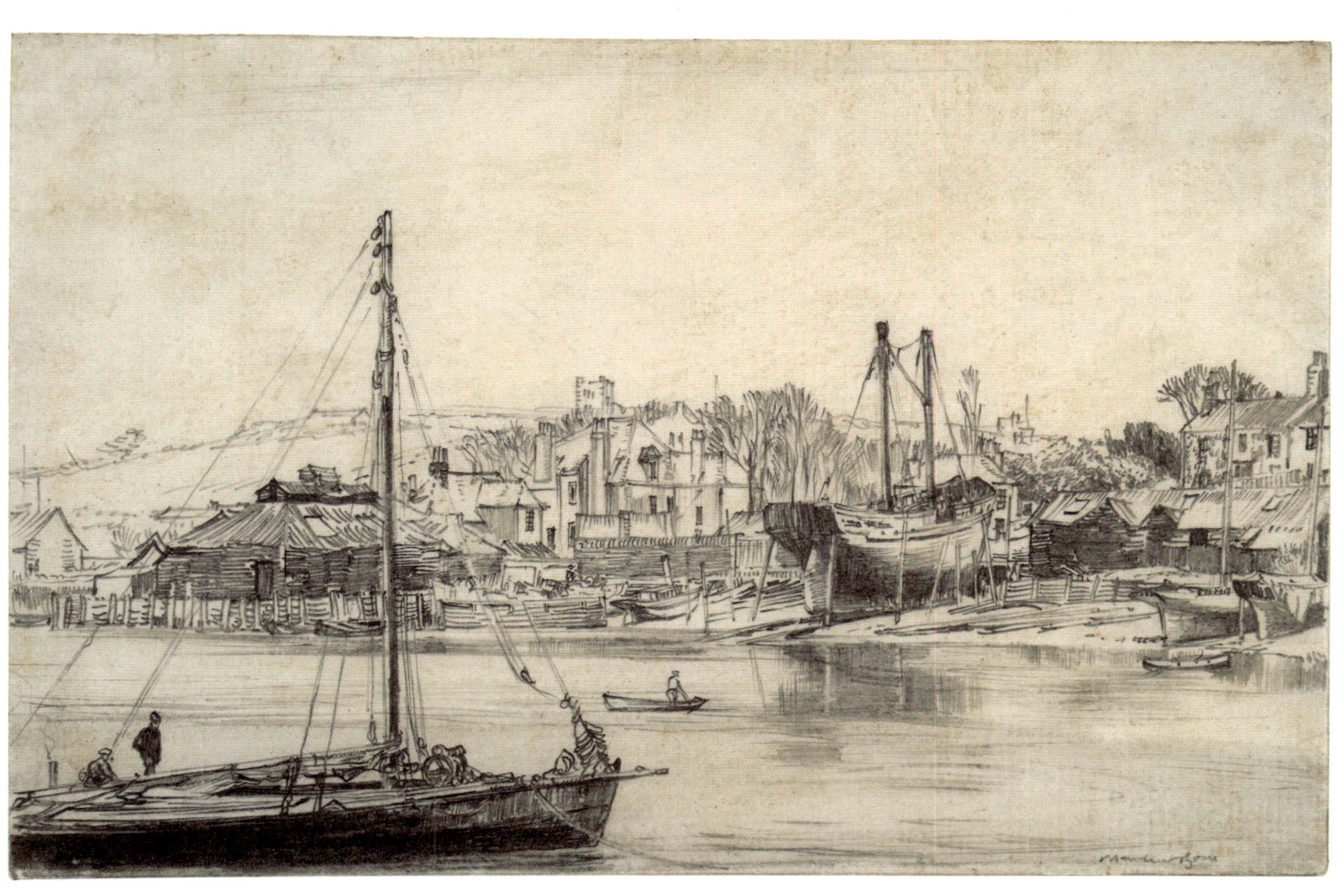

France, Italy, Holland, Spain, Turkey) and trips to New York, especially in the period between the wars. ¶ In comparison with his later, more dramatic and elaborate compositions, this small drawing, entitled *Shipbreaking Talmouth,* is probably an early work dating from around 1899. ¶ It shows a commonly depicted scene in the artist's work: shipbuilding and repair work, the dry docks, the boats along the coastline and the bustle of the fishermen. Bone depicts a tranquil maritime scene, introduced with a mirror-like body of water that recedes back towards the sandy coast. In the foreground a boat is anchored on the left which balances the composition and draws the eye towards the ship-repair yard. On the beach are numerous small boats, among which a larger ship awaits its future fate. ¶ The drawing is executed using short parallel lines in graphite, with only the shaded areas showing a more jagged touch. Some of its features are rendered in meticulous detail (i.e. the houses and the boats along the edge), and are harmoniously organised. Human figures, although shown on a much smaller scale than the other elements in the composition, are very much present, as it is they who are the protagonists of the routine action. ¶ Two years after the outbreak of the First World War, David Muirhead Bone, who had been living in London since 1901, was recruited by the British Minister Charles Masterman, the man responsible for the British War Propaganda Bureau, to accompany the Allied Forces on the Western Front as the "Official War Artist". He documented the dramatic events that he saw there with numerous drawings that were later published and performed the same role during the Second World War. He was knighted in 1937. ¶ With an artistic career that lasted over half a century, Bone left a vast portfolio of graphic work that included many hundreds of etches and thousands of drawings, most of which are in British and European public collections.

PROVENANCE

Unknown.

·

EXHIBITIONS

LISBON, 1998, no. 154, pp. 178–79, p. 178 (repr.).

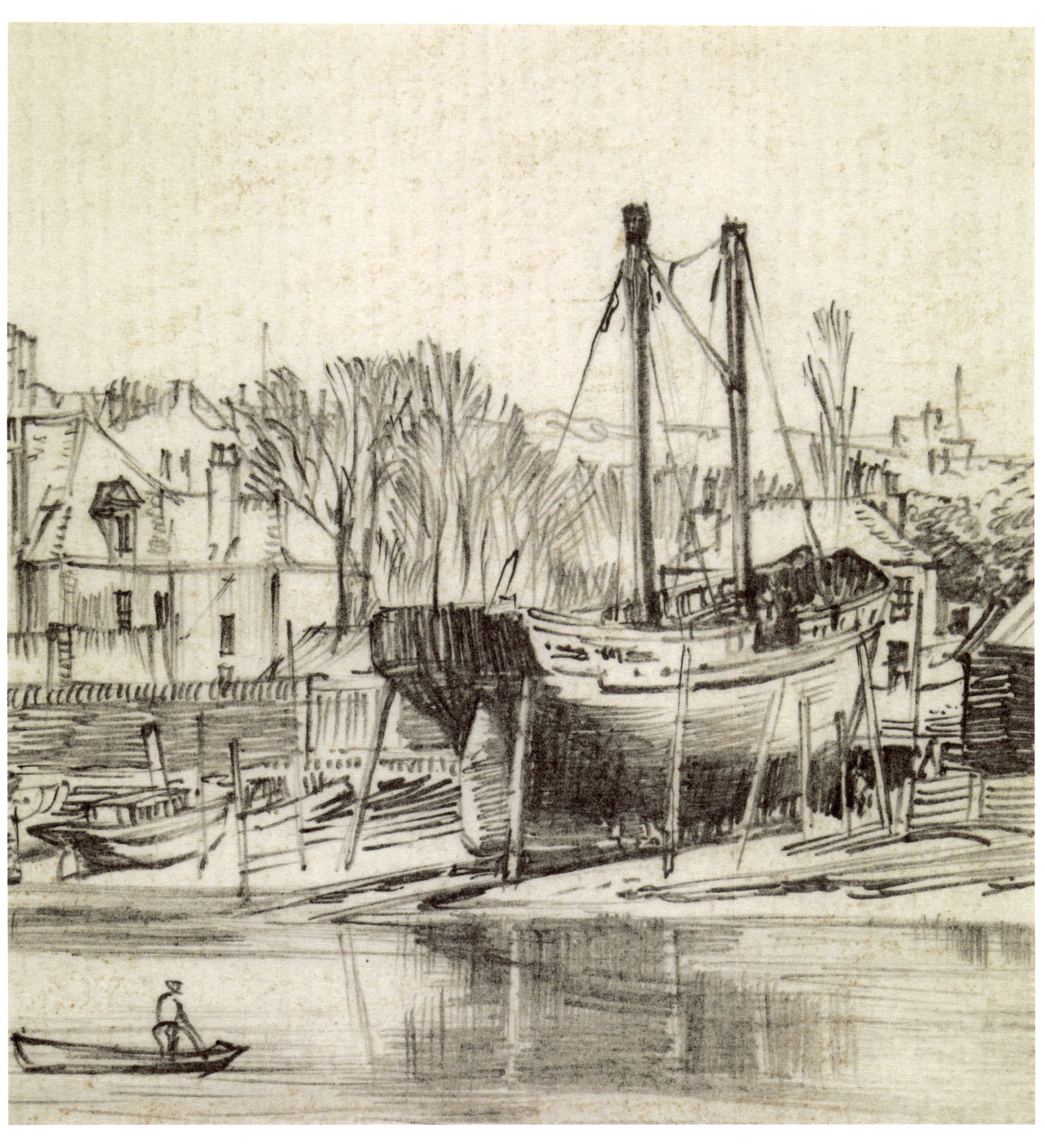

[28]

LA FONTAINE'S FABLES

Various artists.
France, nineteenth-twentieth centuries.
Inv. 462 (1–57)

The fifty-seven watercolours listed below, which illustrate various fables by Jean de La Fontaine (1621–1695), were created by thirty-five artists, either French or working in France during the late nineteenth-early twentieth centuries[1]. ¶ Worthy of note, each item in this collection highlights the important role played by private collectors, who were responsible for encouraging the use of the watercolour technique and for ensuring that this technique came to be accepted by official and academic bodies. It should be remembered that this genre was rejected in the early nineteenth century and only became re-established in France in the romantic era thanks to the influence of English painters such as Turner (1775–1851) and Bonington (1802–1828). This new acceptance was fostered by artists such as Eugène Lami (1800–1890) who set up the French Watercolourists' Society in 1879. The society's exhibitions included contributions from many of the artists responsible for the watercolours now being presented. ¶ In the case of the works in question, the collector Alfred Baillehache, besides commissioning representations of La Fontaine's fables from contemporary watercolourists, also purchased other watercolours on the same theme when the collections of Alfred Hartmann and Antony Roux (1833–1913)[2] were put on sale in April 1899 and May 1914 respectively. It was this group of works, originating from three different collections, that Calouste Gulbenkian purchased on 23 May 1922 when the Baillehache collection went on sale at the Hôtel Drouot in Paris[3]. ¶ This set of watercolours has also served to intensify the ever-growing interest in the illustration of La Fontaine's fables because, as Alain-Marie Bassy states, "illustration reinforces the meaning of the *Fables*"[4]. This has been the case ever since they were published for the first time in three collections, distributed across twelve books, and then published in Paris in 1668, 1678–79 and 1693 respectively[5]. ¶ In the *Fables*, La Fontaine revisited themes dealt with by Aesop, Phaedrus and Ovid as well as in the fables of the Middle Ages and in Indian and Arabic literature. Once the best prologues had been selected, the fabulist revived them through his poetical lyricism and gave them new life, applying a layer of humour and irony which allowed his razor-sharp portraits of the human condition to be aimed at the society of his time, from the common people and the bourgeois to the nobility and the clergy. Thus the characters to whom the fabulist gave life, whether they be people or animals, secretly lead the reader to confront his or her own existence. ¶ From François Chauveau (1613–1676), the illustrator of the first edition of La Fontaine's fables, artists in every era have developed his themes in painting, drawing, printmaking, sculpture, tapestry or ceramics, opting to use the broadest range of techniques. The text and

1. These works, which were used in books and tapestries on seat furniture, appeared in the exhibition curated by Manuela Fidalgo and Maria Fernanda Passos Leite, "No Tempo em Que Os Animais Falavam" ["Once upon a time when the Animals Talked. La Fontaine's Fables in the Calouste Gulbenkian Collection"]. Lisbon, Calouste Gulbenkian Collection, 1994–95.

2. Antony Roux, who was Baillehache's uncle, deserves a special mention for the role that he played in this regard. A wealthy Marsellaise art dealer, he invited renowned artists of the time to represent La Fontaine's well-known fables in watercolours. In May 1881, at the Durand-Ruel Gallery, a large number of watercolours resulting from this project were exhibited (specifically, around one hundred and twenty by various artists and twenty five by Gustave Moreau). The success of the initiative, especially the acclaim received by the works of Moreau, led Roux to make another commission from this artist. In 1886, sixty three watercolours and an allegory in fable form were exhibited at the Goupil Gallery in Paris. This group of works was sold sometime before May 1914 (the date of the sale of Anthony Roux's Collection). Only one watercolour from this group belongs to the Gustave Moreau Museum in Paris, an institution that also owns several preparatory sketches for the aforementioned works. See GREVERAND, 2002, p. 27.

3. See *Ibidem*, p. 29.

4. "l'illustration fait corps avec les *Fables*". See BASSY, 1986, p. 11.

5. The first collection, entitled *Fables choisies mises en vers par M. de La Fontaine*, gathered together 124 fables, previously published in six books, into a single volume which was preceded by a dedication to the then six-year-old Louis, Dauphin of France, the son of Louis XIV and Maria Teresa of Austria. The second collection appeared on two consecutive dates: the first, containing 45 fables, was published in 1678 (books VII and VIII) and the second, containing 42 fables, in 1679 (books IX, X and XI). Lastly, the third collection was published in 1693 (book XII). It contained 27 fables combined with four poems by the same author.

the images thereby become accomplices in such a way that "regardless of the technique used, artists sought to turn text and its illustration into the front and back of the same aesthetic object"[6]. ¶ The creators of the works now being discussed opted to use the watercolour, a genre whose spontaneity allows the constant changes of nature to be interpreted with great veracity. It also allows the whole composition to be imbued with the sense of freshness arising from the transparency of the shades used on the white of the paper and from the way that the brightness of the coloured pigments is diffused in infinite light-coloured hues. ¶ The originality of the imaginaries of each of the thirty-five artists who worked on this collection is evident in the choice of the exact point in the prologue which they each aimed to illustrate. A good example of this is the fable *The Shepherd and the Sea*, which was depicted in the watercolours of both Georges Clairin (inv. 462-17) and Félix Ziem (inv.462-20). Clairin chose the moment when the shepherd, regretting the previous adventures that had led him into poverty, rejects the offers of riches from the sea through a beautiful mermaid. The chosen shades are in some way related to the tension of the moment. For his part, Ziem uses warm and bright colours, enhanced by the transparency of the watercolour, to depict the poetic atmosphere surrounding the peaceful existence of the shepherd and his flock on a broad beach washed by the waters and the breeze. ¶ Set against a broad range of scenic backdrops, the action in most representations of these works takes place in the open air among forests, woods, mountains or wide plains through which streams flow. In works such as *The Frog and the Rat* by Saunier (inv. 462-14), *The Snake's Head and Tail* by Jacquemart (inv. 462-47), and Heilbuth's *The Hare and the Frogs* (inv. 462-3), *The Heron* (inv. 462-55) and *The Cricket* (inv. 462-56), the landscape takes on such importance that the composition is transformed into a hymn to nature while the characters become mere accessories. In all of them, the evocation of the fabulist's theme is no more than a pretext for the treatment of the landscape in the composition. ¶ At times, as in *The Oak and the Reed* by Harpignies (inv. 462-1), whom Anatole France called "the Michelangelo of trees," nature takes on an allegorical meaning in the poetic world of the fable and the natural elements play out the confrontation between moral values that are common to all humanity. ¶ The unlikely nature of some of La Fontaine's texts, such as *The Mountain in Labour,* was wisely expressed in the watercolour by Thornley (inv. 462-38) through an almost magical atmosphere in which a burst of colour is suddenly and harshly imposed. ¶ Entitled *Idylle Antique* in the former Antony Roux Collection, the fable *The Fishes and the Shepherd Who Played the Flute* (inv. 462-39) appears together with a composition that is also dominated by a landscape conveyed with the transparency of the watercolour and subtle indefinite touches of colour. Painted by Giuseppe de Nittis, an artist who was close to the Macchiaioli group and the impressionists, the bucolic and idyllic setting in which the shepherd tries to attract the fish with the sound of his flute is combined with the elegant treatment of the female nude. ¶ Among the best-represented artists in this series of watercolours is Elie Delaunay, with twelve works. He tended to choose themes of a historical, philosophical, mythological or allegorical nature in which compositions with classical outlines were rendered with denser and more vigorous shades. *Simonides Saved by the Gods* (inv. 462-12) is a good example of the artist's work and, in the textual context, a eulogy to poetry. ¶ A unique group of works within this series is that comprising the four watercolours by Isidor Rosenstock, a painter of landscapes and views of the gardens of Versailles. The latter, together with his sculptural groups, served as settings in

6. « …quelle que soit la technique utilisée, les artistes ont cherché à faire du texte et de son illustration le recto et le verso d'un même objet esthétique. » See COMPÈRE, LUCOT, GREVERAND, 1994, p. 56.

which to represent the fables selected by the artist, such as *The Crow and the Fox* (inv. 462-42). ¶ For his watercolour, Henri Gervex chose one of the best-known stories of all time, *The Grasshopper and the Ant* (inv. 462-34). Curiously enough, this was the first fable in the first book of the first collection published, as mentioned above, in 1668. Like Gustave Doré, Gervex chose to interpret the two small insects in an anthropomorphic manner, taking advantage of the two levels on which the fabulist's text can be read. Thus, Gervex evokes the conflict between the two heroines, representatives of two mutually hostile social classes distinguished by their dress and their physical posture. In this case, in contrast to Doré's approach, the cricket is shown to be begging, not in front of a wealthy house, but against the backdrop of a carriage which the ant is entering with a haughty bearing. This work was wonderfully well-served by the watercolour technique in the depiction of the cricket's colourful quasi-gypsy clothes, the sober black of the ant's dress and fur-hemmed cloak and, above all, in the cold, lightly suggested wintery setting of bare-branched trees. Just a light touch of colour between the branches provides a counterpoint, albeit a slight one, to the spirit of the narrative. ¶ Gustave Doré was responsible for one of the most beautiful illustrations in this series, *The Eagle and the Magpie* (inv. 462-43). While, in a somewhat unlikely encounter, the two characters 'converse' in a dark and secluded spot, the countryside opens up beyond the trees, which rise to form a natural barrier. From the distant mountains, which are painted in a play of red and orange shades, a light emanates that floods the sky in successively changing hues, lending the work a visionary quality that is enhanced by the pictorial characteristics of the watercolour. This method can also be seen in the background of Giacomelli's watercolour *The Vultures and the Pigeons* (inv. 462-40), in which a palette that is now warm and vibrant, now luminous and transparent, evokes the raw violence of the carnage that has just taken place through an explosion of reds. ¶ One group of illustrations sets La Fontaine's text in indoor spaces. In this context, in which the protagonists are human beings, three watercolours stand out: *The Doctors* (inv. 462-28), by Toudouze, and two works by Leloir, *The Young Widow* (inv. 462-25) and *The Old Woman and the Two Servants* (inv. 462-18). In the first, in which the decorative elements and the characters' clothing evoke the period in which La Fontaine lived (the seventeenth century), two illustrious doctors spend so long discussing the treatment to be given to a patient that the latter is left to suffer in increasing agony. To accentuate the ridiculousness of the situation, Toudouze uses a caricatural language to depict the features of the wise doctors, who do nothing to save the patient. All of the focus falls on the two conceited men in the foreground while the patient, who is practically ignored, wastes away on the far side of the room. ¶ In this group of watercolours, Leloir, an artist who excelled in the study of clothing, is the outstanding illustrator of interior scenes. In *The Young Widow*, we once again see the evocation of a seventeenth-century environment characterised by ostentatious decoration in which the main character appears in the foreground, fastidiously dressed and carefully attending to her toilette. *The Old Lady and the Two Servants* is set in a more modest space, the quarters of the servants who are forced to work at the pace imposed by the mistress. Of note in this watercolour is the compositional beauty arising from Leloir's decision to express the conflict by granting an essential role to the harsh, yellowish light that shines from the lantern hidden behind the gloomy old lady, tormenting the two young women. ¶ In 1930, some years after buying this series of watercolours, Calouste Gulbenkian commissioned Jean

Dunand (1877–1942), a lacquerwork expert with professional and social[7] ties to the Collector, to mount the fifty-seven works on special paper and to create a binding with a slipcase that would protect them more effectively (fig. 28.1)[8]. ¶ For the slipcase, a box with a suede-lined interior and an opening at the side, Dunand opted for a black lacquer covering decorated on all of its surfaces with a multicoloured sprinkling of small red and cream-coloured particles. The use of these different-sized particles, some of which are minuscule, gives rise to an optical play of multiple depths. ¶ The brown morocco-leather binding is decorated in such a way as to allude to the theme of the watercolours, with representations of animals, the protagonists of the fabulist's prologues. On the uppermost surface a circular metal plate, lacquered in blue, represents the fable *The Heron*. In a landscape dominated by the course of a stream, on the banks of which fantastic vegetation is sprinkled here and there with gold, a heron looks at the various species of fish circling around it without finding any that might be good enough to serve as a meal. The whirlpool caused by the circular movement of the fish in the water is accentuated by the various concentric circles that are embossed and printed in silver as well as by circular plates of black lacquered metal. To create the white areas of the heron's body, Dunand used the eggshell technique. The upper back cover is completely covered by a plate with a black lacquer background on which several exotic fish move among the luxuriant vegetation of the riverbed, releasing air bubbles that rise to meet the rays of light shining through them. The volume of each of these elements is accentuated by a light relief. ¶ Jean Dunand's signature appears on this binding three times: once on the plate decorating the upper surface, once on the lacquer of the upper back cover and again on the lower back cover.

7. See correspondence held in the archives of the Calouste Gulbenkian Museum.

8. See LISBON, 2001, p. 243, no. 105.

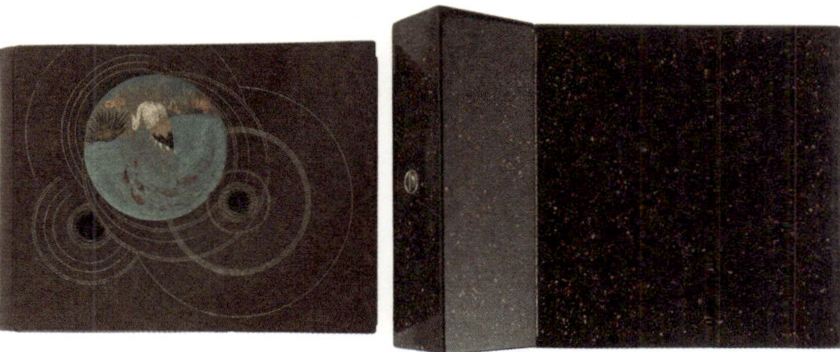

– fig. 28.1 –
Jean Dunand (1877–1942), Binding and case for the watercolour album (*La Fontaine's Fables*), France, ca. 1930. Binding: 38.7 × 49.4 cm; Case: 43 × 57.2 cm. Lisbon, Calouste Gulbenkian Museum

Photo: Carlos Azevedo

PROVENANCE

Antony Roux Collection: inv. 462-14 (lot no. 113), inv. 462-24 (lot no. 94); inv. 462-41 (lot no. 76); inv. 462-54 (lot no. 93); inv. 462-39 (lot no. 101, under the title *Idylle Antique*); Hartmann Collection: inv. 462-47 (lot no. 88); Alfred Baillehache Collection (owner of the set comprising the fifty seven watercolours). Acquired by Calouste Gulbenkian at the latter collection's sale, through Graat et Madoulé, Paris, at Hôtel Drouot, 23 May 1922, lot nos. 64 to 120.

•

EXHIBITIONS

LISBON, 1994–1995; LISBON, 1998, pp. 260–62, nos. 271–274 (repr.)

•

LITERATURE

GRÉVERAND, 2002, pp. 28–29, no. 32 (p. 30), pp. 76–77 (repr.), pp. 78–79 (repr.), p. 103 (repr.), pp. 110–111 (repr.), p. 118 (repr.), pp. 112–123 (repr.), pp. 164–165 (repr.), pp. 180–181 (repr.).

[28–1]
Georges-Jules-Victor Clairin
(1843–1919)
The Shepherd and the Sea
(book IV, fable 2)
31.5 × 25.2 cm
Signed on the lower
left-hand side: *G. Clairin*
Inv. 462–17

[28–2]
Jules-Elie Delaunay (1828–1891)
Death and the Wretched Man
(book I, fable 15)
23.3 × 29.2 cm
Signed and dated on the lower
left-hand side: *Elie Delaunay 1881*
Inv. 462–4

[28–3]
Jules-Elie Delaunay (1828–1891)
The Child and the School-Master
(book I, f 19)
20 × 24.7 cm
Signed and dated on the lower
left-hand side: *Elie Delaunay 1880*
Inv. 462–6

[28–4]
Jules-Elie Delaunay (1828–1891)
The Dove and the Ant
(book II, fable 12)
25 × 20 cm
Signed and dated on the lower
left-hand side: *Elie Delaunay 1880*
Inv. 462–7

[28–5]
Jules-Elie Delaunay (1828–1891)
Jupiter and the Traveller
(book IX, fable 13)
23.4 × 29.3 cm
Signed and dated on the lower right-hand side: *Elie Delaunay 1880*
Inv. 462–8

[28–6]
Jules-Elie Delaunay (1828–1891)
Simonides Saved by the Gods
(book I, fable 14)
22.2 × 29 cm
Signed and dated on the lower
left-hand side: *Elie Delaunay 1881*
Inv. 462–12

[28–7]
Jules-Elie Delaunay (1828–1891)
The Old Man and His Sons
(book IV, fable 18)
20.3 × 24.7 cm
Signed and dated on the lower
left-hand side: *Elie Delaunay 1881*
Inv. 462–15

[28–8]
Jules-Elie Delaunay (1828–1891)
The Old Man and the Three Young Men
(book XI, fable 8)
20 × 24.8 cm
Signed and dated on the lower
right-hand side: *Elie Delaunay 1880*
Inv. 462–24

[28–9]
Jules-Elie Delaunay (1828–1891)
Daphnis and Alcimadura
(book XII, fable 26)
30.4 × 22.3 cm
Signed and dated on the lower
left-hand side: *Elie Delaunay 1881*
Inv. 462–41

[28–10]
Jules-Elie Delaunay (1828–1891)
The Two Cocks
(book VII, fable 13)
30 × 23.4 cm
Signed and dated on the lower
left-hand side: *Elie Delaunay 1882*
Inv. 462–45

[28–11]
Jules-Elie Delaunay (1828–1891)
The Ingratitude and Injustice of Men Toward Fortune
(book VII, fable 14)
30.3 × 24.3 cm
Signed and dated on the lower
left-hand side: *Elie Delaunay 1880* (?)
Inv. 462–52

[28–12]
Jules-Elie Delaunay (1828–1891)
Love and Folly
(book XII, fable 14)
31 × 22.7 cm
Signed and dated on the lower
right-hand side: *Elie Delaunay 1880*
Inv. 462–57

[28–13]
Jules-Elie Delaunay (1828–1891)
Philemon and Baucis
(poem published in book XII, fable 25)
23.2 × 29.6 cm
Signed and dated on the lower
left-hand side: *Elie Delaunay. 1882*
Inv. 462–54

[28–14]
Paul Gustave L. C. Doré (1832–1883)
The Eagle and the Magpie
(book XII, fable 11)
23.9 × 31 cm
Signed on the lower
left-hand side: *G. Doré*
Inv. 462–43

[28–15]
Ernest-Ange Duez (1843–1896)
The Bird-catcher, the Hawk and the Lark
(book VI, fable 15)
29 × 22 cm
Signed on the lower
right-hand side: *E. Duez*
Inv. 462–33

[28–16]
Gabriel Ferrier (1847–1914)
The Woman and the Snake
19.5 × 35.2 cm
Signed and dated on the lower
left-hand side: *Gabriel Ferrier, 188* (?)
Inv. 462–44

[28–17]
François-Louis Français (1814–1897)
The Fox and the Grapes
(book III, fable 11)
30.5 × 23.2 cm
Signed and dated at the bottom,
respectively on the left and
right-hand side: *Français, 1880*
Inv. 462–50

[28–18]
Henri Gervex (1852–1929)
The Grasshopper and the Ant
(book I, fable 1)
28.5 × 21.9 cm
Signed on the lower
left-hand side:
H. Gervex
Inv. 462–34

[28–19]
Hector Giacomelli (1822–1904)
The Vultures and the Pigeons
(book VII, fable 8)
26.4 × 21.5 cm
Signed on the lower
left-hand side: *H. Giacomelli*
Inv. 462–40

[28–20]
Alexandre-Gaston Guignard (1848–1922)
The Crow Who Wanted to Imitate the Eagle
(book II, fable 16)
30.5 × 22.8 cm
Signed on the lower
right-hand side: illegible
Inv. 462–9

[28–21]
Henri-Joseph Harpignies (1819–1916)
The Oak and the Reed
(book I, fable 22)
24.5 × 19.4 cm
Signed and dated on the lower
left-hand side: *Harpignies 79*
Inv. 462–1

[28–22]
Ferdinand Heilbuth (1826–1889)
The Hare and the Frogs
(book II, fable 14)
24.5 × 30.2 cm
Signed on the lower
right-hand side: *F Heilbuth*
Inv. 462–3

[28–23]
Ferdinand Heilbuth (1826–1889)
The Heron
(book VII, fable 4)
24.9 × 29.5 cm
Signed on the lower
left-hand side: *F Heilbuth*
Inv. 462–55

[28–24]
Ferdinand Heilbuth (1826–1889)
The Cricket
24 × 19 cm
Signed on the lower
right-hand side: *F Heilbuth*
Inv. 462–56

[28–25]
Jules-Ferdinand Jacquemart (1837–1880)
The Ass and the Pup
(book IV, fable 5)
25.5 × 21.7 cm
Signed and dated on the lower
left-hand side: *J. Jacquemart 79*
Inv. 462–37

[28–26]
Jules-Ferdinand Jacquemart (1837–1880)
The Snake's Head and Tail
(book VII, fable 17)
28.7 × 22.5 cm
Signed and dated on the lower
right-hand side: *J. Jacquemart. 79*
Inv. 462–47

[28–27]
Gustave Jean Jacquet (1846–1909)
The Drowned Wife
(book III, fable 16)
22.2 × 28.2 cm
Signed and dated on the lower
right-hand side: *G Jacquet 1880*
Inv. 462–2

[28–28]
Henri Jourdain (1846–1931)
The Stag Who Sees Himself in the Water
(book VI, fable 9)
23 × 28 cm
Signed on the lower
left-hand side: *Henri Jourdain*
Inv. 462–46

TWENTIETH CENTURY

[29]

JOHN SINGER SARGENT

Florence, 1856 – London, 1925

THE CHURCH OF SANTA MARIA DELLA SALUTE, VENICE

Venice, ca. 1904–9

Watercolour with touches of gouache
and graphite traces on cardboard
36.7 × 53.8 cm
Inv. 75

Like other artists represented in the Gulbenkian Collection, such as Félix Ziem [25] and Paul Jouve [30, 31], John Singer Sargent was also a painter-traveller who spent his life moving around from place to place. The child of American parents who decided to leave their country and live in Europe as part of a constant quest for new cultural experiences, Sargent, who had been exposed to this influence since childhood, hardly settled in one place for long. In his search for renewed inspiration for his work, he left behind evidence of the numerous trips that he undertook to the United States, Italy, France, England, Germany, Austria, Spain, Portugal, Turkey, Norway, Greece, Swiss, Palestine and Egypt, among other places[1]. ¶ The many towns and cities in which he lived – in the United States of America, the Middle East, and Northern and Southern Europe – all marked important stages in his life. These cities included Florence, where he was born and where he studied at the Accademia delle Belle Arti; Paris, where he continued his artistic training under the painter Carolus-Duran (1837–1917) and where he later achieved great success with his exhibitions at the *Salons*; London, which offered him a regular flow of work as a portrait painter; Boston, which entrusted him to decorate state-owned buildings such as the public library; and, finally, Venice, which became his favourite city of all. ¶ After returning in 1880–1881 and 1882 to the city that he had known since childhood, Sargent never excluded it from his travel itineraries and revisited it virtually every year after 1900. In fact, in a letter to his friend Vernon Lee[2], written when he was still studying in Paris, Sargent already hints at the importance that Venice was to have in his art: "Well, we [his family] have decided to spend the winter here [Paris]. I am sorry to leave Italy – that is to say, Venice, but on the other hand I am persuaded that Paris is the place to learn painting in. When I can paint, then away for Venice!"[3] With its architectural beauty, romantic atmosphere and echoes of history, Venice fired his imagination, leading him to produce numerous works in oils and watercolours. He depicted the most famous places of the inimitable Adriatic city not through

1. See KILMURRAY, Elaine – "Chronology of travels", *in* ADELSON *et al.*, 1997, pp. 237–42.

2. Pseudonym of the English writer Violet Paget (1856–1935).

3. Letter from Sargent to Vernon Lee, 4 September 1874, private collection. See KILMURRAY, Elaine – "The light of Venice, John Singer Sargent", *in* BASEL, 2008 (pp. 121–40), p. 121.

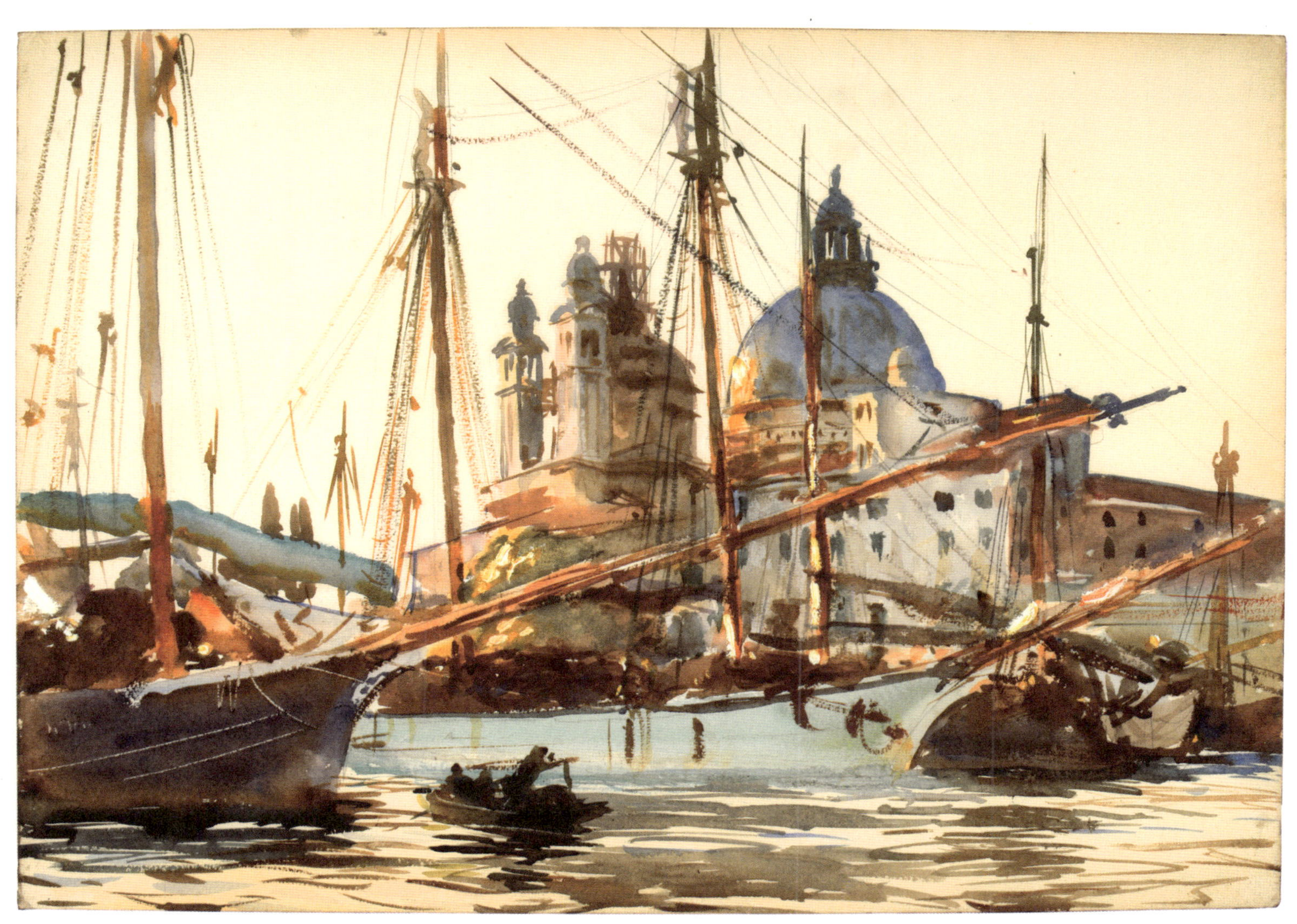

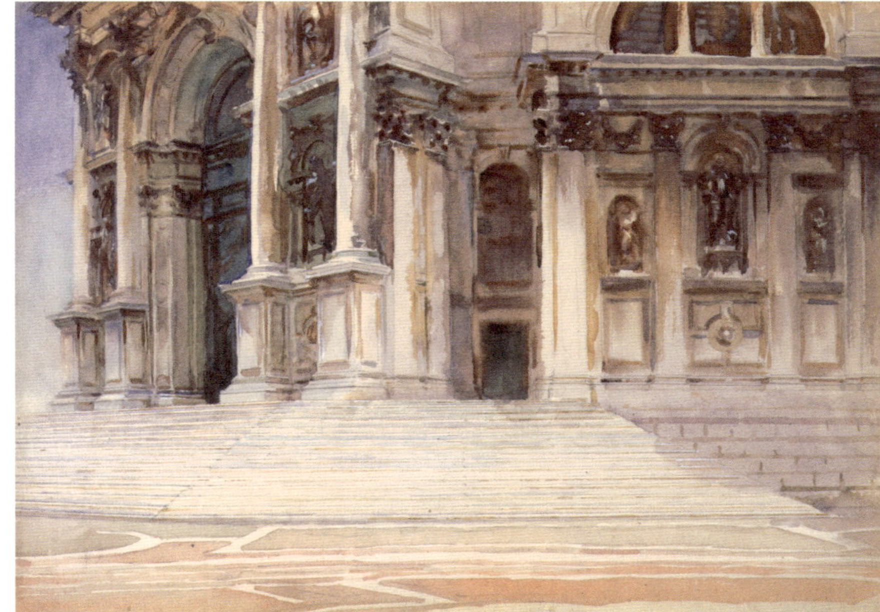

– fig. 29.1 –
John Singer Sargent (1856–1925), *Santa Maria della Salute*, 1906–1909. Watercolour on paper, 36.8 × 53.6 cm. Joslyn Art Museum, Omaha, Nebraska. Museum purchase 1946.29.

expansive vistas but through large scenographic planes that give the spectator a close-up view of architectural details, fragments of buildings and old palaces, bridges and narrow back streets where, curiously, human figures are either absent or play only a secondary role in his melancholy expressions. ¶ Frequently using an impressionist style, Sargent painted these urban portraits from a gondola. With great sensitivity, he managed to capture the vibrating outlines of buildings and boats mirrored in the lagoon's sparkling waters and the oscillating effects of the light reflected in them. He concentrated on capturing the watery atmosphere and the play of light, allowing his earlier, more limited, palette of cooler shades to give way to a range of soft yet bright, occasionally intense, colours in which pinks, lilacs, yellows, sapphire-blues and violets predominate. ¶ The subjects of the painter's studies of Venice are easy to identify due to the wealth of detail that he gave them. This is the case of the imposing baroque basilica of Santa Maria della Salute, which was built in the mid-seventeenth century by the architect Baldassare Longhena (1598–1682). Situated by the Punta della Dogana, at the entrance to the Grand Canal, the building can be seen in many of the painter's works, including some of his most complex compositions, in particular his exquisite watercolours. ¶ This is the edifice that gives its title to the watercolour acquired by Calouste Gulbenkian at the sale of the William Newall Collection (1851–1922) in London in June 1922. When it was purchased, the work was accompanied by a signed letter from Sargent to Mr Newall, dated 16 December 1909[4], which may help to establish an approximate date for the work. ¶ This church is the subject of a series of watercolours and oils which Sargent began in 1904. Fascinated by the magnificent towering monument, the painter never portrayed it in its entirety, choosing instead to offer syncopated views in which a fragment takes on the dynamic greatness of the whole, as in the watercolour *Santa Maria della Salute*, owned by the Joslyn Art Museum, Omaha[5], which excludes the grand domes and focusses on the decorated façade with its columns, pillars, niches with stone sculptures, and

4. "Dear Mr. Newall, I acknowledge with thanks the receipt of your cheque for… [word or number erased] guineas and I am glad to think that a watercolour of mine will be in your possession. I sent it today to Brown's Hotel, Dover Street. Yours sincerely – John S. Sargent." See Archives from the Calouste Gulbenkian Museum, also see ORMOND, KILMURRAY, 2009, no. 1120, p. 170, note 1.

5. ADELSON, *et al.*, 1997, no. 206, p. 203.

– fig. 29.2 –
John Singer Sargent (1856–1925), *Santa Maria della Salute, Venice*, ca. 1903–1907. Watercolour on paper, 34.9 × 53.5 cm. Isabella Stewart Gardner Museum, Boston, inv. P3W31.

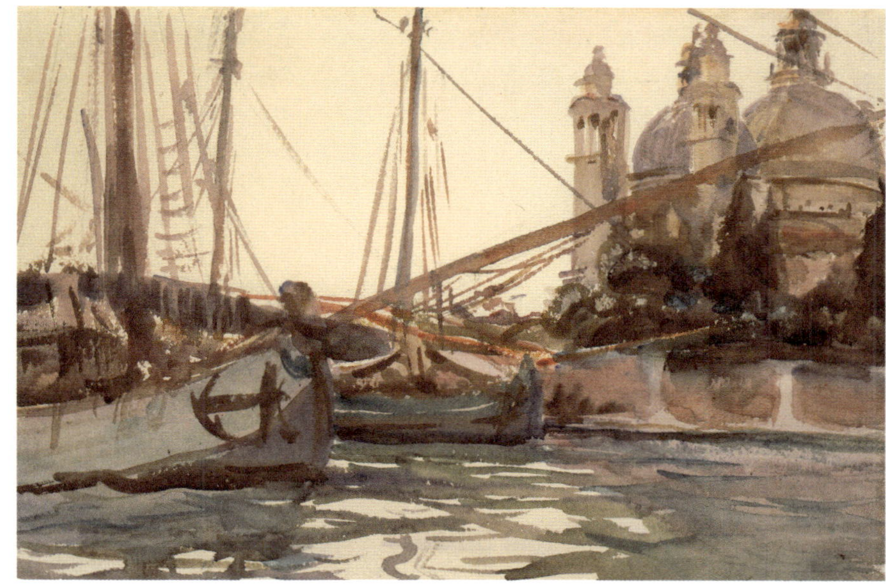

the flight of steps leading up to the main entrance (fig. 29.1). ¶ The Gulbenkian watercolour is part of a group in which the central motif is not actually the church itself, which appears as a backdrop. The actual subject of this composition is the intense maritime activity taking place on the Giudecca Canal, a wide stretch of water running parallel to the Grand Canal which Sargent, facing north-west, painted from his gondola. From the rear of the Santa Maria della Salute, Sargent recorded, "in all its balletic grace"[6], the coming and going of the numerous sailboats, fishing boats and commercial vessels gliding across the water or anchored at the Fondamenta delle Zattere. Several different-sized vessels enter the composition from the left and are seen in profile; the foreground is taken up by the black prow of a boat whose long bowsprit cuts diagonally across the composition, crisscrossing the masts, sails and rigging of the surrounding vessels. The pictorial space is punctuated by strong vertical and diagonal lines, some of which extend beyond the boundaries of the work. ¶ Sargent's main point of interest in this watercolour essentially lies in the reflection of the blue of the sky and the shimmering water on the hulls and sails of the boats, conveying the sunlight with sparkling shades and colours that stimulate a sense of joy. Through the mesh formed by the vessels and their rigging the imposing Santa Maria della Salute appears in the distance with its back to the Grand Canal. In this example, Sargent shows both of its domes (one of which appears to be covered in scaffolding) and their belfries, bathed in the warm golden light of a Venetian afternoon. ¶ This work truly shows Sargent's ability as a watercolourist. Taught by his mother, he first employed the technique as a child before going on to use it in academic works and preliminary studies for other works. In the early twentieth century, he began to explore the inherent qualities of the watercolour, particularly its transparency. At this point in his life, his box of watercolours became an essential item that he took with him whenever he travelled. However, as early as 1892, when he wrote the introduction to the catalogue for his friend Hercules Brabazon's (1821–1906) first solo exhibi-

6. JANIS, Donna Seldin, "Venice", *in* ADELSON, *et al.*, 1997, p. 205.

7. Quoted in BLAUGRUND, Annette – "Sunshine captured: the development and dispersement of Sargent's watercolors", *in* NEW YORK, 1986; CHICAGO, 1987, p. 219.

tion, Sargent already valued the watercolour and hinted at what was to be his own destiny a decade later: "Each sketch is a new delight of harmony and the harmonies are innumerable and unexpected, taken from Nature, or, rather, imposed by her... Only after years of the contemplation of Nature can the process of selection become so sure an instinct; and a handling so spontaneous and so freed from the commonplaces of expression is final mastery, the result of long artistic training"[7]. ¶ In this watercolour, Sargent followed his usual custom of working on a support dampened with light washes, taking advantage of the white of the paper and the transparency of the pigments that he used, which came from a palette of colours limited to browns, blues, pinks, greens and yellows. In the play that he created between greenish-browns and the white of the paper, the broad watery brushstrokes highlight the shimmering waters. The watercolourist's versatility is evident in the way that the entire composition emanates the kind of shimmering light that can be seen only in Venice and that brings the scene to life. ¶ Of the many watercolours that Sargent painted of the city, *The Santa Maria della Salute, Venice*, which belongs to the Isabella Stewart Gardner Museum of Boston (fig. 29.2), is the most similar to the piece owned by the Gulbenkian Museum. Both works were probably painted on the same day, although the latter was likely to have been painted later on, when the weather conditions no longer allowed the paint to dry so quickly, giving rise to some visible drips at certain points.

PROVENANCE

William Newall Collection. Acquired by Calouste Gulbenkian at the sale of this collection, through Colnaghi, at Christie's, London, 30 June 1922, lot no. 67.

EXHIBITIONS

LISBON, 2006b, no. 22, p. 140–41, p. 141 (repr.); BASEL, 2008, p. 126, p. 138 (repr.).

LITERATURE

ADELSON, *et al.*, 1997, no. 212, p. 206 (repr.).

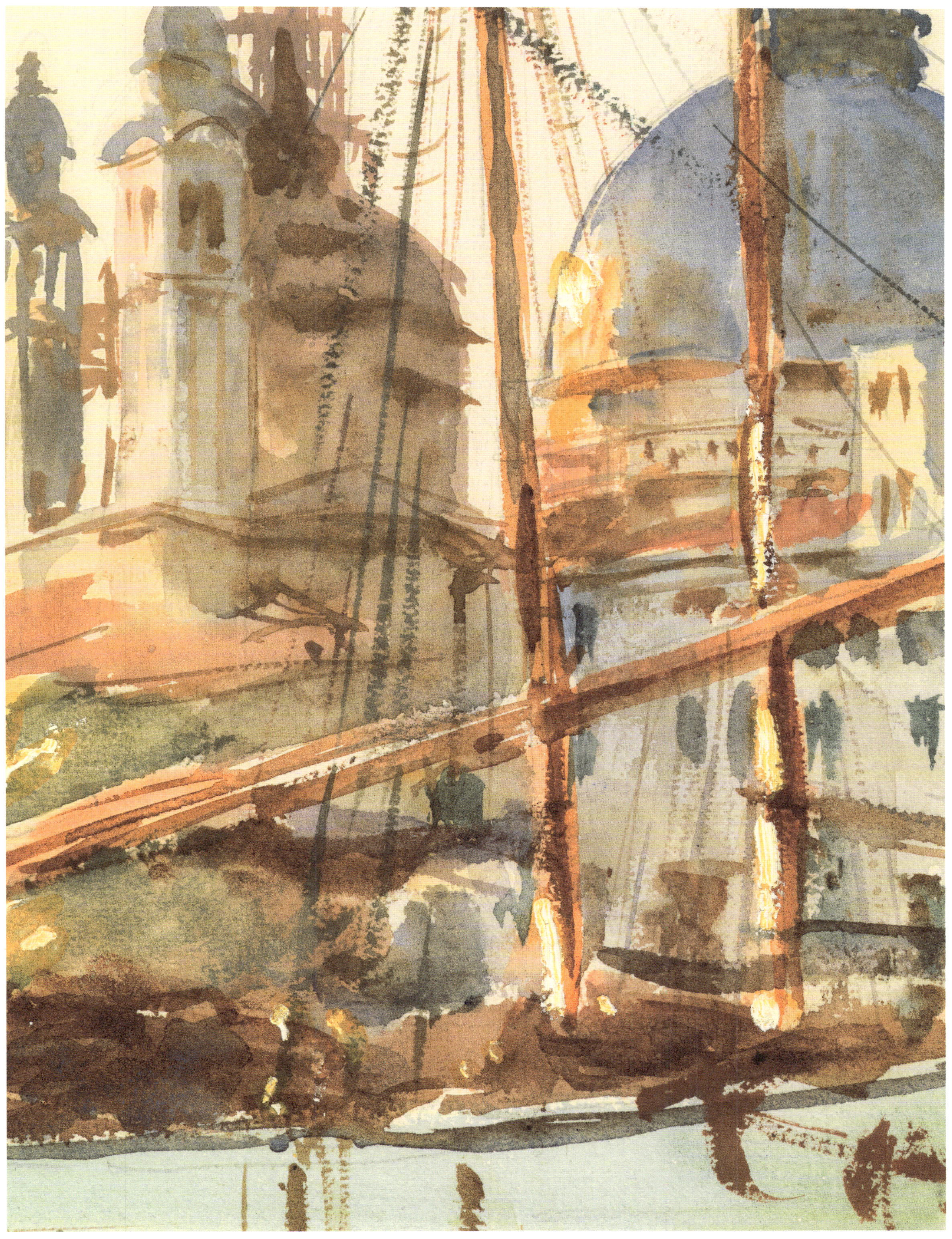

[30]

PAUL JOUVE

Bourron-Marlotte, 1878 – Paris, 1973

ROYAL EAGLE

France, ca. 1914

Conté crayon, white chalk, stump,
with touches of ochre pencil on paper.
54.5 × 76.3 cm.
Signature on lower left-hand side: *P. Jouve*.
Inv. 2219

1. Paris: Le Livre contemporain, 1919, no. 5, printed for Henri Lenseigne from a run of 125. Paul Jouve's compositions were engraved by François-Louis Schmied (1873–1941). Lisbon, Calouste Gulbenkian Museum, inv. LM381.

2. Lausanne: Gonin et Cie, undated [1932], no. 52 of a run of 150 prints. Paul Jouve's compositions were engraved by J. L. Perrichon. Lisbon, Calouste Gulbenkian Museum, inv. LM437.

The painter, sculptor, illustrator and engraver Paul Jouve is represented in the Gulbenkian Collection by two magnificent drawings [30–31] and by two equally noteworthy books illustrated by him: *Le Livre de la Jungle* [The Jungle Book] by Rudyard Kipling[1] and Colette's *Paradis Terrestre*[2]. By acquiring these four works for his collection on separate occasions between 1923 and 1939, Calouste Gulbenkian showed his particular interest in the artist's graphic work. ¶ Born in Bourron-Marlotte, near the forest of Fontainebleau, Paul Jouve lived in Paris from the age of two. The artistic temperament that he revealed from an early age was recognized and cultivated by his father, a painter and ceramic artist who allowed him to study at the École des Arts Décoratifs. However, the young Paul was interested neither in the traditional vocabulary of the arts nor in studio exercises, and he preferred to make studies directly from nature and in particular from the animal kingdom, which became the overriding theme of all his work. ¶ A painter of animals by his own choice and passion for the subject, he showed an early love of nature and was keen to study the anatomy and behaviour of animals in his quest to understand their relations with their own environments. He liked to observe them directly, firstly in captivity, depicting them in the European zoos, markets and museums that he often visited in his search for different models and new inspirations. However, these depictions of imprisoned animals set outside their natural environments lacked verisimilitude. It was only later, when Jouve saw them in their own habitats during his numerous trips to Africa, the Far East and India, that his interpretations took on the quiddity that enabled them to rank alongside the greatest works of the animal painters of the previous century such as Barye (1796–1875) and Delacroix (1798–1863). In his foreword to Camille Mauclair's monograph on Jouve, Pierre Bellanger managed to sum up this ability: "I recall hearing, in one of your exhibitions, a foreigner, excited with your lions, elephants, tigers and panthers cry out: 'Oh! That Jouve, he is the king of animals'. Let me say, in a less lapidary fashion, that you have solved the problem

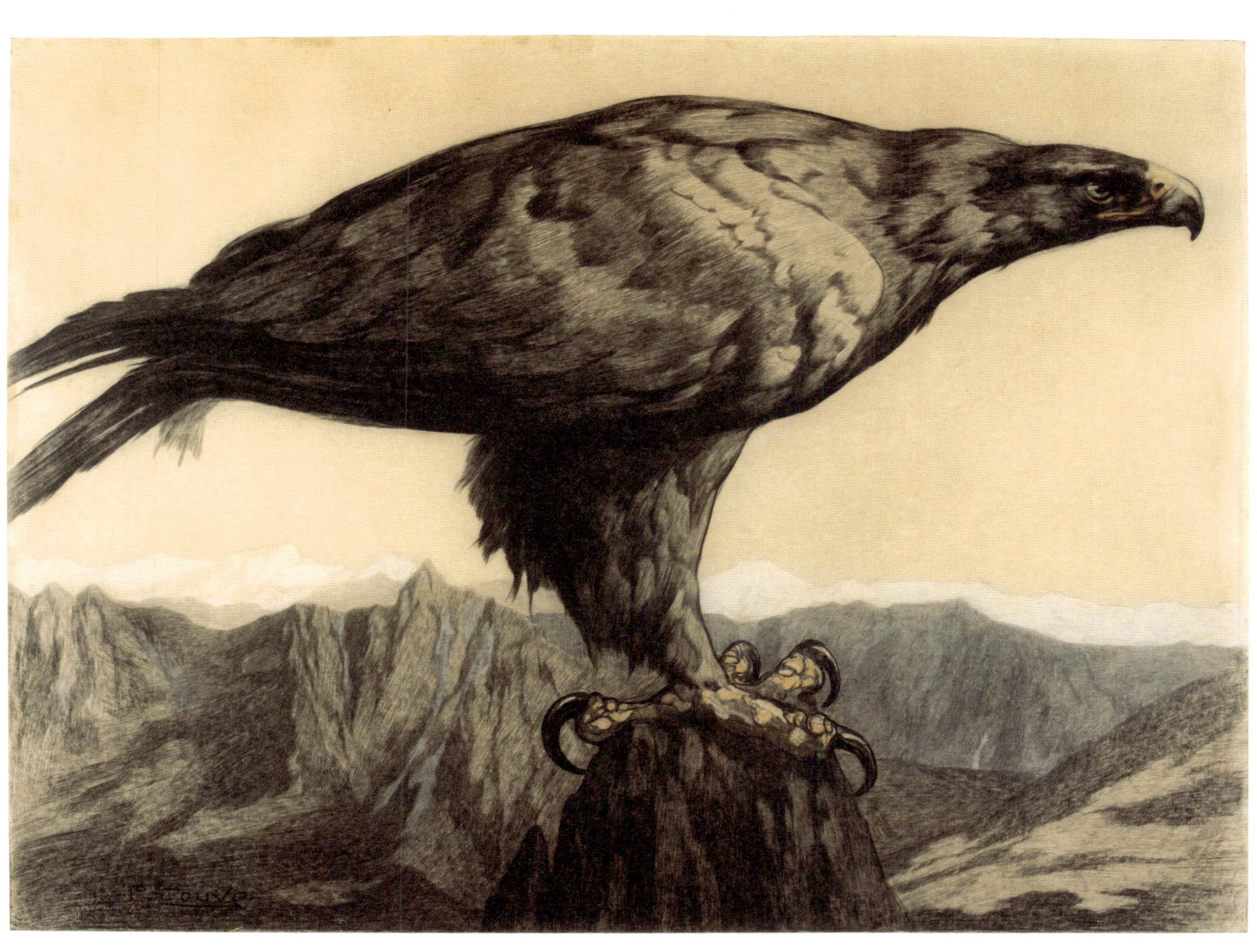

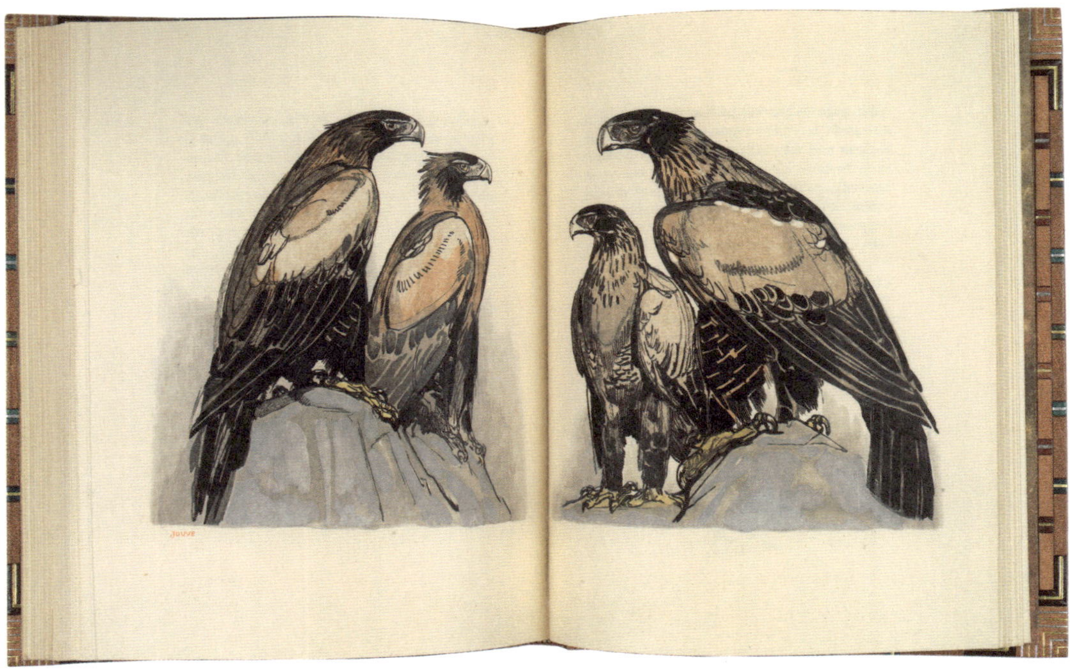

– fig. 30.1 – Illustrations designed by Paul Jouve (1878–1973) and en graved by J.-L. Perrichon, *in* Colette's, *Paradis Terrestres*, chapter X, p. 114–15. Lisbon, Calouste Gulbenkian Museum, inv. LM437. Photo: Catarina Gomes Ferreira

that already troubled Plato: thanks to you, animals have a soul"[3]. ¶ Jouve persevered in his observation of animals; he was fascinated by their every move, their attitudes, expressions, the way that their muscles flexed and relaxed. He wanted not only to convey the reality of their anatomical forms on paper (to which ends he also initially visited local slaughterhouses) but also to understand the secret lives and subtle psychological states of each species. This approach led the art critic François Monod to state in a comment on his drawings: "His studies present a beautiful and easy vigour that denote an intuitive temperament, served by a meticulous consciousness [...], he only focus himself on the indispensable details and he does not burdens his vision, which is always clear and typical, excellent to translate the redoubtable indolence of lions, the cautious flexibility of felines, the melancholy of old horses, the disdainful impertinence of apes"[4]. ¶ This drawing in the Gulbenkian Collection shows a royal eagle, a bird that recurs throughout Jouve's body of work. The piece was probably made around 1914, the same year in which the already lauded artist was awarded a grant by the Government of French Equatorial Africa to work on the African continent[5]. The outbreak of the First World War meant that he had to delay his visit, which took place only in 1931. ¶ As mentioned above, this particular bird of prey is the subject of countless of the artist's drawings, pastels, prints and paintings. However, far from being repetitive, it is always portrayed in different ways. Sometimes depicted alone, sometimes in the company of other birds, its wings may be outstretched or it may be shown devouring its prey or sharing it with its young. It is sometimes lightly sketched and sometimes drawn in meticulous detail. It may be perched on a solitary rock or an old tree-trunk, either as part of a landscape or portrayed against a neutral background, wounded or about to set off to hunt. As Camille Mauclair wrote: "Jouve tells us everything about the eagle. He shows the latter to us with its armour of black and grey feathers, dressed with its wings bent as a royal mantle, supported on its huge claws as curbed knives of horns [...]. Jouve shows us the eagle hunting, hovering with its wings wide open, in the glacial air, under the sun,

3. «Je me souviens d'avoir entendu, à l'une de vos expositions un étranger, enthousiasmé par vos lions, vos éléphants, vos tigres, vos panthères, s'écrier: 'Oh ! That Jouve, he is the king of animals.' Laissez-moi vous dire, sous une forme un peu moins lapidaire, que vous avez résolu le problème qui inquiétait déjà Platon: grâce à vous les animaux ont une âme." *In* MAUCLAIR, 1931, facsimile of a letter, s.p. h*ors-texte*.

4. "Ses études sont d'une belle vigueur facile qui dénote un tempérament d'intuitif, servi par une conscience méticuleuse [...], il ne s'attarde qu'aux détails indispensables et n'alourdit pas la vision qui est toujours nette et caractéristique, excellant à traduire l'indolence redoutable des lions, la souplesse cauteleuse des félins, la mélancolie des vieux chevaux, l'impertinence dédaigneuse des singes." In *Art et Décoration*, March 1905, quoted *in* MARCILHAC, 2005, p. 33.

5. I would like to thank Madame Amélie Marcilhac and Paul Jouve's heir for sharing her opinions on this drawing (2011).

or returning to its domain infected with the fragments of cadavers disputed over by eaglets"[6]. ¶ This large drawing in the Gulbenkian Collection shows the eagle perched on a cliff top. Jouve used the crayon to convey the changing shades of its thick plumage, the vigorous and robust volume of its body and, in particular, its huge talons, curved beak and keen eyes that scan the horizon. Touches of colour with the ochre pencil imparted to the bird's body, claws and beak add to the realism of the composition and accentuate the features that, in a fight, could have devastating effects. Jouve's skill in depicting the bird goes beyond its anatomical reality and allows observers to share in the tension of the moment: motionless, the muscles under its feathers are so taut that the body remains horizontal and the nearly imperceptible movement of the head to focus its gaze leads us to think that it is about to set off after a target. ¶ The eagle is shown on a peak against the backdrop of a mountain range. The mountains glimpsed in the distance are still covered with snow that is highlighted in white chalk, while on the visually more detailed rocky outcrops that lie closer to us it is possible to make out the ice that is starting to melt in rhythms of blue, indicating that winter is coming to an end and that the eagle will begin to find survival less of a struggle. The relationship between the constitutive elements of the composition is impressive. The sense of the bird being at a great height is reinforced by the truncated view of the cliff on which it is perched and by its position well above the line of the horizon. The deep perspective of the landscape, depicted in successive stretches, comes from the interception of the different masses of rock that are geometrically drawn with thick dense vertical, horizontal and diagonal lines. ¶ Jouve's representations of eagles share affinities with the Gulbenkian Collection's work, among which the artist's original drawings that were made into wood engravings by J-L. Perrichon to illustrate chapter 10 ("Rapaces") of Colette's *Paradis Terrestres* (fig. 30.1). ¶ In devoting his long life (he died at the age of 95) to exalting the animal kingdom, Paul Jouve, whose first contribution to the art world was a long frieze of marching animals created to decorate the triumphal gateway of the Place de la Concorde at the Paris World's Fair in 1900, lived long enough to achieve recognition for his ability to adhere to the modernity imposed by time. His innovative approach and decorative style, combined with a technique that united simplicity and nobility, brought him worldwide acclaim and recognition as an illustrious representative of the aesthetics of Art Deco.

6. "Jouve nous dit tout de l'aigle. Il nous le montre dans son armure de plumes noires et grises, vêtu de ses aigles repliées comme d'un manteau royal, appuyé sur ses serres énormes hérissées de courbes couteaux de corne [...]. Jouve nous montre l'aigle en chasse, planant de toute l'étendue de ses rémiges, dans l'air glacial, dans le soleil, ou rentrant dans son aire infectée par les fragments de cadavres que se disputent les aiglon." See MAUCLAIR, 1931, pp. 33–34.

PROVENANCE

Madame J. Danthon Collection. Acquired by Calouste Gulbenkian at the sale of this collection, through André Schoeller, at Hôtel Drouot, Paris, 24 May 1933, lot no. 8 (repr.).

[31]

PAUL JOUVE

Bourron-Marlotte, 1878–Paris, 1973

BLACK PANTHER AND SERPENT (PYTHON)

France, early 1920s

Conté crayon and thick ink applied with brush
on paper glued on to cardboard.
50.8 × 100.8 cm.
Signed on the bottom left-hand side: *Jouve.*
Inv. 625

This drawing, which Calouste Gulbenkian acquired directly from Paul Jouve in 1923, dates from early in that decade, when the painter had already reached artistic maturity and was enjoying public acclaim. Hoping to renew and add to his repertoire of models, and responding to requests from others, Jouve continued with his customary travels during this period. He travelled to Algeria in 1921 and, with a grant awarded by the Indochina government, to the Far East in 1922. These journeys would undoubtedly have an impact on his artistic vision, helping him to gain an intuitive understanding of the behaviour of each animal that he depicted. ¶ Initially rather academic, Jouve's drawings gradually moved towards a realism that was sometimes unsettling, a point highlighted by the art critic Charles Saunier: "The animals drawn by Mr. Jouve breathe and live in freedom"[1]. In the early 1920s, exhibiting his total mastery of the creative process, Jouve represented animals in action through a more simplified line that demonstrated a perfect understanding of their anatomy and reactions, using a synthetic rather than an analytic style in which the overall vision of the composition took precedence over detail. As the critic Jean-José Frappa stated after the artist's exhibition at the Danthon gallery, Jouve expressed the play of muscles beneath the skin, as well as the effort involved in a particular movement, with just a few strokes of his pencil[2].The artist subsequently simplified his composition and palette and evolved towards a more stylised and decorative aesthetic language. ¶ The wild animals portrayed by Paul Jouve are not generally characterised by tension or gratuitous brutality, except where his concern is to emphasise the survival instinct. In the compositions in which a greater sense of violence reigns, the artistic choices made by Jouve demonstrate that, when animals kill, it is not through cruelty but in response to the demands of life, such as hunger, procreation and defence. ¶ This is precisely the theme of the Gulbenkian drawing, and it is one that is very common in the artist's work. The confrontation between snakes and animals as powerful as lions, tigers or black panthers fascinated him and he depicted it with great passion,

1. "Les animaux déssinés par M. Jouve respirent et vivent libres", in the magazine *Art et Décoration*, April 1906, quoted *in* MARCILHAC, 2005, p. 60.

2. *Monde Illustré*, 3 June 1921, quoted in *Ibidem*, pp. 108–9.

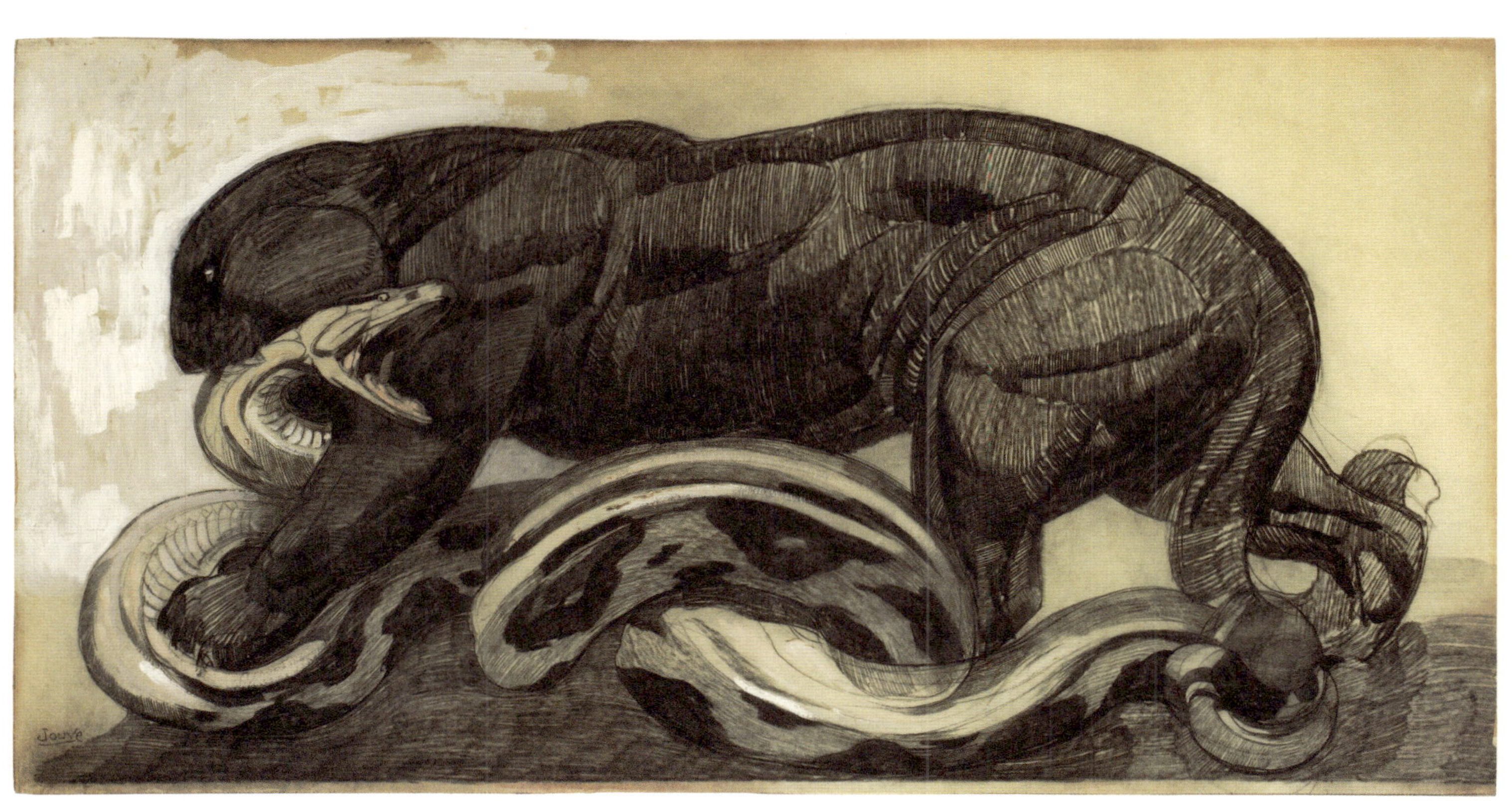

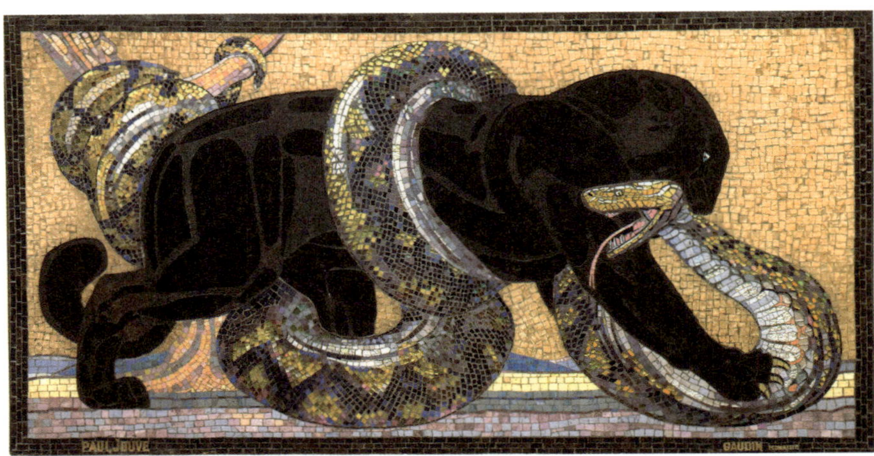

– fig. 31.1 –
Panthère noire combattant un serpent python. Panel executed by Gaudin, after a drawing by Paul Jouve (1878–1973). Coloured mosaics and gold, 88 × 175 cm. Académie des beaux-arts collection, Paris, deposit at Musée des années 30, Boulogne-Billancourt. Reproduction kindly authorized by the Académie des beaux-arts.

always offering the viewer an insight into the potential outcome of the struggle. ¶ This drawing, which is of huge dimensions, depicts a relentless fight to the death between a black panther and a python. The two animals are shown in close-up in all their physical power. Caught mid-action, they present a stark contrast to a background that is neutral apart from a few white brush strokes on the top left-hand side. ¶ Jouve used thick, dense strokes of crayon to create contrasting areas of light and shade which bring out the anatomical modelling of the bodies and the pulsating muscles, particularly those of the panther, who is already shown in a pose suggestive of victory. The lines that describe the snake are looser and supplemented by touches of coloured ink to represent the snake's multi-coloured skin. Although there is still power in the coils that the snake intends to wrap around its opponent, it is clearly at a disadvantage against the fangs which the panther sinks into its body. Neither the power of its unyielding bite nor the brute force of the coils designed to squeeze the bones and immobilise the muscles of its prey have been to any effect. On this occasion, nature has favoured the black panther, sparing it from death. The same situation can be seen in the oil painting *Panthère noire combattant un python*, from around 1930, which belonged to the Dray Collection[3]. However, in the mosaic panel created by Gaudin after one of Jouve's compositions (*Panthère noire combattant un serpent python*[4] (fig. 31.1), from 1932), the outcome is uncertain: although the snake is between the panther's jaws, it is already coiled dangerously around the panther's back. ¶ Paul Jouve was very familiar with the dramas of survival in the jungle that are so well expressed in this drawing. Once again, in this episode, the power of the laws of nature is evoked. These laws are inescapable, since they are the only path to upholding universal order, in which life and death sustain each other in order to maintain each species in the correct proportion. Paul Jouve's talent was to understand this principle and to be able to convey it in his work.

3. MARCILHAC, 2005, pp. 167–69 (repr.).

4. *Ibidem*, pp. 222–23 (repr.).

PROVENANCE

Acquired by Calouste Gulbenkian directly from the artist, through Graat et Madoulé, Paris, 31 December 1923.

•

EXHIBITIONS

LISBON, 2006b, no. 81, p. 237 (repr.).

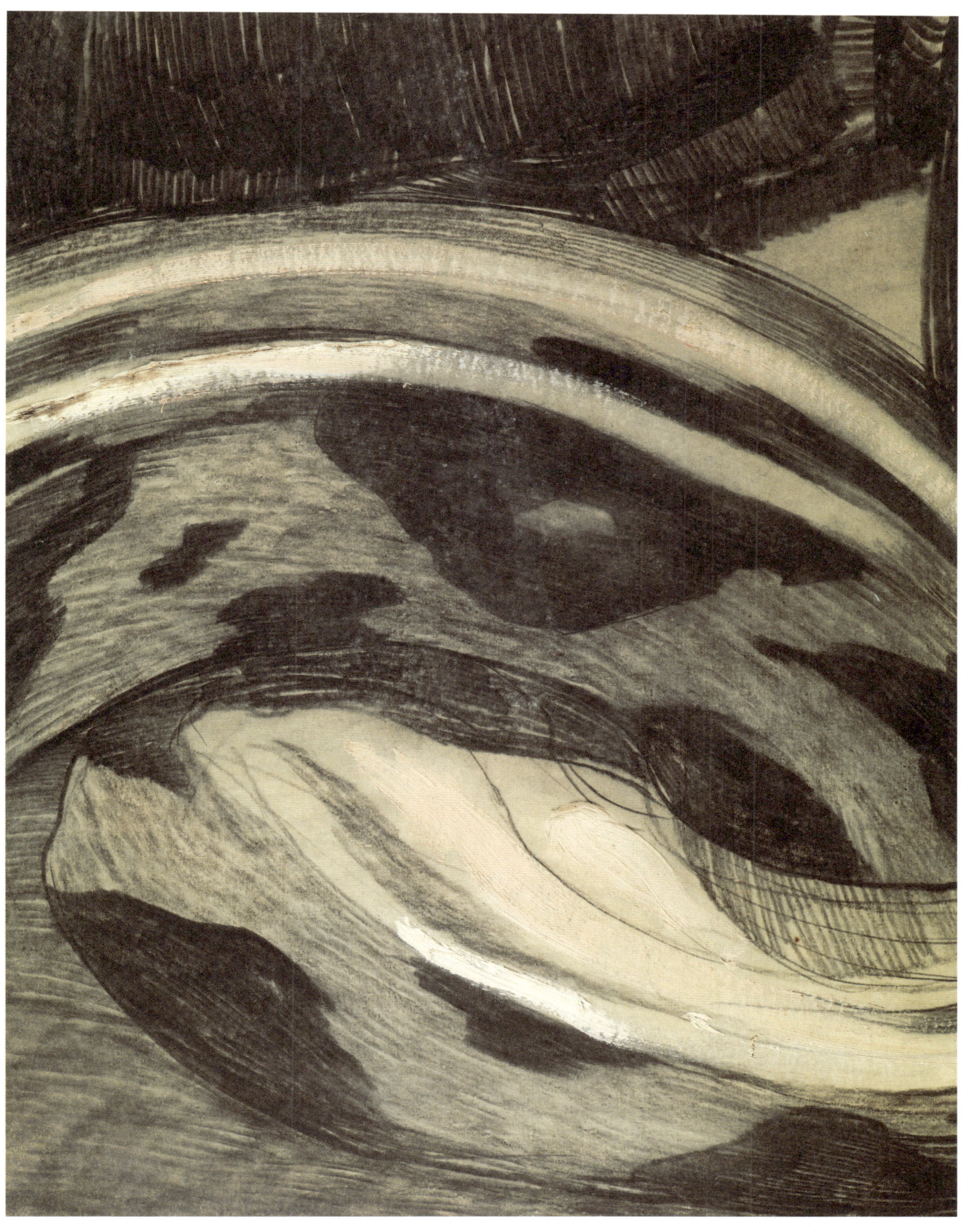

[32–35]

LÉONARD TSUGOUHARU FOUJITA
Tokyo, 1886 – Zurich, 1968

LANDSCAPE — TOKYO
France, ca. 1927

Pen and ink on paper.
26 × 37 cm.
Signed: *Foujita*.
Inscription: "Tokio" (in western and Japanese characters).
Inv. 2465

LANDSCAPE — KYOTO
France, ca. 1927

Pen and ink on paper.
25.7 × 37.2 cm.
Signed: *Foujita*.
Inscription: "Kioto" (in western and Japanese characters).
Inv. 2463

LANDSCAPE — TOKAIDO
France, ca. 1927

Pen and ink on paper.
25.5 × 37 cm.
Signed: *Foujita*.
Inscription: "Tokaido" (in western and Japanese characters).
Inv. 2464

LANDSCAPE — ENOSHIMA
France, ca. 1927

Pen and ink on paper.
26 × 37.3 cm.
Signed: *Foujita*.
Inscription: "Enoshima" (in western and Japanese characters).
Inv. 2462

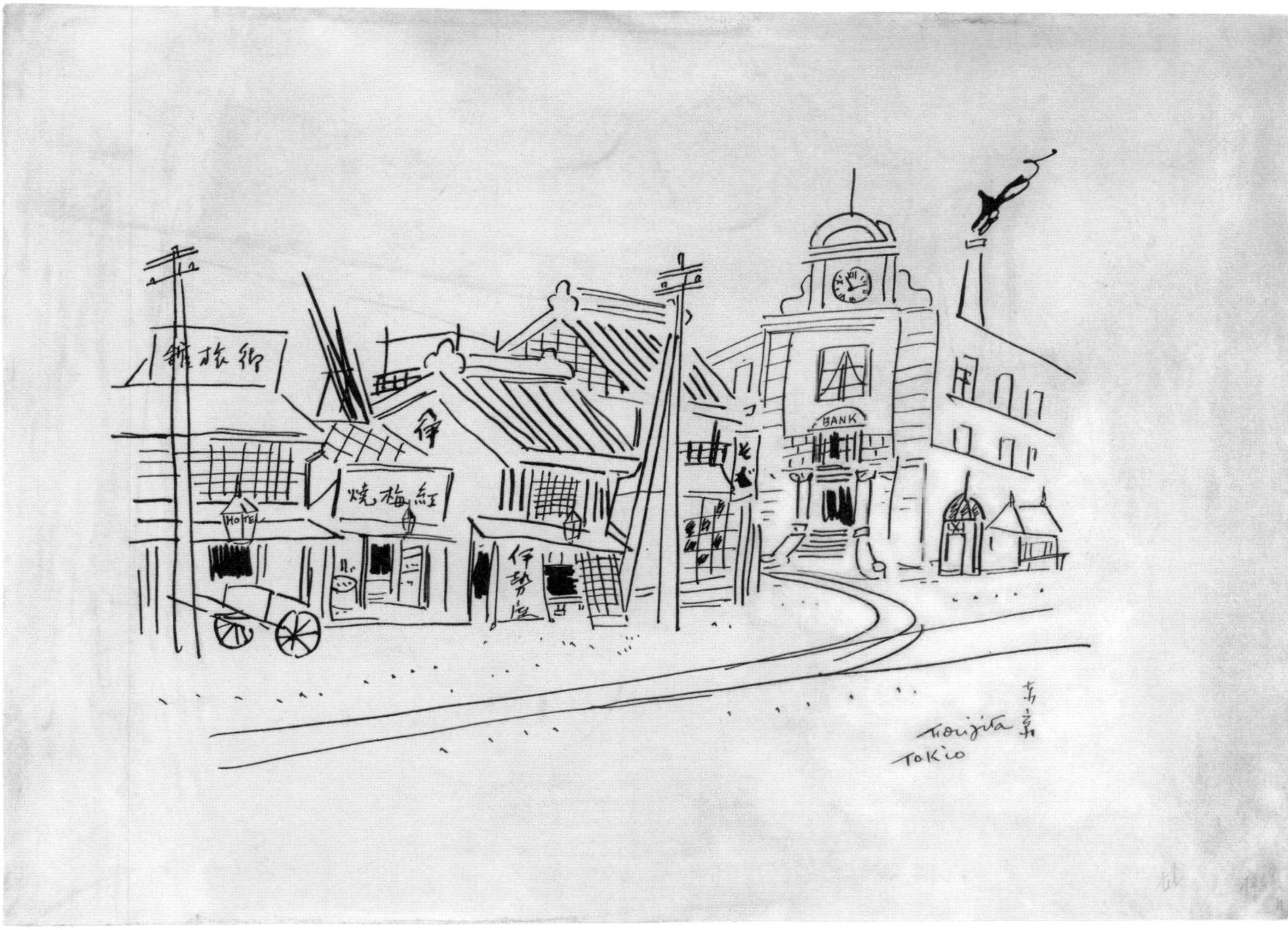

Foujita 東京
Tokio

Foujita 京都
Kioto

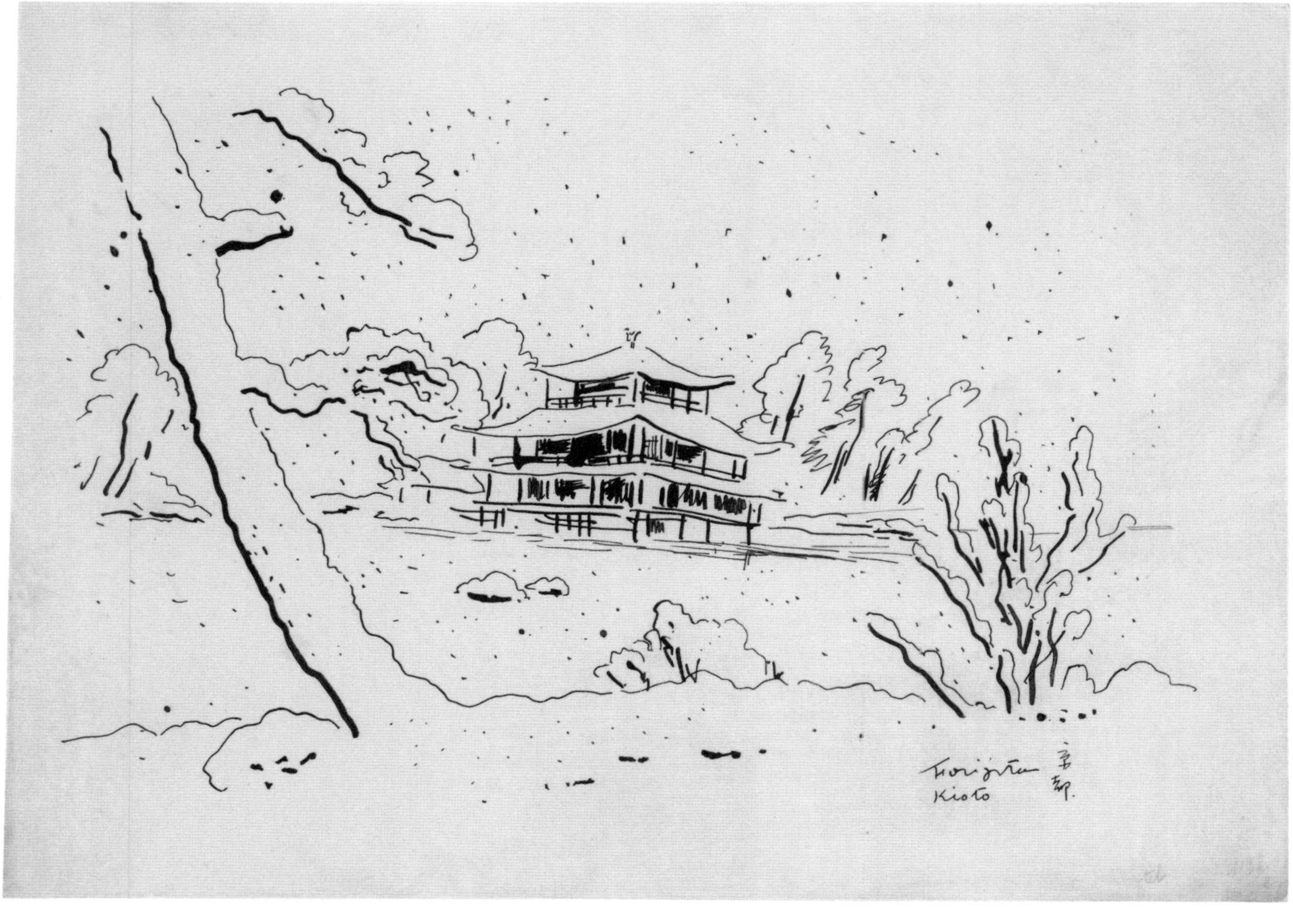

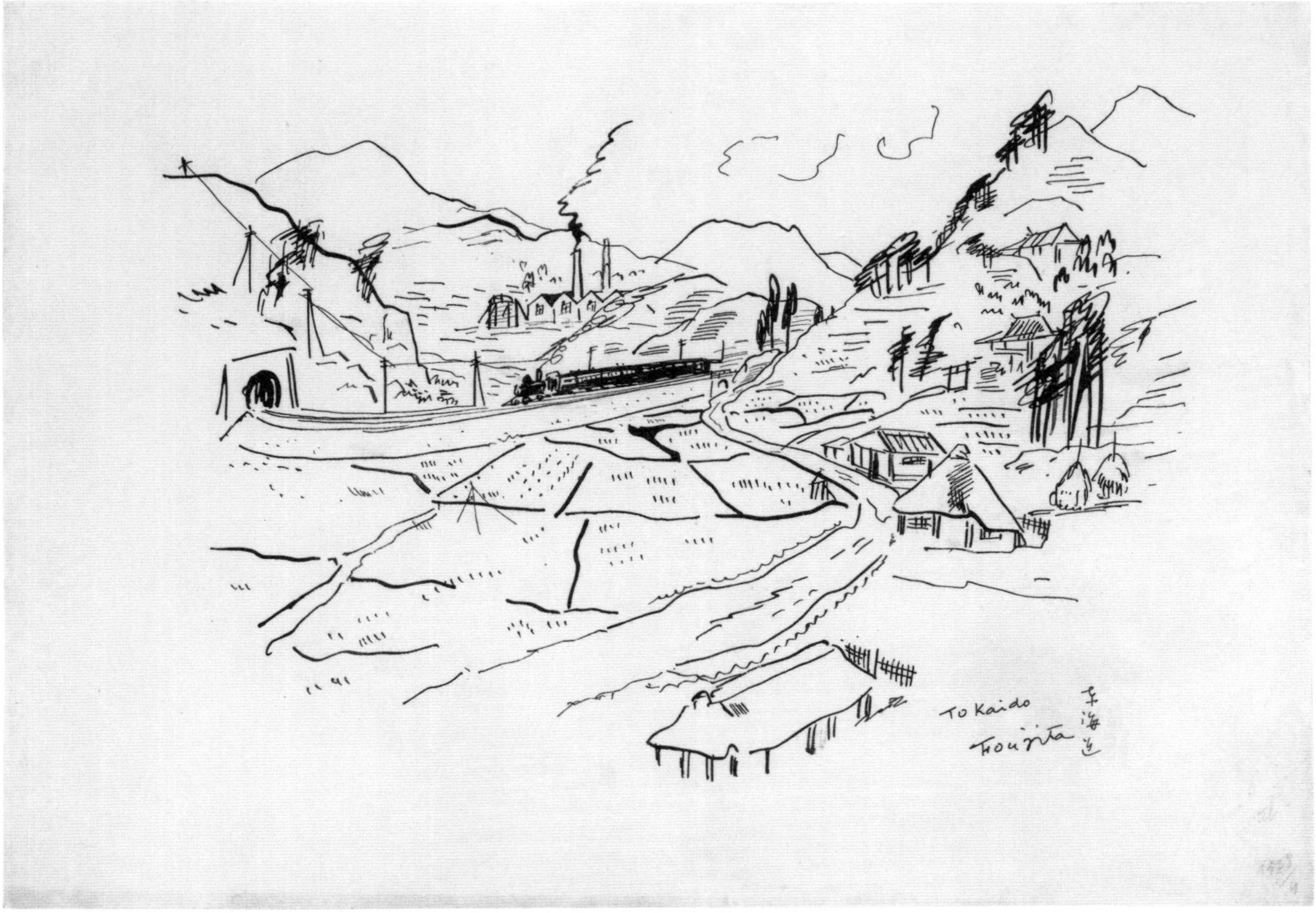

Tokaido 東海道
Foujita

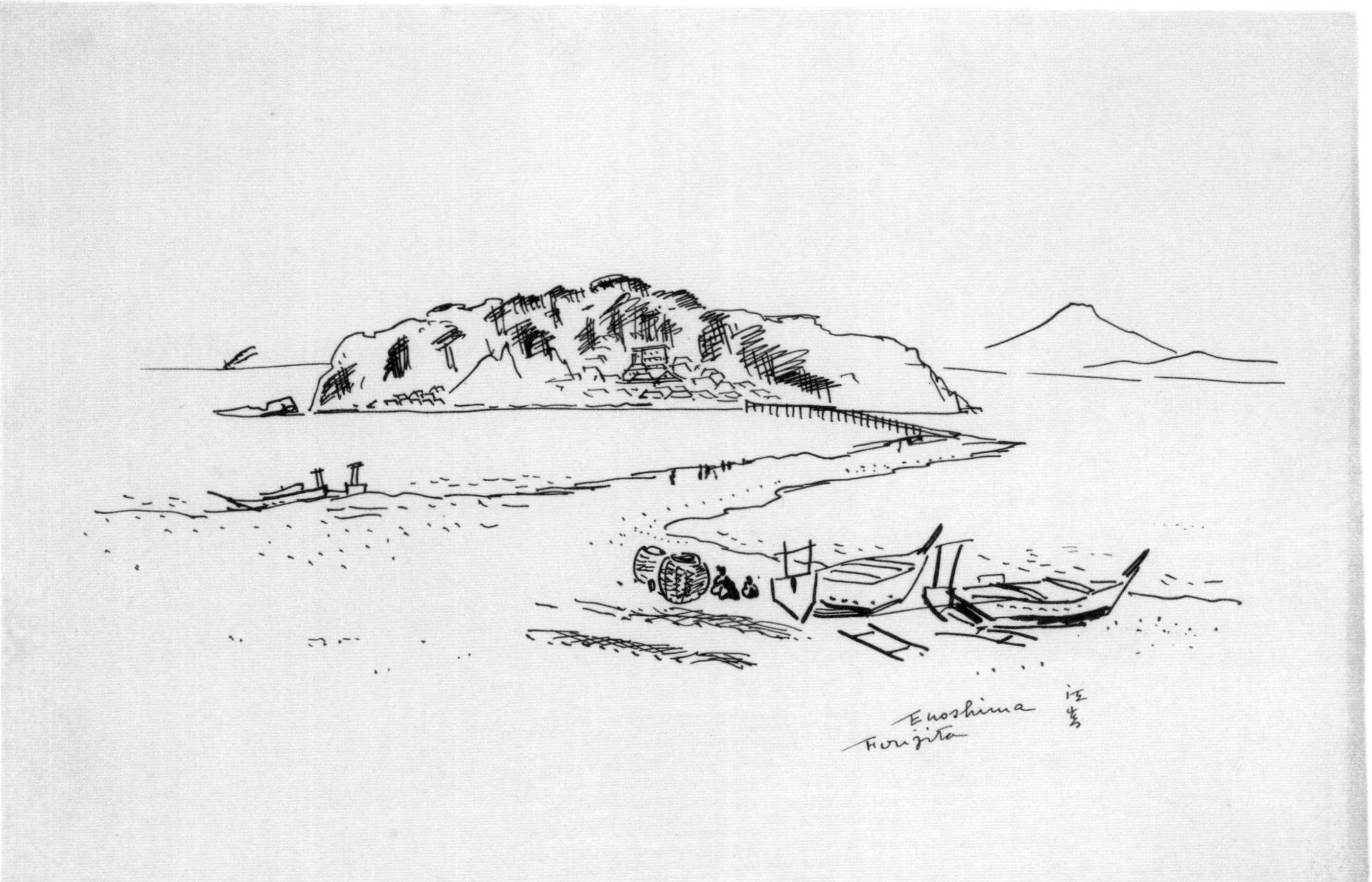

Enoshima 江島
Foujita

These four drawings[1] are among the many compositions produced by Tsugouharu Foujita to illustrate *Les huits renommées*[2], a book by Kikou Yamata (1897–1975) that was published in 1927. They were acquired by Calouste Gulbenkian at the sale of the Christian Lazard Collection in Paris in 1939, together with the first copy of the edition referred to, and the remaining original drawings produced by Foujita for the book, assembled in a second volume of the same edition (fig. 32.1). ¶ Though all the drawings for *Les huits renommées* were produced using the same style and technique, what distinguishes these four works from the others is their larger size, which meant that they could be reproduced as double-page illustrations. ¶ Kikou Yamata, who was of French and Japanese descent, spent the formative years of her artistic development in Japan, and also a period during the Second World War), but it was in France, where she returned in 1923 after the death of her father, that she established a literary career which benefitted from her encounters with the great literary names of the period. The history of Japan and the figure of the Japanese woman are dominant concerns in the writer's work, as are themes which express the duality of her own existence, characterised by her adoption of two very different cultures – western and eastern. ¶ The pages of *Les huits renommées* are filled with descriptive memories of everyday life and the picturesque features of Japan: the cities and their neighbourhoods, avenues, canals, parks and temples; historic monuments; natural spaces with local flora and fauna; traditional tastes and smells; tea houses; the characteristic sounds of the street; geishas and their kimonos. The reader encounters a language that is sometimes poetic, with phrases that are almost telegraphic in their brevity, sometimes revealing the euphoria of rediscovery, at other times evincing a certain nostalgia for the traditional culture that is disappearing. ¶ The success of this book was in part due to Foujita's illustrations, which as always revealed his oriental roots. He produced a total of fifty-one illustrations of the book's themes, all of which are characterised by the coherence and harmony typical of Japanese culture. ¶ Foujita's talent as an engraver and draughtsman earned him a solid reputation with the publishers of high-quality limited edition books. Throughout his career, between 1919 and 1964, the artist illustrated more than forty literary works[3]. ¶ The drawings shown here are landscapes which refer to four different Japanese locations, identified next to the artist's signature. In all of them, Foujita used a pen and black ink to bring a great linear simplicity to his interpretation of each scene, achieved through a clear and fluid line characterised by surprising precision in his treatment of details. ¶ The first drawing depicts a view of the city of Tokyo, where tradition and modernity exist side by side. It should be remembered that much of the city had been destroyed by an earthquake in 1923 which was followed by reconstruction. It is thus not surprising that in this street tightly packed traditional buildings coexist with a more modern building with a wide flight of steps and a sumptuous entrance. In the foreground of the drawing there is a thoroughfare with a variety of constructions which signal the bustle of urban life: a bank, topped by a pediment with a clock, a hotel, various open shops awaiting customers. Curiously, the signs are written in a combination of western and Japanese script. ¶ The second drawing is of the city of Kyoto, the capital of the Japanese empire until 1868, when the government was transferred to Edo, subsequently renamed Tokyo. The city has numerous temples, one of which is shown in a wintry landscape, just as it begins to snow, turning everything white. It is possibly the famous temple of Kinkaku-ji, sur-

1. I am grateful to Sylvie Buisson, specialist in Foujita's work, for her opinions on these drawings (2011).

2. Kikou Yamata, *Les huits renommées*. Paris: A. Delpeuch, 1927. Unique copy, no. 1 on Japanese paper of an edition of 320, with Foujita's original drawings and a separate series of prints of the illustrations. Lisbon, Calouste Gulbenkian Museum, inv. LM441A/B.

3. BUISSON, BUISSON, 1987, pp. 563–64.

rounded by the calm waters of the lake Kyoko-chi. Also known as the "Golden Pavilion," it is, apart from the ground floor, covered in gold leaf. The roof is crowned by a Chinese phoenix, which is also gilded. ¶ In the third drawing, it was Foujita's turn to depict the famous Tokaido Road, the main land route through feudal Japan, which linked Edo (Tokyo) and Kyoto. The road was famous for its fifty-three "stations', which functioned as checkpoints and also offered services and provisions to travellers. These stations were spread out over the entire length of the route and were immortalised in prints by artists such as Ando Hiroshige (1797–1858)[4]. In the Gulbenkian drawing, there is a magnificent landscape of mountains in the distance and cultivated fields in the foreground, punctuated by small dwellings. A train can be seen heading towards the tunnel which cuts through the base of the mountain range; following the construction of the first railway line alongside the ancient route (1889), the time needed to make this trip was dramatically shortened. ¶ Finally, in the fourth of the Gulbenkian drawings, Foujita depicts the small island of Enoshima, at the mouth of the Katase River. Due to the existence of a temple dedicated to Benten, an important Japanese goddess and the guardian of good fortune, wealth, knowledge and music, this island became very popular. In the foreground of this study, Foujita depicts fishing boats beached on the sandy shores of the opposite bank of the river. Next he sketches the approximately 600-metre-long bridge which links this side of the coast with the island

4. The Calouste Gulbenkian Collection holds a set of Japanese prints dated ca. 1845, signed by three great masters: Hiroshige (1797–1858), Kuniyoshi (1797–1861) and Kunisada (1786–1865), showing the "53 Stations of the Tokaido", Lisbon, Calouste Gulbenkian Museum, inv. 2437.

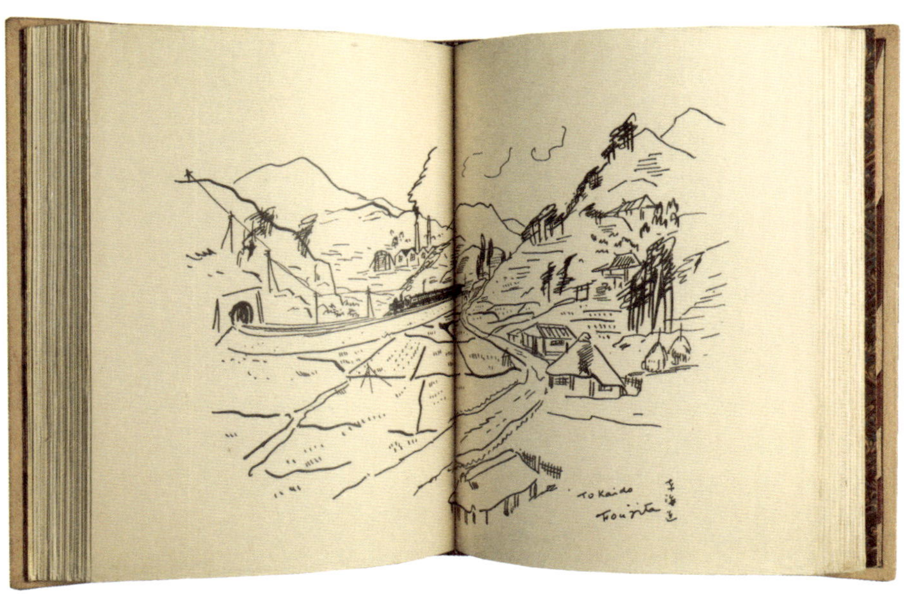

– fig. 32.1 –
Illustration from an original drawing (inv. 2464) by Tsugouharu Foujita for *Les huits renommées* by Kikou Yamata.
Lisbon, Calouste Gulbenkian Museum, inv. LM441A.

Photo: Inês Oliveira e Silva

where, with a very subtle broken line, the rows of houses and various buildings of the shrine are depicted. In the distance, the imposing form of Mount Fuji is delicately suggested. ¶ In his illustrations for Kikou Yamata's book, Foujita's style and artistic technique stay within the conventions of Japanese cultural tradition. However, his vast artistic legacy of paintings, drawings and prints generally reveal a harnessing of the traditions of Japanese art, above all in terms of technique, to the themes of western modernism. ¶ Of all the artists who settled in Paris between the two world wars, becoming part of the École de Paris group[5], Foujita – born in Japan into an aristocratic family – was without doubt one of the most famous. Having received a solid art education in Japan, Foujita felt that his future could only lie in the west. He said himself at the time: "People predicted I would be the painter number one in Japan, but I wished to be the painter number one in Paris. I needed to go to the sources"[6]. ¶ Arriving in France at the age of 27, he set himself up in Montparnasse, where he met the most important artists of the time. When he stated "I must have fallen amidst the best"[7], he was undoubtedly referring to Picasso, Matisse, Rousseau, Soutine, Léger and above all Modigliani, among others, who welcomed him into their circle and offered true friendship. ¶ The doors of the Parisian artistic and literary worlds soon opened up to Foujita and his favourite themes, which were always figurative: portraits, self-portraits, the female nude, still lifes, landscapes, children, series of cats and also religious themes, with French-inspired settings and European figures, but a schematic, Japanese approach to line. ¶ Intelligent, agreeable, good-natured, elegant, exotic and a hard worker, Foujita led a life of unquestioned success, achieving public and official recognition. He travelled constantly around the world, often going back and forth between Japan and France. He married several times and was the urbane gentleman of the wild 1920s and of the non-stop bohemian party that was Montparnasse. ¶ Japanese blood flowed through his veins, but his heart belonged to France. And so, justifying a brief return to that country after spending several years in Japan, he recognised that "I need Paris; hence my return to France"[8]. Having lived in Japan during the Second World War, Foujita returned to France in 1950 and left no room for doubt as to his intentions: "I return to stay. I wish to die in France and to be buried in the Montparnasse graveyard, next to Modigliani"[9]. Five years later, he took French nationality and, in 1959, was baptised at Reims Cathedral, adopting the name *Léonard* in tribute to the great Renaissance painter. He also took the name *François* in memory of Saint Francis of Assisi and *René* in recognition of his godfather, René Lalou, head of the *Mumm* champagne house in Reims.

5. Designation given to the group of foreign artists who arrived in Paris in the 1920s, hoping to find in the French capital an environment conducive to artistic development. Above all, they settled in Montparnasse. Among them were Marc Chagall, Pablo Picasso, Pascin, Amadeo Modigliani and, of course, Tsugouharu Foujita.

6. "On me prédisait que je serai le premier peintre du Japon, mais c'était le premier peintre de Paris que je rêvais d'être ; il me fallait aller aux sources." BUISSON, BUISSON, 1987, p. 27.

7. "Je suis bien tombé au milieu des meilleurs." *Ibidem*, p. 35.

8. "Il me faut Paris, voilà pourquoi j'ai repris le chemin de la France." *Ibidem*, p. 184.

9. "Je reviens pour rester. Je veux mourir en France et être enterré au cimetière Montparnasse auprès de Modigliani." *Ibidem*, p. 206.

PROVENANCE

C. L. (Christian Lazard) Collection. Acquired by Calouste Gulbenkian together with Kikou Yamata's work *Les huit renommées*, at the sale of the above mentioned collection, through Giraud-Badin, Paris, 7 June 1939, lot no. 176.

GLOSSARY

BINDER

Transparent medium made from animal or plant matter that serves to bind together the coloured powders that make up pigments.

BISTRE

Paint made from the soot produced by burnt wood dissolved and boiled in water or other liquids. The colour, which ranges from a light yellowish-brown, close to saffron, to a deep blackish-brown, varies in accordance with the wood used and the carbonization time. It has a warm and transparent tone.

BLACK CHALK

Also known as Italian stone, this material is a slate clay containing carbon particles which give it a tone that can range from grey to matt black. It produces a vigorous and a less regular line. Black chalk was widely used in the fifteenth century and remained a popular technique for drawing in the following century. Its use declined in the eighteenth century due to the difficulty of obtaining high-quality material and the emergence of the Conté pencil.

BROWN INKS

Experts acknowledge the difficulty of correctly identifying the origin of the components of the various inks used in old drawings when the original colour has changed naturally due to ageing or oxidation (unless laboratory tests are carried out). The different materials that have this colour (particularly bistre or sepia) are therefore known as 'brown inks'. Where the Gulbenkian Collection's drawings are concerned, the difficulty is augmented by the fact that a number of its works were immersed in muddy water during the floods of 1967 and were subsequently treated with products in order to restore them.

BRUSH

Instrument consisting of bristles, hairs, threads or other natural or synthetic filaments attached to the end of a handle that is normally made of wood. Brushes come in different thicknesses and formats.

CHALK

Material originating from a type of calcareous rock (calcite or calcium carbonate). When reduced to a powder and mixed with water and a binder, small sticks can be formed that are white, red, or a different colour depending on the pigments used. White-chalk highlighting emerged around the fifteenth century when the use of paper became more common. When applied, chalk can be confused with pastel. However, it is more stable and produces a harder line.

CHARCOAL

The first material to be used for drawing, charcoal is produced from small branches (willow, walnut, rosemary and grapevine, among others) tied together and carbonized in a sealed container so that they burn slowly and are not reduced to ashes. This method produces small, highly friable, cylinders that leave particles on the fibres of the paper, allowing intense black tones to be obtained by crushing and layering the material. The hardness and density of the grey-black line varies according to the carbonization time. Fixatives are often used in charcoal drawing to ensure that the work retains its definition.

CRAYON (CONTÉ PENCIL)

The forerunner of the modern pencil, the Conté pencil consisted of lead made from a mixture of graphite powder and clay that was hardened by fire and placed inside a wooden covering. It was invented in the late eighteenth century (1795) by the Frenchman Nicolas-Jacques Conté (1755–1805), after whom the material is named. The line that it produces varies in intensity and tone depending on the firing time and the percentages of graphite and clay used in the composition.

FIXATIVE

Prepared from resins, gum or natural glues diluted in water or other substances such as alcohol, fixatives are normally applied as a spray to lend adhesive properties to the materials used on the surface of the paper, thereby preventing their constituent particles from breaking apart.

GOUACHE

Mixture composed of ground pigments, Arabic gum and opaque white pigments that lend it opacity and covering power, a characteristic that distinguishes it from watercolour and allows dark colours to be overlaid by light ones.

GRAPHITE

Also known as 'black lead' or plumbago, graphite, a crystallised form of carbon, is a solid dark-grey mineral with metal reflections. Greasy to the touch, it was discovered around 1560 in the mines of Cumberland in the north of England. It was not used frequently until the mid-seventeenth century, firstly for tracing and only later for finished drawings.

GUM

Substance obtained from some trees, shrubs or seaweeds that are insoluble in alcohol and soluble in water. Gums are used as adhesives and as binding agents for paints and pigments.

HIGHLIGHTS

A means of accentuating certain areas of a drawing by introducing lighter patches or texturing, imbuing the work with new values by using different materials such as gold, sanguine, white chalk, gouache, and watercolour, among others.

INDIAN INK

Ink probably invented in China around 2500 BC. Black in colour, it is made from carbon (soot) bound with gum Arabic, creating a mixture that was initially moulded into small ingots. This carbon pigment was later traded from India, hence the name India or Indian ink. When used in its pure state it tends to create a brilliant black line. When diluted in water it allows a broad range of grey tones to be obtained. Once it has dried it is indelible.

METALPOINT

Metal-tipped rod made from lead, silver or gold which allowed the artist to draw on a paper support, normally coated with a ground. These instruments left a groove on the support with varying degrees of tonality, depending on the material used.

PAPER

Invented in Han-dynasty China (206 BC 220 AD) around the year 105 AD. Knowledge of paper manufacturing reached Europe through Arabic civilisation and, in the fifteenth century, this craft technique had been mastered in practically every country, coinciding with the emergence of the printing press developed by Gutenberg around 1450. Early paper was made from rags by means of a complex process that is still used today to create traditional paper. Paper began to be industrially manufactured from wood pastes in the nineteenth century and became the preferred support for drawing in the fifteenth century, replacing previously used materials such as parchment or vellum.

PARCHMENT

The skin of an animal such as a goat, or sheep that is treated with lime water and then rubbed smooth with pumice stones. Finally, it is dried out and stretched to serve as a support for writing and drawing. It takes its name from the Greek city of Pergamon in Asia Minor, where it is believed to have become widespread around the third century AD, replacing papyrus as a support for writing.

PASTEL

Mixture of pigments that are powdered and bound together with gum or glue. Small cylinders are then moulded which are used after they have dried, usually on painted and flocked paper. Being a highly unstable and extremely fragile material, it must be used with a fixative. Use of pastel reached a high point in the eighteenth century.

PEN

Originally associated with writing, evidence of this instrument's use in drawing dates back to the Middle Ages. Three types of pen of differing origins can be identified: quills, pens made from plants, and metal pens. Quills, which are known to have been used since the sixth century, were made from the feathers of different species of birds such as ducks, swans and crows. Crow quills were used for more delicate work. Pens made from plants (reed, bamboo) were less flexible and produced a broader and rougher line due to the square shape of the tip. Industrially produced metal pens entered general use in the nineteenth century.

PIGMENTS

Coloured particles made from mineral, plant or animal sources that are ground and mixed with binding agents. Modern pigments are also made from synthetic substances.

SANGUINE (RED CHALK)

A mixture of clay and hematite whose tone varies from orange-red to brownish-red. The name sanguine was coined by analogy with the colour of blood. It is the perfect colour for representations of the human body, portraits and landscapes and in the eighteenth century it became widely used as a complement to other techniques such as three-crayons drawing, in which it was employed in conjunction with black chalk and white chalk.

SEPIA

The only paint created from animal sources that is used in drawing. It is made from the liquid found in the ink sacs of squid, cuttlefish or other molluscs, which gives it a dark-brown tone. It is often confused with bistre although its tone is colder and it was not until the eighteenth century that it came to be used in art.

STUMP

A small roll of paper, cotton or chamois leather with pointed ends that is used to soften lines or drawn areas. The use of a stump allows varying tones to be obtained from lines or patches made with materials such as charcoal, chalk or pastels.

THREE-CHALKS (TROIS CRAYONS)

The name of a technique, much in vogue in the eighteenth century, which combines the use of black chalk, red chalk (sanguine), and white chalk, sometimes on coloured paper.

WASHES

Water-diluted inks normally applied with a brush. Washes are used in drawing in conjunction with other techniques such as pen. Expressing tonal variations by exploring chiaroscuro effects, they also impart values to the forms of the composition. Grey wash is obtained by diluting India ink in water, allowing a broad spectrum of grey tones to be created. The most common washes are those made with brown paint, the colours of which range from the lightest tones to the darkest.

WATERCOLOUR

A mixture of coloured pigments and gum Arabic (a binder that takes its name from an Arabic acacia plant) that is diluted in water without white being added. When white is required by the composition, it is created by 'reserving' a blank area of the paper. Watercolours are essentially characterized by the transparency of the colours and by the immediacy with which they must be executed. The proportion of pigments and water determines the transparency and intensity of the colours as well as their luminosity and tonality, which can range from the palest tones to the darkest. With watercolour, it is only possible to work from the lightest colours to the darkest. It is often used in combination with more opaque materials such as gouache.

–

Glossary made with the assistance of Helena Nunes, and upon consultation of the following works:

LEYMARIE, Jean ; Monnier ; Geneviève ; Rose, Bernice, *Histoire d'Un Art. Le Dessin*. Genève 1979.
PARRAMÓN, J.M. (Trad. d'Anne Montange), *Le Grand Livre du Dessin*. Paris, 1986.
SÉRULLAZ, Arlette, *100 Dessins du Musée du Louvre*. Paris, 2012.
TEISSIG, Karel, *Les Techniques du Dessin*. Paris, 1986.

SELECTED BIBLIOGRAPHY

This bibliography presents a selected series of titles which include books, articles, auction, collection and exhibition catalogues.

BOOKS, ARTICLES, AUCTION AND COLLECTION CATALOGUES

A COLLECTION OF DRAWINGS, 1917
A Collection of Drawings by Deceased Masters. London: Burlington Fine Arts Club, 1917.

ADELSON ET AL., 1997
Warren Adelson, *et al.* – *Sargent Abroad: Figures and Landscapes*. New York, London, Paris: Abbeville Press Publishers, 1997.

ALTDEUTSCHE MALEREI, 1963
Altdeutsche Malerei. Alte Pinakothek München. Katalog II. München: Verlag F. Bruckmann, 1963.

ANANOFF, 1961, 1963, 1968, 1970
Alexandre Ananoff – *L'Œuvre dessiné de Jean-Honoré Fragonard (1732–1806): catalogue raisonné*. 4 vols. Paris: 1961, 1963, 1968, 1970, vol. IV.

ANANOFF, 1966
Alexandre Ananoff – *L'œuvre dessiné de François Boucher (1703–1770): Catalogue raisonné*. Paris: F. de Nobele, 1966.

ANANOFF, WILDENSTEIN, 1976
Alexandre Ananoff, Daniel Wildenstein – *François Boucher*, 2 vols. Lausanne, Paris: La Bibliothèques des Arts, 1976.

ARMSTRONG, 1902
Sir Walter Armstrong – *Turner*. London, Manchester e Liverpool: Thos. Agnew & Sons; New York: Charles Scribner's Sons, 1902.

BACOU, 1975
Roseline Bacou – *Millet dessins*. Fribourg (Suisse): Office du Livre, 1975.

BANDERA, FIORIO, 2000
S. Bandera, M. T. Fiorio – *Bernardino Luini e la pittura del rinascimento a Milano. Gli affreschi di san Maurizio al Monastero Maggiore*. Milano: Skira, 2000.

BARNES, DE POORTER, MILLAR, VEY, 2004
Susan J. Barnes, Nora De Poorter, Oliver Millar, Horst Vey – *Van Dyck. A Complete Catalogue of the Paintings*. New Haven and London: Published for The Paul Mellon Centre for Studies in British Art by Yale University Press, 2004.

BASSY, 1986
Alain-Marie Bassy – *Les Fables de la Fontaine. Quatre Siècles d'Illustration*. Paris: Éditions Promodis, 1986.

BERALDI, PORTALIS, 1880–1882
H. Béraldi, R. Portalis – *Les Graveurs du XVIIIe Siècle*. Paris: Damascène Morgand et Charles Fatout, 1880–1882, 3 vols.

BERENSON, 1967
Bernard Berenson – *The Italian Painters of the Renaissance*. London: The Phaidon Press, 1967.

BIASS-FABIANI, FABRE, 1994
Sophie Biass-Fabiani, Gérard Fabre – *Félix Ziem, Journal (1854–1898)*. Arles: Actes Sud, 1994.

BINAGHI OLIVARI, 2007
Maria Teresa Binaghi Olivari – *Bernardino Luini*. Milano: 5 Continents, 2007.

BORTOLATTO, 1974
Luigina Rossi Bortolatto – *L'Opera Completa di Francesco Guardi*. Milano: Rizzoli, 1974.

BRETON, 1896
Jules Breton – *Un peintre paysan: souvenirs & impressions*. Paris: Alphonse Lemerre, 1896.

BRETTELL, BRETTELL, 1983
Richard R. Brettell, Caroline B. Brettell – *Les peintres et le paysan au XIXe siècle*. Geneva: Skira, 1983.

BRION, 1976
Marcel Brion – *Guardi*. Paris: Henri Scrépel, 1976.

BROOS, 1992
Ben Broos – "Willem van Mieris: 'Tarquinius and Lucretia', a drawing and a painting," *The Hoogsteder Mercury*. The Hague: Galerie Hoogsteder, 1992, no. 13–14, 1992.

BROWN, 1982
Christopher Brown – *Van Dyck*. Oxford: Phaidon Press Limited, 1982.

BUISSON, BUISSON, 1987
Sylvie Buisson; Dominique Buisson – *La vie et l'œuvre de Léonard-Tsuguharu Foujita*. Paris: ACR Édition Internationale, 1987.

BURDIN-HELLEBRANTH, 1998
Anne Burdin-Hellebranth – *Félix Ziem, 1821–1911*. Bruxelles, 1998, 2 vols.

BUROLLET, 1980
Thérèse Burollet – *Musée Cognacq-Jay: 1, peintures et dessins*. Paris: Ville de Paris, 1980.

CATALOGUE DES DESSINS, 1884
Catalogue des dessins de l'École Moderne. Paris: École des Beaux-Arts, 1884.

CATALOGUE RAISONNÉ DES DIFFÉRENS OBJETS, 1775
Catalogue raisonné des différens objets de curiosités dans les sciences et arts qui composaient le cabinet de feu Mr Mariette [...] *par F. Basan, Graveur*. Paris: chez l'auteur, 1775.

COLMACK, 1970
Malcolm Colmack – *The Drawings of Watteau*. London, New York, Sydney, Toronto: Hamlyn, 1970.

COMPÈRE, LUCOT, GRÉVERAND, 1994
Gaston Compère; Yves-Marie Lucot; Gérard Gréverand – *Au pays de La Fontaine. Un homme, une œuvre, un lieu*. S.l.: Casterman, 1994.

DACIER, VUAFLART, 1929
Émile Dacier, Albert Vuaflart (Jacques Hérold, ed. lit.), Société pour l'étude de la gravure française (Ed. scientifique) – *Jean de Julienne et les graveurs de Watteau au XVIIIe siècle. I. Notices et documents biographiques* (par Jacques Hérold & Albert Vuaflart), 1929; II, *Historique*, 1922; III, *Catalogue*, 1922; IV, *Planches*, 1921. Paris: Pour les membres de la Société [etc.], 1921–1929.

DELLA CHIESA, 1956
Angela Ottino Della Chiesa – *Bernardino Luini*. Novara: Istituto Geografico de Agostini, 1956.

DODGSON, 1918
Campbell Dodgson – "Two new drawings by Dürer in the British Museum," *The Burlington Magazine for Connoisseurs*, XXVIII, no. CLI, 1918 (p. 7–14), p. 8, note 3.

DODGSON, 1920
Campbell Dodgson – "Study of a dead duck," *The Vasari Society for the Reproduction of Drawings by Old Masters*, First series, Part X (1914–1915), no. 19. Oxford: The University Press, 1920.

EISENMANN, [1890]
O. Eisenmann – *Ausgewählte Handzeichnungen älterer Meister aus der Sammlung Edward Habich zu Cassel*. 3 Aufl. Lübeck: Berhard Nohring, [1890].

EISLER, 1991
Colin Eisler – *Dürer's Animals*. Washington and London: Smithsonian Institution Press, 1991.

FERRARI, 2006
Simone Ferrari – *Jacopo de'Barbari. Un protagonista del Rinascimento tra Venezia e Dürer*. Milano: Bruno Mondadori, 2006.

FLECHSIG, 1936
Eduard Flechsig – *Albrecht Dürer – Sein Leben und seine künstlerische Entwicklung*, I. Bd. Berlin 1928, II Bd. Berlin, 1936.

FOSTER, 1994
Carter E. Foster – *Charles-Nicolas Cochin The Younger*. The Philadelphia Portfolio. Bulletin Philadelphia Museum of Art, Summer 1994, vol. 90, 381.

GAUTHIEZ, 1928
Pierre Gauthiez – *Luini, biographie critique, illustrée de vingt-quatre reproductions hors texte*. Paris: Henri Laurens, cop. 1928.

GILTAY, 1980
J. Giltay – "De tekeningen van Jacob van Ruisdael", *O.H.*, XCIV, nos 2–3,1980.

GONCOURT, 1875
Edmond de Goncourt – *Catalogue raisonné de l'œuvre peint, dessiné et gravé d'Antoine Watteau*. Paris: Rapilly, 1875.

GONCOURT, GONCOURT, 1880
Edmond de Goncourt, Jules de Goncourt – *L'Art du Dix-huitième siècle*. Paris: A. Quantin, 1880, premier volume.

GONCOURT, GONCOURT, 1882
Edmond de Goncourt, Jules de Goncourt – *L'Art du Dix-huitième siècle*. Second volume. Paris: A. Quantin, (1865), 1882.

GORDON, 2003
Alden Gordon – *The Houses and Collections of the Marquis de Marigny. Documents for the History of Collecting, French Inventories I*. Los Angeles: The Getty Research Institute, 2003.

GRÉVERAND, 2002
Gérard Gréverand – *La Fontaine et les Artistes*. Tournai: La Renaissance du Livre, 2002.

HARDIE, 1969, 1971
Martin Hardie – *Watercolour Painting in Britain*. London: B. T. Batsford, 1969, 1971, vol. 3.

HENRIOT, 1928
G. Henriot – *Collection David Weil*, 3 vols., Paris, 1928.

HERBERT, 1973
Robert L. Herbert – "Les Faux Millet, *Revue de l'Art*", 21, 1973, p. 56–65.

HOLLSTEIN, 1949
F. W. H. Hollstein – *Dutch and Flemish Etchings, Engravings and Woodcuts, ca. 1450–1700*. Amsterdam: Menno Hertzberger, 1949.

JEAN-RICHARD, 1978
Pierrette Jean-Richard – *Musée du Louvre, Cabinet des Dessins…École française*. Vol. I, *L'Oeuvre gravé de François Boucher dans la Collection Edmond de Rothschild*. Paris: Éditions des musées nationaux, 1978.

JOMBERT, 1770
Charles-Antoine Jombert – *Catalogue de l'œuvre de Ch. Nic. Cochin fils*. Paris: Prault, 1770.

JOSI, 1821
C. Josi – *Collection d'imitations de dessins d'après les principaux maîtres hollandais et flamands, commencée par C. Ploos van Amstel, continuée et portée au nombre de cent morceaux…*, 2 vols., London, 1821.

KELLY, SCHWABE, (1931), 1972
Francis M. Kelly, Randolph Schwabe – *A Short History of Costume and Armour, 1066–1800* (1931). Newton Abbot, David & Charles Reprints, 1972.

KILLERMANN, 1953
Sebastian Killermann – *A. Dürers Werk: Eine natur-und kulturgeschichtliche Untersuchrung*. Regensburg, 1953.

LAWSON, 1999
James Lawson – *Van Dyck, Paintings and Drawings*. Munich, London, New York: Prestel Verlag, 1999.

LEPOITTEVIN, 1971
Lucien Lepoittevin – *Jean-François Millet*. Vol. I: *Portraitiste*; Vol. II : *L'ambiguité de l'image*.Paris: Léonce Laget, 1971.

LIEB, STANGE, 1960
Norbert Lieb, Alfred Stange – *Hans Holbein der Ältere*. München, Berlin: Deutscher Kunstverlag, 1960.

LIPPMANN, 1929
Friedrich Lippmann – *Zeichnungen von Albrecht Dürer in Nachbildung*, begründet von F. Lippmann, 7. Bd., hrsg. von Friedrich Winkler, Berlin, 1929.

LONGSTREET, 1966
Stephen Longstreet – *The Drawings of Watteau*. Alhambra: Borden Publishing Company, 1966.

LUGT, 1921–1956
Frits Lugt – *Les marques des collections de dessins etd'estampes*. Amsterdam, La Haye:Vereenigde druckkerijen: Martinus Nijhoff, 1921–1956.

LUGT, FRITS
http://www.marquesdecollections.fr/aide.cfm

MARCILHAC, 2005
Félix Marcilhac – *Paul Jouve, peintre, sculpteur, animalier, 1878–1973*. Paris: Les Éditions de l'Amateur, 2005.

MAUCLAIR ET AL., 1931
Camille Mauclair – *Paul Jouve*. Paris: Henry Babou, 1931.

MAYER, (1990)
E. Mayer – *International Auction Records 1990*, 24 (1990).

MICHEL, 1987
Christian Michel – *Charles-Nicolas Cochin et le livre illustré au XVIIIe Siècle*. Genève: Librairie Droz, 1987.

MICHEL, 1993
Christian Michel – *Charles-Nicolas Cochin et l'Art des Lumières*. Rome: École Française de Rome, 1993.

MIQUEL, 1978
Pierre Miquel – *Félix Ziem, 1821–1911*. Maurs-la-Jolie: Martinelle, 1978.

MOIR, 1994
Alfred Moir – *Anthony van Dyck*. New York: Harry N. Abrams, Inc., Publishers, 1994.

MORASSI, [1973]
Antonio Morassi – *L'Opera completa di Antonio e Francesco Guardi*. Venezia: Alfieri, [1973].

MORASSI, 1958
Antonio Morassi – *Dessins vénitiens du dix-huitième siècle de la collection du duc de Talleyrand*. Milano: Edizioni Daria Guarnati, 1958.

MORASSI, 1984
Antonio Morassi – *Guardi: L'Opera Completa*. Vol. I, *I dipinti*; Vol. 2, *I dipinti* (illustrations); Vol. 3, *I disegni*. Venezia, 1984.

MOREAU-NÉLATON, 1921
Étienne Moreau-Nélaton – *Millet raconté par lui-même*. 3 vols. Paris: Henri Laurens, 1921.

MOSCHINI, 1956
J. Vittorio Moschini – *Francesco Guardi*. Milano, 1956.

MURARO, 1993
Michelangelo Muraro – *Os Guardi da Colecção C. Gulbenkian / The Guardi Paintings of the C. Gulbenkian Collection*. Lisboa: Museu Calouste Gulbenkian, 1993.

MUSPER, 1953
Helmuth Theodor Musper – *Albrecht Dürer: Der gegenwärtige Stand der Forschung*. Stuttgart: W. Kolhammer, 1953.

OGÉE, 2010
Frédéric Ogée – *J.M.W. Turner: les paysages absolus*. Paris: Éditions Hazan, 2010.

OLD MASTER PICTURES, 1989
Old Master Pictures. Amsterdam (Christie's), 28 November 1989.

ORMOND, KILMURRAY, 2009
Richard Ormond, Elaine Kilmurray – *John Singer Sargent: Venetian Figures and Landscapes, 1898–1913*. New Haven and London: Yale University Press, 2009.

OSKAR REINHART COLLECTION, 2005
Oskar Reinhart Collection 'Am Römerholz' Winterthur. Complete Catalogue. Basel: Schwabe; London: Holberton, 2005.

PALLUCHINI, 1965
Rodolfo Palluchini – *Francesco Guardi*. Lisboa: Fundação Calouste Gulbenkian, 1965.

PANOFSKY, 1948
Erwin Panofsky – *Albrecht Dürer*, 2 Bände. Princeton, New Jersey, 1943; 3. Aufl. 1948, 2 Bd.

PARKER, [1931]
Karl Theodor Parker – *The Drawings of Antoine Watteau*. London: B.T. Batsford, Ltd [1931].

PARKER, MATHEY, 1957
K. T. Parker, J. Mathey – *Antoine Watteau. Catalogue complet de son oeuvre dessiné*, 2 vols. Paris: F. de Nobele, cop. 1957.

Perdigão, 1969
José de Azeredo Perdigão – *Calouste Gulbenkian Collector*. Lisbon: Calouste Gulbenkian Foundation, 1969.

PIEL, (1983)
Friedrich Piel – *Albrecht Dürer: Aquarelle und Zeichnungen*. Köln, (1983).

PORTALIS, 1877
(Le Baron) Roger Portalis – *Les dessinateurs d'illustrations au dix-huitième siècle*. Paris: Damascène Morgand et Charles Fatout, 2 vols., 1877.

PORTALIS, 1889
(Le Baron) Roger Portalis – *Honoré Fragonard, sa vie son œuvre*. Paris: J. Rothschild, 1889.

POSNER, 1984
Donald Posner – *Antoine Watteau*, London, 1984.

PUYVELDE, 1964
Leo van Puyvelde – *Van Dyck*. Bruxelles: Éditions Meddens, 1964.

RATCLIFF, 1982
Carter Ratcliff – *John Singer Sargent*. New York: Abbeville Press, 1982.

RÉAU, 1956
Louis Réau – *Fragonard: sa vie et son œuvre*. [Bruxelles]: Elsevier, 1956.

RIDING, JONES, 2013
Christine Riding, Richard Jones – *Turner & the Sea*. London: National Maritime, 2013.

RODARI, 1994
Florian Rodari – *Fragonard. L'instant désiré*. Paris: Herscher, 1994.

ROSENBERG, 1928
Jakob Rosenberg – *Jacob van Ruisdael*. Berlin, 1928.

ROSENBERG, PRAT, 1996
Pierre Rosenberg, Louis-Antoine Prat – *Antoine Watteau, 1684–1721. Catalogue raisonné des dessins*, 3 vols. [Paris]: Gallimard; [Milano]: Electa, 1996.

ROUX, 1946
Marcel Roux, Bibliothèque nationale, Département des estampes – *Inventaire du fonds français, graveurs du XVIIIe siècle*. Paris . Tome V, Cochin fils (Charles-Nicolas) – H. Dambrun. Paris: Bibliothèque nationale, 1946.

RUSKIN, (1904)
The Works of John Ruskin, E. T. Cook,Alexandern Weddesburn (eds.). London: Georges Selon; New York: Longmans, Green, and Co., 1904.

SAMPAIO, 2009
Luísa Sampaio – *Painting in the Calouste Gulbenkian Museum*. Lisbon: Calouste Gulbenkian Foundation; Milano: Skira, 2009.

SCHILLING, 1933
Edmund Schilling – "Zur Zeichenkunst des Älteren Holbein," *Pantheon*, Band XII, 1933, p. 315–22.

Schönbrunner, Meder [1896–1908]
J. Schönbrunner, J. Meder – *Handzeichnungen alter Meister aus der Albertina und anderen Sammlungen*. Wien: Gerlach & Schenk [1896–1908].

SENSIER, 1881
Alfred sensier – *La Vie et l'œuvre de J.-F. Millet*. Paris: A. Quantin, 1881.

SHANES, 1981
Eric Shanes – *Turner's Rivers, Harbours and Coasts*. London: Book Club Associates, 1981.

SHANES, 1990
Eric Shanes – *Turner*.Paris: Hazan, 1990.

SHAW, 1951
J. Byam Shaw – *The Drawings of Francesco Guardi*. London: Faber and Faber, 1951.

SIMON, 1930
K. E. Simon – *Jacob van Ruisdael* (diss.). [Berlin, 1927; trade edition reprinted with additions and corrections]. Berlin,1930.

SIMONSON, 1904
George A. Simonson – *Francesco Guardi, 1712–1793*. London: Methuen & Co., 1904.

SLIVE, 2001
Seymour Slive – *Jacob van Ruisdael. A Complete Catalogue of His Paintings, Drawings and Etchings*. New Haven & London: Yale University Press, 2001.

STECHOW, (1966), 1968
Wolfgang Stechow – *Dutch Landscape Painting of the Seventeenth Century*. National Gallery of Art, Kres Foundation Studies in the History of European Art. Number one. New York: Phaidon Publishers Inc. (1966), 1968.

STRAUSS, 1974
Walter L. Strauss – *The Complete Drawings of Albrecht Dürer*, 6 vols. New York, 1974.

STRIEDER, 1981
Peter Strieder – *Dürer*. Mit Beiträgen von Gisela Goldberg, Joseph Harnest, Matthias Mende. Königstein im Taunus, 1981.

STURGES (1982), CA. 1987
Hollister Sturges (ed.) – "Jules Breton, creator of a noble pleasant image," *The Rural Vision: France and America in the Late Nineteenth Century*, Proceedings of a symposium held at Joslyn Art Museum, Omaha, Nebraska, November 6, 1982, in conjunction with the exhibition *Jules Breton and the French Rural tradition*. Omaha, Nebr.: Distributed by the University of Nebraska Press, ca. 1987.

SUIDA, 1929
W. Suida – *Leonardo und sein Kreis*. München: F. Bruckmann, 1929.

THIRION, 1885
Henri Thirion – *Les Adam et Clodion*. Paris: A. Quantin, 1885.

TIETZE, 1951
Hans Tietze – *Dürer als Zeichner und Aquarellist*. Wien, 1951.

TIETZE, TIETZE-CONRAT, 1937 BB.
Hans Tietze, Erica Tietze-Conrat – *Kritisches Verzeichnis der Werke Albrecht Dürers*, Bd. II, Der reife Dürer, I. Halbband, 1505–1520. Basel, Leipzig, 1937 bb.

TORRE, 1714
Carlo Torre – *Il Ritratto di Milano*. Milano: Per gl'Agnelli Scult. & Stamp, 1714.

VACHON, 1899
Marius Vachon – *Jules Breton*. Paris: A. Lahure, 1899.

VAN BREUGEL (1985) [DELFT 1987]
Emke Elen-Clifford Kocq Van Breugel – "Tekeningen van Willem van Mieris (1662–1747) in relatie tot zijn schilderijen," *Leids Kunsthistorisch Jaarboek*, 4 (1985) [Delft 1987].

VAN BREUGEL, 1992
Emke Elen-Clifford Kocq Van Breugel – "Sculpturen van Francis van Bossuit getekend door William van Mieris," *Delineavit et Sculpsit*, 8, Leiden, October 1992.

VENTURI, 1925–1929
Adolfo Venturi – *Storia dell'Arte Italiana. La Pintura del Cinquecento*. Parte II. Milano: Ulrico Hoepli, 1925–29.

VEY, 1962
Horst Vey – *Die Zeichnungen Anton van Dycks*. 2 vols. Brüssel: Verlag Arcade, 1962.

WAAGEN, 1857
G. F. Waagen – *Galleries and Cabinets of Art in Great Britain*. London: J. Murray, 1857.

WILDENSTEIN, 1960
Georges Wildenstein – *Les Peintures de Fragonard*. [London]: Phaidon, 1960.

WILDENSTEIN, 1976
Ananoff et Daniel Wildenstein – *François Boucher*, 2 vols. Lausanne, Paris, 1976.

WILLIAMSON, 1900
George Charles Williamson – *Bernardino Luini*. London: Charleston: BiblioLife, [2010]. Reimp. George Bell, London, 1900.

WILTON, 1987
Andrew Wilton – *Turner in His Time*. London: Thames and Hudson, 1987.

WINKLER, 1929
Friedrich Winkler – "Dürerstudien, I. Dürers Zeichnungen von seiner ersten italienischen Reise (1494/95)," *Jahrbuch der Preussischen Kunstsammlungen*, 50, 1929, (p. 123–166), p. 137.

WINKLER, 1932
Friedrich Winkler – "Dürerstudien, III. Verschollene Meisterzeichnungen Dürers," *Jahrbuch der Preussischen Kunstsammlungen*, 53, 1932 (p. 68–89), p. 86, note 2.

WINKLER, 1938
Friedrich Winkler – *Die Zeichnungen Albrecht Dürers*, 4 Bände. Berlin 1936–1939. 3 Bd. 1938.

WINKLER, 1957
Friedrich Winkler – *Albrecht Dürer: Leben und Werk*. Berlin, 1957.

WOLTMANN, 1872
Dr. Alfred Woltmann – *Holbein and his time*; translation by F. E. Bunnètt. London: Richard Bentley and Son, 1872.

ZAMPA, 1968
Giorgio Zampa – *L'Opera completa di Dürer*. Milano, 1968.

EXHIBITION CATALOGUES

ARRAS, QUIMPER, DUBLIN, 2002
Jules Breton: La chanson des blés. Arras: Musée des Beaux-arts (16 March–2 June); Quimper: Musée des Beaux-arts (15 June–8 September); Dublin: National Gallery of Ireland (23 September–15 December). New Haven and London: Yale University Press, in assoc. National Gallery of Ireland, 2002.

ATHENS, 2009
Le Goût à la grecque. La Naissance du néoclassicisme dans l'art français. Chef-d'œuvres du Musée du Louvre. Athens: La Pinacothèque Nationale – Musée Alexandros Soutzos (28 September 2009–11 January 2010).

AUGSBURG, 1965
Hans Holbein der Ältere und die Kunst und die Kunst der Spätgotik. Augsburg: J. P. Himmer, 1965.

BASEL, 2008
Martin Schwander (ed.) – *Venice from Canaletto and Turner to Monet*. Basel: Beyeler Foundation (28 September 2008–25 January 2009).

BERLIN, 1910
Ausstellung von Werken französischer Kunst des XVIII. Jahrhunderts. Berlin: Königliche Akademie der Künste, 1910.

CAMBRIDGE, 2000
Nicholas Turner – *European Master Drawings from Portuguese Collections*. Cambridge: The Fitzwilliam Museum (16 May–13 August 2000).

CHARLEROI, 1994
J. M. W., 1775–1851. Aquarelles et dessins du legs Turner: Collection de la Tate Gallery, Londres. Ville de Charleroi: Palais des Beaux-Arts, 1994.

CHARTRES, 1983
Exigences de réalisme dans la peinture française entre 1830 et 1870. Chartres: Musée des Beaux-Arts de Chartres (5 November 1983–15 February 1984).

KARLSRUHE, 2011
Von Schönheit und Tod. Tierstilleben von der Renaissance bis zur Moderne. Karlsruhe: Staatliche Kunsthalle (19 November 2011–19 February 2012.

L'ISLE-ADAM, GRASSE, 2001–2002
Fragonard et le voyage en Italie, 1773–1774. Les Bergeret, une famille de mécènes. L'Isle-Adam: Musée d'Art et d'Histoire Louis-Senlecq (20 May–30 September 2001); Grasse: Villa-Musée Jean-Honoré Fragonard (1 June–30 September 2002).

LEIDEN, 1988
Emke Elen-Clifford Kocq Van Breugel – *Leidse fijnschilders: van Gerrit Dou tot Frans van Mieris de Jonge, 1630–1760*. Leiden: Stedelijk, Museum De Lakenhal (10 September–4 December 1988).

LISBON, 1973
Turner (1775–1851). Desenhos, Aguarelas e Óleos / Drawings, watercolours and paintings. Lisbon: Calouste Gulbenkian Foundation (June–July 1973).

LISBON, 1976
Exposição Evocativa de Calouste Gulbenkian. XX Aniversário da Fundação, 1956/1976. Lisbon: Fundação Calouste Gulbenkian (June–October 1976).

LISBON, 1985
A Colecção Calouste Gulbenkian. Um Olhar sobre as Reservas. XXX Aniversário da Morte de Calouste Gulbenkian. Lisbon: Fundação Calouste Gulbenkian, July 1985.

LISBON, 1994–1995
Manuela Fidalgo; Maria Fernanda Passos Leite – *No Tempo em Que os Animais Falavam. Fábulas de La Fontaine na Colecção Calouste Gulbenkian*. Lisbon: Fundação Calouste Gulbenkian, 1994–95.

LISBON, 1998
Art and the Sea. Lisbon: Calouste Gulbenkian Foundation (18 May–30 August 1998).

LISBON, 1999
A Arte do Retrato. Quotidiano e Circunstância. Lisbon: Fundação Calouste Gulbenkian (October 1999–January 2000).

LISBON, PORTO, 2000–2002
Desenhos de Mestres Europeus em Colecções Portuguesas. Lisbon: Centro Cultural de Belém (12 October 2000–7 January 2001); Porto: Museu Nacional de Soares dos Reis (22 November 2001–17 February 2002).

LISBON, 2001
The World of Lacquer: 2000 years of History. Lisbon: Calouste Gulbenkian Foundation (30 march–10 de June 2001).

LISBON, 2003
Sea and light. Turner's watercolours from the Tate Collection. Lisbon: Calouste Gulbenkian Foundation (20 February–18 May 2003).

LISBON, 2005
Designing the Décor. French Drawings from the Eighteenth Century. Lisbon: Calouste Gulbenkian Foundation (19 October 2005–5 January 2006).

LISBON, 2006 a
From Paris to Tokyo: Art of the Book in the Calouste Gulbenkian Collection. Lisbon: Calouste Gulbenkian Foundation (19 July–8 October 2006).

LISBON, 2006 b
The Collector and his taste, Calouste S. Gulbenkian, 1869–1955. Lisbon: Calouste Gulbenkian Foundation (19 July–8 October 2006).

LISBON, 2008
O Gosto «à Grega». Nascimento do Neoclassicismo em França, 1750–1775. Lisbon: Calouste Gulbenkian Foundation (14 February–4 may 2008).

LONDON, 1836
A Catalogue of 100 Original Drawings by Albrecht Dürer and Tizian Vecelli, Collected by Sir Thomas Lawrence. London: Woodburn Gallery, Eighth Exhibition, May 1836.

LONDON, 1878
Twenty-six Drawings by Watteau, Property of Miss James. London: South Kensington Museum, Bethnal Green Branch, 1878.

LONDON, 1913
Catalogue of a Collection of Pictures, Drawings, etc., of the French School of the Eighteenth Century (edited by Sir Claude Phillips). London: Burlington Fine Arts Club, 1913.

LONDON, 1917
A Collection of Drawings by Deceased Masters. London: Burlington Fine Arts Club, 1917.

LONDON, 1974
Turner, 1775–1851. London: The Tate Gallery (16 November1974–2 March 1975). London: The Tate Gallery and The Royal Academy of Arts, 1974.

LONDON, 2000
Turner. The Great Watercolours (with essays by Evelyn Joll, Ian Warrell and Andrew Wilton). London: Royal Academy of Arts (2 December–18 February 2001). London: Royal Academy of Arts, 2000.

LONDON, 2001
Eric Shanes – *The Golden Age of Watercolours: the Hickman Bacon Collection.* London: Dulwich Picture Gallery (19 September 2001–6 January 2002). London: Merrell, 2001.

LONDON, 2004
François Boucher. Seductive Visions. Londres: The Wallace Collection (30 September 2004–17 April 2005).

LONDON, FLORENCE, 2010–2011
Fra Angelico to Leonardo. Italian Renaissance Drawings. London: British Museum (22 April–25 June 2010); Florence: Galleria degli Uffizi (1 February–30 April 2011). London: The British Museum Press, 2010.

LONDON, 2011
Watteau. The Drawings. London: Royal Academy of Arts (12 March–5 June 2011).

LONDON, 2013
Christine Riding, Richard Jones - *Turner & the Sea.* London: National Maritime Museum(21 November 2013–21 April 2014), Thames and Hudson, 2013.

LONDON, NEW YORK, 1984
Muirhead Bone, 1876–1953. London: Gaston & Cooke; New York: C&J Goodfriend, 1984.

LONDON, WASHINGTON, BOSTON, 1998–1999
John Singer Sargent. London: Tate Gallery (15 October 1998–17 January 1999); Washington, National Gallery of Art (21 February–31 May 1999); Boston, Museum of Fine Arts (23 June–26 September 1999).

LUINO, 1975
Sacro e profano nella pittura di Bernardino Luini. Civico instituto di cultura popolare (9 August–8 October 1975). Luino: Silvana Editoriale d'Arte, 1975.

MADRID, 2002
Dibujos Europeos en las Colecciones Portuguesas, 1500–1800. Madrid: Museo Nacional del Prado (10 May–21 July 2002).

MADRID, 2007
El gusto "à la griega." Nascimento del neoclasicismo Francés. Madrid: Palacio Real (25 October 2007–6 January 2008).

MANCHESTER, 1857
Art Treasures of the United Kingdom. Manchester, 1857.

MARTIGUES, 1994
Félix Ziem, Peintre voyageur, 1821–1911. Peintures. Martigues: Musée Ziem (28 June–30 October), Actes Sud, 1994.

NEW YORK, 1999
Only the Best: Masterpieces of the Calouste Gulbenkian Museum. Lisbon. New York: Metropolitan Museum of Art (16 November 1999–27 February 2000).

NEW YORK, CHICAGO, 1986–1987
John Singer Sargent. New York: Whitney Museum of American Art (7 October 1986–4 January 1987); Chicago: The Art Institute of Chicago (7 February–19 April 1987).

NEW YORK, DETROIT, PARIS, 1986–1987
François Boucher, 1703–1770. New York: The Metropolitan Museum of Art (17 January–4 May 1968); Detroit: The Detroit Institute of Arts (27 May–17 August 1986); Paris, Galeries nationales du Grand Palais (18 December 1986–5 January1987). Paris: Editions de la Réunion des musées nationaux, 1986.

NEW YORK, FORT WORTH, 2003–2004
Les dessins de François Boucher. New York: The Frick Collection (8 October–14 December 2003); Fort Worth, TX, Kimbell Art Museum (18 January–18 April 2004). New York: American Federation of the Arts; London, Scala Publishers Ltd, 2003.

OEIRAS, 1965
*Obras de Arte da Colecção Calouste Gulbenk*ian. Oeiras: Palácio Pombal, 1965.

OMAHA, NEBR, MEMPHIS, TENN, WILLIAMSTOWN, MASS, 1982–1983
Jules Breton and the French Rural Tradtion. Omaha, Nebr: Joslyn Art Museum (6 November 1982–2 January 1983); Memphis, Tenn: Dixon Gallery and Gardens (16 January–6 March 1983); Williamstown, Mass: Sterling and Francine Clark Art Institute (2 April–5 June 1983). Omaha, Nebr: Joslyn Art Museum in association with the Arts Publisher, Inc., New York, 1982.

OTAWA, 1980
The Young van Dyck / Le Jeune van Dyck. Otawa: The National Gallery of Canada / National Museums of Canada for the Corporation of National Museums of Canada (19 September–9 November 1980).

PARIS, 1921
Exposition d'œuvres de J.-H. Fragonard [Rédaction M. Georges Wildenstein]. Paris: Musée des Arts décoratifs. Pavilion de Marsan, Palais du Louvre (7 June–10 July 1921).

PARIS, 1967
Le Cabinet d'un Grand Amateur, P.-J. Mariette 1694–1774: Dessins du XV e au XVIIIe siècle. Paris:Musée du Louvre. Paris: Réunion des musées nationaux, 1967.

PARIS, 1975
Jean-François Millet (1814–1875). Paris: Grand Palais (7 October 1975–5 January 1976). Paris: Editions des Musées Nationaux, 1975.

PARIS, 1978
Albrecht Dürer 1471–1528, Gravures, Dessins. Paris: Centre Culturel du Marais, 1978.

PARIS, 1979
L'Art en France sous le Second Empire. Paris: Grand Palais (11 May–13 August 1979). Paris: Réunion des musées nationaux, 1979.

PARIS, 1992
Clodion, 1738–1814. Paris: Musée du Louvre (17 March–29 June 1992).

PARIS, 1994
Paysages, paysans. L'art de la terre en Europe du Moyen âge au XXe siècle. Paris: Bibliothèque nationale de France (25 March–26 June 1994). Paris: Bibliothèque nationale de France; Réunion des musées nationaux, 1994.

PARIS, 2003
François Boucher hier et aujourd'hui. Paris: Musée du Louvre (17 October 2003–19 January 2004). Paris: Éditions de la Réunion des musées nationaux, 2003.

PARIS, 2006
Dessins de Jean-François Millet. Paris: Musée d'Orsay (30 May–3 September 2006). Milan: 5 Continents; Paris: Musée d'Orsay, 2006.

PARIS, 2008
Alexis Merle Du Bourg – *Antoon van Dyck, Portrait.* Paris: Musée Jacquemart-André (8 October 2008 –25 January 2009). Bruxelles: Fonds Mercator, 2008.

PARIS, NEW YORK, 1987–1988
Fragonard. Paris: Galeries nationales du Grand Palais (24 September 1987–4 January 1988); Nova Iorque: Metropolitan Museum of Art (2 February–8 May 1988). Paris: Éditions de la Réunion des Musées nationaux, 1987.

PARIS, SYDNEY, OTAWA, 2003–2006
François Boucher et l'art rocaille dans les collections de l'École des beaux-arts. Paris: École nationale supérieure des beaux-arts (16 October–21 December 2003); Sydney: Art Gallery of New South Wales (5 March–1 may 2005); Otawa (16 September 2005–1 January 2006). Paris: École nationale supérieure des beaux-arts, 2003.

PORTO, 1964
Artes Plásticas Francesas de Watteau a Renoir. Colecção da Fundação Calouste Gulbenkian. Porto: Museu Nacional de Soares dos Reis, 1964.

ST ANDREWS, GLASGOW, 1986–1987
Muirhead Bone. Portrait of the Artist. St Andrews: St Andrews University Printing Department, 1986 (exhibition organized by the Crawford Centre for the Arts, University of St Andrews. Crawford Centre: 28 November–21 December 1986); Glasgow Art Gallery (25 January–9 March 1987).

ST IVES, 2006
Light into Colour. Turner in the South West. St Ives: Tate St Ives (28 January–7 May 2006).

ST PETERSBURG, FL, 1982
Fragonard and His Friends: Changing Ideals in Eighteenth Century Art. St. Petersburg, Florida, Museum of Fine Arts (20 November 1982–6 February1983).

THE HAGUE, CAMBRIDGE MA, 1981–1982
Jacob van Ruisdael. The Hague: Mauritshuis (1 October 1981–3 January 1982); Cambridge: Fogg Art Museum (18 January–11 April 1982).

THE HAGUE, WASHINGTON, 2005–2006
Frans van Mieris 1635–1681. The Hague, Royal Picture Gallery Mauritshuis (1 October 2005–22 January 2006); Washington, National Gallery of Art (26 February–21 May 2006). Zwolle: Waanders Publishers, 2005.

VERSAILLES, 2004
Esquisses, pastels et dessins de François Boucher dans les collections privées. Versailles: Musée Lambinet (12 October 2004–9 January 2005). Paris: Somogy, Éditions d'Art; Musée Lambinet, 2004.

VIENNA, 1985
Albrecht Dürer und die Tier – und Pflanzenstudien der Renaissance. Vienna: Graphische Sammlung Albertina (18 April–30 June 1985). Munich: Prestel-Verlag, 1985.

WASHINGTON, 1990
Anthony van Dyck, Washington: National Gallery of Art (11 November 1990–24 February 1991).

WASHINGTON, PARIS, BERLIN, 1984–1985
Watteau 1684–1721. Washington: National Gallery of Art (17 June–23 September 1984), Paris: Galeries nationales du Grand Palais (23 October 1984–28 January 1985), Berlin: Schloss Charlottenbourg (22 February–26 May 1985).

WASHINGTON, CAMBRIDGE, MASS, NEW YORK, 1978–1979
Drawings by Fragonard in North American Collections. Washington: National Gallery of Art (19 November 1978–21 January 1979); Cambridge, Mass: Fogg Art Museum, Harvard University (16 February–1 April 1979); New York: The Frick Collection (20 April–3 June 1979).

WASHINGTON, DALLAS, LONDON, 2007–2008
J.M.W. Turner. Washington: National Gallery of Art (1 October 2007–6 January 2008); Dallas: Museum of Art (10 February–18 May 2008); New York: Metropolitam Museum of Art (24 June–21 September 2008). London: Tate Publishing, 2007.

WILLIAMSTOWN, MASS, PITTSBURGH, PENN, AMSTERDAM, 1999–2000
Jean-François Millet. Drawn into the Light. Williamstown, Mass: Sterling and Francine Clark Art Institute (June–September 1999); Pittsburg, Penn: The Frick Art and Historical Center (September–October 1999); Amsterdam: Van Gogh Museum (October 1999–January 2000). London: Yale University Press, 1999.

NO.	INVENTORY NO.
1	140
2	457
3	426
4	141
5	861
6	518
7	2300
8	66
9	865
10	515
11	172 A
12	172 B
13	459
14	2872
15	458
16	2297
17	2299
18	2226
19	2298
20	2871
21	375
22	374
23	864
24	867
25	373
26	460
27	2158
28	462 (1–57)
29	75
30	2219
31	625
32	2465
33	2463
34	2464
35	2462

AUTHOR		NO.
Bone, Muirhead, 1876–1953	–	27
Boucher, François, 1703–70	–	8, 10, 11–12,
Breton, Jules-Adolphe-Aimé-Louis, 1827–1906	–	26
Clairin, Georges-Jules-Victor, 1843–1919	–	[28–1]
Cochin, Charles-Nicolas, 'the Younger', 1715–90	–	13, 14, 15
Da Vinci, Leonardo, ca. 1520–(?), artist from the circle of	–	3
Delaunay, Jules-Elie, 1828–91	–	[28–2]; [28–3]; [28–4]; [28–5]; [28–6]; [28–7]; [28–8]; [28–9]; [28–10]; [28–11]; [28–12]; [28–13]
Doré, Paul Gustave L. C., known as Gustave, 1832–83	–	[28–14]
Duez, Ernest-Ange, 1843–96	–	[28–15]
Dürer, Albrecht, 1471–1528	–	1
Edridge, Henry, 1769–1821	–	23
Ferrier, Gabriel, 1847–1914	–	[28–16]
Foujita, Léonard Tsugouharu, 1886–1968	–	32–35
Fragonard, Jean-Honoré, 1732–1806	–	16, 17
Français, François-Louis, 1814–97	–	[28–17]
Gervex, Henri, 1852–1929	–	[28–18]
Giacomelli, Hector, 1822–1904	–	[28–19]
Guardi, Francesco, 1712–1793	–	[20]
Guignard, Alexandre-Gaston, 1848–1922	–	[28–20]
Harpignies, Henri-Joseph, 1819–1916	–	[28–21]
Heilbuth, Ferdinand, 1826–1889	–	[28–22], [28–23], [28–24]
Holbein, Hans, *the Elder*, c. 1460/65 – 1524, copy after	–	[2]
Igonet, Marie-Madeleine, act. 1744–60	–	9
Jacquemart, Jules-Ferdinand, 1837–80	–	[28–25]; [28–26]
Jacquet, Gustave Jean, 1846–1909	–	[28–27]
Jourdain, Henri, 1846–1931	–	[28–28]
Jouve, Paul, 1878–1973	–	30, 31
Lami, Eugène Louis, 1800–90	–	[28–29]
Latenay, Gaston de, 1859–1943	–	[28–30]
Leloir, Maurice, 1853–1940	–	[28–31]; [28–32]
Le Mains, Gaston, 1860–1929	–	[28–33]
Machard, Jules Louis, 1839–1900	–	[28–34]
Michel, Claude, known as Clodion, 1738–1814, after	–	19
Millet, Jean-François, 1814–75	–	24
Morot, Aimé Nicolas, 1850–1913	–	[28–35]; [28–36]; [28–37]
Nittis, Giuseppe de, 1846–84	–	[28–38]
Palizzi, Giuseppe, 1812–88	–	[28–39]
Penne, Charles Olivier de, 1831–97	–	[28–40]
Pille, Charles Henri, 1844–97	–	[28–41]
Raffaëlli, Jean François, 1850–1924	–	[28–42]
Rosenstock, Isidor, 1880–1956	–	[28–43]; [28–44]; [28–45]; [28–46]
Rötig, Georges Frédéric, 1873–1961	–	[28–47]
Rousseau, Philippe, 1816–87	–	[28–48]; [28–49]
Ruisdael, Jacob van, 1628/1629–82	–	5
Sargent, John Singer, 1856–1925	–	29
Saunier, Octave Alfred, 1842–89	–	[28–50]
Thornley, William or George William, 1858–98	–	[28–51]
Toudouze, Edouard, 1848–1907	–	[28–52]
Turner, Joseph Mallord William, 1775–1851	–	21, 22
Unkown author	–	18
Van Dyck, Anton, 1599–1641, attributed to	–	4
Van Mieris, Willem, 1662–1747	–	6
Vayson, Paul, 1842–1911	–	[28–53]
Vignal, Pierre, 1855–1925	–	[28–54]; [28–55]
Watteau, Jean Antoine, 1684–1721	–	7
Worms, Jules, 1832–1924	–	[28–56]
Ziem, Félix, 1821–1911	–	25, [28–57]

PROVENANCE / COLLECTIONS	NO.
Adrien Fauchier-Magnan	20
Alfred Baillehache	28
Alfred Beurdeley	13, 18
Amédée Constantin	16
Andrew Fountaine	2
Andrew James	7
Antony Roux	28
Archduke Frederich of Habsburg-Lothringen	2
Artist's studio (Jean-François Millet)	24
Artist's studio (Jules Breton)	26
C. Langton	22
Camille Marcille	16
Ch. Philipe	5
Charles Sackville Bale	4
Christiaan Josi	5
Christian Lazard	32-35
Conde de Greffulhe	7, 17
David David-Weill	16, 19
Duque de Talleyrand	20
Edward Habich	2
Émile Norblin	16
Ernest Le Roy	25
Gaston Le Breton, Paris, 1921	15
General-Conde Antoine-François Andréossy	1
Graphische Sammlung Albertina	2
Gustave Adolphe Guyot de Villeneuve	15, 19
H.H.A. Josse	7, 16
Hartmann	23
Hubert Robert	16
John Dillon	22
John Farnworth	22
John Postle Heseltine	4
Madame de Polès	16
Madame J. Danthon	30
Marie Joseph François Mahérault	17, 19
Marquis de Biron	11, 12, 16, 19
Marquess of Landsdowne (5th)	3, 5, 10, 23
Max e Maurice Rosenheim	8
Max J. Bonn	1, 4
Neyman	5
Pierre-Jean Mariette	1
Prosper Henry Lankrink	4
Roux Traissinet	25
Saint	16
Sarah Ann James	7
Sir Horace Walpole (not confirmed)	1
Sir Thomas Lawrence	1
Thomas Dimsdale	7
Varanchan de Saint-Geniès	16
Vicomte de Greffulhe	17
William Mitchell	2
William Newall	29
William Quilter	22

LAST COLLECTION	DATE OF SALE	NO.
Alfred Baillehache (1870–1922)	1922	28
Alfred Beurdeley (1847–1919)	1905	13
Christian Lazard	1939	32–35
Comte de Greffulhe (1848–1931)	1937	7, 17
Ernest Le Roy	1926	25
Gaston Le Breton (1845–1920)	1921	15
Jules Breton (1827-1906), artist's studio	1911	26
Madame J. Danthon	1933	30
Marquess of Landsdowne (1845–1927)	1920	3, 5, 10, 23
Marquis de Biron (1859–1939)	1914	11–12
Max J. Bonn (1880–1943)	1922	1, 4
Max Rosenheim (1849–1911) and Maurice Rosenheim (1851–1922)	1923	8
Paul Jouve (1878-1973), bought directly from the artist	1923	31
William Newall (1851–1922)	1922	29

DATE OF ACQUISITION	NO.
1905	13
1911	26
1914	11, 12, 22
1915	24
1916	21
1917	9
1920	3, 5, 10, 23
1921	15
1922	1, 4, 28, 29
1923	8, 31
1925	2
1926	25
1932	18
1933	30
1937	7, 16, 17, 19
1939	32–35
2002	20
2003	14
Unknown	6
Unknown	27

GENERAL CO-ORDINATION
João Castel-Branco Pereira, *Director*
Nuno Vassallo e Silva, *Deputy Director*

EDITORIAL CO-ORDINATION
João Carvalho Dias, with the assistance of
Carla Paulino and Inês Antunes (interns)

TEXTS
Manuela Fidalgo

DESIGN AND
GRAPHIC CO-ORDINATION
Sílvia Prudêncio

ADMINISTRATIVE SUPPORT
Maria de Fátima Vasconcelos
Augusto Ferreira
António Coelho Alves
José Leal

DOCUMENTAL SUPPORT
Biblioteca de Arte
Ana Barata
Cristina Ramos

CONSERVATION AND RESTORATION
Helena Nunes

PHOTOGRAPHY AND PHOTO EDITING
Catarina Gomes Ferreira

PHOTOGRAPHIC ARCHIVE
Marta Areia

REVISION
antónio alves martins

PRINTING
AGIR – Produções Gráficas

COVER
Jean-Honoré Fragonard (1732–1806),
Qu'en Dit l'Abbé. Pormenor do [16].
Foto: Mário de Oliveira (1957)

p. 26, detail of [4]; p. 54, detail of [7]; p. 115, detail of [19]; p. 147, detail of [25]; p. 164, detail of [30], p. 171, detail of [29]; p. 179, detail of [31].
Photos: Carlos Azevedo

www.museu.gulbenkian.pt
www.gulbenkian.pt

English edition: 1000 copies
ISBN: 978-972-8848-93-4
ISBN: 978-972-8848-92-7 (Portuguese edition)
LEGAL DEPOT: 375438/14

ACKNOWLEDGEMENTS

The creation of this book, which is small in size but highly complex due to the multifaceted nature of the works that it concerns, was made possible only by the trust and encouragement shown to me throughout the process by João Castel-Branco Pereira, the Director of the Calouste Gulbenkian Museum, to whom I am profoundly grateful. This gratitude obviously extends to Nuno Vassallo e Silva, the Deputy Director of the museum. ¶ I am also deeply grateful to João Carvalho Dias, who oversaw the production and publication of this book with the competence that has long characterised his work. I will never forget the fraternal and comradely way in which we shared the discouragement caused by obstacles encountered and the enthusiasm over the discoveries made throughout the different phases of the project. ¶ For the very special contributions that they made to the research carried out on the authorship and dates of the works in this catalogue, I would like to thank Kate de Rothschild, Ben Broos, Angela Dillon Bussi, Albert Elen, Annette Bourrut Lacouture, Alastair Lang, Giorgio Marini, and Eunice Williams. ¶ I am also greatly indebted to the wise advice given by experts in the various areas of knowledge which the nature of the works entailed, the expert help provided by professional colleagues, and the support of those who, in the normal course of their duties, responded quickly and selflessly to the requests that I put them. ¶ For the reasons given I am truly grateful to António Coelho Alves; Marta Areia; Carlos Azevedo; Katharine Baetjer; Ana Barata; Jean Belaubre; Daniella Ben-Arie; Sophie Biass-Fabiani; Maria Teresa Binaghi; Jonathan Bober; Alexis Merle du Bourg; Sónia Brito; Sylvie Buisson; Anne Burdin-Hellebranth; Alvin L. Clark Jr.; Leopold Deliss; Barbara Dossi; Augusto Ferreira; Catarina Gomes Ferreira; António Figueiredo; Peter Fuhring; Miguel Fumega; Mons. Enrico Galiati; Jacqueline Genser; Gisela Goldberg; Ana Paula Gordo; Alden Gordon; Robert L. Herbert; Leile Jarbouai; Pierrette Jean-Richard; A.D. Fraser Jenkins; Richard Johns ; Fritz Koreny; Pascal de La Vaissière; Lionel Lambourne; José Leal; Amélie Marcillac; Félix Marcillac; Raphaële Martin-Pigalle; Anne Louise Mason; Christian Müller; Annick Notter; Helena Nunes; Benjamin Peronnet; Cristina Ramos; Constança Rosa; Louis--Antoine Prat; Jacinto Ramos; Pierre Rosenberg; Rachael Sadinsky; Marie-Pierre Salé; José Miguel dos Santos; Fernando Maia Santos; Livia Schaafsma; David Scrase; Seymour Slive; Perrin Stein; Anna Tempesti; Christian Theuerkauff; Nicholas Turner; Maria de Fátima Vasconcelos; Ian Warrell; Harriet West; Daniel Wildenstein; Rui Xavier and Ana Zúquete.

SPONSOR
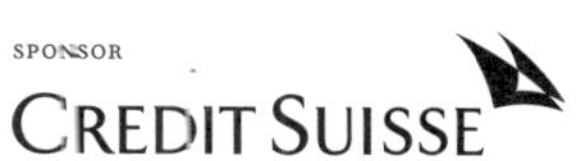